# A Literary Life

# A Literary Life

## Reflections and Reminiscences
### 1928 – 1990

## MORLEY CALLAGHAN

*Exile Editions*

*Publishers of singular*
*Fiction, Poetry, Non-fiction, Drama, and Graphic Books*

2008

Library and Archives Canada Cataloguing in Publication

Callaghan, Morley, 1903-1990
   A literary life : reflections and reminiscences, 1928-1990 / Morley
Callaghan.

ISBN 978-1-55096-099-0

   1. Callaghan, Morley, 1903-1990.  2. Novelists, Canadian (English)
--20th century--Biography.  I. Title.

PS8505.A43Z475 2008        C813'.52        C2008-902304-8

Design and Composition by Digital ReproSet
Typeset in Garamond at the Moons of Jupiter Studios
Printed in Canada by Gauvin Imprimerie

The publisher would like to acknowledge the financial assistance of
the Canada Council for the Arts and the Ontario Arts Council, which is an
agency of the Government of Ontario.

Published in Canada in 2008 by Exile Editions Ltd.
144483 Southgate Road 14
General Delivery
Holstein, Ontario, N0G 2A0
info@exileeditions.com
www.ExileEditions.com

Canadian Sales Distribution:      U.S. Sales Distribution:
McArthur & Company               Independent Publishers Group
c/o Harper Collins               814 North Franklin Street
1995 Markham Road                Chicago, IL 60610
Toronto, ON  M1B 5M8             www.ipgbook.com
toll free: 1 800 387 0117        toll free: 1 800 888 4741

*Whatever I was,*
*whoever I am,*
*is in my work.*

—Morley Callaghan

# CONTENTS

# INTRODUCTION

Of a late November evening two or three years before he died, I was sitting with my father in his library, his old typewriter by the window of the study at the front of the house, and around him were old books, photographs, a clutter of magazines, broken pipe stems, the stain of years of smoke on the walls, the drapes drawn against a chill wind. He'd settled into a nest of shawls, chewing on his pipe, feeling the cold deeper in his bones now that he was nearing ninety.

We were talking 'about the singer Tina Turner.

He said: "She cut loose from that thug of a husband . . . she's recreated herself. Watching her, it makes me want to write, I think creation is something you can pick up on, creation can be contagious . . ."

The television was on, the sound low, and he had one eye on a college football game somewhere . . .

"You mean you and your guys in Paris all had the same head cold?"

He chuckled, as he sideways glanced at the screen to watch a wide sweeping run by a scatback in a game he didn't care about, some boy running beautifully, and he said, "Well, what've you been reading?"

"Nothing."

"Didn't you read that nitwit today in the *Globe* about Jerusalem?"

"Just the same-old same-old."

"I was going to read this guy Doctorow but then I decided that there's something too secure in writing about brave deeds done back in someone else's time. I put it aside . . ."

"So it's you, me, and the TV."

"Not exactly . . ."

"Guess I'll hit the road."

"I was going to talk to you about a thing I've been working on, a way of doing all my talks and stuff about writers over the years, and other stuff, too, without it being like everybody else's old thing . . . stale stuff stacked together like sliced bread . . ."

He showed me thirty or more pages of some newsprint pages torn in half, torn into little oblong piles of pages that he shuffled back and forth as we talked.

Over the decades, I knew he had written the occasional book review, some newspaper and magazine essays, and the odd column. Also, for more than twenty years, he had appeared on the CBC Radio program, *Anthology*, invited by its editor/producer, Robert Weaver, to talk about whatever was on his mind. Through the first years of his radio appearances he spoke off-the-cuff, using notes he had scribbled before and after breakfast on the backs of envelopes. Then, after it was suggested that he should think about his archives, he began to type his talks on pink and yellow and green sheets of newsprint, typing sentences that had words left out, on pages that soon had holes – letters like o – punching through the papers as ● because his old Underwood roller had hardened to stone over the years. And then he would make corrections on those pages in a ballpoint hand that my mother described as "a slurring of letters in which some vowels just never show up."

"I want this thing to have the feel of my just talking, just that . . ."

In fact, what he was trying to do was put his horribly typed notes into a kind of off-hand narrative flow, as if the reader might be on the telephone with him or sitting with him late at night in his library, listening to him in an easy intimacy as he rehearsed whatever was on his mind.

"And maybe," he said, "I could drop in the actual reviews I wrote when I was young, and other later stuff – you know, I remember I wrote a very pointed piece a few years ago about surveillance and the police, and you remember when you were in college I wrote those sports columns for the *Telegram* . . . Somehow, this thing, if it was set up right, could have a freshness of effect, it could be a new way of getting at a literary life, maybe some teasing anecdotes thrown in . . ."

He handed me a box of papers.

A few weeks later, we got to work and agreed on how the book should begin: with *The young in one another's arms* . . .

"And Marquez should be near the beginning, too," he said.

Since we had just come back from a trip to Paris together: "Paris, that piece I wrote about Rodin, that could be great toward the very end . . ."

•   •   •

In what turned out to be the last year of his life, he started to write a novel; he'd written a draft of the first hundred pages . . . it was called, *In the Park*. "I like this woman," he said. "She's something new for me, and the park: every great city has a great park and ours is out there in the west end, High Park, and she lives with her lawyer-father over-looking the park . . ."

"What about your book of talks, the young in one another's arms, and all that stuff?"

"It can sit for a while."

Then, he fell and broke his hip.

He convalesced in a nursing hospital. He read novels and all the newspapers, received visitors, and watched the Blue Jays baseball games on a small bedside TV. "I don't get it," he said. "I have never dreamed in words. I've always dreamed in pictures, Monet, Cézanne, Matisse, but last night I dreamed in words, words under my eye, like Joyce obviously dreamed in words, words that had to be the phantoms of his dreaming mind when he wrote *Anna was, Livia is, Plurabell's to be* – because you can sing those words, they sing themselves, they're the music of his dreams about the Liffey River, the Lethe, a music I'd never heard before, the music of Lethe."

The broken bone knitted, he healed very quickly, and after two weeks he was home and walking. He picked up a stack of pages he had written about Solzhenitsyn. He read them. "Great," he said. "Got to get back to this." He did not finish the manuscript at hand himself – but he had set up an anecdotal pace, he had established a tone, and he had revised two-thirds of his talks – so I decided that enough of his intent was there before me to go ahead, to not only complete the text, but to achieve the overall effect he had hoped for.

While selecting pieces that best conveyed his habit of mind, I tried to maintain his ongoing conversational tone, and tried to give the feel of a Morley narrative backbone that was not constrained by chronology. Morley didn't believe in "divisions by decades." He wanted this book to reflect the "way his mind worked," and to achieve that end, he preferred resonance and reverberations to any storytelling arc or any strict thematic unity.

Morley's published book reviews and essays are indicated and identified on end by the periodical year of publication. His reflections and pensées, nearly all written for this text, are identified by their having no date in place of publication. In some cases, titles, where there were none, have been provided. His radio pieces, most of which he had tossed into boxes or manila envelopes, post-broadcast, were undated. They are identified on end by *CBC Anthology*.

For about a year (1957-58) he wrote a weekly sports column for the *Toronto Telegram*. He wrote about baseball and hockey and a lot about boxing, much in the manner of a *feuilletoniste* and I have printed five such columns in rapid succession – separated only by "pensées" – to give the effect of his sudden appearance and disappearance in the then second largest newspaper in the country.

In one of the ironies of life, I became the Literary Editor of the *Toronto Telegram* in 1966, and I stayed in that position until 1971. In that period, I hired Morley to write several essays and book reviews. Most are reprinted here.

Also, a few lines and stanzas from Ezra Pound appear throughout the text. I'm not sure that Pound was his favourite poet; I'm not sure that he had a favourite; but he could and would quote prodigiously, most often declaiming, with a boyish pleasure in his eye, Pound.

The few, strange little anecdotal linkages that seem to have their root in his travels across the country as a broadcaster, going from hotel to hotel during the war years, are from those parts of Morley's manuscript that he had completed before he died.

The reader of Morley's oeuvre will recognize that the structure he chose for this text is similar in spirit to the method followed in his *Complete Short Stories*, which he insisted were to be printed without original publication dates. That this process frustrated a certain kind of professional academic pleased him to no end. He liked to think that his short stories were of such consistent quality that no reader would be able to tell which stories had been written first and which had been written last. All that mattered to him was the story in and of itself.

A little over a week after he had reread his Solzhenitsyn piece, after he had gone back to work on the organization of his book, he was found lying in his own blood in his vestibule to the house. Before he was taken to the hospital, he asked for "one of those little Laura Secord rice puddings from the corner store."

After two months in the Intensive Care Unit, after two months in which he lay cocooned inside his bloated body, two months in which he never opened his eyes, never said a word, he died.

•   •   •

Silence.

As for all the talks with my father! We had talked on the phone or in his living room or library almost every night of my adult life.

He was a great talker.

He was a great listener, too, which is why, I think, women liked him.

He liked to talk about everything he'd read or heard and sometimes it felt like he was mischievously rehearsing what he wanted to say on the radio. So he said what he said, and maybe the next day, he'd say it again (with a twist), and sometimes he wrote it down, two-finger typing on that old beaten-up portable, and then he said it again on radio.

I have not, since, been able to describe the silence in the night in my life without that voice, without that talk. But now that I am done with shaping his literary reminiscences, his reviews and his reflections, getting hold, I believe, of the book he wanted them to be, I know that his voice is on the page, the tone of his temperament so consistent from the beginning, and I hear him on the page as I remember him, and I am sure that Morley's readers, especially those who used to hear him on radio, will recognize his voice and will learn what it was like to sit with him, sometimes in the dark, and to listen to him, and to rejoice – whether you agree with him or not – in the way his mind worked.

*Barry Callaghan*
Toronto, 2008

## EDITOR'S NOTE

In considering this text I have consulted with the documentary filmmaker David Sobelman, who is also a story editor and poet, testing for placement and resonance, piece by piece, knowing he'd recognize anything out of whack with Morley's tone. And why not? After all, meeting by "regular chance" while Morley was alive, they often sat together on a bench in front of the old Bloor Street Dominion Store, having a talk after shopping for groceries.

*I beg you, my friendly critics,*
*Do not set about to procure me an audience.*

*I mate with my free kind upon the crags;*
*The hidden recesses*
*Have heard the echo of my heels,*
*In the cool light,*
*In the darkness.*

—Ezra Pound

# THE YOUNG IN
# ONE ANOTHER'S ARMS

*The young in one another's arms.* The young in one another's arms. The Yeats line repeating and repeating itself in my head while listening to the English journalist Malcolm Muggeridge explain to his television audience that copulation indulged in without procreation in mind is squalid and silly, and I was hoping that if I, too, am to grow old – and I am eighty – I will not find myself wallowing in this pathetic falsification of life, this barnyard breeding view of a man and woman in bed . . . The young in one another's arms. The young in one another's arms . . .

# BARONESS ORCZY:
## *THE SCARLET PIMPERNEL*

⁂

At the age of twelve, I was given for Christmas an English annual, *Chums*, a huge volume, about fourteen inches by ten and nearly five-inches thick. Though years had passed since Mother or Father had mentioned Santa Claus, we had kept the belief that my brother and I should not know what we were getting for Christmas. We should wake up in the morning and there beside the bed would be our presents.

I used to lie awake long past midnight on Christmas Eve when I was thirteen and fourteen, making no noise, pretending to be sound asleep, listening intently, and finally I would hear the stealthy step on the stairs, my father or mother groping in the dark to the foot of the bed, and then the rustling sound of parcels on the floor, and I would try to guess by the sound whether the big book, *Chums*, had been laid there once again, and then the withdrawing footsteps and the dark. I never had the effrontery to turn on the light. I would fall asleep contented, knowing the book was there.

In the morning, I flopped the book open, going rapidly through the list of pirate stories, the war stories, the boxing stories, to see if this year again there would be a long story by the Baroness Orczy about the Scarlet Pimpernel. Ah, the wonder of her hero, Sir Percy Blakeny, who dedicated his life to rescuing lovely and noble aristocrats from the terrible guillotine and those wild ruthless thugs of the Revolution, especially the terrible, cold, cunning Robespierre.

Sir Percy Blakeny, an English aristocrat himself, clever, cunning, elusive, never failed in his mission, and to this day I can hear myself repeating: *They seek him here, they seek him there, they seek his shadow everywhere. Is he in heaven, is he in hell, that damned elusive Pimpernel.*

The Baroness recorded how she'd once caught a glimpse of the man in Temple Station while waiting for an Inner Circle train. She said: "I saw him in his exquisite clothes, his slender hand holding up his spyglass. I heard his lazy drawling speech, his quaint laugh." Yes, there he was, as he was to be in all her stories: the romantic daring dandy in a field of French thugs.

Years had to pass before it seemed odd to me that I, a boy in the heart of a democratic American continent, should have given my heart not only to this dazzling clever foppish aristocrat, but to his cause as well, year after year, his cause growing in my imagination, a view of the French Revolution that would have delighted any Bourbon. Yes, years had to pass before I woke up, or grew up and saw that I had everything all wrong about the great French Revolution.

What is involved here still interests me. There is magic in the words of a good storyteller, and the good story will outlast the actual facts even if the facts are recorded, and the power of the story as the truth is broken only when the reader outgrows the storyteller and seeks for better and more moving stories in real people. As I grew older, I couldn't go on reading a boy's book, *Chums.* I couldn't go on listening for the step on the stair in the dark, and so the Orczy view of the French Revolution and aristocrats became just as boyish a thing as waiting for the step on the stair. Orczy had shown, however, how a writer could shape a young mind, and shown, too, that when great events are concerned, many minds remain forever young.

No matter, the Baroness had done one remarkable thing for me. She had worked over enormous research on Paris buildings, streets and places, all marvellously accurate. So, she was the one who first took me into Paris.

By the time I was sixteen, I had left the Baroness and moved on to the Dumas, father and son, yet still the streets and places were familiar. They were my places now, and of course, after Dumas I had gone to the Paris of Balzac, and on and on in those same streets and in those same places, and I remember that when I actually did get to Paris and I was sitting at the Café de la Paix, I looked around with a feeling of comfort, no, elation. Though I was seeing the streets and the places for the first time with my own eyes, I actually felt at home, and it was then that I remembered fondly the Baroness Orczy, the Baroness, the enchantress who had first taken me to Paris.

# JOHN CHEEVER:
# IN THE DARK, READERS

I heard John Cheever say that the reading public, those who read good adult fiction, are the keepers of civilization. This is interesting. The writer never knows who these people are, these readers who are never in touch with each other as a group. Only a very few of them get in touch with the writer. Yet they are there.

Cheever thinks these quiet people, all separated, perhaps reading in lonely rooms, yet sharing the life of the imagination as it is ordered for them by a thousand different artists, are the ones who have always held civilizations together. It may be that the temperament these people share, a need in their hearts and in their heads that they have to keep feeding, is what has always kept civilization alive – especially in the noisiest and most barbaric times. But how does a good writer reach this public?

Every unknown writer has to believe this public is out there waiting for him and will welcome him and read him if only they will discover him, how good he is. Yet, I believe it is harder now for the new writer, the man of quiet singularity, to get commercial publication, and a public. It is not that editors in the great commercial houses won't recognize his talent. They will, but they will recognize, too, with a wonderful quickness, that the more singular he is, the less chance he has of any commercial success.

The other day, at a booksellers convention, one of the dealers said, "It's all hype now. Hype. Hype. Anything can be sold with the right hype. The right promotion!" A book that is a piece of trash, or a work that doesn't hurt or disturb anyone, can indeed be hyped, maybe into a million-dollar success. But what that dealer doesn't know is that this kind of Boffo promotion can only carry a very good book so far. Sooner or later the popcorn trade will find the book so out of the ordinary, so unfamiliar, they will drop it.

The hope, the eternal hope for the honest writer is that any and all gaudy promotion, if he can get it, may push his book toward that far stream – the unknown public, the quiet ones who are out there in the dark – who have no faces – to whose ears the writer's voice is just a whisper in the dark, in the most intimate of relationships, the capturing of imaginations in a deep awareness of compassion, or sorrow, or ecstasy – a view of life – nothing in the abstract; experience really felt and shared by the writer and the reader who never meet . . .

When he is young the good writer believes he only has to write a perfect story and it will be read by these unknown people who keep literature alive through the ages. When James Joyce wrote his stories, *Dubliners*, he couldn't find a publisher. His brother Stanislas wrote to him reassuringly that there always would be people somewhere who would want to read a good story. Maupassant said that if a poet were to write only one perfect sonnet he would be immortal in French literature. I used to think so, too. Now I'm not sure. There are so many impediments to the recognition of any kind of uniqueness. There is so much typing going on – thousands of poets in North America, thousands of storywriters, reams and reams of trash being churned out – all getting in the way of the one good smaller thing, stuff and more stuff gobbling up shelf space. Millions of dollars are to be made from stuff. So, the perfect sonnet, the perfect little story, would have to appear in some obscure small magazine. A magazine that might disappear in six months. And yet

– I can't accept that the obscure but great writer can get lost forever. His works are somewhere in the stream now, though the
stream may be flowing underground. Years may have to pass as the
work remains submerged, as civilization is so often submerged, but
some day that work will be discovered and it will be discovered by
those nameless readers alone out there in the dark.

*CBC Anthology*

# MARIAN ENGEL: *BEAR*

I have always believed in mystery, the wonder of a thing in itself. The separate thing. I've shied away from visions, I've shied away from trying to see one thing through other things. I've always been uneasy about elaborate metaphors. They are a form of flight from the mystery of the thing under the eye. The separate thing in itself. "A daffodil was not a daffodil to him." It had to be something else. A symbol. Symbolism, several things deployed in a pattern, is supposed to enlarge a separate thing, so that it becomes quite different, so that it takes on another meaning, a meaning outside itself.

Marian Engel wrote a novel called *Bear*.

A plain young woman who is a librarian in our north country is bent on seducing a bedraggled bear and getting it to mount her. She brings the bear to its knees between her knees. The bear is good at oral sex. When the bear isn't licking her, she gets laid by a neighbouring farmer. When the farmer isn't able, and she can't find the bear, she masturbates. The book, it has been said, is not about this woman but about something else, something bigger – female sexuality. We all know that female sexuality is bigger than any one woman. So, the bear must be more than a bear, too. I've found that people like Robertson Davies, Margaret Laurence and Northrop Frye, see a myth-making symbolism in cunnilingus by a bear. Others say that the bear is a symbol of the national lover. Have Margaret Laurence and Robertson Davies ever been downwind of a bear? Facts mean something; facts matter if symbols are to work.

And then there is this: no one talks about the actual woman, this librarian. She's a woman devoid of wonder, she's a woman who excites no wonder. Incredulity, yes, but no wonder. Symbols aside, if the woman there on Engel's page is a portrait of a woman of our time, and of our place, God help her, heaven pity us.

*Be in me as the eternal moods*
*of the bleak wind, and not*
*As transient things are —*
*gaiety of flowers.*
*Have me in the strong loneliness*
*of sunless cliffs*
*And of grey waters.*
*Let the gods speak softly of us*
*In days hereafter,*
*the shadowy flowers of Oreus*
*Remember thee.*

—Ezra Pound

# JERZY KOSINSKI:
# A CANDLE BURNS

Sometimes I feel my belief in man's essential humanity isn't right for the time. I know it is a part of man's nature to have a liking for imaginative violence, especially if he leads a sedentary life. Yet, some books, like *Last Exit to Brooklyn* and *The Painted Bird*, are aesthetic failures, not only because of the monotony of the violence but because they deliberately falsify life in their diminution of human experience.

The Jerzy Kosinski book, *The Painted Bird*, dear to so many devoted students of the concentration camps, has a terrible, even a contrived falsification. In the book, set in the time of the Second Great War, a homeless wandering little boy, going from one peasant cottage to another in Eastern Europe, encounters only the unmitigated horror of humanity. Though each line, each paragraph is brilliantly crafted, each chapter is a bestial shock. While reading, I kept saying – How can the next chapter possibly be more shocking? Can he do it? Especially after the poor boy, thrown into a cesspool by church-going people, comes up for air and is mute.

Kosinski managed to keep the depravity mounting, but it was incredible to me that the boy – wandering in all those villages – wouldn't encounter one act of kindness or gentleness. All you can say is that living in the shadow of the concentration camps – death being the order of the day in those camps – they didn't kill him.

But then, a village is not a concentration camp. Death is not the order of the day in a village, and if it is – then it's not a village, or a camp is not a camp. You can't have it both ways. Kosinski, who is a very quick-witted man – alert, as if a candle string of energy were burning down in his brain as he tried to stay one step ahead of the ash-end of his inner darkness – came around to the house one day with my son, Barry, and we had an amiable talk, trying to share separate nostalgias – separate worlds of writers who might somehow be friends – but after an hour, as he left, as he stepped out on to the front porch, he put his arm around my son's shoulder and I heard him say, "A lovely man, but he doesn't know what we know about life, does he." I thought I saw my son flinch.

I have to believe that even in a ruthless environment, and under the most sadistic conditions, some one man would reveal what I might call human feeling. Some one man! I'm not contending for Rousseauistic romanticism, the natural goodness of man dear to so many nineteenth-century novelists. Having seen what I've lived through, how could I believe men are naturally good? But now, there is another wild romanticism abroad, a fervent faith that man is naturally vicious, cruel, brutal, ruthless and sadistic. This is romanticism, too. It makes Kosinski's *The Painted Bird* very attractive to the young. I think it is a sentimentality about man. In its way, I believe it is just as great a falsification of life as the old-time Horatio Alger books, or *Anne of Green Gables*.

So, I go on believing that a few people, just a few people, at a given moment will stand up and demonstrate that man has buried within him a sense of inherent dignity, or some sense of conscience. Maybe I've wasted many years as a writer trying to hold to this conviction about man, though I always knew that even at the Crucifixion the disciples had failed. Of course, they wrote about it, they talked about it afterwards, that dignity. And I suppose Kosinski knows this, and I suppose, too, that when you know this as a writer, it frees you from refinements and sentimentalities, and the job of writing becomes more cruelly exciting.

The joke is that many of the writers urging this snakepit view are incorrigible moralists themselves. They exalt in the discovery that men, at heart, are pigs and apes when they are not clowns and frauds. These writers are the children of that dreary Old Testament figure, Ezekiel, with his hysterical view of Jerusalem. I'm sure that Jerusalem in his time wasn't like that at all, any more than peasants are as Kosinski depicts them in *The Painted Bird*. I can't prove this, of course. I can only rely on my own observations of towns and people.

I'm fascinated by the excitement, pleasure, and the sense of vindication some young men and women get out of books like Hubert Selby Jr.'s *Last Exit to Brooklyn*. The Ezekiel satisfaction! There seems to be a craving for this kind of violence, maybe the desire to kill or even be killed, and then comes the strange sense of relief and vindication, even a sense of righteousness. I'm sure the prophet Ezekiel knew this. He wanted to be listened to. Most novelists know that people go through their daily lives following drab routines, trained in polite amenities, half of them afraid of the dark, and of course they are afraid of recognizing or acknowledging the depths of violence and brutality in the half-starved part of their natures.

A literature which doesn't recognize this craving for violence simply does not recognize man as he is and always has been. That's true, but this part of the reader's heart is also the great natural marketplace for the eager writer. All that is required is an uncomplicated, primitive, and rather simple-minded view of man. When Hemingway wrote his little story about the barroom fight in which one of the fighters very expertly gouges out the eyes of the other and lets the eyeballs fall out like grapes, his early admirers, and I was one of them, thought Hemingway was going crazy. I am sure, now, that he was crazy like a fox. He recognized that there was going to be a new fashion, a new crowd of readers who would love exhibitions of incredible violence. He was far from crazy. He was moving into one of the great streams of history, even Christian history. Onward Christian solders! Think of the religious wars of the Middle Ages. Think of all the pious justifications of the hunger for violence.

Yet, there may be one good aspect to the contemporary lust for violence in movies and books. It brings something out into the open. This new violence does not purport to be Christian violence directed at evil. Just bestial violence for its own sake. Man as he is! There is no sloganeering on behalf of the Lord God of Hosts, no Old Testament satisfaction in the slaughter of enemies, but only violence out in the open, killing as killing, slaughter as slaughter. Man and his works are an abomination! I want none of this. It's an awful view, but it's good to have this view itself out in the open for what it is. Man incapable of love or disinterested goodness: the old twisted Puritan contempt for the natural man.

*CBC Anthology*

# GABRIEL GARCIA MARQUEZ

On the other hand, the discovery of a great writer has always filled me with wonder and curiosity. It is hard to do something so new with words that a book, all of a piece, has its own sense of reality. Genius, the way material is caught and looked at, seems to depend on the inner eye of the artist. A great writer, new to me, though known no doubt to thousands, is Gabriel Garcia Marquez, the Colombian author of *One Hundred Years of Solitude*. The only other South American whose work is familiar to me is Jorge Luis Borges. Borges is celebrated internationally; laurel wreaths are placed on his brow wherever he goes. He is a great craftsman who translates into our language beautifully; his style is so finely honed that you must salute him as an artist when you finish one of his little stories. Yet for me, Borges offers none of the fresh sense of wonder I get from Marquez. Borges is full of echoes from Europe, echoes from nineteenth-century European idealistic philosophy. From him, I get no sense of discovery, only my recognition of his craving for a perfection.

But this man Marquez, he bursts upon you with all the wild opulence of the jungle, the swamp, the crazy dreams of people, their piety, their brutality, their amazing courage, their betrayals and loyalties. The talent comes at you with the rush of a torrent, such a rush that a reader accustomed to English literature, draws back at first, thinking, Oh, this is all too exotic, and then caught up, he perceives that he is in the wild flow of limitless life. Mind you, dreams and fantasies and tall tales, miracles and nonsense, are a part of every man's life. We know this. Here it is. With his masterly style Marquez has achieved this extension of reality. He has done it in a way far beyond the scope of the naturalistic writer.

I'm not concerned with the factual story of *One Hundred Years of Solitude*. The outline gives none of the book's flavour. It is a story about the birth and death of a mythical South American town called Macondo. Where is it? Maybe in Ecuador. Maybe in any other country in Latin America. It is the story, too, of the rise and fall of the Buendia family. The founder of the town, old José Buendia, is succeeded by his son, Colonel Buendia, who makes endless revolutions, is defeated again and again, keeps coming back, triumphs, sees the eternal failure of his revolution, becomes a national hero, then suffers an awareness that revolutionary triumph is a kind of ghastly tragic joke. His town is rotting in the corruption all around him. But outlasting all the wild political events, all the lust and the follies of the town, all the births and deaths, the mad fantasies, the famines, the executions, is Ursula, the mother.

Ursula, the mother. Ursula, the wife of the town's founder. What a great character she is. She is the eternal wife, the everlasting mother, with her own superstitious sense of earthly reality. The prosaic one, holding the family together with her own completely feminine wisdom. For me, in Ursula's hundred years, she is almost crying out, "Before the town was, a woman was, before all the wild fantasies of men with their lust and crazy political brutalities, a woman was," and when her men in their dreams are wildly on the side of death, she is prudently trying to husband her own patch of soil. Her house, her family, her faith must survive, as she survives till the time comes when she is old and blind. Even then, while life flickers on in her, she knows her house so well that her kinsfolk are compelled to forget she is blind.

Ursula the mother is among the great characters of fiction. I have been emphasizing Ursula's greatness of character but what I'm really interested in is the wonder of the Marquez method.

If you are going to write the chronicle of a mythical town covering one hundred years, how do you get it down in a way that will convey all the superstitions, all the lying, all the lust, all the massacres in a straight, naturalistic style, or even in the poetic style of a Turgenev? The particular psyches of the characters would be separated, as people are separated. We would know when one character was dreaming, one telling the truth, another telling lies. When it was all put down this way we would be able to see that behind the putting down was the author's own critical sense of reality – something apart, making us aware of the difference between fact and fantasy.

But Marquez, with a magnificent insight into the power of style, a power that can create its own transcendent reality, handled the problem with the quick sureness of genius. The story, then, is to be told in a straightforward lucid, natural style. Using this style, Marquez is as literal as Tolstoy. The journey, the march that results in the founding of the town, is done as directly, as factually, as Xenophon did it in the *March of the Ten Thousand.* The recording of events! But here is the trick. What are the events in the life of a town, any town, any life? The provable facts that might be noted by any rational bookkeeper?

No.

The events of this mythical town are the things that happened and the things the people imagined happened, and the things that became legend, and, as legend, later on became facts; and the lies, too, related as facts so that they are believed later on and are not to be questioned. These things are put down in a literal style, all as events given equal weight. Sometimes the telling is very terse. A wonder is related laconically. A girl is said to have vanished at her death, a direct ascension into the clouds, no doubt: this is told as casually as the naturalistic telling of how another girl sucked her thumb. From this style so devoid of all psychological probing, of all the baggage of fidelity to the naturalist flow of thought, comes a startling and believable picture of the soul of a community, the swirl of life, a more complete life without and within the strange figures we call men and women. With this style, treating all things great and small as fact, pure fact, everything is in motion, all is action.

A woman who had read this book said to me, "But surely it is all symbolic. Surely the old man's obsession with his life's work, the fine metalwork, the making of little fish out of gold, surely that stands for the Church, doesn't it?" Fish: the Church? "I don't know," I said. Another reader said to me: "When the old man grows decrepit and senile, they put a rope around his neck and tie him to a tree in the sunlight, where he lives out his days. Surely, that has some great symbolic meaning." Maybe. Again, I don't know. I look at these things as part of the whole, part of the fantastic town life, part of the imagination. I seek and recognize the fantastic unity of the book, an original work, a rare thing. Let the academics, if they will, take it to pieces, symbol by symbol, till the unity of the imagination is torn to shreds. I like to feel the unbroken impact of this great writer, keeping incredibly the child's sense of wonder, held only by the spell of his method.

*CBC Anthology*

# JOYCE CAROL OATES

The poet's eye is supposed to roll in a fine frenzy, as if he were possessed. Poets do get carried away, it is true, but I have never encountered anything that struck me as possession in the work of a writer in our time until I came upon Joyce Carol Oates.

I have been reading her novel *Bellefleur*, the book which for the first time, after all her other works, has put her on the bestseller list. It should not surprise Oates to hear me say that an alien novel, coming from only God knows where, took her over and used her as a pipeline, for she herself has calmly told us how she was possessed some time ago by the spirit or voice of a dead young Portuguese and found herself writing a group of Portuguese stories. You may take this claim with a grain of salt, as I did at the time, but the fact is that those stories have a style and flavour utterly unlike the rest of her work. Indeed, I think that style is superior, clean, controlled, stripped, accurate, all characteristics often alien to her. I said to myself at the time, "Well, who knows how many voices there are in all of us."

But this tumult of a book, *Bellefleur*, is another matter. First, you have to understand that the nature of the *Bellefleur* material lies in all the standard elements of the old Gothic novel: the great half-ruined castle of a house in the hills, the vastly rich family, a whole tribe of them dominating their countryside, men who ride and drink and gamble, a tall woman so beautiful and strong she could have been Queen of the Amazons, who has for a pet a spider big as a sparrow, and there are rats, too, that turn into beautiful cats. All these characters are a shebang of gargoyles like those on mediaeval cathedral walls brooding over the town around the cathedral. My instinct is to turn away from this kind of material. I find the world around me, as it is, shocking and mysterious enough, but as soon as I started to read *Bellefleur*, I was touched by the mad energy in the writing, the headlong rush of this energy, the vast knowledge of people and things, and while my own aesthetic judgement was rejecting what was being done on these pages, the creative surge, the power of this wild and distorted imagination filled me with amazement.

There was before me a created thing. What was happening within this world was true to the law of the creating, even though I might draw back, blink my eyes and say, "This is rubbish." It is as if the material itself claimed Oates and took her over. Where it came from I don't know, but this should be said; I don't think any writer, doing research on a period, or a set of characters in a period, could have all the little facts come bubbling out the way they do here. Let's say someone's aunt is mentioned, which leads us to the husband of the aunt, then maybe, the father and so on, going back and back – as though the material was literally forcing itself out, having been given a small blowhole, in thousands of words, never pared down – and in phrases sometimes brilliant, sometimes banal, with insights, too, that are often brilliant.

Then come repetitions in a style that dulls the senses, the whole thing in a style that is so often lurid and overheated. And yet, this is what is fascinating; one begins to believe it couldn't have come out any other way because Oates had no choice. She was the pipeline, and so the material seems to take control of the words. Frenzied material. Frenzied words. It is all so far removed from the monumental, studied objectivity of a Flaubert where the artist is not only in complete control of the words but the words make the magic. A Flaubert works on his pages for years because he is the proud self-contained artist. Oates, as a pipeline, has to let it all pour out with an amazing energy giving the thing, or letting the thing, have a wild life of its own, and one wonders in the end if she sits back stunned, pondering over where it all came from.

If I seem to be drawing a long bow in suggesting that Oates in this book was by some other voice possessed, remember her Portuguese stories. It may be that all powerful artists are like mansions with many rooms, one big room, the living room, used in the main – but with other voices in other rooms waiting to be heard if the artists will only listen at the right time in the right way.

I, for one, don't like to think I might be taken over by a voice I could not control, an act somewhat different from what might be called inspiration. Inspiration is the heightening of all the senses when involuntarily the artist draws from the deepest well of his talent, and it becomes easy for him to do so even if something had to happen to prime the pump. When the work is finished he knows it is gloriously himself.

But as for those other voices, those extraneous voices – how does a writer, how does Oates know whether they are superior in wisdom and insight to her own voice? Where did those other voices come from? What opened Oates' imagination to all those devils and ludicrous demons, all those lusts, all the violence, all the hatred, all the vengeance? The creative energy is simply stunning. Were those voices really extraneous, are they really alien to her? Or does she in fact contain a stampede of voices? Is that who she is? It may be that Oates is more unique in herself than in anything she writes.

*CBC Anthology*

# IN A JUGULAR VEIN:
# HEMINGWAY

*A Moveable Feast* opens with the young Hemingway sitting at a café on the Place St. Michel, and straightway the old familiar and terribly determined elegiac note is sounded. It is very disquieting. Is he going to try to recapture the rhythms *of A Farewell to Arms*, I wondered unhappily? But soon, and mainly because he is able to recapture some of the feeling he had had for his first wife, Hadley, and their small son in those Paris days between 1921 and 1926, the style gets straightened out; this sad, disturbing and often funny book gets going in its own right. Once again after all these years we seem to see him sitting alone at a café, writing and hoping. It is very moving. We see him, too, as he watches the fishermen on the banks of the Seine, or goes into the Musée du Luxembourg to study the paintings of Cézanne, and wonders if he could get the same landscape effects in prose.

It was the time when he was writing those little stories that were something new in the language. Working in poverty, and in love with his wife, he was strangely happy. Having given up newspaper work, he was committed to writing and was turning out a kind of story that was so suggestive, so stripped, so objective, so effective in capturing pure sensation that it became a unique kind of poetry. Never again was he to be as original or as objective as he had been in those days. When the time came to write this book, maybe he knew what he had lost. And maybe this knowledge explains the book's bitter tone.

But in those days he wasn't as self-absorbed or as isolated as he makes out. In fact, long before he wrote *The Sun Also Rises*, he had had a peculiar underground fame, and the wonderful thing about him at the time was that he had a generous interest in the work of other unknown writers, was in touch with them, and would go out of his way to try to get them published in the little Paris magazines. Did he forget about the young writers who adored him? Why is it that the main thing he wanted to remember, or get down on paper, was that he had found perfect happiness in isolation, work and love – till other people came into the picture? And the only wisdom he has to offer now, looking back on it, is that other people, any people, are always the enemies of those who are in love, and the enemies of the artist also. They smell out happiness, they move in to destroy it. It is always people, never himself, who are to blame.

And so he manages to give the impression that two star-crossed lovers, himself and Hadley, the *Farewell to Arms* theme again, had their happiness destroyed by *the* great enemy – people. A man's fate is in the people who are interested in him, and if you are skiing in the Alps with your girl and people find you there, you can't prevail against them. This is, surely, a pretty childish view of life.

Some of the people to be looked down on are done in the book as set pieces, and not at all in a flow of memories. This faulty structure is the great weakness of the book. And what frightening sketches of people who at one time knew and liked him! There is Ford Madox Ford, who, as editor of the *Transatlantic Review*, had printed some of Hemingway's early work, and who, even before the triumphant appearance of *The Sun Also Rises,* had written a front-page article in the *Herald Tribune Books*, New York, calling him the best young writer in America; Ernest Walsh, the Irish poet, an editor of *This Quarter*, who had first printed "Big Two Hearted River" and "The Undefeated;" Gertrude Stein, once his motherly friend, who had belittled him in print; Wyndham Lewis, who over the years had deplored Hemingway's love of violence; Pascin, the painter, and Scott Fitzgerald, who as he says, had been a loyal friend for years – until they fell out.

The touch he uses in these portraits is controlled, expert, humorous and apparently exact; he is like a proud pool player, who lines up the balls with his cue, says, "That one in the corner pocket," and sinks it cleanly. But underneath the surface humour – it's really a gallow's humour – there is a long-nourished savagery, or downright venom, and in his portraits there is the quick leap for the jugular vein.

What a relief it is to find him expressing tenderness and respect and loyalty to Ezra Pound – or affection for Sylvia Beach. And a relief, too, to discover there was a young poet named Evan Shipman whom he liked. Otherwise, one could gather he had no capacity for friendship at all. In a prefatory note he says there were many good friends. There were indeed. It is unfortunate that he didn't get some of his old simple friendliness into the book. How much fairer he would have been to himself in revealing what he was really like in those days. He was actually an attractive, interesting, fascinating companion, dark and brooding though he might be, with strange shrewd hunches about people that turned into grudges. He was likeable and simple in manner, too. The savagery that was in him only broke out when he went berserk, as in this book. He is a mockingly amusing cold killer with a weapon he often controls so beautifully – his own prose.

In those days he would tell you he disliked Ford. He would openly scoff at him. Yet his brother, in his hero-worshipping book, tells how Ford had been sent by Ernest to visit the Hemingway family home in Chicago. Yet in the Hemingway sketch of Ford, the two of them sitting at a café, a very expert, very funny sketch, he pictures Ford as a liar and a clown who gave off a body odour that fouled the air. Was this all there was to Ford? Of course not, and he knew it.

It is true, too, that Wyndham Lewis was a difficult man to meet. He was so self-conscious, so worried that his importance would not be recognized, that he was always ill at ease and without any grace of manner. Hemingway and Lewis met in Pound's studio when Hemingway was teaching Pound to box. Looking back on the meeting, he believed he hated Lewis on sight. He can hardly express his loathing for the "meanest-looking man I ever met." Yet here, again, Hemingway overdoes it. And why? Only God knows! He had no more interest in trying to understand Lewis than he had in understanding Ford. Yet these highly prejudiced, personal reactions are interesting. In them may be found the keynote to the brilliance of much of his work. With him, everything was personal, his work became the projection of his personality. He was not concerned with fairness or charity, or moral judgements, just with his own sensations.

Mind you, I, for one, don't care whether he was fair to Gertrude Stein or not. That domineering woman had talked her way into a reputation, and she had taken her snide cracks at him. So, he's gone to work on her. It's the literary life, I suppose.

The best and happiest writing in the book, and in some ways the fairest picture he gives of anyone, is of Scott Fitzgerald. The writing turns free and easy. He forgets the Biblical rhythms. He is at home and happy with his subject. The description of a trip to Lyon with Fitzgerald is simply hilarious; it is more than that; he gives a wonderfully vivid glimpse of Fitzgerald in all his changing moods, drunk and sober, and recognizes his talent. Yet on end, aside from recognition of the talent, Fitzgerald is so cut down as a person – well, as Hemingway tells it, even the bartender at the Ritz, where Fitzgerald spent so much time, can't remember him, but promised to try to do so, if old Hem would only write about him and make him memorable.

As for the terrible disorder in Fitzgerald's life, Hemingway blames it on Zelda. Poor crazy Zelda, who, he says, was jealous of Scott, and liked to see him get drunk, knowing he wouldn't be able to work. And what may be just as fantastic is Hemingway's explanation of why he began to shy away from Scott. He saw that Scott liked walking in on him to interrupt him, and saw that it was all a plan to make it impossible for him to work. This leaves us with Fitzgerald doing to Hemingway what Zelda was doing to Fitzgerald. It gets mixed up and very complicated. But you remember they were two men who dramatised everything, simply everything, including each other.

As the book draws to an end there is a curious revelation which is almost shocking in its candour. The idyllic love between Hemingway and his wife had continued up to the writing of *The Sun Also Rises*. When they are skiing happily in the Alps, some rich people seek them out. A rich girl moves in with them, and in no time Hemingway has two women, and then finally he has only one and it isn't Hadley any more. "Then you have the rich and nothing is ever as it was again," he says, and his life took another turn, and with sourness, he blames the rich for moving in on him and taking away his happiness. Was he so weak and helpless in the presence of the rich? It is such a surprising revelation one can't at first quite believe it, and then comes the thought, it must be true, for it is the first time Hemingway has ever deliberately put himself in a bad light.

*The Spectator*, 1964

# E.J. PRATT:
# MUSCULAR GAIETY

People who are well liked, whose stance in life seems to depend on their being well liked, are hard on their friends. How can anyone bear to have an argument with them, an argument that brings an angry flush to the face. How can anyone, without apparently letting down all men of good will in the world, bear to wound them by being sharply and honestly critical.

If the enormously well-liked man is a writer, he must be baffled when he reads a luke-warm or disapproving appraisal of his work by a stranger, someone, who has had no chance to get to like and admire him as a man. The poet, E.J. Pratt, or Ned, as he was known to his friends, was a well-liked man. In fact, he had the warm approval not only of hundreds of students who passed through his hands in the years when he was an English professor at Victoria College in Toronto, but his contemporaries, the poets and the critics, seemed to love him as a man.

Pratt was a generation ahead of me, yet, as soon as I had broken into print late in the twenties and had had some success in New York, he came to see me. He was generous, he was warm. I soon forgot the difference in age. Without noticing it, I soon entered into a male conspiracy with him, wherein was celebrated in a dozen small ways the love of comradeship, masculine vehemence, the primitive virtues, a recognition that there were men in this world who were scoundrels and twerps who didn't belong, and above all – the sharing of the splendours of the stag party. His cronies met at his house quite often and had dinner, drinks, and good conversation, with never a woman coming to spoil the happy comradeship that was so important to this well-liked man.

When you share food, drinks and jokes you tend to share opinions and approvals. Ned Pratt had a very infectious smile. There was a kind of warm intimacy in this smile. He was a generous man, generous with his food, his liquor, his praise. The generosity of his praise seemed to leave me tongue-tied, sometimes leave me feeling churlish, because I did not have this kind of generosity. I could not praise when the praise was unimportant to me. So infectious was his humour and the sense of comradeship he conveyed, that when you found him denouncing some poet, some heel, some scoundrel who had offended his sensibilities, I couldn't bear to disagree with him.

I saw Ned Pratt at many parties, I played golf with him, I always enjoyed his company, but I had begun to notice that I never discussed his work with him, and he never discussed mine. It didn't seem to be necessary. Instead, there was this shared approval. We would have lunch, he would ask me to come to his college. Sometimes, I would tell myself it was unnatural that two writers who respected each other weren't saying, occasionally, "Look, I wrote this poem," or, "Look, I wrote this story, what do you think?" So, I said nothing, even when he told me that the younger academics were going in for "that man, T.S. Eliot." I was going in for him myself at the time. To have offered a word of objection to his point of view, it seemed to me then, would have been a violation of the liking I and all other acceptable men had for Ned Pratt, and which I am sure he counted on in matters that were important to him.

Over the years, while never having a cross word, I can see now that Ned Pratt never knew what was going on in my head, and what all the liking amounted to was this: I never made a critical remark that could possibly upset him. My view of his poetry I kept strictly to myself. I doubt that this even aroused his curiosity because he must have been able to tell that I liked him, as if this liking had to take in everything. The fact was, I admired the way he could take language that others would not think right for poetry and use it with poetic power. But I liked his shorter poems far better than I liked the celebrated long narratives, which I thought overrated. I remember that when Pratt's poetry failed to make much of an impression in the United States or England, I regretted that he hadn't appeared frequently in New York and London . . . appeared in person.

In the war years, Ned Pratt wrote a poem, "Dunkirk." In those days, when a poet of the stature of Pratt wrote a poem about such a heroic and moving event as Dunkirk, it was considered an important event. The publisher, Hugh Eayres, and Dr. Pelham Edgar of Victoria College, the distinguished commentator on Henry James, organized a dinner for about twenty citizens of the York Club, dinner for a poet in this exclusive bastion of the bourgeoisie. But by this time, Ned Pratt had become the national poet. At this dinner he was to read the new long narrative poem.

It was a very good dinner, with drinks and cigars and hearty conversation, the tone subdued on the advice of Dr. Edgar. But we all knew each other. If there were some at the tables I didn't like, this didn't matter. They all liked Ned Pratt.

Finally, Dr. Edgar, an elegant figure himself, and a man who read far more widely than did most of his university colleagues, rose and talked a little and then Pratt rose and began to read the poem. It is a long poem. It was getting a very good clear reading. At first, I listened with great curiosity, a writer's curiosity. I wanted to see how Ned Pratt would handle this vivid story material; yet, after a while, I felt a loss of concentration. I wasn't being genuinely moved, and then, off by myself, yet feeling secure because no one could hear what I was saying to myself, and after all I was a prose writer, I said irritably, "Too much cataloguing. Too much cataloguing," feeling quite safe in my secret irritation, because in all the faces around me there was the same rapt concentration of approval.

The reading was over. The applause was warm and happy.

Dr. Edgar, rising, said it struck him that it would be interesting to get – first of all – the opinion of a younger man. "What would you like to say, Mr. Callaghan?" Mute, flabbergasted, I stared at Dr. Edgar, feeling like a discovered Judas who deserved this humiliation, having to reveal himself at last. There was Ned beaming at me. Here I was among the local literary gentry, I who had never talked about poetry with Ned, at last flushed out and with nothing in my head. Pratt was waiting with all that warm goodwill, that confident generosity in his face, while I tried to look as if I were meditating. To my astonishment I found myself saying, "I was struck by the muscular gaiety . . ." When this strange phrase brought a happy grin to Ned's face and an appreciative nod from Dr. Edgar, I knew I was home free. I talked for five minutes about muscular gaiety, which I said was the essence of Ned Pratt. The phrase seemed to show how much I liked him, and how who he was could not be separated from his work. Afterwards, with warm appreciation, he said, "Muscular gaiety. Oh, I liked that very much."

# RAYMOND KNISTER

In 1925, when I was in my second year at law school and my stories had begun to appear in the avant-garde literary magazines in Paris, I saw the name of another Canadian storyteller, Raymond Knister, in one of those magazines. Astonished, I sat down and read the story. And in that same issue this Knister also had a sheaf of farm poems. I liked the farm poems. I could smell the farm in them. They were simple and direct. They were effortlessly authentic. The story had some of the same quality. I could see that Knister had the honest eye and neat skill to get down precisely what his eye caught. This remarkable gift didn't quite work for me in the story because without the rhythmic flow of the poems the meticulous observations seemed a trifle laboured. I sat up and took notice because here was a writer from my neck of the woods who aspired to be first-rate.

I suppose Knister was as curious about me as I was about him, for, about a month after I read him, he came to see me. He walked in on me, saying simply, "I'm Raymond Knister," smiling as if he fully expected I would know about him. He was of medium height with a very high forehead, a nice-looking man a few years older than I, a man with a stutter he tried to control by talking in a singsong tone. Welcoming him like the long lost brother, I wanted to know where he was from and how it came about that he was appearing in such an international magazine. He was from a farming family, he said. He could not explain how it was that a boy from a farming family, who had spent a little time at Victoria College in

Toronto, should have an innate taste for the best in literature. In 1923 he had gone off for a year to Iowa City to serve on the editorial board of *The Midland*, which was certainly one of the best little literary magazines in America. In the summer of 1924, he told me, he had lived in Chicago, writing during the day and driving a taxi at night. Musing, I said he must have come from a very cultured farming family. No, he didn't think so, he said, smiling. He was the only one who had literary talent. Then, as young writers do, getting the feel of each other, we talked about the writers we loved, found some splendid agreements and new excitements. He had read all of Sherwood Anderson, Virginia Woolf, Katherine Mansfield, Dorothy Richardson, Joyce's *Dubliners*, and Turgenev. He loved Turgenev. Well, I parted with him reluctantly and was sure I had found a treasure.

The next time he came to see me, he brought a copy of the issue of *The Midland* that contained his story, "Mist-Green Oats." I liked the story. It had, of course, that splendid authenticity of all his farm work, but it was brought close to me by a lyric prose flow.

I had introduced Raymond to Loretto, whom I was to marry, and I remember one charming evening in the summer when the three of us walked along Toronto's lakeshore, west, all the way out to Sunnyside, to the boardwalk and dance pavilion, walking slowly and exchanging profound insights into the other contemporary writers we thought important. Raymond talked about e.e. cummings. He declaimed loudly, "when on a pale green gesture of twilight . . ." This was a beautiful poem, he said fervently. He would have liked to have written those lines. He began to talk about his own work. He began to stammer. Then suddenly in a rather loud voice, free from all stammering because he was really singing, he declaimed:

*The trees cry loud, "Oh, who will unchain us!"*
*They gasp crying, but deep mould never stirs.*
*Never in this life shall they go whirling:—*
*The storm's great burrs.*

Then, laughing, he said, "I wrote that last week and showed it to Charles G.D. Roberts. He told me it was all right except for the last line. What do you think?"

Though I thought of Raymond as a stranger in town, the astonishing thing about him was that he knew all the local literati. At that time I knew none of them. He knew E.J. Pratt, Wilson Macdonald, the older Roberts, and Mazo de la Roche, who at that time lived with her cousin on central Yorkville Avenue and was as poor as a church mouse. Obviously, he wasn't at all shy. I found he simply presented himself to anyone he really wanted to meet.

My own private world, which at that time was in Paris, was widening quickly. All those experimental magazines now wanted stories from me. I wondered if Raymond was getting left out. At the time I owed Hemingway a letter, and when I wrote him, I asked, "By the way, did you notice in that second issue of *This Quarter* the work of another Canadian, Raymond Knister? I know him. What about him?" In a month or so Hemingway answered my letter but did not mention Raymond Knister.

Before he met me, Raymond had written some pieces for the *Toronto Star Weekly*. The bit of money he got from those pieces had been important to him, he told me. Now he found that this market was drying up for him. I introduced him to the *Weekly* writer, Greg Clarke, who could tell him what the *Weekly* wanted from him. Their meeting wasn't fruitful. Raymond's luck seemed to have run out. "The *Weekly*!" I remember him saying with exasperation, "if they will only tell me exactly how they want it written, I can write it exactly that way." And he actually believed this. Not only was he wrong about this, he was wrong-headed about himself and foolishly stubborn in believing he could make any style his own. He could only be Raymond. He wasn't a hack. Yet he had this strange stubborn faith in himself – a writer with a hundred arrows to his bow. It was this stubbornness at the time which made him so remarkable in this country. He really believed that he could support himself writing uncommercial stories, and not only himself, for he was planning to get married.

I learned how annoyingly stubborn Raymond could be. A new issue of *This Quarter* had come out, featuring a story of mine and using nothing of Raymond's. He came to see me and told me that *This Quarter* hadn't paid him for the prose and poetry they had used in their previous issue. I remember how he kept looking at me strangely as he told me this. What happened to that payment? he wanted to know, waiting grimly for my comment. Well, I knew he needed money, but I didn't know what was on his mind till a week later when he asked me point-blank if they hadn't sent his money to me, believing I would give it to him. I was astonished. A few days later he confronted me again. "Had the money come to me?" he asked. I shouted at him, "Why the hell should they send your money to me? How can you be so stubborn?" Yet I wasn't angry. He was the isolated writer, the hard-up lonely writer grimly determined that his talent should be rewarded by someone some-where, even if the someone had to be me.

By 1928, knowing I had a novel and a book of stories published in New York, and having finished law school, I got married and went to Paris. For over a year I saw nothing of Raymond. When I returned to Canada, the Depression had begun. Those were hard and terrible times for writers. Many stopped writing. I can't remem-ber seeing Raymond for two or three years. I heard that he had gone to Montreal, married, and now had a daughter. I couldn't imagine how he could be earning a living, although he had written his novel, *White Narcissus*, which Pelham Edgar had praised highly. Edgar was right. It is a remarkable book, remarkable in that it seems to demonstrate so perfectly the aspects of Knister's talent that were so strong. The book is a kind of *The Return of the Native* book. A young man returns to his native hearth, the family farm, and the life he had lived there. The woman he was to love is there, too. It is the real Knister and he reveals all his power to create a farm atmosphere and do it all so effortlessly that we never think, here is a writer deliberately creating atmosphere.

I saw Raymond for the last time one afternoon in Toronto when he dropped in at my place on Avenue Road and stayed a few hours. He looked very much like himself. He talked about the Montreal literati. Apparently he had met them all. Then he sat down and read a story of mine that was in the *New Yorker*. Smiling, he said enigmatically, "You're now like the ancient mariner." Instead of exploring that one, I asked him how he planned to live, and he told me that his friend Pelham Edgar had a friend who owned a nice cottage at Port Hope and Edgar had arranged for him to live there. Right now he was trying to finish a story titled, "Peaches, Peaches." He wanted to enter the story in a big contest being staged by an American magazine. There was $10,000 in it for the winner. I wished him luck.

Later on he sent me a copy of "Peaches, Peaches," which he had worked feverishly to get in to the magazine just under the wire. His wife, he said, had worked just as hard as he had, copying the manuscript. They had high hopes. I read the manuscript. It was full of good work and wonderfully authentic, and yet it was weak in narrative power. I couldn't bear to tell this to him when he still had such high hopes.

A little later, at his uncle's cottage at Stoney Point on Lake St. Clair, Raymond went swimming by himself and drowned.

"Afterword," 1990, from *White Narcissus*,
a novel by Raymond Knister

*By the time he was twenty-five, Morley had hit his stride. Goodwill and happenstance had come his way. His stories had appeared in little magazines like* This Quarter, Max Perkins' Scribners, *and the commercial magazines, too. He was a presence in New York. He was a presence in Toronto. He'd published a collection of stories and a first novel,* Strange Fugitive, *the first gangster novel in America. Even after the 1929 crash, as he passed out of the what he called his morning glory stage, he believed he could stay alive as a writer in the ten-cents-a-dance days of the Depression, he believed he could keep a wife and a son by writing not only novels but more and more non-commercial stories for magazines like* The New Yorker, Harper's Bazaar, *and* Esquire.

*In Toronto, he'd begun to write book reviews for the national magazine,* Saturday Night. *A writer for that magazine, Bernard Preston, wrote a long profile of him in which he said:*

"And what does he talk about, this laxly intent artist, this indolently active thinker? The answer is: everything! Everything, that is, that bears relation to life. He is passionately opposed to ignorance, he must have awareness, and so spends hours daily reading newspapers from all over the world. He loves the crowd at a prize fight, at a football or a hockey game. He is intensely interested in politics, in the wider sense of the word, and used to speaking in public . . . he will discuss ships and sealing wax with equal impartiality. He is also so thoroughly detached mentally that he feels readily at home in any realm of thought or any part of the globe. . . . Contact with alert minds is as the breath of his nostrils to him. He admits readily, with no sense of confession, that he likes New York better than any other place.

He finds doubtless that there he can enjoy not only a freer interchange of ideas, but that ideas are much more rife and original than in most centres. The very air teams with stimulation . . . He reconciles a profound knowledge of the world and a mature youthfulness with an apparently artless ingenuousness and young wisdom, and exercises keen critical ability with seeming carelessness. In other words, he embodies equipoise, balance, sanity . . ."

*In Toronto, however, many reviewers had talked about Morley's style being like Hemingway's style. But they weren't anything alike. In fact, Morley's style was recognized in New York as being so much his own that in 1930, when he was only twenty-seven,* The Saturday Review of Literature, *published three parodies of his stories — under the title, "Canada Dry," by a writer named Christopher Ward. To be only twenty-seven, to have written only three books, and to have a style so singular as to be open to parody, is remarkable. Typically, Morley had forgotten all about this, but I thought it would be amusing to reprint* The Saturday Review *heading and one of the parodies (in which, surprisingly, he appears as a character), anticipation some of the book reviews he was then beginning to write for* Saturday Night, *the reviews of an engaged young writer responding to the styles of other emerging writers.*

◆   ◆   ◆

# "PAYING THE PIPER"
# BY M-RL-Y C-LL-GH-N

Bassett Murphy had big hands. He had been intended for a school-teacher, but it snowed so hard that winter that the old folks got restless. There was no reason why they should feel the way they did about it. There were plenty of other people in Toronto. There was a young Jew from New York at the Gaiety, a dancer, who wore grey trousers, but that didn't help much.

Bassett's father had white hands and a gold watch that had been given to him on his twenty-first birthday by his Aunt Norah, who lived in Montreal. He was a chess expert and had long nourished an ambition to be elected coroner. Bassett borrowed ten dollars from him and went north. His mother had on her best silk dress.

At North Bay, he got off the train and ate a roast beef sandwich with lots of gravy in a Greek restaurant. The Greek's wife did her washing standing up.

Bassett winked at the Greek and said, "Pretty cold, eh?"

"Sure Mike! Every hour on the hour," the Greek said.

Walking along the street, he saw a lot of houses. He was disappointed, so he got a room in one of the houses. Three days later there was a railroad accident in Manitoba and snow on Pike's Peak.

Bassett went back home. His father was busy with his postage stamps, but his mother was glad it was no worse. With that, all pretense was abandoned and Bassett called on the people next door. Their name was Carboy.

Mildred Carboy was a nice girl. She was out when Bassett called.

He got a job on a Toronto paper. There he met Morley Callaghan. They used to take long walks together.

"You ought to write stories for the American magazines," said Morley.

"Stories?"

"Yes, stories."

"For the American magazines?"

"Yes, for the American magazines. They aren't hard to do. You just pick out somebody you know, like me, for instance, and describe him. Tell all about his clothes and his family and what he does. It doesn't matter what he does, just so you tell all about it and how many panes of glass there are in the bedroom window and whether he wears a grey fedora. Your man doesn't really have to do anything at all. The story doesn't have to have any beginning or any end, and there's nothing particular in the middle. When you've written enough you just stop. Then the critics say, 'He has great restraint, a fine economy of means. It's the things he leaves out that make him important.'"

"Then the more you leave out the more important you are?"

"Sure."

"Then I'm the most important of all. I leave out everything."

by Christopher Ward,
*Saturday Review of Literature*, 1930

# INTRODUCING
# ERNEST HEMINGWAY

So many brilliant post-war writers are discovered every day by enterprising critics that one is apt to overlook the importance of Ernest Hemingway. Reviewers discussing the American short story have grown accustomed to mentioning his volume, *In Our Time* and his work has been praised by Sinclair Lewis, Sherwood Anderson, James Joyce, almost everybody of importance, excepting H.L. Mencken. It is appropriate that Hemingway should have dedicated his new book, *Torrents of Spring*, a satire on modern writers, to Mencken "in admiration."

Irrespective of critical acclaim and literary fashions, I believe Hemingway is writing the best short stories coming from an American today. It is too bad his vogue is limited, for his prose has a classical quality, a direct simplicity and earthy flavour quite foreign to the King's English and the literary language of professors, which makes it a spoken language with a feeling for the natural rhythms that are colloquial. The short stories of *In Our Time* show his complete mastery of his material, his fine regard for the value of a word and a disdain for mannerisms and vanities dear to the heart of many good writers. He is a fine naturalist, who, instead of piling up material and convincing by sheer weight of evidence, in the manner of Dreiser or Zola, cuts down the material to essentials and leaves it starkly authentic.

Hemingway lives in Paris, his first slender volumes were published by Contact and the Three Mountains Press, and so he is often associated with that Paris group: Ford Madox Ford, Ezra Pound, James Joyce and Robert McAlmon. But Hemingway, having none of Ford's affectations of style, has more intensity and control of himself and his material than McAlmon, and unlike John Dos Passos, he has not come under the influence of James Joyce.

*In Our Time* consists of fifteen short stories with brief interposed "chapters" in italics. These fiercely concentrated moments of energy and vitality are extraordinarily vivid; a British officer in the garden at Mons, bullfights, a hanging, an evacuation, all having a permanent quality, the words used at one with the subject matter. He has refused to succumb to the temptation of the splendid word, the devices of those who wish to be mistaken for English stylists. Stories like "Cat in the Rain" and "The Doctor and the Doctor's Wife" show a temperamentally different attitude to the short story. "Cat in the Rain" catches a mood, a short feeling of opposition between husband and wife in a hotel room. A young boy watches a quarrel between his father and a half-breed in "The Doctor and the Doctor's Wife" and the reader understands intimately the relation between the Doctor and his Christian Science wife. In "Out of Season," a depressing, irritating mood is caught and held. "The Three-Day Blow," two boys getting drunk and trying to remain thoroughly practical, is a happy and subtle piece of writing. Finally the story, "Big Two-Hearted River," is as good a piece of descriptive writing as I have ever read. Nick goes fishing. Nothing stands between the reader and Nick's movements. So accurate is Hemingway's reporting that this movement has an exhilarating reality in these days of the psychological novel. One moves with his people, knows what they are thinking, feels the wind, sees the hills and gets the smell of burnt timber.

Hemingway's new book, *The Torrents of Spring*, is a robust and lively satire on the affectations of some modern writers, done in the style of Sherwood Anderson's *Dark Laughter*. Hemingway hates affectations and poses, which to him are the source of the truly ridiculous. Here, he hilariously carries Anderson's manner to a logical but ridiculous extremity, and incidentally, hits out at Dos Passos' studies in futility and D.H. Lawrence's affected awareness of the primitive. It is healthy and good to find a writer of Hemingway's calibre wielding the slapstick on celebrated writers, even as one acknowledges that Anderson's *Dark Laughter* remains a distinguished and beautiful piece of work.

*Saturday Night*, 1926

# THE WANDERER:
# ALAIN FOURNIER

*The Wanderer* by Alain Fournier is a book done so quietly and softly that it leaves the impression of being overheard. But it is not a fairy tale. In the deluge of critical praise that greeted the publication of the book, in America there was much talk of its unreality, or rather of the loveliness of its illusion. And it was compared with the plays of Barrie, largely, I imagine, because the critics felt that the book had charm and, as everybody knows, Barrie is the last word in charm.

But Fournier has none of Barrie's "delicious sentiment." His writing is so simple, so intensely real, so devoid of all sleight-of-hand gestures that critics reading it are startled, and so accustomed are they to conventional prose with its conventional world that they can only account for the strange reality of this book by calling it a lovely illusion.

Fournier died at the age of twenty-seven, a sacrifice to war as surely as was Rupert Brooke. This was his only novel, though he started several others, and it reveals how he had abandoned naturalism and how he had caught some of the lyrical feeling for country and for simple people vaguely conscious of an ideal world that is in many of the novels of the English countryside. This is merely a groping effort to classify Fournier, and the English novel is mentioned because he is closer to the English than to the French tradition. One would imagine that a young man in his time would have caught some of the glamour of Zola, for he was thinking of writing at a time when naturalism had apparently swept all before it, but Zola might just as well have not existed for all the influence he had on *The Wanderer*. Nor does Fournier bear any resemblance to the young Gide, or to Proust or to the young modern Frenchmen such as Breton. One can simply say that the novel seems to have fallen outside the tradition of the modern French novel, a little later than naturalism and yet a little too old-fashioned in its telling to show the effect of a study of modern technique. If one suggests that the story is slightly old-fashioned in its telling, it should be remembered that it was first published about fifteen years ago, that it attracted little attention and that it might never have been reprinted had not a few men, especially Cocteau after the war, recalled the book, wondering what had happened to it. So it was reprinted in France and now one hears that the younger men regard it as an important influence. But still it occurs to me that it is almost good that Fournier left only this one book, which seems to reveal so much of his own life and leaves an impression of something wispy and fragile caught in the moonlight that would have disappeared forever at the dawn. Other books might have marked more definitely just where Fournier stood in relation to other novelists of his time but this one book is left as his own story. And it has the truth of a life, a reality so quiet and so intense that it appears to be an illusion.

I can see that some might associate this book with Thornton Wilder's *Bridge of San Luis Rey*, but *The Wanderer* is, I believe, a better book because of its lack of that artificial arrangement of material that is very often mistaken for form. *The Wanderer*, taken causally, is the country story of a boy named Meaulnes, who has the instinct for wandering. He leaves school one night and stumbles upon an old manor house where a feast is prepared for an expected bridegroom. Meaulnes has little more than a glimpse of a beautiful fair girl and a few words with her. The night passes, he is back at school, but he cherishes the memory of the night as an ideal of perfection, the greatest possible perfection in this world, and so he searches for years for the beautiful fair girl, trying to recapture that youthful notion of perfection. But even when he finds her and marries her, something is lacking; she is beautiful, but the illusion of the night of the feast, which was for him the magic land of youth, has passed away into a story that is almost fairy-like and fantastic, but as an illusion, and this is the mystery of the writing, it is inexplicably all the more real.

*Saturday Night,* 1928

# ALFRED KAZIN:
# ANTENNAE OF THE RACE

When I was reading Alfred Kazin's *Bright Book of Life: American Storytellers from Hemingway to Mailer*, I came upon that much quoted dictum of Ezra Pound's: "Writers are the antennae of the race." Kazin says that Pound knew exactly where the future was heading, and the revealed future is now – it is here, says Kazin, in contemporary American fiction.

Kazin is always interesting, he comes up with insights that are often profound and challenging, and after I put the book down, feeling rather depressed by the view of American life as it is drawn by Kazin out of the work of Mailer, Capote, Cheever, the Jewish novelists, and Joyce Carol Oates, Pynchon, Salinger, and Updike, I got to wondering about the Pound observation that writers are the antennae of the race.

Has the disappointment with America, the fascination with absurdity in their work added up to a rejection of man's importance on this earth? Has this malaise, this malfeasance of the heart, this helter-skelter sense of helplessness, been picked up by the antennae of the writers of our time because it is *actually* there (as it was *not* there for the young Pound, nor for the young Hemingway who, as Kazin says, believed in glory, high art, and the splendor of form) or have they, surrounded by normal people, come to share in a pathology, an endless scrutiny of the self that is poised to act, yet paralyzed. If so, none among them could touch a theme of moral grandeur, or be awed by the dignity of self-respect without feeling that he was indulging in sentimental fantasies, lying about his own time?

A writer looks around. His own eyes, his own heart, dictate what he sees and records. The seen things will be the grist for the mill that is his own heart, his own spiritual condition. But the artist is a shaper and maker as well as a recording machine. He is not like an interpreter in the police court of life. Such interpreters are nothing in themselves. No. The artist's antennae send out signals as well as picking them up. These signals, when heard, may result in the shaping of a whole society. It is my belief that society, even all of history, is shaped as much by men's fantasies as by — let us say — economic forces, the means of production, or the medium of exchange. Since the novelist and poet are makers of their own fantasies, which they submit to other men's conceptions of imaginative truth, then they are acting upon society as much as society is acting upon them. If, in a particular time in America, the human spirit as it is revealed in novels is twisted or apathetic or completely disillusioned, then the flaw, the spiritual flaw, may be in the artist as well as in the lives of others.

Disillusionment. Again and again Kazin mentions disillusionment. But disillusioned with what? A writer sits at his window on the world. In the twenties, when I started to write, the disillusionment with politics, with war, with academics, with the democratic process, was so vast it became an energetic force; it became a kind of general good health for artists.

Off with the old corruption. On with the new. And in the recognition of corruption and phoniness there was a splendid zest. Boundless energy was released. Given the fierceness of that past rejection, what seems childish to me now is that our current writers and philosophers and preachers, looking at the world of our time, can shudder and really believe that never was the world so out of joint.

Out of joint? Compared with when? For the American writers, and I do get this impression from Kazin, there was a time, there must have been a time, the good old days, when there were sunlit days of belief in the American dream, whatever that was. But, were the good old sunlit solid times in the nineteenth century? If sensitive American writers shuddered watching the national dream vanish in Vietnam, surely they would also have shuddered in the nineteenth century watching the slaughters, the genocide of the native American tribes. But these slaughters didn't trouble Edgar Poe or Henry Thoreau or Walt Whitman.

In Europe, in that same nineteenth century of pieties and faiths, so many wars were being fought, so many empires enlarged, so many coloured races subjugated and so many workers ground into poverty, that the mind now goes awry with dismay, yet it was the age of optimism, of progress – at least, these were the accepted fantasies.

The personal lives of eminent Victorians were as twisted and snarled as any lives being lived in Palm Beach or Manhattan (there were 75,000 working prostitutes in London at the time), yet the English writers, Dickens, Thackery, Tennyson, the antennae of their race, quivered with a bouncy will to live and live well, even if their personal lives were full of duplicity and the dirty little secrets that are now the natural material for disillusioned American writers.

With pipe dreams vanishing, I suppose it comes down to this: if the great national dream once existed, the American writer, to judge from the Kazin analysis, has nothing to fall back on now but himself. But why not? It was always this way for great artists. The question arises; how does a writer see himself? What does he think of himself, aside from the consoling bluff that he just picks up the sights and sounds around him and gets them in order? Take the case of Salinger as he appears under the Kazin microscope.

Salinger, Kazin says, believes in nothing but the Glass family, which he created in his own fiction. In Salinger's world, the whole of rotten society is pitted against this one perfect admirable and interesting family. Of course, there is a violent world outside Salinger's mind, and of course one family is more admirable than another – as Salinger has it. But I believe the writer sees what he sees in order to satisfy his own fantasy. I, as a novelist, am not satisfied to imagine that Salinger is merely the recording antennae for his time, caught up in the net of his society. I am too much of a personalist. I want to know what happened in Salinger's own life. Why does a writer have to see life in his own particular pattern?

If you believe we live in incredibly debased and corrupt times devoid of all spirituality you will be satisfied with the writer simply as a recording angel. But if you believe as I do, that there never was a period in history when men weren't violent, politicians weren't corrupt, men lustful and greedy and cynical and saying one thing and doing another, then you might be inclined to say that in our time we suffer only from the loss of fantasies. It is as if the old fantasies have all worn out. That boundless optimism, that Dream. But this also means that the young writer has enormous room to manoeuvre, enormous room to shape the world in his own image. A young writer, at his window, if he be alive and confident, should say, "There it is out there, the human race, still squirming and suffering and missing love. I can make anything I want to make out of it and I will!"

*CBC Anthology*

# PROTECTION MONEY

*"After all, money is for the throwing off the backs of trains."*
—GENE FOWLER, a Hollywood screenwriter

I remember the first story I ever sold to a little magazine in Paris. Great young writers were being printed in that magazine, *This Quarter*. I was in Toronto. When they printed my story and sent me eight dollars, that trifling bit of money was a treasure far beyond the thousand dollars or two thousand dollars I might have got from the *Saturday Evening Post*, the big money market of the time. To try for the big money I would have had to study the market, learn the formula, give them what they wanted; I would have been their man. My eight-dollar sale meant that someone I esteemed wanted to pay me for being myself. Two thousand dollars? Yes, I would have blown it, but I hung on to the eight dollars. I kept it around. It told me that my life might have to be very frugal but there could be money for me somewhere in the world – on my terms.

All those stories that get bandied around about the wild liberality and spendthrift madness of bohemian writers and painters are heart warming, and I feel restless and eager to go again in search of such a life, but since I am one who has lived in the Quarter in Paris, and in Greenwich Village, I know that the sums of money involved in such madcap living were pathetically small, if men and women of real talent were involved. Nearly all young writers and painters are poor. The charm of it is that they would rather be poor doing what they are doing than making ten times as much in the business world.

When I was twenty-two I had met a young writer in New York named Nathan Asch, living in Greenwich Village. Living as a writer! Hemingway had told me that Nathan Asch was the first of his friends that he'd let read *The Sun Also Rises*. Nathan could have had advantages. He was the son of the great Jewish novelist, Sholem Asch. Yes, Nathan could have lived well. But no, he was a writer himself. He came to Toronto to stay close to me one summer. How he lived, I just don't know. A small cheque would come from New York. In the meantime, he would have pawned his typewriter. He had one pair of socks. His big toe finally put a hole in one of the socks. I was with him one day in Woolworth's and we passed a counter on which was a pile of socks. The store, if you remember, was more or less a five, ten and fifteen cent store in those days. The display sign announced: Socks – fifteen cents apiece. Nathan picked out the right colour, selected one sock, and handed it to the sales-girl. Fifteen cents! It was absurd, she said. She refused to sell him one sock. Nathan couldn't afford thirty cents for two socks. They argued. She got indignant and told him to go away. He demanded that she bring the manager to him. When this man came, he listened, stunned, told Nathan he was absurd, and tried to leave. But Nathan, following him, told him that the sign, fifteen cents a sock, meant that he was contractually obliged to sell the sock. The sign was an offer; he accepted it. Of course he was right. The bewildered manager told the girl to sell Nathan one sock and she wrapped it up. Well, that fifteen cents was very important to Nathan, the young writer, and he wasn't trying to outsmart a storekeeper. He was using all his wits to hold on to trifling sums of money that were the protection of his freedom to live, writing only what he wanted to write.

Protection! That's the thing! Money as a protection for the artist. I suspect that people who stand at hotel windows, or on the rear platforms of trains, tossing dollars away have nothing left to protect, nothing that they deeply respect. They have caved in at their own heart's core, their youth's dream long gone, that aspiration gone long, long ago. Even a popular mystery writer like Agatha Christie who became like the old woman who lived in a shoe and had so much money she didn't know what to do, was generous beyond words, but in the main – only with her relatives, or intimates, suggesting that she had an enormous respect for money. Anyway, I'm not talking about her kind of writer.

There is the artist who has to be continually in the business of trying to get more money for his work so there can be new work coming from him. So that someday he may be in a position where he can't be continually belittled by the affluent peasants who surround him in his daily life. I imagine there is a deep, deep satisfaction for such a man as he watches a financial wall, an off-product of his heart and soul, grow around him. I rejoiced when I heard that great painters like Matisse grew very rich. Why not? Their work has enriched everyone else and they were the ones who knew in the early years how desperately important it was to have protection money. I like that, the artist working to pay himself protection money, a one-man mob taking out a one-man contract on himself. I was glad that Eugene O'Neill finally made money. I was glad when I heard Hemingway had left a couple of million dollars. Money. Money earned by the artist for his own work. Money, first and foremost as a protection that he will always need to guard his talent among seemingly more munificent men who stand on the back platform of trains throwing it away, money that reminds them, I suspect, of something else they had wanted to do.

*CBC Anthology*

# LOOKING AT
# NATIVE PROSE

When I picked up *Tristram Shandy* the other day I intended to see if there was any truth in the rumour that out of Sterne had come many of the Joycian parodies in *Ulysses*. It would have been more accurate, I imagined at the time, to have said that Joyce, in spots, had recaptured some of the spirit of Sterne, the broad comedic tilt to the prose so characteristic of the English, a tilt that has been almost forgotten since the French realists took possession of the field. For example, in the first half of *Tristram Shandy*, there are two or three places where I'd swear Sterne was making a parody of the Lord's Prayer, just as Joyce parodied the Creed.

But I went on reading, marvelling at the sheer happiness in Sterne's writing. Here was pleasure in the mere putting down of words on paper, the qualities of a vigorous, active mind and a sense of humour reflected in the words. He had all the gusto of an amateur, his story pattern was the personal arrangement of an amateur, and surely he left the impression that it mattered not at all what his next-door neighbour or his neighbouring professional thought of his work.

In Toronto, and I daresay in all of Canada, writing has nothing to do with a free happy spirit because no one, or at least very few, are at all interested in prose for the sake of prose. They are all interested in markets, the study of markets, and they are as avaricious for the dollar as any other collection of needle-and-thread men swapping big talk about large markets.

Prose in this country is, I believe, more degraded than in any other civilized country on earth. Even the local poets, for all their wishy-washiness, have more dignity than the local prose writers, and I believe that is because they are more forlorn, they realize instinctively that the audience for their work is so small that they can never be paid, they can never be honoured to any extent in the community: and so their verses, when they appear at all, have a little more dignity than the work of the fiction writers because the poets expect less.

I have heard it said by hack writers in good standing locally, that they are tremendously handicapped in Canada because there are no big markets in the country. The truth is, they already get far more than their wares are worth. There is no reason on earth why a gent from a correspondence school, who has just finished the short story course, should be encouraged to force his miserable warbling upon an indifferent public in the name of Canadian Literature. Of course, every country has its teachers of the short story, its schools, its associations for studying the markets, but in most countries there is an intellectual minority that finds such associations amusing and realizes that the "teachers" are know-nothings. Oddly enough, in this country, "the teachers" are the heroes. The "associations" preserve and protect the local cultural standard.

But Lawrence Sterne in *Tristram Shandy* had a good feeling about writing. The good feeling that is so sadly lacking in practically all Canadian prose. How many prose writers are there in this country who have a feeling for words alone? Take specimens from the work of those writers who are most venerated locally, examine them carefully, and then, let us hope for something different in the next generation. The best of the lot, Frederick Philip Grove, has great importance in Canada. He is one of the few writers the land has produced who has tried to face the country and its culture honestly and sincerely. Younger men will come along later and write much better prose than he does, but they will be indebted to him, a kind of Canadian Dreiser, for stubbornly, awkwardly breaking the way for them.

Often, I have wondered if the ladies and gentlemen of the Canadian Author's Association, and other such tradesmen's organizations, when bewailing the lack of opportunity in this country to emerge with an overflowing money bag, appreciate what a writer with an artistic conscience is up against, particularly if he is interested in modern technique.

Is there a single publication in the country where he may be received royally? Would a single magazine, able to pay money for words, touch him with a ten-foot pole? Granting that they must make money, the fact remains that there is no publication in the country interested in the publication of decent prose and poetry for its own sake, and until such a periodical appears, there will be no local expression in literature. It has often seemed to me that the trouble is mainly that we in Canada have no nationality, that the people, with the exception of two or three painters, have no feeling for the place, neither landscapes nor city streets.

Perhaps I should have made it clear some time ago that my indignation is an indignation of the spirit rather than the flesh, because I know that it is a custom in this country for the few authors who are making any money to smile patronizingly at young men who have silly notions about "art." To these fellows, and at the same time, to young men or women who are willing to go on working independently, I take great pleasure in announcing from the housetops that it is worthwhile to stick to it, and in a few years the market-minded gentleman may be envious of their returns. And in the meantime, read *Tristram Shandy*, because it dispenses with all the academic notions of good writing.

A rereading of *Tristram Shandy* would be especially helpful to all our prose writers, far more helpful than a close study of modern English writers like Galsworthy, or Ford Madox Ford, or Aldous Huxley, or Katherine Mansfield, because Sterne's gusto, his eagerness for life, his broad strokes are closer to the character of this continent. English prose, in his day, was finding a beginning, and so his own work embodies some of the most characteristic traits of great English prose, the spirit of slapstick satire, and a sheer joy in writing.

At that time, modern French prose had not left an impression on English fiction. Today it is very difficult to find a piece of respectable English prose that does not show the influence, in some degree, of Flaubert; or the spirit and purpose of Balzac. The greatest of modern English writers turned away from their English source and became English Balzacs – as in the case of Arnold Bennett and his *Old Wives' Tale*, or those first cousins of Flaubert, writers like John Galsworthy.

But I do believe that today there is a tendency to turn away from French prose, to search along easier, freer lines, for the ready word, the happy word, which, when offered by the artist, will become the inevitable word. We are coming closer to Sterne and his happy eagerness to record out of his own personality. D.H. Lawrence, for example, is openly careless of style, he shrugs his shoulders at it; he is ready with words that are very often close to speech, and the result is that he is a great stylist, a far greater stylist than Joseph Hergesheimer, who takes such infinite pains with a sentence.

Any page of Sterne, opened at random, offers fresh and racy speech, not quite the speech of our day, but what was obviously speech of his own time. That is, I believe, why Sterne is so interesting to many modern writers. He got close to the very heart of the living force in prose by using a lively speech. And that is why he should be of especial interest to people in this country, who either grope hopelessly toward present English models, or flounder about sorrowfully because we have no tradition. Surely the way, the departure, is obvious. The way lies through the acceptance of whatever speech we have in this country, and a prose employing it will have the colour, the raciness, the flesh and blood of the people of this section of the American continent. Because of the soil, we are American. Not United States, but American.

It seems to me to be stupid to want to write in Canada and carry on the tradition of Galsworthy, or Hardy, or to write in the manner of Huxley. Economically, socially, geographically, we are far, far away from England. We belong to a new world, and the whole struggle should be to find our roots in this world. Nor do the best English critics rejoice when a Canadian writer pretends that the Canadian farmer or backwoodsman is like one of Hardy's peasants. They have the common sense to know that that is a fake. The gesture, old-fashioned and pathetic, toward London's critical praise, is downright absurd, and we should have grown out of it long ago. The opportunity awaiting the honest Canadian prose writer is so large that I believe many are appalled, laugh weakly, and prefer to go on writing fairy tales after the fashion of Oscar Wilde. One half of the American world awaits the prose writer, awaits his recording, awaits his acceptance of it, the new world of the plain, the bush country, and the skyscraper.

Bernard K. Sandwell, the well-known local editor who recently reviewed *Canadian Short Stories* in *Saturday Night*, doubted whether our younger writers, using a plain, conversational language, could ever equal the achievement of the older men, Roberts, D.C. Scott,

Gilbert Parker, etc. What Mr. Sandwell overlooked is that the few young men in the country, Raymond Knister, Tom Murtho, etc, who are interested in prose, are attempting to find a beginning on their own soil, and they are on absolutely solid ground. The older generation, regarded so seriously now, never found a beginning, were not interested in technique, and had no identity. The older writers, who spend a good deal of time wondering what the London critics will think of their books, should pass the time away by reading *Tristram Shandy*.

*Saturday Night*, 1928

# GREY OWL:
# LANGUAGE OF THE EYES

In our seemingly staid town in the thirties, literary gents and their ladies used to dress up of an evening. The very proper publisher of the Macmillan Company had big champagne socials. The people we knew held swank supper parties in their homes, men with black ties, the ladies in gowns. Loretto always wore a silk or silver fox evening wrap to lectures by visiting poets like Yeats or George Russell, and to the theatre, too. At the York Club, I met the naturalist, Grey Owl, who had successfully presented himself to the world as a full-blooded Indian. It was the night I used the language of the eyes.

Pascal said the heart has ways of knowing what the mind does not understand. This is a way of saying that there is something in the mind that goes leap-frogging over the rational process, and then waits for the slow steps of reason to catch up. Sometimes we know with certainty – and then must wait to understand or justify how we knew with such certainty.

But if the heart has this way of wisdom, then the eye, too, has the strange power of jumping ahead of the mind and recording a kind of knowledge – particularly if it meets the eye of someone else. The exchange of glances. The sudden glance. Nothing need be said. Nothing has to be figured out, but it is as if a hundred messages are transmitted and sorted through.

There may be, in the exchange of a glance between two persons who've never met before, a recognition as profound – and of the same order – as that old intense Greek recognition of a blood relationship or bondage. This kind of eye knowledge, from a language that comes when eyes suddenly and unexpectedly meet, has always fascinated me.

It is now known that Grey Owl, a remarkable man, had become an Indian in thought, word and deed, although he was an Englishman without a drop of Indian blood. But in the thirties, he was having a splendid success in Canada and England where he was taken for what he pretended to be, a full-blooded Indian. Moreover, his publishers both in Canada and England, having talked to him and investigated him, had no doubt that he was the real thing. He came to Toronto, he was wined and feted, he made public appearances, and when newspapermen tried to investigate his background and come up with some explanation for his beguiling literacy, they failed to damage his pretensions; instead, they made him more of a nine-day wonder, and so it came about that he was accepted as a native Indian, his book was widely read, and there was great local pride in him.

The Macmillan Company was his publisher. Hugh Eayres, his editor, was a man who liked to do things with a flourish and some style, and since he also had the greatest confidence in Grey Owl, having met him and talked with him and judged him, he gave a dinner for him at the York Club. At this dinner were twelve guests. I was one of them. We all knew each other quite well. The fact that Grey Owl, the native Indian right out of the bush, was there in the staid sedate and exclusive York Club, meeting the local intellectuals at a splendid formal dinner, was an event of such grandeur that no one could have imagined Grey Owl showing up if he were an impostor. Or, it may have been that by this time the strangely talented man had become in his own mind the other man he claimed to be, as he lived and thought like this other man, and so had no fear whatever of questions from strangers.

At the dinner table, I was sitting almost directly opposite Grey Owl. He was a good-looking man, reticent, courteous, who conducted himself with a quiet dignity. I didn't say a word across the table. I didn't speak to him at all. At first glance, he didn't look like an Indian. But then, what is an Indian supposed to look like? When we were kids we used to say that all Chinese looked alike, and then we discovered later that the Chinese could joke, too, about all white men looking alike. Why should an Indian have it written on his skull and in his face that he is an Indian?

So, as the dinner wore on, I listened to snatches of his conversation, eyeing him thoughtfully, just wondering, just curious, and satisfied that I was not there at all as a presence for him. Then came that peculiar moment when he half-turned his head from the man on his left who was talking to him – I forget who it was – as if he were suddenly aware of my silence. His eyes met mine in just one glance, a swift but full meeting of the eyes. My own eyes shifted away. I can't know what went on in him; but for me – just for me – there came a moment of certainty; it came from reading the language of the eyes, a thousand words in the exchanged glance. For me, there was recognition of him. Inwardly, though surprised, I was satisfied with my private recognition: there was no Indian blood in him. He was an Englishman.

When the dinner party broke up Hugh Eayres said to me, "Well, what do you make of Grey Owl?"

"An interesting man. But he's not an Indian."

"He is an Indian. Don't say that."

"His eyes."

"His eyes?"

"Our eyes met."

"That's all you've got to go on?"

After some time passed, a couple of years, it was finally revealed that Grey Owl was in fact an Englishman who had loved the woods and wild life and he was no more an Indian than I was, but this didn't particularly interest me. I remained far more interested in that moment when our eyes had met. From then on, I found myself watching for the language of the eyes, the recognition of someone that comes in a glance. But beware: you may discover in the eyes of the other a sudden unwelcome recognition of you.

# THE WAR YEARS:
## DOS PASSOS

The novel *1919* by John Dos Passos has so much fine energy so
nicely controlled, such a sweep in scene and action, such magnificent colour and smell of four or five countries and a passionate
worship of justice and truth that it seems, at first, beyond criticism.

*1919* carries on the scheme started in Dos Passos' *The 42
Parallel*, which ended at the outbreak of the war. The new book
goes through the war years with America up to the 1919 burial of
the unknown soldier in Washington, and it is, in reality, a portrait
of that generation living and dying against the background of one
of the maddest periods in the world's history. Dos Passos offers four
or five characters. Joe Williams, a sailor and drifter; Anne Elizabeth, a pampered daughter from Texas; Dick Savage, a Harvard
boy; Eveline Hutchins, a minister's daughter from Chicago; and
Ben Compton, an intellectual Jewish radical in the American work-
ing-class movement.

These characters become the nerve and muscle of America:
they gain in strength, they move forward, the nerves leap in
response to the panacea of the Wilsonian democracy of the period,
the muscles strain, and then life is broken or twisted by all the fake
panaceas, the false ideals, the disillusionment following the great
peace botch that left us all tense, waiting for the spring of nations
at one another's throats.

The stories of these individual lives is often full enough of tragedy and a kind of wild savage beauty, but gradually I began to sense that each individual case was simply pathetic, and only a portent for a whole generation, for all of modern America that is cursed by materialism, that is without spiritual values and with a democracy that is dead as a doornail, democracy tied to the stake, democracy ready for the burning while big business chants and beats the tom toms.

Too rapid a glance through the book might indicate that the form is difficult. On the first page is a collection of newspaper clippings of the time when the Germans were trying to take Verdun. These clippings seem to be taken at random from any part of a paper, front page, stock market, society column, anywhere, and released without any precision. Again and again these pages bob up through the book till they become a kind of March of Time. About halfway through the book, one begins to get irritated by these bulletin boards because the narratives of the four or five characters are being broken off, and for a time I began to feel there was nothing so dead in the world as last year's newspapers.

It was only after I had left the book and was considering the way the separate narratives, the separate lives of the characters, were carried on as they joined the Red Cross in France, in Italy, in Paris, Rome or London, in a colloquial vivid prose richer, juicier, more alive and sensitive than anything in our time, that I was suddenly aware of a whole modern world seeping through the narrative, a feeling that the restlessness of the people of Europe was a profound challenge because it was a restlessness that came out of centuries of senseless beatings, carried on to the tune of comic lies. It may be that those clippings had had that powerful effect on me because we remember the headlines; they belong to our time, they touch off sparks to the imagination, but I also had to remember that in a few years these headlines will also belong completely to the ashcan. So Dos Passos is a writer who writes for his own time. I can't imagine him being interested in what tomorrow, or tomorrow's embalmers, might think of him. He's too authentic for that sort of thing.

Perhaps it is through the use of what he calls "The Camera Eye" that he gets this feeling of immediate depth in the background, and that makes me wonder if, after all is said and done, the clippings couldn't have been dispensed with. This "Eye" appears suddenly through the narratives, a few pages of large type, a kind of impressionistic poem, very personal to the author, as though they were his own recollections of particular incidents of the time in a kind of dream form; they have the effect of the trembling of a veil. Often very beautiful, they seem to touch at something vaster than can be said in cold crisp prose.

While Dos Passos is telling in narrative prose the story of a few people, he is also trying to touch off a portrait of the whole time; the book is a kind of spiritual history of a period, and these portraits of President Wilson, the house of Morgan, Jack Reed, Teddy Roosevelt, are just as much part of the background as are the hills, waterfalls, or dank pools of an artist painting a picture of a wilderness. What portraits! Wilson is more than a tragic idealist; for Dos Passos sees through him to the very marrow; he is neither tragic nor an idealist.

In his study, *Expression in America*, Mr. Ludwig Lewisohn dismisses Dos Passos rather lightly. Mr. Lewisohn feels that Dos Passos does not carry the human spirit forward, and I'm afraid that other people looking at this book and seeing that the author tries simply to tell what happens, will make the same rash mistake: the characters seem to be extroverts interested only in action rather than thinking. But Dos Passos writes of his characters with simplicity and humility in his prose; there is complete effacement of the author; he is interested in seeing the object there to be seen. Dos Passos is wise enough to know that the job of the artist is to "make" and not talk, and so he not only has "made" his major characters, but he has done so with proportion and clarity: the conception is big and gorgeous, the "spiritual" implications are so vast one is left a bit stunned.

*Saturday Night*, 1932

# THE JEW IN THE CITIES: SHOLEM ASCH

This tale of *Three Cities* by Sholem Asch, the cities of Petersburg, Warsaw, and Moscow, is the work of a very great novelist. Asch writes of the Jewish people and he writes in Yiddish, and this book is a translation from the Yiddish, but the world he creates, and the world that is inside himself, is so large that it becomes a part of the whole European stream of life.

When he writes of Petersburg before the war, he is concentrating on the Petersburg of the wealthy Russian Jews, capitalists and lawyers and their women. There seems to be assembled so many fragments of the Jewish temperament, fierce idealism, avariciousness, sensuality, greedy materialism, that one becomes conscious of aspects of the soul of a people, and this soul begins to expand so that it soon becomes large enough to become the soul of all people.

These people in the old capital had only their own luxury, their own pride and their own race consciousness to feed on. Many of the young Jews continually pondered the question of becoming orthodox Christians. To them, the personal problem, the human ego, was more important than the happiness of a whole people. There were no great causes among them. Even a great Jewish advocate, who pleaded the cause of his oppressed people when they were dragged before the bar of Russian justice, turned out to be an empty muddle-headed liberal completely seduced by the sounds of the words that rolled from his glib tongue, loving the role he played among his own people.

But out of this parasitical society emerges one young man, Zachary Mirdkin, the son of a man of great wealth, hopelessly in love with the memory of his mother, who becomes stifled by the intensity of his personal problem, who longs to penetrate deeper into the consciousness of the people of his race, and who in the end abandons Petersburg for the Warsaw society of poor but enlightened Jews. So from Petersburg to Warsaw the stream of life on these pages keeps moving along, slowly, sometimes delayed in wide pools of still water, but always broadening.

The life that Zachary encounters in Warsaw is the antithesis of all he knew in Petersburg, except that Jews are so much the same wherever they are. There is always the same Jewish problem to face with no solution. But this Warsaw world is much closer to the longing and struggle of a people, and by this time it is not just the Jewish people, but all the workers and peasants of the rest of Europe. In Warsaw, Zachary rids himself of his twisted pathological love for the mother-woman which was strong enough in him to be almost a will to death. He gains a social consciousness. He becomes one, not only with his own people, but with the masses of the European nations. By this time the Great War has broken out. The stream of life in the book has so broadened that one watches it as though one were watching something inevitable in the destiny of Europe.

In Moscow, we get the culmination of the Bolshevik revolution that followed the Kerensky regime. This Moscow book is full of great writing. A whole people, blinded, made stupid, yet groping their way forward, has become conscious of its power. Now, there does not seem to be the old sharp distinction between Jew and Gentile. The one revolutionary world is there for both Jew and

Gentile, a world demanding assent or rejection. Zachary has joined with the Bolsheviks, not because he was one of their party, but because he felt that they were closer to expressing, in action, the hopes of a people crushed by a thousand years of servitude. This Moscow section contains some truly remarkable writing, scenes pictured in a full vividness that will be remembered . . .

As far as the technique is concerned, Asch has little to add to the novel. He sticks to narrative and avoids experimentation. In a sense, he is an old-fashioned novelist. He writes with the eye of God, which is to say that he tells what he wants to tell about anybody or any place at any point in the book. If the book has faults, looseness of construction is one of the most obvious, although the book has such power that it drives through these faults and makes them seem petty and inconsequential.

Asch is not and never will be a writer like Turgenev, moulding, shaping, refining and polishing. He has, instead, the scope of a Tolstoy, but it is only when one compares him to such a great master as Tolstoy that he seems to be so much less of an artist. Of all the Europeans, he is probably closer to Balzac because he loves the richness of detail, the movement of large masses, the whole social structure. There are times when, as a reader, I've questioned Balzac's sincerity, when I've wondered if he was not just pulling strings to make the story interesting, but no one may question Asch's integrity of purpose.

It is this integrity of purpose that is the great distinction of the novel and of the writer. It never falters. He is able to touch everything and touch it cleanly. No matter how he fumbles or loses himself in detail there remains in him this vast patience and willingness to adhere to his purpose.

A great many sagas have appeared in English recently: the Galsworthy books, the Walpole efforts, all running around a thousand pages. One should compare this book with these English novelists to realize how fine a European writer Asch actually is. The Jewish world made him one of their classics years ago. But with this book he belongs to the whole of Europe.

*Saturday Night*, 1933

# SAUL BELLOW

There was an interview with Saul Bellow in the *New York Times* and when I read it I felt baffled. What is going on with Bellow? He is the darling of the New York critical establishment: they see him as the most intellectual of contemporary writers. One could brood over "intellectual" and wonder whether the designation should please Bellow, but it is better to get on with what he said in the interview.

Two of his arguments baffled me.

First: Bellow now believes that America needs big public novelists rather than small public ones. The big public voices, of course, will have a social awareness. Bellow gives us the names of some small public voices: James Joyce, Marcel Proust, and T.S. Eliot; their devotees in the academic groves, he says, have taken pride in the fact that they are coterie darlings, and the coterie gives the impression that these writers are the cream of the crop in modern letters.

Bellow protests against this continuing trend in criticism. What we need now, he maintains, are writers like Dreiser and Sherwood Anderson, big public novelists.

But surely Bellow is forgetful. Sherwood Anderson never had a big public. With Anderson dead for so long, his *Winesberg, Ohio,* has become an American classic, but he never published a book that sold well until the end of his life when he wrote *Dark Laughter*, and even that, if I remember, only sold about thirty thousand copies, and today, that novel, his one public success, is hardly read at all. For that matter, it is hard to find students who have read the *Winesberg* stories. If Bellow were to look back to his own beginnings, or no . . . maybe I should tell him about mine.

In those days, Anderson was very much a coterie writer. One could even say that he was almost a writer's writer, for every young storywriter in America sought out those beautiful Anderson stories. We all came under his influence. Though his work appeared in the anthologies, few of the commercial magazines would print his stories. He had to wait until he was past sixty for this kind of publication.

I can remember back in 1927 when H.L. Mencken complained that Anderson was becoming the darling of the Greenwich Village intellectuals. He had won his own little core of critical supporters – even as Bellow has done today. But he never had Bellow's success. It is safe to say that he never had big public commercial popularity, so it would seem to me, looking back on the record, that Bellow has picked on the wrong kind of writer for his argument. One could, with more authority, put Anderson and what happened to him alongside the life stories of Pound, Joyce, Proust, and Eliot, whom Bellow calls the small public writers.

Theodore Dreiser, with his *American Tragedy* and his vast social awareness was a writer of quite a different order from Anderson, who sought so painfully and persistently for lyrical relationships among his characters. Dreiser, as Bellow might say, was always aware of the social forces that shaped his people. Yet the fact is, Dreiser, who seemed to have in his heart and hands all the materials for the big public address to a great audience, couldn't find that audience.

For most of his life, through the days of *Jennie Gerhardt* and *Sister Carrie*, he was a small public novelist. When, at the age of sixty he finally broke through with his *American Tragedy*, he complained bitterly that his success had come too late. It strikes me that Dreiser couldn't write the kind of novel Bellow writes, nor could

Bellow write the Dreiserian novel. The men are worlds apart. So it amounts to this. Great authentic writers hewing to their own line have difficulty in becoming what Bellow would call "big public socially aware novelists." Small bands of admirers have to keep pushing the work of these giants until a big public is ready to welcome them. In short, the same thing happened to Anderson and Dreiser that has happened to the writers Bellow irritably inveighs against – Pound, Joyce, Eliot, and Proust.

In the case of Pound, one thing should be remembered. No academic group, no critical coterie, is responsible for Pound's survival and his present eminence. Pound survives because young poets discovered him, and as long as there are young poets reading him and learning from him it won't matter what that academic world thinks, although they will be smart enough to be aware of his continuing influence on the young. Because of his poetic line, a line that has always moved me, Pound has survived his own political opinions, he has survived hatred.

As for Proust – would Bellow contend that Dreiser is more socially aware than Proust? I trust not. If in the graduate schools, Proust or Joyce, or even Eliot go up and down – it doesn't really matter; for these writers will always be there for other writers to read.

Second: I am particularly baffled by Bellow's remarks about Jewish novelists; himself, Malamud and Roth, and I'm troubled, too, because he makes me feel wary about dealing with any Jewish writer. It seems to upset Bellow that he, Malamud, and Roth are separated from Anglo-Protestant writers, and that certain critics persist in dealing with them as Jewish writers. Here, I am stumped.

For me, if Malamud writes a novel about a Jewish family being persecuted in a *shtetle* in eastern Europe I can't help believing I'm reading a Jewish novel written by a Jewish writer, and when Philip

Roth wrote *Portnoy's Complaint* and Portnoy and his family were so comically revealed in what seemed to be such an authentically Jewish tone, and when the non-Jewish girls who came into the book seemed so alien to his imagination, and when the novel resolved itself in Israel, how could I help but believe that I was reading a Jewish novel?

Bellow apparently wants to strike a blow at Anglo-Protestant critics. This seems to me to be very much beside the point. I think it is utterly wrong, even in literary circles, to think that fashions in esteem settle down to a battle between Anglo-Protestants and writers who are Jews, for surely this kind of battleground for a tossing of shoulders in wounded irritation is only a very, very small parcel of the land that is urban life in North America.

My grandfather was Irish. If I wrote a book in which every character, except perhaps one girl, is Irish, I shouldn't be surprised if the critics talk about me as an Irish writer. Is it wrong to think of William Kennedy – a writer, God bless him, that Bellow championed – as an Irish writer? Almost everyone in Kennedy's *Albany* trilogy is of Irish descent, of Irish temperament, and lives by Irish rituals of love and abandonment. On the other hand, Scott Fitzgerald, who was of Irish background, is not talked about as an Irish writer and should not be talked about as an Irish writer because there is no single flow of Irish life in his books. Am I wrong about this? Or am I right in thinking that Bellow was not at his best in that interview?

*CBC Anthology*

# DUELS NOW ARE ABSURD

Most men, never having stood for anything in themselves, have relied on others to tell them what to believe in, and how to live with each other. Thousands of years have rolled on, rolling over one code after another, but always there have been rituals of the taboos, a kind of sacred tabulation that has made one act more important than another. These codes have always provided the dramatic framework for the great novelists. But what is a novelist today to do looking out on a world in which there are no longer any taboos in human behaviour? No longer any great acts that bring shameful social ostracism. The poor novelist has had all his stage props swept aside. How can he now, in his providential art, deal with the ways of men; all the characters he sees around him are free, loose and immune from any condemnation of moral depravity. Everything is to be judged only by the excitement, the rush of the experience. The novelist now faces a world in which there are no real criminals. There are only the hunters and the hunted. The losers are those who get caught. Obsessed as I am now by this awareness, I grow more fascinated by the hunger for more and more police stories on television – fascinated because I, as a novelist, can see that the cops are simply tougher than the thugs, and I keep asking myself which set of characters are supposed to be the thugs? It is supposed to matter to me as a viewer that the one in uniform is on my side. But which side am I on? Does it matter?

I look around and say to myself, "If I can't interest people now in adultery, thieving or lying, not if there is to be any shame attached to these activities, what can I turn to if I have, in my antique fashion, a conception of a moral order? Honour? A man's honour? Joseph Conrad used to put this virtue at the very core of his men. But I hardly hear the word used now. If a public man stood up and declared that his honour had been sullied, would anyone take him seriously? Honour seems to be a throwback to those days when a man sought revenge for a slight upon his integrity and sought satisfaction in a duel. Duels now are absurd. Maybe even points of honour have become absurd.

In the old days it was simple. The world was full of thugs, thieves, whores and con men who dressed in black. Harry Lime in the sewers of Vienna. People generally agreed that the conduct of such men was shameful. That's why artists dressed them in black. That's why such rogues came to a bad end.

Now, money not only talks and walks, it sings. The man in black has come to a good end. He is in show business. He is Johnny Cash. He is Johnny Paycheck. He is common currency, the rogue singer. Such a rogue only comes to a wretched end if he is a loser, and if he is a loser he is in prison, and if he is in prison Johnny Cash will come and sing to him.

In this scheme of things, the big whore, the big rogue, if he is really *Ed Sullivan* or *60 Minutes* big, will appear on television, too, a celebrity like any other celebrity, the ultimate social triumph being "name fame." If the name becomes big enough, the bearer – no matter the crime he has committed, even murder – can go anywhere, certainly anywhere on the networks. For the writer, this could be a fine ironic tale, but only if there were enough readers to understand that it was a savage satire on society.

I was on to "name fame" as the ultimate social triumph years ago, in the thirties, when I wrote a novel about a reformed bank robber who was wined and dined as a celebrity. I would do the public reception of such a man quite differently today. Now, I would have this man, as soon as he was released from prison, get an agent. And the agent would book him on a talk show, and then another, and he would make the rounds of all the talk shows and campuses at a fee that got bigger and bigger as his name got bigger, his crime not a moral stain but his first-name to fame.

So, as my kind of novelist I'm up against it. If the old moral structures aren't there for me as a novelist, I am then faced with a choice. I can attempt to impose my own order out of my own vision, which may make me inaccessible to many readers, or I can do as so many novelists are doing: simply deal with characters in terms of the sensation of the experience. Just the experience! The surge! But maybe that's already a dead end. André Gide could have been called the prince of the quest for experience. They tell me, however, since his death, his reputation has been in rapid decline.

As for me, a writer who's always looked awkward trying to march in step with the temper of the time, I know that I can't really care if the guidelines for the old novelists, the great moral structures, have broken down. I can't do anything about it. I think that a man like me – not given to shifting truths but sifting through truths – has to do his writing out of a structure within himself. I'm watching and listening very carefully, and as far as I can determine, my own structure hasn't fractured, hasn't fallen apart, so I'll have to go on doing as I have always done, fitting everything I see into myself.

*CBC Anthology*

# THE FAULKNER RIDDLE
## SOLVED

With every book that Faulkner publishes, he becomes less and less of a problem child. That he is a man of a very peculiar and extraordinary talent no one denies, but just what he has a talent for, whether he has profound insight into the human mind and heart, or whether he has great skill at delineating everything horrible in terms of fantastic action, ought to be settled for all time in *The Wild Palms*.

It's not really one story. It's two stories and they haven't any relation whatsoever to each other. They are just two stories broken up, and you're fed a chapter or two of one, and then a chapter or two of the other. In the first story a young doctor runs off with a married woman who leaves two children behind her. They live only for their love, both understanding and expressing the notion that love never dies, it only leaves people when people are unworthy of it. The woman dies when the doctor tries to perform an abortion on her.

The second story is about a convict who, with his companions, is rushed out of a prison to help do relief work when Old Man River is flooding, and the convict is swept down the river with a pregnant woman he has rescued from an overhanging tree. All the poor fellow wants to do really is get back to his prison refuge from the hard world, but the river carries him on down with the woman, and her child is born on a little bank with snakes swimming all around, and the convict helps in the delivery. This story ends when the convict is successful: that is, when he is able to give himself up and is returned to the prison haven with an extra ten years tacked on to his sentence.

I think the first story about the two lovers is a complete flop, if you're looking for any revelation of the hearts or souls of two people in love. Yet, it makes some astonishing reading. If you remember, D.H. Lawrence also had some rather striking, even astonishing notions about women in love. But when he got hold of *Lady Chatterley* and got right down to cases, Lawrence actually succeeded in creating an awareness of an ecstasy that is universal.

I wonder if there can be such a thing as an irrelevant ecstasy? There ought not to be such a thing. Yet here they are, irrelevant ecstasies, on Faulkner's pages in this particular love story, a maddening, perverse piece of work.

All the Faulkner talent for giving you the quality of a moment, or rather the external appearance of a moment, is there, the thing happening in a room, the thing seen, the bright important flashes of the gestures made between two people. It is there on the page as real as a bright dream, but there is something wrong. Nine times out of ten the thing that is wrong is what was supposed to be going on inside the people. It just isn't true. With a fervent poetic eloquence he calls upon you to believe a thing that isn't true, and you know it isn't true, but Faulkner keeps on working at it and at last he hits you on the head with a set of shocking facts: with the flash of stars that comes from the impact and in a dazed condition the reader almost believes.

But afterwards, when you look back, you know what was true in the book, and you know that Faulkner's great talent is for the delineation of externals. He could, if he wanted, be a wonderful straight action writer, but no, he wants to deal in psychology, and the psychological business in these stories, especially in the love story, when there is an effort to probe deeply into human motives, to reveal mysterious underlying depths of feeling, results only in a most extraordinary display of stylistic fireworks. What a flow of language the man has! Some of it gets muddy and some of it is incredibly bad, but some of it is overpoweringly eloquent and poetic. Only don't ever ask him to make you feel what it was like between two people so that you will say to yourself afterwards, "That's it. I was there."

Some of the best writing Faulkner ever did is in the other story that threads through *Wild Palms*, the story about the convict drifting down the river. Since the convict obviously is a simple type, most of Faulkner's talent goes into showing what it was like going down the river as the river flooded. I don't know anybody who could have done it better. It is an extraordinary piece of work.

But sooner or later someone is going to ask one important question, not only of William Faulkner, but of all American writers. It's a simple question, and it's just this: *what is a man, what is he doing on earth?* What's your conception of a man? All the big writers understood that question and tried to give some kind of an answer, from Chaucer to Gorki, and even a revolutionary novelist like the Frenchman, André Malraux. Try reading this last book of Faulkner's with this question in mind, and various answers, some of them pretty juvenile, will keep springing up on the pages.

*Saturday Night*, 1939

# REMEMBERING
# THE UNREAD

Back around the time I was reading Faulkner's *Wild Palms*, the poet W.W.E. Ross – who was as laconic among loquacious men as his initials – said to me, "Yes, I remember that story." I said, "Well, that's not saying much for the story, is it?" He said, "What more can you say? That's the greatest thing you can say."

I was irritated. But as the years passed I came to believe in his wisdom, and came to believe a man might play a very odd game with himself, if he will be strictly honest. Of all he has read and praised, let him ask what he remembers. If he can't remember a story . . . no, this, I can see, may lead to a little difficulty. Many a man has had a desperate love affair with a girl and later on in life he finds that he can hardly remember her. It's very troubling. Was it really desperate? The test of a story and what it meant in your life, or even if you think it meant nothing at the time you read it, is this: can you remember it now? If you can, the story must have had some sharpness, some edge, some overhanging flavour, perhaps some form of its own.

For you, a book may have its excellence, yet not cut into you. I read Malcolm Lowry's *Under the Volcano* when it first came out. Years later, talking to the poet Earle Birney, I told him I must have missed something; I couldn't remember the story. He urged me to read it again. I did so. I still find that I have to struggle with my memory to see the book. I know that Lowry is a remarkable writer, maybe even a great one, but if I'm to be honest I have to say that he has no place in my private sense of literature.

If you play this game with yourself, and you are sufficiently ruthless, you'll be astonished at how many great works fall by the wayside. You have sloughed them all off. There was a time, the time when you were a student, when your eyes were hard, your head hard, too, and your heart most easily stirred, and the stories I thought great in those days stand up for me surprisingly well. I'll never forget reading *Madame Bovary*, curled up on a couch, and dreading that the book would come to an end and poor Emma would meet her fate. Years later, re-reading the book, I relived all my youthful dread and admiration. So, that book surely belongs with me wherever I go. And I remember standing under a bedroom light trying to finish Dostoevsky's *Crime and Punishment* before getting undressed. Years later, I could still feel the same awe and excitement.

Then, still drawing out of this memory bag, I was in for some shocks. The Solzhenitsyn book, *The First Circle*, which I read just a while ago – so big, so overwhelming! Now I'm painfully aware that the canvas is too crowded. What I remember of the book is the ambience, the overwhelming atmosphere of terror and repression, a human condition. This atmospheric effect I'm sure I'll always remember.

Doesn't this then open up another vista on memorable stories? Atmosphere, mood, a quickening, a restlessness in you, hanging forever in your memory. You see something going on in your life and say, "It's like a Chekhov play or a story." The total effect of a man's work, his view of life, may have dug its way into your continuing awareness of things, it may have even altered your view of life, though you may be hard put to outline a single story. I can remember more single stories of Maupassant that I can of Chekhov's, yet I seem to hear Chekhov again and again. Something other than story line must be there, and completely memorable.

Of all the crop of recent funny dirty books, how many scenes or effects can I remember? Richler's *Cocksure*? No, just the joke about the lady teacher, a joke I had remembered before the book was written. *Portnoy's Complaint*? How quickly that one must have raced through my mind. But books of another order – Margaret Laurence's novel, *The Stone Angel* – I remember that old woman, I remember vividly my feeling for her and my feeling about the writing. As for her novel, *The Fire-Dwellers*, I grope my way, trying to remember. I can't.

This challenging of one's memory, of one's sense of retainment, becomes rather horrifying in its lack of respect for persons. Saul Bellow? *Mr. Sammler's Planet*! What was that one about? A good old Jew, displaced, who read H.G. Wells. That's all it is to me now. And those letters in *Herzog*, in that book hailed as a classic in alienation, I can't remember one of those letters and doubt that anyone else can either. Yet Bellow's less celebrated book, *The Victim*, I remember it quite well. For me, Saul Bellow is a writer who wrote a novel called *The Victim*.

Then, still looking back, to my surprise I find I can remember Dreiser's *American Tragedy* and his *Sister Carrie*. Dreiser! I didn't like the way he wrote. Evidently it doesn't matter what I liked or disliked at the time. Dreiser was able to get into my memory most masterfully. Other strange stuff: *The Spoon River Anthology* by Edgar Lee Masters. Does anyone read him now? The book is always there for me . . .

Sitting alone with *Spoon River*, trying to remember *Herzog*, I soon found myself brooding over books I had forgotten to read. A dozen such fine books are here on the shelf. Why didn't it torment me that I had not read them? A few years ago Edmund Wilson asked me if I had read much of Dickens. "Not all of him," I said. "Try *Bleak House*," he said. I went out and bought the book. The story opened splendidly, I was all admiration, I read a hundred pages. I kept the book on the table beside the bed. One night I forgot to pick it up. I haven't touched it since. Why? I don't know. But it is unlikely I'll ever finish the book.

And here's something else. Will the fact I forgot to finish reading the book prevent me from talking about Dickens and *Bleak House*? Not at all. Having no direct experience with a thing never prevents a man from talking eloquently about that same thing. I remember one night in New York a young writer told me he had read a story of mine and thought it beautifully Chaucerian. We had an exhilarating discussion about Chaucer, and when I left him, my imagination was aglow. At home I suddenly said, "Chaucer? I haven't looked at Chaucer since I was at college." The young writer was in the same position. I suppose it was easier to talk about Chaucer than about my story.

Unread books are so easy to talk about! The biggest aspidistra of them all, for me, is the Bible. I knew the Gospels and had read through them many times, and occasionally I had dipped into the Old Testament. In conversation, argument or discussion, I had the general biblical baggage. Then, I was given a bible, the Jerusalem Bible with all the scholarly comments. It looked so interesting that I started to read, but not, I confess, as one reads holy writ. Just as a reader.

I read book after book, and in the end I got an impression related in no way to the impression I had carried around for years. I won't say that my religious experience was deepened. It wasn't. It would have been better if I hadn't done this reading. I would have remained happily receptive to the general opinion; the state of the good citizen.

Such a reading of a book may upset all your strong opinions, opinions that have been ground into you. Opinions you are willing to fight and die for. No writer in modern times has aroused as much controversy as Karl Marx. Men have dedicated their whole lives to fighting against all he stood for. I daresay, not one in a hundred thousand of these fighters against communism has read Marx's *Das Kapital*. Would it be wise, then, for any one of them to read the book. I doubt it. They could only be puzzled. They could even be made to feel guilty of having the outlaw instinct for wanting to have some direct contact with the thing that they like talking about.

I remember the neo-scholastic revival that was to lead to a new Middle Ages. The light was to be found in Thomism, the philosophy of St. Thomas Aquinas, and I used to marvel at how few of the devotees had actually read St. Thomas. It wasn't necessary. There were splendid commentators, and besides, it was sometimes difficult to understand St. Thomas. It was safer to trust in the insights of the commentators and leave the original work unread.

Even if you don't read commentators, I find you can have a sound, tested recognizable opinion about a book. For example, I have read very little Thoreau, yet I have such good opinions of him that I am often deeply moved when I talk about his work. But what if I really read him, and it turned out to be like my reading of the Old Testament, and I found I didn't take to him? No, Thoreau I admire, and like any other man, have succumbed to name fame. Which explains why there are so many writers so famous that people feel entitled to have deep personal antipathies to their unread work. I have found this to be true of Hemingway. Again and again I run into men who scoff at his novels, call him a phoney, belittle his courage, and then, under pressure finally confess they haven't read him, and didn't need to. What he stood for was now common knowledge, wasn't it?

And here I pause: can a writer become so famous that no one has to bother reading him? Oh, the unread writers! I have never read Sam Slick, Natalie Sarraute, Heinrich Boll, Amos Oz, Eudora Welty, several English women novelists who all have three names, John Barth, Nadine Gordimer, and some of them I certainly should read. Yet I would have no trouble talking about them, if I wanted to be accommodating, knowing of course that they meant nothing to me at all. Well, why don't I read them? Why don't I finish *Bleak House*? Secret apathy, I suppose. A reader draws back instinctively when he feels this apathy. Or maybe, stubbornly, I don't want my second-hand opinions, the opinions that make me a law-abiding citizen, that make up the dead part of my person, to be upset.

But remember this. Our whole culture is held together by a general agreement to live by second-hand opinion, to avoid any personal sharp contact with real things, with real emotions. The educated, highly disciplined man, is an expert at living in other people's emotions, in other people's minds. He knows how to swim standing still in the best-tested opinions on all things living and dead. In this way, his life is held together – just as a whole community is often held together. On the other hand, the man who wants to have a direct personal contact with life or books, who wants to make his own judgements, depending on his own sensibilities, is a kind of outlaw who can suffer the excitements and terrors of the outlaw if only in the badlands of his own living room.

*CBC Anthology*

# STEINBECK:
# THE HUMAN STAMPEDE

If you begin to wonder about *The Grapes of Wrath* you find you don't know whether to think of it as a novel at all. Maybe that's the greatest possible tribute you can pay to it. I don't know.

After all, what is a novel?

If it is simply a flow of life churning along to some end, then *The Grapes of Wrath* is magnificent, and the things you hold against it are beside the point.

The Joad family are from Oklahoma and, like hundreds of thousands of other people in Oklahoma, they gradually lost their land to the banks, land taken for cotton growing, and they decided to pile their people and their household belongings into old Fords and Hudson super-sixes and start a great trek to the promised land of California. When they got there, of course, they found that the natives didn't want them and treated them like scum, and they became homeless serfs.

This isn't told with the controlled phrasing of Henry James; it isn't just a faithful document: it's a wild impassioned battle hymn, and when Steinbeck decides that maybe you're missing the point, he takes time out for a chapter of social indictment, or a chapter which is often a blank verse exhortation to the hearts of all Americans.

The story opens with Tom Joad returning from a few years in the penitentiary to the home of his people only to find them getting ready to trek to California. This part of the book struck me as being magnificent. Tom, and a backsliding preacher friend, Casy, just drift around the neighbourhood for a while, talking and looking at things, but the way the country and the people come alive through their eyes is astonishing. Such natural dramatic dialogue I haven't heard in years. And there are beautiful glimpses of the country in easeful prose. In fact, looking back at it now, I'm wondering if that part of the book isn't the part I'll remember years after I've forgotten the rest. I know this would be tragic. You might even say this was sentimental, like looking back on a piece of land you had been tied to, looking back when everything else was lost. But it is in this part of the story that everything seems so astonishingly fresh. Dialogue, anecdotes, incidents, haven't had a chance to repeat themselves. The author doesn't seem to be trying: it has all come easily.

On the way to California, what Steinbeck does is tell you every little thing that happened, just keeping right at it, and keeping it moving under your eyes. If a car breaks a part in the engine, if they have a blow out, if they have a good meal, if they put their feet in the river, if they wash their faces – all the repetitious little things they say, even their smallest grunts, are faithfully recorded. What holds it all together, and makes it hard to put down, is his poetic emotion for the characters, or if you don't like that phrase, his passionate sympathy.

I, however, got a little bored with the economic interpolations along the way. "Stop, go on, I get it. I get it." The piling on got to be ham-fisted. Blunting the effect. For example, at one point there's a chapter on what is wrong with America and how the machine is killing everything, and in a mechanical way this is followed by another little chapter about a waitress in a hamburger joint along the way and how she liked truckers because they were free and generous. Then, a couple of little kids and their old man come in to buy a piece of bread from her, which she shouldn't sell, not when she has sandwiches for sale. It seemed to me that everything Steinbeck had been trying to say about the all-encompassing economic wrench in the lives of people – and trying to say it for about a hundred pages – he'd said movingly here, beautifully, around that piece of bread, so that your heart was breaking and he'd said it in only five pages.

Out of this welter of detail, this dulling of effect, one magnificent character emerges – drawn on the grand scale, and that is the mother, or "Ma," as she is called throughout the book. In some ways, she is just another farmwoman in the American west, but if there is such a thing as a noble character drawn out of lowliness on the heroic scale it's this Joad woman. She shines like a great beacon light. Remember, all she wants is self-respect, the dignity that she is entitled to as a human being with a family to look after, but arrayed against her, bent on destroying her noble qualities, are brutal, sinister, all-enveloping social forces, economic materialism, and if Steinbeck's economic, almost doctrinal point of view is enough for you, in itself, then the book is a great book. If, however, you feel that there is a rigidity of line to Steinbeck's view, to his hewing of it – then, despite the wide scope of his intent – you may feel he has sung a wild impassioned battle hymn while wearing blinkers.

*Saturday Night*, 1939

# THOMAS WOLFE'S
# APPETITE FOR LIFE

It is hard to read *The Web and the Rock* by Thomas Wolfe without feeling a profound personal regret that Thomas Wolfe is dead. If I ask myself why I feel such a sense of loss then I begin to get at the source of his power as a writer. Such gusto he had, such passion and a kind of wide-eyed eagerness for everything that touched him at every hour of the day, that his work for me became a celebration of life itself: it seemed to be important just to be alive while Wolfe was around writing.

Perhaps this great quality was simply something in Wolfe's heart that was greater even than his achievement as a writer: this I do know, that you go on reading from page to page even when you are let down, even when you feel he has repeated himself a hundred times and you wish once and for all he would say exactly what he meant. He was like an old-time knight in search of the Holy Grail, only for Wolfe it was the pieces of a magic tapestry that were to be sought, pieces apt to be found hidden on the persons of small boys, or stuck away in garbage pails up some back alley, or held in the hand of some little waitress, or around the neck of some beautiful lady; in short, wherever there was any kind of human activity – wherever people loved and felt and thought – there might be found a piece of the pattern, and Wolfe went there eagerly with his hand out and his heart open, examining, probing and celebrating and taking what he found and seeing if it would fit into the pattern of a magic tapestry.

Only it came about, in the search for pieces of his pattern that might be found in any corner of America, that a strange thing happened to Wolfe, the seeker. In his search he fell in love with every fragment of life and every object that he examined: a great nostalgia grew in his heart for the places where he had wandered; it got so that he couldn't reject anything. And when he worked away fiercely assembling the pieces he had picked up, there was the bright thread of the magic pattern shining through it, but it was broken and disconnected: the stuff that he couldn't bear to reject was always there to blur and break the line.

This sort of search and capture of brief glory and the stretches of failure would have marked Wolfe's work even if he had lived to be a hundred. The trouble was that his voracious appetite for experiencing and remembering was far greater than his sense of discipline as an artist. Maybe he would have wanted to have it this way. In any event, in *The Web and the Rock*, he is the same Wolfe. After the first two hundred pages his hero, Monk, from the South, not a giant this time, but a middle-sized man with simian characteristics, becomes the old Eugene Gant, whirling around on the rock of Manhattan.

Yet, in the first part of the book that deals with the life of the boy, Monk, in his native southern town, there are wonderful pieces of writing. Surely Wolfe never wrote better or was more completely successful than in these opening two hundred pages. The portraits of the people take on a big, bold, striking line: they loom up powerfully, they quiver with life and they have that largeness and bursting quality that were so dear to Wolfe's soul. There is a stretch of writing about "three o'clock in the afternoon," when a boy is, or ought to be entitled to lie around doing nothing, that is breathtaking: and there is a portrait of a butcher's wife that is simply unforgettable.

But after Monk leaves the town and goes on to college, the truly magnificent qualities of penetration in line and feeling fade out for quite a long stretch. Not that the book isn't good in here, but there is no particular revelation that isn't above the capacity of a half a hundred talents actively employed in the same writing business in our time. And so it goes for quite a stretch into the New York experiences. Wolfe seems to be much more self-conscious about the people in New York than he was about those on Monk's native heath. But once Monk meets up with the half-Jewess, Esther, a woman years older than he, rich and working as a designer in the theatre, Wolfe seems to dig in again and the book starts to roll and rumble in the true Wolfe tradition.

The character, Esther, with her grey hair and her fineness and her consciousness of her Jewish blood, is a very remarkable portrait of a woman. Her love affair with Monk is exciting going. At its best, when it is clear and straightforward, it is full of penetration and insight. At its worst, it takes on a kind of imitation Wagnerian sound that isn't very impressive, and it blurs; oh, it blurs again and again simply because Wolfe can't bear to let go, as if he feels that intensity will be lost if he doesn't keep thrusting again and again.

Among the greatest admirers of Wolfe, who rank him with the great masters, there seems to be some confusion about what constitutes intensity. To put it in a way that can be seen; did you ever watch the late Harry Greb fight? Greb was a great fighter with a windmill attack, his arms pumping all the time, mauling away. But was he more intense in action than a fighter like Kid Chocolate, who moved like a dancer and whose every thrust was beautiful to watch in its deadly precision? No sir, whether in fighting or in writing, the man with the sure sharp thrust is the one who is truly intense.

I could go on picking away endlessly at this book, saying what is wrong with it, and yet in the end there is nothing to do but feel humble before the inevitable recognition of Wolfe's mysterious power, which is this: he could make you feel like living, he could make you feel like writing, he could make you feel that fashions in literature were unimportant, he could make you like people, he could enliven your ambition for yourself even if you were never sure of the intellectual source that directed his own ambition.

*Saturday Night,* 1939

# A GOOD WORD
# FOR BOOK REVIEWERS

Some authors say they don't bother to read reviews, that they glance at the review page to see whether their work has been given good space, and then they use the page to wrap the fish they've had for dinner. I don't believe this story.

All too often, you are compelled to read each notice carefully. If you find the reviewer is very stupid, you have to remember that the editor who printed the review probably thinks his man is bright enough and acidic enough to get under your skin, so never write a complaining letter to the editor. A letter should be written only if there has been a falsification in the review. Or, if you believe that the editor is a little brighter than the man he chose to do your book, you might believe that he may be embarrassed himself, and if he is embarrassed he may even drop you a line to say he does not share the opinion of his reviewer. That's a pale hope, but it has happened to me. Even so, what can you do?

And of course, there is author baiting. A reviewer, sometimes sadly a failed writer, may resent a good writer's fame, or his prestige, or even his sales, and so he will deliberately needle the author. The whole point of the review will be to open a wound in the author's self-esteem. If an editor prints such author baiting, the editor is really revealing himself. The reviewer is doing a hatchet job. The editor has handed him the hatchet. Even so, I don't think the author should take pen in hand. The editor and his hatchet boy will only chuckle.

But, here, I begin to sing their praises, all those critics muddled, malicious and goofy. They are an absolutely necessary part of the author's life. He needs them as he needs those men and women who become the characters in his work. They are telling him – one by one – in their own peculiar and often astonishing ways – how people feel about his view of life, how close it is to the commonality, how singular it is. More than that – they are a democratic babble of voices, there to constantly remind the writer that where one man swears he sees a horse, another man will see a dog.

I always go to CBC Radio, where I know the radio reviews of my novels have always been scrupulously honest, full of integrity. I know because I have always had an amiable relationship with the CBC. No one that I know of has ever set out to scuttle me. I have always had the feeling they wished me well. Yet, their reviews of my novels have been awful.

When I wrote *The Loved and the Lost*, a novel that a few people scattered throughout the world think is awfully good, the lady who spoke about it for the CBC laid herself on the line, as only an honest woman could do. She said that I had written a book about the Negro problem and in thirty years I hadn't learned anything about writing because I had nothing to say to settle the Negro problem: I had left it where it was.

This fascinated me. I knew the lady. I knew her husband. I had a good opinion of them, but now I knew them as I had never known them. She had told me something about her psyche that she would never, in guarded moments, have told me. She had even told me something about myself that I hadn't dreamed of – that I had written a book about the Negro problem.

When I wrote *The Many Coloured Coat*, a professor, a writer from Edmonton, said that the book broke in half! The first part hardly seemed to belong to the second part. This was a personal perception that could only have come out of utter candour and the reviewer's loyalty to himself. No one else anywhere in the world has ever had that perception, so I remember it for its singularity. As for my book, *A Fine and Private Place*, the lady who did it by way of Halifax, after pointing out that I had been overrated for years, went on to say, with a tone of earnest concern, as if for my well-being, that I had waited thirteen years to write *A Fine and Private Place*, and better I had waited a lot longer.

I regard these reviewers as friends. My esteem and warmth doesn't depend on my judgement of their perceptions. That's unimportant. They have been – as only your best friends are willing to be – brutally frank with me about themselves.

So, I am putting in a good word for honest book reviewers. Warts and all, obtuse, sometimes movingly perceptive, or just dreadfully ordinary, they are something more than the usual mill-run of people. They talk back to the writer, who is often alone. They, without knowing it, are telling him about themselves in their relationship to his work, and ultimately, to him. Since that is all you can ask of people, the writer should listen with compassion.

*CBC Anthology*

# THE HEART'S WAY
# OF KNOWING

Some women have a way of making writers want to open their hearts to them, to talk about their work and their most complicated problems with the work. They seem to take the reactions of these women with far more seriousness than they would the observations of the most learned critics.

These women rarely have any lofty academic qualifications, have rarely written anything themselves, and yet, there is something in them that the writer recognizes as being necessary to him, something that seems to free his imagination. It is as though he were talking to himself in bed, knowing that the one lying beside him would be sympathetically and warmly involved, even if not quite understanding his problem. No, understand is the wrong word. Her understanding would not be of the intellectual order, it would be of the heart, and the heart's way of knowing.

I was reminded of this when reading *The Letters of Gustave Flaubert*. Flaubert had a mistress named Louise Colet, and in his letters to her, he tried to reveal all the anguish that went into his art. It is true that he also wrote to another woman, George Sand, a remarkable writer herself, but the passion with which he sought an intimacy of understanding about his artistic concerns is not in the letters to Sand. Flaubert, that isolated provincial by choice, the most dedicated to his art of all writers, chose an obscure woman he liked sleeping with as his confidant. The greatest intellectuals of

Europe would have loved to have had him involve them in his work. No, it had to be this one woman who even was given to nagging him about getting along with his career in the world.

So, what is it that this woman offers? I think it must be that there is some kind of an awareness in the writer that in the female, when she is attractive to him, there is a kind of intuitive excitement about seeing things come together and make a harmony. Of course, I don't know.

But take Balzac. Unlike Flaubert he knew everybody and was engrossed in the literary life of Paris, but whose opinion was it he really wanted and sought? Again, an obscure woman who lived out in the country. At one time she may have been his mistress, but no matter! When he wanted a view of a book he had written, he went to her.

Some years ago I had a friend, a Chicago man named Chapman who came to Toronto to study medieval philosophy, Thomas Aquinas. I grew to love this man whose mind teemed with rich ideas. Someday, he said, he hoped to write a novel; in the meantime he was a metaphysician. We had wonderful Athenian evenings, sitting till dawn shouting and laughing, and the same woman was always there with us, listening and laughing and giving us drinks and food.

My friend finally went to teach in New York. Every time I went to New York I stayed with him and in the evenings we sat in a tavern drinking and talking. It worried me that the intellectual gaiety was gone. We were still enormously interested in each other, but we didn't shine or revel in our eagerness and after an argument we didn't embrace each other. The excitement was gone, and wondering about this I said, "Do you remember those evenings in Toronto, and how alive we seemed?"

"Wonderful evenings, I'll always remember them," he said.

"And the same woman. Always the same woman was there with us."

"You know," he said with a little laugh, after he had pondered. "I can't remember a thing she ever said. And as a matter of fact, I couldn't tell you anything about her, I hardly remember her."

"Oh, I do," I said. "Would that she were here, would that she were here," and I smiled with an indulgent air, for I knew now that he would never write that novel. He was an academic, he never would be a fiction writer.

# CALENDAR YEARS:
# THE DEPRESSION

ᘛᘜᘙᘚ

How can anyone believe that an expression of life can begin or end with calendar dates? In North America, of course, where writers seem to have short-lived glory, it is natural to mention the decade in which they flourished. But in Europe, where a writer is supposed to grow fine and mellow as the years pass, and be in vigorous production even to the end of a long life, what has he to do with the spirit of any particular decade?

André Gide actually had a friendship with Oscar Wilde, so the bookkeepers of literature might easily pinpoint him with the writers of the '90s but, unfortunately for them, he reached the peak of his influence in France in the 1930s, '40s and even into the '50s. In short, he belonged to no particular decade.

Nor did Thomas Mann. Nor does Faulkner. Nor does Marie-Claire Blais or Mavis Gallant. When the talent is big enough it bridges the years, and if the historian, mulling over the work of these writers, notes changes as they grow older, the changes are usually in spirit as the writer either grows wiser or as the talent fades and ceases to be adventurous, and it has nothing to do with the impact of the fads and enthusiasms of any particular bracket of years.

One night I was listening to a woman writer talking about her upbringing in the '50s and how restricted that life had been, how cribbed, cabined, and confined women were and how naïve girls were expected to be, and how she had nearly suffocated under the puritan repression of those days, and how exultant she had become about herself under the great liberating influence of the '60s.

I remember the 1950s well, just as I remember the '30s, and the '20s, and I listened to this talk about the '50s with a kind of blank astonishment, as if I were hearing a tale about my grandmother's time.

I had written *The Loved and the Lost*, about a Montreal girl of the day who had certainly gone winging it on her own. I had thought these girls were all around me. Obviously, the '50s for me were one thing, and for the woman writer I had been listening to, quite another. And maybe this is the way it always is when we talk about the spirit of any one of the decades. We tell our own story. If three or four writers and eight or nine newspapermen have shared the same restricted life in a small pocket of a particular time, and they tell their story very well, then we take it as a picture of the toss and temper of life lived in those days, although others who lived at the same time might shake their heads in wonder.

What we all hope for, I'm sure, at the end of a year when the bells ring out the old, is that they are also ringing in a new period of creative energy, one of those strange magic periods that come in human history and are like circles of light around a number of years. If such a period comes, and no one knows when it will ever come, and it surely has nothing to do with the calendar or the ending of a decade, then we do have groupings and then new directions, and the mystery of it is that no one can quite name the year or the decade when the light began to become a circle, a slow creeping circle around a time of dullness.

So, I come to a decade, and a story that is being told about that decade again and again. This repeated story seems to have become the one true story, but it is not my story at all, though I lived most actively in this decade, the '30s.

I read magazine articles, I watch show after show on television about survivors of the Depression years, all telling their dismal stories, singing their dismal songs:

*When I was in that railroad wreck, who took the engine off my neck . . . ?*

In this country, there is a danger of the '30s forever after being called the Ten Lost Years. What a blinkered, one-eyed, bloodshot, view of life. No one has ever come to ask me about the Depression years. Why? I was a writer, I had a wife and a small child. I, too, was faced by the great depression. I was in a city like millions of others. I was not riding the rods. I was not seventeen or twenty and footloose, I was not able to hole up in a college.

What I know about the Depression is what I had then felt in the fabric of life, as I touched it in big cities like New York and Toronto.

It's true that over and over on the street I would encounter a man I knew who was out of work. I myself, in the first two difficult years, scrounged on my own, and I counted on my wife's family; I was their poor relative at the door. On the streets downtown in front of the missions, I saw the line-ups at the soup kitchens. That was the first real shock I'd got in '32 in New York, seeing the huge line-ups of shabby, shuffling men at the mission places and hundreds of other men selling apples on the streets, but you'll just have to take my word for it that by '33 the pressure was lifting, and, unless you are completely seduced by the Ten Lost Years nonsense on television, you might possibly believe that in those days a spirit touched writers and artists and intellectuals, and it got into the community, too, a spirit that came out of a sense of warmth and concern.

I was talking to the painter, Carl Schaefer, a few months ago about those years, that time, this spirit, and though he had been broke and hadn't known from one week to another whether he would starve, he seemed to think that there had been something wonderfully creative about those years, creative in the way people drew together. The social conscience! That was the phrase. It may not have amounted to much more than a slogan, but there was at least a longing for some real human warmth behind the slogan.

I was in New York a lot in those days, and knew many of the writers, and I knew how this secret intimate warmth got into all their stories. It is not accidental that no one at that time wanted to read the stories of the more glittering world of Scott Fitzgerald. A simple moving human touch, and a comedic wink as well, was in the stories of Erskine Caldwell and William Saroyan, James T. Farrell, and John Steinbeck. And the theatre had come alive, too. O'Neill was writing, and the Group Theater was established and Clifford Odets was in full flower. Thomas Wolfe, in his big exuberant way, was still loving America for all he was worth, in spite of the Depression. No, they weren't lost years. They were moving creative years. Years that are creative are never lost.

You may say that I didn't ride the rods looking for work, I did not have my mortgage foreclosed on a western farm as a result of the drought, nor did I believe that the only way out of those years was to join the Mackenzie-Papineau division and go marching off to Spain to defend Madrid against the hated Franco.

I did none of these things. I tried to live from day to day in the cities, and I went on being a writer, and I am outraged when someone who wasn't there at the time calls the period the Ten Lost Years and gets away with it. The truth is, I only felt depressed toward the end of the decade, in 1938, when I could see, the skull beneath the homburg hat, when I could see with all its dreadful murderous falsifications, the Second World War coming.

*CBC Anthology*

# THE DEATH
# OF A REVOLUTIONARY

The other day Ernest Toller, the famous German poet and drama-tist, committed suicide in exile in New York. Much has been writ-ten about his death. I have just read a piece by Dorothy Thompson and a poem by W.H. Auden. That he chose to die by his own hand seems to have profoundly shocked the intellectual world because he was a revolutionary poet who dreamed and worked for a new and free society. So his death has great political significance. The world proclaims him a martyr to fascism.

But I've been wondering how the doctrinaire Marxians, Trot-skyites, and Stalinites actually feel in their hearts about Ernest Tol-ler's death. I've been wondering what kind of a pang came into the hearts of revolutionary leaders all over the world.

Remember, this man chose to destroy himself by his own hand. He looked over the world and was full of despair. Suicide is the final personal act of despair: it is the last possible personal gesture that separates a man from all mass movements.

The good Marxian can shrug his shoulders and say, "Sure, it's true Toller gave his life to the revolutionary movement, but the way he dies is just a demonstration of petty bourgeois defeatism. He didn't know the right answers. Or if he did know them he wasn't trained in them. Anyway, look at his origins. He was never a true proletarian. Hence in a crucial period in revolutionary politics he resorts to such a bourgeois gesture as a personal suicide. Personal problems are unimportant in the movement." If that sounds too *trite*, and *unfair* to Marxians, I am sorry, but basically it must be the Communist approach to Toller's death. Mind you, I don't mean in the hearts of individual revolutionaries: they got the same shock that everybody else did: but they must subscribe to the routine answer.

And it is these routine answers that begin to infuriate me. Maybe Toller felt the same way about it. Maybe, driven into exile by fascism, he saw no hope for his new world and his dream because in our time revolutionary and counter-revolutionary movements leave little hope for man as a man — as a human being.

If Toller's death would thrust the personal problem or the fate of the single individual right back into the teeth of the revolutionary leadership throughout the world, it would be a great death and have great meaning. But I don't think it will. For the revolutionists have experienced that same sense of shock before and managed to recover very nicely. I have in mind the death of the celebrated Russian poet, Mayakovsky, whose suicide, after he had been so widely acclaimed as the poet of the new order, created such a tremendous stir among the communist intellectuals in Russia. Mayakovsky's death did at least have a temporary influence in Russia. The watchdogs, who sniffed around Russian writers, telling them, in the name of the party line, what they ought to write, were, for a time, driven into the kennels.

Well, there was Toller, in a strange country, with his people being hounded in his homeland, nursing his private despair. It's too bad he couldn't have spoken to the men who know the right answers and had them point out to him that he was out of date, going around as he was, with death in him. Or what a break it would have been for him if he had run into the author of a piece on Dostoevsky I read a few months ago. The author, a good Marxian, was pointing out that a book like *Crime and Punishment*, while a great book in its day, could have little meaning for us today because it dealt with the problem of an individual soul. Such rubbish drives you mad. It is this fundamental stupidity that crushes the humanity out of the revolutionary dream.

And these suicides, tremendous personal assertions of despair, which have no place in the Marxian pattern for the modern revolutionary mind, will keep happening: they are challenging individual blows, blows to the conception of man such a pattern offers. How are people who have no interest in the fate of individuals to explain the suicides of revolutionaries? Surely such conduct on the part of men who understand history and mass movements and the whole dialectic is disturbing, just as the conduct of the old Bolsheviks at the celebrated Trotsky trials was disturbing.

I think of walking down a street in New York one afternoon with a young writer who had swung far to the left at the time of the trials. He was greatly disturbed; not so much by the probable guilt or innocence of the old Bolsheviks, but by an explanation of their peculiar conduct offered to him by a man who had been one of the editors of the *New Masses*, the leading communist review in the United States. My friend had been told very earnestly that if people were finding the behaviour of the old Bolsheviks hard to understand at the trials it was because they didn't understand the Russian soul: if they would read Dostoevsky, however, they would understand it. Not Marx, Engels, Zola, or any one of a number of materialistic writers, but the reactionary Dostoevsky, with his Christian and mystic insights into the Russian soul.

Yes, Toller's conduct, too, will be hard for many a young revolutionary to understand. His personal problem, his personal despair, became bigger for him than his revolutionary hope. If the trouble is that he was what they call an "imperfect Marxist," then, like a lot of other liberals and socialists who belong to the political left wing, the years in Europe must seem like limbo.

When Toller came to America he brought with him, inside him, all that had happened in Europe in the last decade. It added up to death. He and his people had been persecuted. Everything he stood for had taken a bad beating.

Every time Toller sat down in a restaurant by himself he must have wondered how it all could have happened so quickly. First the great hope of a new social order after the war, his struggle for it in Germany, his fame as a writer. Then the rise of fascism in Italy, the collapse of the revolutionary movement in Germany where it had been so strong – a sudden almost voluntary surrender. Then Hitler; then Austria. The bombardment and destruction of the socialist apartment houses in Vienna must have shown him clearly what the end of his dream was to be. The rise of the popular front in France may have given him a brief hope, and the new Spanish republic surely exalted him, but how long did they last? That was all dead or dying when Toller came to America.

Toller knew when they'd rung down the curtain. They did it at Munich and in some style, too. There's a nettling thing about Munich. People still go around talking about the big mistake Neville Chamberlain made in talking with Hitler. Mr. Chamberlain was a businessman and not stupid, and when he stood up in the House of Commons, under violent attack on the subject of Munich, he was pretty unperturbed. And with good reason. Outside of a bit of partitioning here and there, Munich did big things for some in Europe: it threw a wet blanket over the revolutionary spirit, a blanket that just about smothered it. If you talked to any of your communist friends around that time, you found that they were feeling Ernest Toller's despair.

So, after Munich, for Ernest Toller there was nothing left. There was still a revolutionary program, of course, there was still Marxian inevitability, if he wanted to believe in it. But when he put these things against his own personal suffering and his own personal despair they were not enough.

*Saturday Night*, 1939

# BARBARA TUCHMAN:
# *A DISTANT MIRROR*

୧୨୨୨୨୨

A month ago I read Barbara Tuchman's engrossing *A Distant Mirror: The Calamitous 14th Century.* I had a particular interest in the book because I had grown up half believing that the Middle Ages, or at least the 13th century, was a time of spiritual unification in Europe, a high bright moment in Western history, a Christian flowering of civilization after the dismal Dark Ages.

If this fine flowering did take place, then how sadly brief was its time! And the seeds of destruction must have been sprouting even in those short hours, for the following 14th century, according to Barbara Tuchman, was one of the most dismal and maniacal periods in all human history.

The evidence, as Miss Tuchman presents it, is overwhelming. She is not a popularizer. Any academic who applies that term to her would be showing envy of her imagination and her sense of storyline. In some seven hundred pages, she has had to cover the Hundred Years War, the outbreak of the bubonic plague and a split in the Church which had one Pope at Avignon and one in Rome. It is inevitable that certain aspects of medieval life should get short shrift from her.

For example, you won't go to Miss Tuchman for a profound understanding of the ins and outs of courtly love. And as for romantic love, she seems to see it as a hard practical necessity because of the system of arranged marriages; loveless marriages arranged for children and to preserve or increase property holdings. Indeed, her perception of romantic love is a far cry from those of Rougemont in his book, *Love in the Western World*. She is grimly flat on the subject. And one other thing: the times, as she describes them, are so terrible, life so cheap, so uncertain, and for common people, so devoid of all ease, that you have to marvel that a man like Chaucer, in every way a man of the times, could have had such humour, warmth and common sense. Chaucer did not write about a miserable unhappy doomed people! And so one wonders if Barbara Tuchman, in spite of her enormous research, was ever quite able to grasp how these people felt about themselves and each other.

The title, *A Distant Mirror*! The implication is that we only need to look back to those witless, irrational, and quite mad, bloodthirsty, devil-haunted times to see our own time of doom approaching. She didn't quite persuade me of this, but to say so is to cavil, to nitpick at a powerful work that gives a honed picture of a doomed century – the ghastly end of something. Or, was it the beginning of something, with the renaissance just around the corner?

Then, a month after reading the book, as I was walking along the street with the 14th century apparently gone from my mind, I found myself thinking idly, "The nobility! The knightly class!" Wherever they were, and no matter the times, were they always so useless and destructive? This must have been what I had really got out of the Tuchman book, this must have been working in the back of my mind.

It fascinated me that those land-owning knights, holed up in their great castles, living on the peasantry, grinding them down with taxes, had contributed absolutely nothing to the society. Nothing but war. They lived only for predatory wars and for hunting and looting and the greedy aggrandizement of themselves. As for their chivalry, the code by which they pretended to live, it applied only to themselves, never to the peasant or the little townsmen. Those knights seemed to understand nothing, not even the art of war. The great French knights in their massive armour despised the longbow because it was used by common English bowmen, and so they suffered the great defeat at Crecy and then blindly used the same dumb tactics at Agincourt and Roncesvalles. They were ruthless and largely witless.

I can imagine a student in some museum, pouring over books, trying to understand the society of those centuries, finally asking himself why people put up with this useless class for so long. Was it the religious sanction – each man had his station? Fantasy? A people with, and of, a powerful fantasy? Though the knights devoted all their energies to war and killing, the only innovations in warfare, the effective use of the foot soldier against the knight, came from the middle class when Swiss merchants resisted the encroachments of the Holy Roman Emperor. When it became apparent that the middle class was needed in actual war planning, the knights were doomed. Anyway, by this time, chivalry was being seen as a boyish and silly dream of men half-mad and in the end was so treated by Cervantes in his *Don Quixote*.

I think any human being looking back into that distant mirror would see himself in sympathy with the peasantry and the slowly emerging middle classes. It is heartbreaking to watch the peasants trying fearfully to free themselves, for they are still within grip of their own fantasy about the nobles and the King. No help came from the Church.

The peasant revolt in England was an extraordinary success until the leader, Wat Tyler, nursing the common fantasy about the sanctity of the King, went idiotically alone to meet his Lord and Master and, of course, was killed. And there were at least three great peasant revolts in France in the 14th century, revolts that ended when the leaders were killed; it is fascinating to watch how those revolts gradually drew in the middle class, and I began to see how utterly inevitable was the French Revolution.

But one other thought stays with me. It is really the confirmation of a view I have had for a long time.

Vast is the power of the imagination, of fiction, in shaping the lives of nations. Miss Tuchman believes the 14th century was a time of pervading insanity. I think it was a time firmly in the grip of powerful fantasies about life and death. I think fantasies shape a society every bit as much as those famous forces described by Marx and Engels – the methods of distribution and production, the medium of exchange and class war. A fantasy, beautiful or dreadful, seizes and drives a society, and then wears out, only to be succeeded by another fantasy. I wish Miss Tuchman could tell us what insane fantasies have us in thrall now.

*CBC Anthology*

# THE POWER OF DARKNESS

Late last night I was sitting with a friend listening to the news from Europe. When I shut off the radio I turned and looked at my friend and I saw there was a little flush on his face and a curious excitement shining in his eyes.

"What's the matter with you?" I asked.

"They don't really know what's going to happen next," he said in a wondering whisper. Then, when he saw me looking at him in such a puzzled way he seemed to grow ashamed: he seemed to guess that I suspected he was fascinated by the mystery of what might be impending in Europe, that it held him in suspense so powerfully that he could not draw away from it and express himself as a rational man without a great effort.

I should say that my friend is a man who hates everything Hitler has stood for. And he doesn't just hate Nazism or Fascism in other countries, he hates every single manifestation of the Fascist temperament in his own country, too. He has often said to me that the authoritarian Fascist or Nazi mind is really a matter of temperament: it has always been in the world and always will be, and there always would be a clash between people of such a temperament and other people who hate it.

Yet, there he was ashamed of himself because I had caught him looking so fascinated by some surprising Hitlerian gesture, and finally he said, "You can't help but be fascinated. Everything that seems to follow logically is just brushed aside. The nations that should hate each other stand together. The economists have always predicted that the have-not nations, for example, would stand against the possessing nations. Yet they don't. Nothing is working out rationally. It is as if the devil himself has got the upper hand in Europe and any terrible and irrational thing is now possible." And then, laughing apologetically, he said, "Of course I don't mean I believe in the devil, but evil, in itself, is fascinating. If you keep on looking at the face of evil it begins to take on a mysterious compulsion. You are drawn to it. It is just as true of people who don't even believe in evil things; they get touched just the same and drawn in. This last year I, myself, a good liberal, have felt the fascination of the compulsion. I'm ashamed of it, of course, yet at least it makes me believe I understand the power Hitler and his coterie have over Europe."

And then he asked me if I remembered the Chicago gang wars and the rise of Al Capone and the way people used to go out and buy papers and follow with a sense of dreadful expectancy the latest moves of a set of first-class thugs. Those men had a fascination for all America, he said. They got into your life, they were exciting, they were ruthless, they destroyed the civilizing social pattern: they touched a primitive jungle, or evil impulse in people. There isn't the slightest doubt that a great many people secretly felt liberated when they read the latest exploits of the most ruthless thugs.

Well, what has been going on in Europe the last few years in the minds of millions of Europeans is something the same, my friend said, only far more sinister. A long time ago you could see the mistake that bourgeois politicians made in dealing with Hitler. Being business men themselves and therefore strictly the product of a commercial world, they always felt that when a showdown came they could show Hitler and his friends that a particular coup wouldn't be worthwhile in terms of dollars and cents. But from the very beginning they had got him all wrong. They were talking a language that he thought was dead. "I remember talking to a very famous French philosopher about five years ago," my friend went on. "He was talking about the difference between Hitler and Mussolini. Mussolini was a practical man, he said. You could take him aside and show him that a certain course of action wasn't commercially profitable. But Hitler was something else. The Frenchman kept tapping his head: it was all in his head, he said, like a big explosive dream that could never be disturbed by a democratic statesman."

My friend then said that once he had got the idea that the men of the Nazi leadership were of a completely different stamp than the leaders of the democratic countries he had started delving into their careers. "Have you followed the career of Goering?" he asked me. "It is fabulous, simply fabulous. Ruthless beyond all measure. But you begin to feel that some supernatural agency has taken him in hand. Such luck, such success, such inhumanity: it's as though the man had made a compact with the Devil. And don't you think that the German people are fascinated by the career of Goering? Oh, they are. From month to month they know in their hearts they follow him breathlessly. Of course the English do not believe this. They still can't get used to men like Goering and Hitler. They think that if Germans read pamphlets and leaflets they will turn on their leadership. But believe me, this they will never do while these fabulous and mysterious and sinister characters are led on to new high points in their destiny. Having looked up the evil that Goering and Hitler can do in a nation, and seeing it turn into paths that are so terribly fascinating and so full of suspense, the German people feel the terrible compulsion of that evil. It has seduced them. They can't turn away from it till the gods, or the devil, or the brooding supernatural forces that are watching over those men make it plain they have deserted them and they are left alone for their enemies to destroy."

While my friend was talking I was thinking of all the speeches of Hitler's I have listened to. Was it possible that people made a mistake in the judging of those speeches? Did they expect a speech such as Roosevelt can make? Were they right in thinking he was such an utter fool?

Maybe with his diabolical intuitions – and make no mistake about it – he is a man of uncanny intuitions, he realizes the forces he touches in people throughout the world. Maybe he knows there are millions of people who feel liberated from all the bonds of conscience and morality as they are understood in the bourgeois world when they listen to him; he knows, indeed, how he fascinates.

"Yes," said my friend, "he broods up there in his mountain retreat like a diabolical child of darkness and unleashed brute force, and behind it is all the power of his sinister intuitions: he broods and murmurs in the darkness, waiting for the sign to be given to him: the sign to be given according to the compact he has made with the supernatural agencies that work with him. And then he comes down out of the darkness of his mountain lair and he speaks and if you listen to him you are swept back in history: you are in the Germany of ancient Roman times. Remember how the Romans could do nothing with those people in their great forest with their tribal gods?

"Well, when Hitler appears among them he appears as an old tribal god: he stirs the ancient racial pre-Christian memories. The hoarse voices shout, wild with eagerness to be led along some tribal way foreign to the rest of civilized Europe, some mad assault, some wild raid justified only with their tribal gods.

"So I can't help being fascinated," my friend said. "I feel that no one knows what is going to happen in Europe, and it is terrible watching. Yet every time I go out on our Canadian streets I feel ashamed of having yielded to this worldwide and terrible fascination. I even feel ashamed of having to explain this."

*Saturday Night,* 1939

# BY THE BLUE
# ALGOMA HILLS

The Algoma Hills on the north shore of Lake Superior: the steamer from Sault Ste. Marie takes you up to a rocky point near the mouth of the Michipicoten River, which is a few miles along shore from the harbour.

It was late in the afternoon. At the dock there was a store and a shed and a government warehouse and a dirt road leading back through the wooded hills. A half-breed with an old motorboat he used for trolling on the lake came along and told us he was sure he could find the tent we were looking for on the point by the river, so we got into the boat. We passed great black slabs of rock jutting out in the lake, hills like cones with vast, wooded slopes, bare in patches where there had been a fire, and the sunlight was gleaming on bare dry boughs: the timber looked like scrub on the great hills; where it had been burned to the rock, it stuck out stiffly, a jumble of matchsticks, but beneath this burned timber was always the rock, slabs of quartz and basalt and granite, and the peaks, shining white in the sunlight, immense rugged cathedrals with dark crevices.

But the sense of grandeur that envelops you as you look up the valleys is almost too inexorable to stand: it seems to be crushing and destroying your own identity as a living thing. By the time we had reached the point by the river, the sun was going down, and it was almost a relief to have it go down. But as soon as we had made a fire and had eaten and were sleeping in the tent, that vast, unyielding stillness of those frightening hills started crushing us again, and it seemed utterly unimportant to be a man on the earth.

In the morning, we saw an old Indian woman with six children in the one canoe, like a city family in a jalopy, on their way home to the reservation. It was good seeing them. Gave you the feeling you soon might be at home in the hills. So that morning we trolled for salmon-trout on the lake, and then we went into the bush, and the black flies were not too bad because it was August, and when we found a little pool that seemed to be full of speckled trout we cut a pile of green brush and lit it and made a smudge and stood where the smoke would blow over our heads and keep the flies away as we fished.

But as soon as we got into any kind of clearing and could look around, there were always the hills. And you can see why the natives are so slow moving: they seem to understand the futility of pitting themselves against so much grandeur. That is what you feel when you go up the river a piece to where the hills open out into a small tributary and where there is a little settlement still called The Mission. It is just two rows of wooden houses, a small white church, a general store with a false front, a dilapidated dock, and an old worm-eaten fishing boat rotting in the sand. The few families are just as much French as Indian, but they'll be Indian as long as they can collect treaty money. They fish and move slowly, and the solemnity of the country is in them, and they have been burying their dead for a hundred years in the little cemetery with picket fences around each individual grave to keep out the encroaching underbrush.

We were wondering what kind of men and dreams could possibly come out of such a country. We couldn't sleep and we kept looking up at the sky. It was astonishing how the hills seemed to thrust us right up close to the stars: they swarmed in an arch over the lake. The loons were wailing down the shore, but we kept looking up, feeling exalted. In the clear air, we were strangely and suddenly free.

The day we headed home, going up the Algoma Central Line, we were half an hour waiting for the train in Hawk Junction, and there we met a young Anglo-Catholic priest from England.

He was starving for conversation; he had left England a year ago and in his zeal had just picked out this part of the country on a map. He wanted to talk about Chesterton and Belloc and the cultivated farmland he had seen passing through southern Ontario. In his loneliness, he dreamed of getting moved down there soon.

When it came time for our train to go, the priest suddenly realized there were a great many things about the possibility of a union between Catholic and Anglo-Catholics he wanted to say and he hadn't had time: and as the train started to move, he began to run alongside, shouting up his arguments at the window, moving faster and falling behind as the train picked up speed. It seemed utterly fantastic in that country, a wild, pathetic gesture against the dissolving force of the inexorable hills.

*Vogue*, 1940

# SAMUEL BECKETT

A writer who is a singular artist, a writer who has a peculiar temperament which he expresses in his vision, a writer who finds that he is at last – after hard years of neglect – recognized by the young as a man for his time, is very lucky. Samuel Beckett was such a man, a private figure, an isolated artist functioning only in the world of his private vision.

In these days when writers strive so frantically to become public personalities, his only advertisement for himself was his imaginative work. I have no recollection of Beckett offering himself as a spokesman for a cause. Camus, a wise man, seemed to be driven to try and tell people how to live. Tolstoy, too, had this compulsion. But Beckett, in his fables, tried to show us the poverty of the human condition without comment. He made fables that had to be a very private experience for me, just as they were for him. Indeed, you may never understand what he had to say; but he couldn't or wouldn't do anything about it. James Joyce, another Irishman, was also an isolated private figure who never went dancing into the spotlight. It was his art alone that made people go looking for him, just as you have to go looking for Beckett without ever finding him.

The only statement the news services could get out of Beckett when they tracked him down in Europe and told him the good news about his Nobel prize, some seventy thousand dollars, was, "I am not grateful." He did, however, take the money. "I am not grateful." It's almost too good a line. A Beckett line. Enigmatic. Disturbing. Was he sour, a little bitter? Cézanne or Dostoevsky or Joyce –

surely they knew in their hearts that the world ought to be grateful to them. How could they pretend to be grateful for something like a prize, a public bauble? False humility would be an insult to their own work. Maybe, just maybe – Beckett was looking at it in this way. But many men who know his work and admire it surely said, "What a pessimist. Always the despairing pessimist. Unable to find hopeful consolation in his bleak vision, even in this great prize."

The common view of Beckett, based on his plays, stories, novels, and poems, is that he was so pessimistic he must be close to everlasting despair; that no man caught in his world could ever feel there was any dignity or joy to be found in being alive; it would have been better never to have left the safety of the womb, better never to have been born at all. Yet, the more I look at Beckett's work the more I am convinced that this view of his vision is all wrong. He had a tragic vision, of course. But in this vision there isn't just a pathetic despairing quest for a little hope. There is a healthy sardonic humour. There is a faith. The faith is masked, always masked, but his faith, something deep in the Beckett abyss, is always there with its own mysterious glow, troubling even when you think you have caught the hang of his more obvious and apparently comic/pessimistic belittlement of human life. What kind of faith is it? Look at this strange bleak world of Beckett's and the creatures stumbling dreamlike through it.

The most familiar glimpse of this world comes through the work most familiar to us; the plays, *Waiting for Godot*, *Endgame*, and *Krapp's Last Tape*. His novels, like *Murphy*, and *Molloy*, excellent though they are as surrealistic fantasies, don't stay in my mind. I know the method. I have no desire to read the novels again. But the short stories, and those prose fragments that are to be found in one of his late prose collections called *No Knife*, are something else. They widen Beckett's visionary landscape. Bleak, bleak man on his last legs, but in this bleak scene there is the continuing mystery of man on this earth and a cry coming out of him. As I hear this cry, it is not a wail of black despair, there is a deep longing in it, a recognition that man's hope, the only light in this bleak world, the only way of redemption, is that he can turn to some other human being for comfort. Astonishingly, he can know moments of love, and these strange, furtive, fugitive moments are what can lighten the way on earth.

Humanity, for Beckett, was beaten up, battered, sick and ailing, yes always sick, physically ill, growing decrepit it seemed, and yet magically, and I insist on this, never completely despairing, because there was some battered remnant of light in his nature. Along the way there was always something frighteningly mysterious going on. The sense of mystery is caught in odd little moments by the characters themselves. As we get used to this bleak world we begin to recognize little signposts of language and gesture. For example, *Krapp's Last Tape* (incidentally, this isn't much of a play. It's a dramatic poem. There are two voices. An old man with his own voice plays a tape he recorded when he was thirty-nine. The scene cuts back and forth from the young voice on the tape to the old man's own voice; so, I suppose this makes for a drama, a conflict of two voices, youth and old age, the most dramatic of all conflicts, you might say. Yet, for me, it always remained a poem). Near the beginning of this piece, Krapp says, "The new light above my table is a great improvement. With all this darkness round me I feel less alone. In a way I love to get up and move about in it, then back here to . . . me . . . Krapp." This struck me as right for Beckett. All the darkness around him. Is it the womb? The primal womb? A man ventures out, then back, back to the safety of himself. What then is to be remembered of the times when a man ventured out? What remains of all the misery? Krapp says:

"What I suddenly saw then was this, that a belief I had been going on all my life, namely great granite rocks, the foam flying up in the light of the lighthouse and the wind gauge spinning like a propeller, clear to me at last that the dark I have always struggled to keep under, is in reality my most (*Krapp curses, switches off, winds tape forward, switches on again*) unshatterable association until my dissolution of storm and night with the light of the understanding and the fire (*he curses louder, switches off, switches on again*) my face in her breasts and my hand on her. We lay there without moving, but under us all moved, and moved us, gently, up and down, and from side to side. Past midnight, never knew such silence. The earth might be uninhabited . . . A chance for happiness."

If the silence and a chance for happiness were missed, they were missed. But a man, being like he is in this lonely Krapp world, can at least know when it was missed. Most men go to their graves without a single moment of awareness that there was a place and a time in their lives when a chance at life and happiness was missed.

There's another little clue to the Beckett vision in earlier lines from Krapp about the dark: "I love to get up and move about in it, and then back here to me. Krapp." More and more, in his later work, Beckett turned inward. The pieces of prose in *No Knife* are fascinating to a writer. No one is doing anything quite like them. They explore what is a new realm of consciousness, or rather, that realm that a man half-asleep, yet still not crippled by the lack of all logic in the dream world, lets his thoughts flow on; the inner voice of a man speaking; the heart is reaching, the spirit is being laid bare, not for a confessor, just the inner voice in a vale of shadows. I doubt that many people will ever read these strange pieces, but if you read them again and again, they begin to haunt you, as your own spirit must sometimes haunt you. Here is an example from *Texts for Nothing*:

> "It's a winter night where I was, where I'm going, remembered, imagined, no matter, believing in me, believing it's me, no need, so long as the others are there, where, in the world of the others, of the long mortal ways, under the sky, with a voice, no, no need, and the power to move now and then, no need either, as long as the others move, the true others, but on earth, beyond all doubt on earth, for as long as it takes to die again, wake again, long enough for things to change here, for something to change, to make possible, a deeper birth, a deeper death, or resurrection in and out of this murmur of memory and dream . . ."

I can't read those lines and think of Beckett as a hopelessly despairing pessimist. The truth is, he seemed to have a vision beyond our own. We see only the man walking around under our noses, the man we're sure of, trivial, in his materialistic false happiness and never aware of what he might be, never a deeper death or resurrection.

The pessimist usually sees life with a flat gloomy certainty. Things will turn to the worst for him. Man always appears in this flat hard light. Yet, there is no certainty in Beckett. Instead, mystery, mystery even in the most trivial details of life. All along the way there are some familiar little clues. In the play, *All that Falls*, the old woman, Mrs. Rooney, is going along the road. She encounters a boy, Christy. She says, "Why do you halt? (*pause*) But why do I halt?" Silence. The insignificant little question that leads to the sense of mystery behind the whole Beckett vision.

What a happy, satisfactory field day the Christian theologians have had with the Beckett vision. Fallen man. Man cast into the lonely darkness, a degraded being, wandering on the face of a desolate earth with only a desperate hope that he may have an appointment somewhere with a redeemer, and nothing to console him in the waiting but a murmuring memory of a love or tenderness encountered somewhere in his life. The flash of grace – even though he has no awareness of grace. He waits for a coming, a rebirth, an encounter with something half-remembered, something planted in him – a part of his nature. You can give this theological structure to Beckett's work, particularly to his great work, *Waiting for Godot*. If you must satisfy yourself that you have found a theological key to the structure – go ahead. Make what you want to make out of it. A work of art should have its baffling mysteries, its Giaconda smile.

Yet, I have one aesthetic objection to the Beckett landscape as he set it up. When man's state is so determinedly bleak and desolate, when man is always spiritually and physically at the bottom of the barrel, any touch of kindness, any expression of love or human need or longing, comes as a very obvious dramatic contrast. Beckett's figures seem to wander on an earth that has just been swept by a plague, or a desolate bombed-out landscape where only the lame, the halt, and the blind remain. One begins to long for Tolstoy's or Chekhov's or Chaucer's world. Everyone knows that all men are not spiritual derelicts. Life is not the last exit from Brooklyn. To say – "Forget the blooming flesh and the good times we have had – in effect we are all spiritual derelicts," strikes me as romantic Jansenism. Beckett, being Irish, may have known the touch of the clammy Jansenist hand. I don't like when it touches me in his work, as in one of his last stories. It is called "The Expelled." The story opens with a drunken derelict being thrown out of his room, into the street; the first paragraph deals with his meditation on counting the steps he tumbles down before he rolled into the gutter. You see again the Beckett figure, the lonely hapless man to whom will come very movingly a little human friendly concern and help from a taxi driver. Then, the drifter wanders into nowhere. It is beautiful. But by this time, I thought, "The pattern is just too Beckettian. There must be some other way out."

His masterpiece is *Waiting for Godot*. Some say this play belongs to the fifties, the theatre spirit of the fifties. This is absurd. It is one of the few plays done in this century which could have had as much meaning in the tenth century as it has now, and as it will have in the next century, or as long as men reach for something outside themselves; an authority over their lives. Two tramps by a tree on a country road turn up again and yet again waiting for someone name Godot who will bring them solace; or at least better their lives. Along the road comes a big-bellied master with his slave on a noose. Vladimir and Estragon, the tramps, encounter the master and slave a second time, after a night has passed, and this time the master is blind, the slave dumb, and they are falling and pleading for help as they stumble on, leaving the two tramps alone. Bewildered and despairing, the tramps nevertheless cling to the hope that Godot yet will come and make things right for them.

The play is a timeless enigmatic fable that can have a hundred meanings, or one absolute meaning. When the great American comic Bert Lahr was playing the role of Estragon I heard him laugh and say that he had no idea what the play meant, yet he loved playing in it. Obviously, he felt a very deep meaning which he couldn't express. Beckett himself might have liked this attitude. Having seen the play two or three times I came to believe the whole Beckett vision, as I understood it, was in this play. In the stories, and in *Krapp's Last Tape*, there are little memories, little recollections of compassion and love, a man's chance at life, a break in his despairing loneliness, his fugitive awareness that we are all bound together just as the slave and the master are bound in Godot, or the two tramps bound in their loneliness and hope. Since *Godot*, it seems to me, is a deeply Christian play, it was fascinating to watch how the two tramps needed each other, and how they showed little touches of compassion and consideration for each other – always so close to that tree. That tree. A man died on a tree. The old language for the Cross. Then I thought, "What if the irony, the Christian irony of this play, is that the two tramps have always looked outside themselves, waiting for an authority outside themselves, Godot, who never shows up? And yet, what if all the time Godot has been there with them? All the time, they have not only had Godot with them, but in themselves.

*CBC Anthology*

# THE UNVANQUISHED:
# WILLIAM FAULKNER

Usually a writer is praised or becomes important because of the worst aspects of his work. These are the aspects that seem to challenge attention and fascinate people. In Faulkner's case, he has been praised very extravagantly for what seems to be his extraordinary psychological penetration into the decay of the South. It's true that almost any reader caught this odour of decay, but it came chiefly out of the deliberate selection of a certain kind of a material and out of his style. The style in itself, which fascinated Arnold Bennett so much that he declared that Faulkner wrote like an angel, actually reeks of decay. Pick up almost any one of the earlier and heavier Faulkner books and try reading them aloud and what you feel in the style is something very literary, something almost antique, something a little rotten that doesn't belong in contemporary life at all: the clean straight line was never there: the effect was crumbling Gothic in our time, and not the Gothic of the American skyscraper either: it was the flamboyant Gothic of a dead time. It was certainly anything but angelic writing, and looking back on it one wonders what Arnold Bennett expected of the angels.

But this present book, *The Unvanquished*, seems to be closer to the rhythms of American life and speech than any of the preceding Faulkner books: the writing is better, livelier, more authentic, more truly visual, although there are still bewildering hangovers from his "angelic" style. For example, the charm of the earlier part of the story and the adventures of the old lady's grandson and his Negro playmate is that what is happening is told as the boy sees it: in fact you get the boy telling the story. It's fine, it's clear, it's direct, it's the eye doing what it does, seeing for itself. And then you get this:

> "Although Vicksburg was just a handful of chips from the woodpile and the River a trench scraped in the packed earth with the point of a hoe, it (river, city and terrain) lived, possessing even in miniature that ponderable though passive recalcitrance of topography which outweighs artillery, against which the most brilliant of victories and the most tragic of defeats are but the loud noises of a moment. To Ringo and me it lived, if only because of the fact that the sun-impacted ground drank water faster than we could fetch it from the well, the very setting of the stage for conflict, a prolonged and well-nigh hopeless ordeal in which we ran, panting and interminable, with the leaking bucket between well-house and battlefield, the two of us needing first to join forces and spend ourselves against a common enemy, time, before we could engender between us and hold intact the pattern of recapitulant mimic, furious victory like a cloth, a shield between ourselves and reality, between us and fact and doom."

This is what the two lads saw in the map they scraped on the ground. But does anyone believe they saw it that way? Isn't it simply literary seeing? And then after paragraphs like this the book will suddenly change in rhythm and race along, alive and exact and powerful.

There is an extraordinary sense of movement in the book, action that never stops: one scene rushes into another, and it's very doubtful if there's another recent book with such a feeling of move-ment, always the eye recording what is seen as it moves. There are a number of very memorable passages: it is hard to forget the smell and feeling of the Negroes fleeing hysterically down the road when the Yankees are not far off. It would be hard to imagine anyone making more striking pictures out of such scenes.

But when the most striking effects are achieved in terms of scenes of action, it is often hard to stop and give insight into char-acter: Faulkner hardly ever stops in this book. And the mind begins to hunger for a pause, some moment of illumination into the souls of the characters. That illumination hardly ever comes; the picture, the action keeps flickering before the eyes: get the illumination out of it if you can, but there must be no stop in the visual recording.

It may be, as I have often felt, that for the most part, when the chips are down and there are to be no fancy motions with the hands and no cards up the sleeves, Faulkner has actually very little illumination of character to offer. Perhaps it has been a mistake to think of him as a prober into dark psychological depths. A good test for any reader then would be to take any one of the earlier Faulkner books, select a page or two, strip it of its decorative effects, get at the real underlying meaning, the actual insight offered, and see how penetrating or fresh it is.

It may be that his flair has always been for action and striking visual effects, great and rare virtues surely in any writer, but it also may be that he has never been what they say he is at all.

*Saturday Night*, 1938

# REPUTATIONS

I have always been fascinated by the creation of reputations, the general acceptance of grandiose statements about writers, fighters, actors, the beauty of particular women, and the greatness of certain critics. How does the word get around? Who puts the word out? I remember when Floyd Patterson was the heavyweight champion. Almost to a man the sports writers agreed that he had the most devastating right-hand punch in the business. Just who made this discovery will never be remembered because no one has to believe it now. And who put out the word that Marshall McLuhan was the greatest earthly authority on the effect of television? And just now the word is going out that Northrop Frye is the greatest critic in the language. How do you get these things believed? Well, a few days ago when I was in New York I got a glimmer of an insight into the whole process.

In Boston there had been a booksellers' convention and an irate merchant, advocating that books should be marketed like bananas, went on to say that reading as an occupation for the elite had gone out of fashion, and anyway, the fact was that no one any longer read John Steinbeck or John O'Hara, or Thomas Wolfe. This struck me as preposterous. Another excited merchant looking for *A Love Machine*, or a *Portnoy's Complaint,* I thought. That night I was at a party where there were writers, actors, and at least one editor, who knew all the other editors in New York and most of the publishers and booksellers, too. "Did you read the report of that booksellers' convention?" I asked in the general conversation. There were some wry and bitter comments made about merchandising books just as you would bananas and coffee and sugar and the loss of all personal relationship between the buyer and the merchant, the days of the charming discussion about the book and the writer, it had all gone, yes, they said. Yet there had been no sense of outrage that a national bookseller had declared that Steinbeck, Wolfe and O'Hara were finished, so I said, "What about it? Do you think it is true?" And to a man everyone in that room agreed it was true. "This is ridiculous," I said. "Young people, all students, love Thomas Wolfe." "Not now," they agreed. There wasn't one dissenting voice. "Students don't read Thomas Wolfe."

Feeling very much out of it, I said, "Then who do they read?" Again came the voices in chorus, "Herman Hesse. *Steppenwolf.*" Well, for the first time I felt good. It was three years ago that I'd heard of the student taste for Herman Hesse and the romantic *Steppenwolf,* and my common sense had told me, and my knowledge of students and their shifting tastes had told me, too, that students couldn't go on making a touchstone out of this one book that came out of nineteenth-century German romanticism. Just as I was about to offer myself as chief mourner for *Steppenwolf,* my distinguished editor, and mind you he was a very knowledgeable man, said, "And no one reads Faulkner anymore either." "Oh, come on," I said. "I don't believe no one is reading Faulkner." He shrugged: "Why should they read Faulkner?" I expected the others to laugh, then join me in saying, "You can't believe that!" Instead, they looked thoughtful.

I began to feel that I was in one of those ancient Delphic caves, the message coming only from a little parochial gathering, the word always coming first from a group around the fire. New York has always had these parochial groups. That is its strength as a centre. In a very small cave the members may easily agree. It is the agreement that is necessary. The outlandish statement, the outlandish display of bad judgement or bad taste is accepted by one's circle of friends, who then repeat and repeat and repeat. And then comes belief. And then a deep respect for this belief, a belief that they have in each other. It gets a little close there in the cave. All literary capitals, of course, are prone to this kind of parochialism. It is not a bad thing. It is the stuff of a literary capital: a deep respect for the belief in itself.

*CBC Anthology*

# JOYCE:
## INTO THE DREAMWORLD

For seventeen years, it is said, Joyce worked on *Finnegans Wake*, and it seems only fair that anyone writing about the work should be given at least a year to get at its full value and meaning. I have been reading the book for about a week. Therefore, all I can pretend to give is some first impressions gathered when first looking into *Finnegans Wake*.

The legend is that Finnegan had a fall and was thought to be dead, and there was a wake that lasted some time, and he suddenly awoke when he heard the word, "Whiskey." With the first line you plunge right into the dream or night world. There is no getting back to the objective rational world of the conscious mind. Not only is there no way of seeing things in clear related outlines, the whole rational or logical structure of language seems to be broken down. It is a little frightening. You are caught in this flow, you try desperately to catch the meaning, to get hold of something that is familiar to the day world which can serve as a guide. It is the apparent meaninglessness that is frightening, for the eye can catch nothing, yet the tireless anti-logical voice keeps sounding, and you have to listen; suddenly the sound itself begins to give a kind of hope or comfort. In this night world where all things are terrifyingly strange, the sense of music is retained.

It is possible, bit by bit, to become familiar with the dream structure, as nearly everyone has found out. Only most mortals dream in pictures. The structure or arrangement of these pictures may or may not be rational; they keep flowing in, often telescoped, the waking sense of time and space readily violated, yet making a perfectly good sense according to the dream reality. But instead of doing it with pictures, Joyce does it with words; they flow, break, are telescoped, or violated, new words are created, old words made into more suggestive sounds by the mind plunged into the dream reality and entirely at the mercy of it, its overwhelming and frightening authority.

Of course the dream flow is of the world of Dublin and Ireland. Much is necessarily lost to a North American reader. But you must never lose sight of the fact that it is an Irish book. In fact, large sections seem to be written in Irish brogue. What seems so strange to the eye can be turned into something very familiar and comical to the ear simply by reading these passages aloud. At other times, as I have mentioned, the dream language seems to be set to music, as in the well-known Anna Livia section. Though there is nothing for the eye, the musical flow of words conveys very beautifully and mysteriously the impression of the waters of the Liffey flowing by and the women by the river with their washing and the water licking the embankment. It is great writing. It is a new sensation in literature, a new way of looking at things perfectly realized, something that can be brought off only by a great master.

Since the greatness of the achievement can be grasped in the Anna Livia section, and in other smaller passages, the mind keeps hungering to grasp the same full meaning in the opaque passages. The flow is so deliberate, so relentless, that is, it is maddening to feel that the mind is missing the significance. You stop and take a paragraph word by word: words that seem to be in there as sounds, or musical notes, words that were never heard before, made by telescoping together the words of many languages that convey the same meaning. Inescapably it comes to you that Joyce is conducting some great prose orchestration out of all the words from all the languages that have flowed through his Irish mind.

It gets that you can follow, or get used to the new word structure, and of all things, you find that again and again it is based upon the pun. There is great wit. And rarely does a page fail to offer some kind of laugh. Parodies of all styles are here. The reader begins to get a curious satisfaction from this all-pervading comedy. It is the lifeline that holds him to the rational world. It is as though the dreamer, out of whom this great flow of words comes, had a vast comic sense and every word was touched by it.

But this very play of words arouses some suspicion and wonder in the reader. Is Joyce actually attempting to produce the dream reality, or is he just using that structure again and again to orchestrate words for their own sake. Of course, the answer might readily be that that was exactly what the dreaming night mind did: get drunk on words. But whatever the intention the result seems to be there over and over again: a literature feeding not on life but on words.

And in that case, the end of the alley is in sight and it is a dead end. Whether it be in painting or writing, the tendency toward pure abstraction can only lead finally to the starvation of the medium. It is a gesture of great intellectual pride and spiritual isolation on the part of the artist. But the pursuit has gone on steadily in our time, and it seems to me that the pursuit is continued on page after page of *Finnegans Wake*: an unholy effort, or if you will, the actual job done, of making pieces of literature with words, simply as words, as the substance.

And that is why you get the impression that in this book you are dealing with the end of something in literature. It isn't just the ivory tower, it is the ivory tower with every window shut and every door locked. It is the great artist retreating completely from life and burning his bridges behind him. For, beside *Finnegans Wake*, *Ulysses* is a simple human document. In the end all one can say is that a great master is going his own way, as a great master should.

*Saturday Night*, 1939

# JOHN MONTAGUE

❧〰❧

The poet John Montague, visiting from Ireland and staying at our house, was talking to me about Saul Bellow, whom he admired. After much elbow-bending, and with the night wearing on, I said, "John, John, of course you have this sympathetic approval of Bellow. And why not, he's an academic, and you're an academic these days, a professor at Cork. You've got to hang together. You recognize the whole academic world working in Bellow."

After a moment's silence, Montague shrugged. "Well, yes, I'm an academic and so is Bellow. But let's face it. These days, we're all in the academic world. Yes, you too."

I went to bed and fell asleep. Two hours later, I woke up, my heart beating heavily, as if I had been in a hopeless struggle. Still half in a dream, I could see I was in a large bare, brightly lit classroom, and all around me were figures who talked gravely to each other. At the blacked-out windows stood several hooded prefects. Others also guarded the doors so no one could get out, or in. Only faint sounds came from the outside world. No one listened or showed any curiosity about these sounds, these cries from the street, because the prefects were watching alertly and suspiciously. And I, staring at the blacked-out windows, my heart beating heavily, was crying out within myself, "What goes on out there? Will we ever know? Will we ever know again?"

# AROUND THE PARISH PUMP

I remember crossing the road from a hotel to a television studio with the writer Dave Godfrey. Just before entering the studio he said he had always taken it for granted that the stories I wrote for the *New Yorker* had been tailored to the tastes and needs of New York editors. Startled, I explained that no editors had ever altered my stories or tried to make them seem like anything else but what they were. This view of Godfrey's must have been on my mind all through the television talk show, and as my wonder grew, I saw that the academic nationalists have had to have some explanation for the American acceptance of my stories. Why my stories? – that was their question. Why had my stories been so readily accepted in New York when they could point in their CanLit calendars to at least six or seven other storywriters who were every bit as good, if not much better, than I was and those writers never could get their stories published in New York? What was the use of explaining that I hadn't headed for the *New Yorker*? When I was twenty-five, the *New Yorker* had come to me, asking me if I had stories they might want to print.

Time passed, then I found myself reading that some fellow, writing about something called "The Canadian Imagination," had just excommunicated me from the national literature. I wrote for Americans, the man said. What was going on in the academic circles of CanLit? By this time, the cool weather had come on, and at the end of the football season, watching the Grey Cup game for the championship of the country, I thought again of the new set of directors of nationalism in our literature, and their quest for a restricted Canadian cultural pattern. What about the football field? Surely football, which vies with hockey for being our national game, ought to express the new and singular Canadian imagination. Indeed, there is a Canadian singularity expressed out there on the field. In our game, we have three downs to make ten yards, not four as in the American game. On a kick, we have to give the punt receiver five yards before tackling him. In the American game, he does not get this protection unless he signals for a fair catch. In our game, the punt is not a pointless appendix. No, the punter gets one point. How about that for peculiarities? And how about this? Most of the highly paid players on the field are Americans, as are the coaches. Still, most of the officials are Canadian. We always like to maintain official control. Do these singularities – like the single point – satisfy the cultural directors or do they drive them a little crazy? Do they refuse to go to our football games? Who knows? But, I know where I come from. Right here. Who are these new directors gathering around the old parish pump?

The other day, when I picked up a copy of the late E.K. Brown's essays, I came to sections that made me think of that old pump. E.K. Brown was not a villager. He was a distinguished professor who had settled in Chicago after Toronto. In his time, the thirties and forties, he was a civilizing influence in Canadian letters. I knew that in one of his essays he had touched on my work. I re-read it. The point he made, and he made it a number of times, was that I had managed to write about Toronto and I had made it seem simply a big North American lake city, and while – in fairness to me – if you followed the story I was telling, the physical details of the city were always accurate and recognizable to anyone who knew the town, the fact was that I had deliberately omitted those little nuances that were peculiarly Torontonian. I suppose he meant I skipped the social structure of the city, the religious clashes, the inner British nature of those people who had the money, and the new people of questionable loyalty who were on the make, and so on.

Years ago, when I first read this I'd been impatient with Brown, because I knew he was an intelligent man. Now I was impatient with him again, because he should have known that a storyteller doing his job has his characters move across a scene, and it is only when one of the characters is concerned with the structure – the sociological structure of a town – that he stops to examine it. Or, when a character has been shaped by the peculiar social structure and this has to be explained. But my characters in the Toronto stories were merely people caught up in a story, and like most people who live in a city, they never sat back to examine – and then record – the peculiar and distinctive parochial marks of their fellow Torontonians. At the time, I believed those alleged signs – those bits of local colour which wouldn't be understood by anyone who didn't live in the city – would soon pass away as the city grew. The city was growing rapidly. I thank heaven I saw it that way, for now in this city of three million, those alleged local nuances have faded as I knew they would. Now, it is Brown who seems completely anachronistic, and if his ghost will forgive me, it's because he's standing beside the old parish pump that is being pumped anew.

In one of my first long stories, "An Autumn Penitent," I had a character living outside the city, come into town one July day and stop to watch the Orange Parade. The editor at Scribners in New York, Max Perkins, going over the proofs, said to me, "There's a thing I don't understand. This Orange Parade."

"That's right," I said. "The Orange Parade. A big local event."

"But there are no oranges grown in Toronto," he said. "Surely it is far too cold for oranges."

I explained that the Orange Lodge was a society that had its origin in Ulster, Ireland. Somewhat baffled, he said that if I was going to mention the Orange Parade, I would have to explain the Orange Lodge; otherwise, readers would be as baffled as he was. I meditated and said, "Just let the character stop to watch a parade," for I realized an explanation would be artificial, and would have nothing to do with my story. Right there, I suppose, I let down the E.K. Brown view. I was eliminating one of the peculiar local bits of colour, and yet I know now from this distance that he, being a sensible man, would agree with the elimination.

In the thirties, William Saroyan wrote a beautiful play called *The Time of Your Life*. It was a play about the flow of life in a San Francisco tavern, and about one character in particular who sat in the tavern night after night as a kind of philosophical judge. The play became a great success. It was much talked about in New York. One night, when I was in a New York bar with a friend, he said to me, "See that guy sitting over there? He's from San Francisco. All week he's been putting out the word that the Saroyan play is a phoney. The guy knows the tavern, the place for Saroyan's play. He even knows the guy who sits in there, and he's telling everybody that Saroyan got it all wrong. The tavern wasn't like that at all."

We joined the guy and we talked to him about the San Francisco tavern. He described it most minutely. I listened to him proving that Saroyan was a lousy reporter and proving, too, that all the local nuances of the life around that tavern had eluded Saroyan. I thought he was crazy. He wasn't interested in the play as a play, a work of the imagination. He had all the power and authority of a man who went every night to the parish pump. He neither knew nor cared about the art of the Saroyan play, but he did care about his pump. I had no doubt that he was telling the factual truth as he described the tavern. He had a hundred details Saroyan hadn't used or had distorted, and a hundred perceptions no doubt shared by others like him who hung around that particular tavern. For this man, in his own little world, the tavern was his parish. If you were interested only in gossip, he held your attention. It never seemed to occur to him that Saroyan, as an artist always does, had leapt out of the parish, dropping in his leap all the irrelevant parochial facts, and the parochial judgements, too, taking with him in his imagination only enough of the particular and the concrete to buttress a flow of life that might be universal.

Here in my own country, I detect in writers who are caught up in the current chummy nationalism, a craving for the comfort, the security, the exclusiveness of a parish intellectual life centred around the old pump. In this little life, all the writers can wear the same badges, they can share the same judgements, they can know who has the right Canadian colonial tone, the right Canadian post-modern tone, the right Canadian multicultural tone, and they can all praise parish publications and parish matters, giving the impression that Canadian literature isn't something you make. It is something you join.

As for those local peculiarities that E.K. Brown wanted me to celebrate, and which I now see as details long since vanished, I am reminded of my early reading of the Russians, Dostoevsky and Chekhov. Dostoevsky's St. Petersburg. I remember I knew I was in a city, I was getting geographical details as the characters moved around but I don't remember the master telling me that the city of Peter the Great was what it was because of Peter the Great. The city lived for me because Dostoevsky's characters lived, Dostoevsky, so utterly unlike Turgenev, utterly unlike Tolstoy, or Chekhov, so unlike his contemporaries that Turgenev said he didn't believe the Dostoevskian characters existed in Russia. That's all right. Because the Dostoevskian imagination existed in Russia. That's what I'd like to see around me, in my town and country. Each writer creating his own strange world.

I don't talk much about specific Canadian writers. I think I know why. I'm baffled by what is going on under my nose. I talk willingly about Marquez or Beckett. But the local writers? And the critics who try to shape the taste and direct the literary traffic? In other countries, writers swing sharp axes. Here, they too often seem to hold hands. No one remembers publisher Jack McClelland's Calgary safari back in the early seventies – or was it the late sixties – when at his behest, all kinds of writers got together and named the hundred best Canadian novels. A hundred! I'm not aware that I'm living in a golden age of any literature, let alone Canadian. But then, all my life I've been interested in individual writers, not organized literatures. I hear every day that in Canada there has been an explosion of writing talent. Everyone is writing novels, stories or poems. I hope they have fun. I'm sure they are, for I remember that Jack McClelland, as he huckstered in our Gold Age, told me that if you couldn't get a novel published in Canada, you couldn't get it published anywhere else on earth. By this time, our times, there is enough stuff around to attract the academic industrialists. There is actually money in the stuff, by way of careers, and some academic power, too.

While wildly applauding this formal showcasing of talent, I am bemused by the ease with which the managers of the new literature reached agreement on what was essentially Canadian in a piece of writing. For years, no matter where I turned, I was told to read *As for Me and My House*, by Sinclair Ross, or Sheila Watson's *The Double Hook*. Why these two books? Why does no one ever say an unkind word about *As for Me and My House?* I tried but I found this little book hard to get into. Let us say, I was not at all carried away.

As for *The Double Hook*, I remember when Edmund Wilson, writing about Canadian Literature, asked me to recommend something and I quickly said, "Around here the scholars go for this book, *The Double Hook*." He'd already looked at it and he had put it aside. I feel like a heel for saying these things, but the agreed-upon celebration of these two little books has always been a nagging botheration for me. Why these two books, born of lonely isolated outposts of civilization, why did these two books become so acceptably Canadian for certain academics? The notion that you have to go to some little town out on the prairies, or near the foothills, where a lonely woman quivers with frustration – go there to get at the real Canadian heart and soul of things – is a falsification of life in this country. There is no reason why masterpieces can't be written about places and lives that are starved and small, but the fact is, whatever is taking place now in the Canadian imagination – a shifting, varied, chaotic, disparate and not to be defined imagination – is taking place in the cities, the great teeming cities far, far away from that banal figure, the lonely prairies housewife or spinster.

What we have now are eight or nine good adult prose writers. Because they are good, it is inevitable that they are not like the fingers on one glove. The world of Robertson Davies is utterly remote from the world of Mavis Gallant, which is exactly as it should be. It is unlikely that the world of Margaret Laurence will ever be touched by the world of Mordecai Richler. The stories of Alice Munro aren't like my own stories, which is why I like reading them. So, what is it that I look for in a Canadian writer? Why, the same qualities I would look for in a good writer in any country. Authenticity. Authenticity of the imagination, and of one's own eyes. If a writer has these qualities, and at the same time, by the grace of God, he or she is an artist with words, then you have a fine native writer.

The qualities I have named may not lead to commercial success. The graduate school's industrial approval may be slow in coming, yet such a writer will always give another writer a real lift, particularly if he's a young writer, a writer who keeps alive the promise of what's to come. I remember the surprise I got reading the first stories of the new writer Marie-Claire Blais, and then Margaret Atwood, she had her own poetic line – that fish hook in the eye – she had it from the beginning, and recently – two fellows I'd never heard of, Amprimoz, who's so quirkily interesting probably no one will read him, and Leon Rooke . . . stories that have a tall tale charm that is his own. And then there's a young woman, a poet, Gwendolyn MacEwen, out there in her own desert world – sometimes it's sand, sometimes it's ice – alive, as is a new young dramatist, and what a strange gift she has for getting inside someone's psychosis, Judith Thompson, with her fresh play, which I read, *White Biting Dog*. Maybe that's what the authentic writer does, she sits alone, times pass, maybe as long as it took for Stendhal, but then – after five or fifty years – she just up and bites you, but because time has passed and tastes have changed, she's not only biting you, you like it, you want her to keep on biting you.

*CBC Anthology*

# LONELINESS

I was in Vancouver with my friend, John Fisher. We got around the town, met many people, and drank as much as possible with new friends in our rooms in the Vancouver hotel. Of an evening at the end of the week, around midnight, I was alone in my own room and quite content to be alone at that hour, for I was tired.

That afternoon, John had met a young woman in another hotel, a very pretty young woman, he said, and over a dinner of Dover sole with me he had celebrated her lush charms. With a gleam of satisfaction in his eye, he told me that she had invited him to come to her house that night at ten. "And oh, she lives alone," he said.

So I, alone now myself and becalmed in my room, and yet content, was standing at the window at midnight watching the moonlight on those faraway snow-capped peaks that were called the Sleeping Beauty. In that nightlight the snowy mountain could indeed take on the shape of a sleeping woman, waiting there in the high hammock of the night. Maybe women had to be on your mind before the snowy forms could make this pattern for you, and maybe they now were on my mind, yet the mountain did have this local name long before I showed up.

Then, the telephone rang. It was John.

"Where are you?" I asked in surprise. "I didn't expect to see you till morning."

"I'm here in the hotel," he said.

"What hotel?"

"This hotel. I'm in my room."

"Alone?"

"No, with someone I want you to meet."

"Bring her around."

"Okay," he said.

I took a bottle from my bag and got some glasses. In ten minutes my colleague came in. "Where is she? What's the matter?"

"I told her I had a little business to discuss with you. It would only take a minute. It's all right. She understands. She's in my room," and he sat down, yet he wasn't like himself at all. Usually he chuckled to himself about these women he caught on the wing, and in fairness to him, he always left the woman feeling he had performed a public service. Now, when he went to speak he sounded apologetic. With a little laugh, he was shaking his head, his face full of bafflement. "Come on," I said. "Didn't it go well? What's the matter with her?"

"This isn't the one," he said. "Now wait a minute," and sitting down he told me how he had got into a taxi earlier in the evening to join that promisingly seductive woman who had whispered, "Come on to my house. Be there at ten," and had given him the address.

The cab driver happened to be a woman, too. In those days just after the war, there were many women cabbies in Vancouver, and he had paid no attention to her till he realized that they had driven miles into the suburbs.

Finally, they had come to a street little better than a mud road. It had been raining. The houses on the street were small. They couldn't find the address, the cab was skidding in the ruts, and then at last the cabbie, a flashlight in her hand, said, "This has got to be it," and getting out with her flashlight she found the number, and she beckoned to him. But the shabby little house was in darkness.

He banged on the door. No one answered. Because the house was in darkness he had told the cabbie to wait, and finally, shame-faced and feeling like a fool, he returned to the cab.

A rear wheel had sunk into a water-filled rut. When the car was started the wheel spun and spun, so he got out with the girl and they rocked the car and kept rocking it till the wheel finally tilted out of the rut. When he got back into the car he sat in the front seat with her. Only then did he notice how fresh-faced and handsome and sturdy she was. They began to talk. She was from the prairies. On the way back to town she asked him all about himself. He had never met a woman with so open and warmly available a nature, and yet so self-sustaining, so confidently alone in herself, and when he asked her to come into the hotel and sit in his room with him, she agreed willingly.

"Well, you're in luck," I said. "Out of one frying pan into another. How did it go?"

"It didn't," he said. "Well, you see – I mean – it would have been too awkward." Again he looked baffled. "I had become a friend. Her new-found friend. A new friend makes her feel so happy. Oh, hell, wait, I'll go and get her. What do I make of her? What do I do with her?"

In a little while he came to the room with the sturdy good-breasted handsome fresh-faced girl. We shook hands. She refused a drink. John sat back watching me while I talked to the woman. For years she had wanted to leave the prairies where it had been too lonely, especially in the cruel winters, and she was very happy in Vancouver. Her father had followed her and now he had a little tobacco store. Here in Vancouver she had found she was always running into someone who soon became a friend. Friends were wonderful, didn't I think so? They could meet, they could write to each other, trust each other, talk on the phone, and she knew in her heart that John, after talking to him for so long, would always be her friend, and they could even write to each other. It was too bad he was leaving town tomorrow. But at nine in the morning he was coming to her father's store, and she intended to give him the most expensive cigar in the shop. For an hour we talked like this about the wonders of friendship. I was aware all the time that John, his eye on me, watched for some sign of cynicism, and yet he was hoping I was as bemused and helpless as he was. When they were leaving I said, "Well, it was a pleasure to be in the company of two who are now such good friends."

"Yeah," John said. He did laugh, but as he walked out, he linked his arm under hers, as if trying to get used to a role he had never played with a woman. So then I was back at the window, by myself, and as I stared at the mountains and the moonlight on the Sleeping Beauty, I felt a little chill as if I were being touched by a terrible winter loneliness.

# IS ALL OF CANADA
# A LONGING FOR SPRING?

Late one night I was at the front window of my Toronto home. It snowed. For hours it had been snowing, the first heavy fall coming in the middle of December. Heavy flakes drifting across the overhanging corner street light masked the familiar fences and trees. Beside me, his paws up on the windowsill while he waited to go out on his run to the corner, was our big white standard poodle, who kept turning his head to me as if he couldn't figure out what was happening to his territory. He was a pup, just six months old. He had never seen snow. But for me it was the beginning of another white winter.

If you said, Tell me about winters, I'd say, What do I know about the winter? I have seen too many of them, they have been with me too long, they are part of my life, I can't separate myself from them, nor would I want to. Though I have said cynically many times that this country was founded on the glowing big-bellied stove and should have on the national flag not the maple leaf but the Quebec heater, and though some of my neighbours now will be preparing for the annual escape to the Bahamas, I am here where I was born, getting some kind of quiet pleasure watching the city get snowed in on this mild winter night. I always feel younger on such a night, especially if the moon comes out after it stops snowing.

My father used to smile and say that Kipling had called Canada Our Lady of the Snows, and the smile was like a wink, warning me that Kipling knew nothing about Canada. But a little Canadian kid doesn't know that there are strange lands where there is no snow. When you are very young you love the winter. A child comes along the street crying and shivering, his wet-mitted hands lifeless at his sides, his neck red from his wet scarf, and his feet soaking wet. But as soon as he gets home and has his mitts placed on the hot radiator, and his socks changed and pants dried, he rushes out again. As soon as he learns to walk he is given a sleigh for Christmas or a toboggan and taken to some hill in a park. If his father says he is too young for skis he makes them out of barrel staves with strips of leather nailed on them as hooks for your feet, and even before he can skate he is playing hockey on the street, or on a hose-frozen rink in his backyard. And if, as he grows older, he hears some teacher refer to the winter as "the great Canadian challenge," he thinks the man is crazy.

On our street, when I was a kid, a man of sixty-five lived alone in a house across from us. In the summer months we hardly saw him. He didn't talk to his neighbours. This woman, a widow, who lived to the left of him, said he was rather surly in his aloofness and she no longer tried to speak to him. He was a tall, stooped, thin man with a drooping grey moustache. When the winter came and the snow fell, this isolated man would come out late at night with his shovel and slowly clear the sidewalk, and then he would stand, leaning on his shovel looking up the street. It didn't matter how deep and heavy the snow was. One night, after he had finished shovelling his own snow, he shovelled the snow of the widow, his neighbour to the left. In the morning the widow came across the street and talked to my mother. She was distressed. She didn't know what to say to the man; if she thanked him he might do it again, and how could she be sure what he was aiming at. She decided to ignore him. When it snowed again he shovelled her walk again, and he kept on. Then, two weeks later, he began to shovel the snow of the neighbour to the right of him, and this woman had a husband. Now the old man had two upset neighbours who would like to have said, "Please stop shovelling my snow," but they didn't like to speak to him. He had always ignored them. All winter long he went on with his shovelling, always late at night, and when he had finished the three places he would stand leaning contentedly on his shovel.

We called him the Snow Man. This man certainly had learned how to use the winter for some personal satisfaction, whatever it was. Maybe it has been the same with me. What is it? It can't come from winter play, the hunting, the ice fishing, the skiing, the snowmobiling. Is it an inner satisfaction never to be quite named? Or it could be a liking for the country's dramatically violent contrasts in climate? Violent summers! Violent winters! After the summer maybe there is some kind of solace for the spirit in the snow and ice. Whatever it is, it gives a man good memories, and he often realizes this when he is in Europe and finds he gets irritated explaining that his country isn't all ice and snow in a long winter night.

One night years ago we were in Paris sitting at our Montparnasse café. An American friend came over to us. He had a pale, slender, sad-eyed, black-haired young Frenchman with him. He introduced him. The Frenchman was a poet. He had heard we were from Canada and he wanted to tell us his story. His lovely girl, to whom he had given everything, had run off with another man, a fellow of no talent, a bum devoid of sensibility, and now he was hurt and despairing and sick of his Parisian life. He had thought of suicide, he said with a wan smile. But that would be cowardly. Instead, he wanted to change his life, hurl himself into a wilderness of ice and snow. Canada was the place. He had read about Canada. He would become a trapper. Could we tell him what furs he could sell? There were otters and beavers and moose and deer and the lynx, weren't there? But above all, what he wanted to know was what kind of sturdy clothes he should have.

"Always remember that in Canada the weasel in winter becomes a white ermine," I began, feeling irritated. Then I blurted out, "Look, you are worrying about the wrong thing. You should be concerned with how little clothing you will be able to wear so much of the summertime in Canada. And the blackflies in the steamy bush. It's hot there. Ice and snow are easy to handle. The heat, the awful summer heat is the thing. In the bush you pray for a wind to blow away the blackflies. In the cities you have to head for a lake. You'll find out what a relief it is when the winter comes and you can put on some clothes."

The young French poet stared at me in astonishment. "Is this true?" he asked. "It is very true about the summer," I said. When he had left, making it plain he was having second thoughts about burying his talents in the ice and snow of Canada, I turned on my American friend. "This is an old story with you Americans," I said, shrugging. "All you know about Canada you get from reading those ballads of Robert W. Service. Yukon ballads. *Look at my eyes, I've been snow blind twice,*" I quoted mockingly. "*Look at my foot, half gone,* or *Out of the night which was fifty below and into the din and glare* . . . Come on, man, why don't you take a look at the map? See where Canada is."

The bleak Arctic view of Canada seems to be set in the European mind, too, and you can't do much about it. It was set a long time ago by those seventeenth-century French chroniclers who visited the early settlements along the St. Lawrence. I'm sure the young French poet had read them. Those journals are so grim they make you wonder why the French were bent on settling here. Or could it be that those chroniclers couldn't understand how men could handle such a winter? They tell of people dressed like bears who buried themselves for the winter. Settlers were found frozen stiff in the snowbanks. Men often had frozen arms or legs chopped off. A cruel, savage, icebound land. But why then did Champlain love the New World along the great St. Lawrence River? Champlain! He had seen the country in the spring. He had known the drama of the seasons. If, as Balzac says, great art exists in contrasts, then New France was one of nature's very artistic jobs. It was full of these contrasts between grim winter and the sudden dramatic grandeur of the green spring and summer. Quebec in the winter! Why was it that so many of the Christmas cards used in Ontario were of scenes in Quebec that told us in bright colours that there was warmth and play in winter?

The only time I ever had the feeling of the cold forbidding bleakness those old writers told about was in February when I was on a train cutting through the Gaspé. I looked out the window. The hills, all snow covered, with deep brown gashes, bare trees that looked ready to crack and break, made me shudder. It looked like an alien world where no man would want to walk alone. On the winter highways cutting through those hills the life was hidden, no – gone, and I felt a terrible sense of abandonment in that scene. French-Canadian writers have told you about this abandonment, this strange kind of French-Canadian loneliness of place in the winter. It is as if the life that was lived there had gone forever, even though you know that in those low-slung farmhouses there are still lighted windows. Yet that winter isolation you feel outside the towns is suddenly broken before your eyes, or in your ears if you are on the highways, by the sight and sound of the snowmobiles scooting over the snow. Hundreds of snowmobiles, maybe thousands, and soon maybe hundreds of thousands of them, till no farm family is locked in by the winter.

Nonetheless, it is there in the winter that you still feel a locked-in feeling, even in the lovely winter city, Quebec. It is because the harbour is locked in, the great St. Lawrence is locked in, too, and even though you are elated by that ethereal winter light, you feel it when the sun glitters on the grey stones in the Old Town. The grey stones are ice-covered and shining, and it is so cold that when you touch these stones with your bare fingers they are held glued as if by a hot living thing. In the strange cold winter light every building is etched starkly sharp against the sky. It is always fiercely cold up on the ramparts, and while I shiver I remember that for me there has always been a kind of special winter opulence in Quebec province; it is not of the beautiful Laurentians, this winter playground with all its ski trails and celebrated ski lodges – it is of Montreal.

This kind of warm opulence has little to do with wealth; it is something that the climate does to the spirit in the setting of the city. When you come into Montreal in heavy snow in zero weather the mountain looks bleak and cold, but around the mountain are a million lights that seem to mock its desolate bleakness. The lights are like warm fires around the mountain. On a cold night it's good to sit in a restaurant, whether it's a little inexpensive one in the east end, or at the Ritz on Sherbrooke, and watch the people come in, their faces tingling from the cold outside. They come into the warmth as if food now has a special pleasure it doesn't have in the warm weather. And women are lovelier in fur coats, and if the coat is rich and she is beautiful you remember her as you could not remember her in the summer, and you have a special winter sense of well-being. It is a seasonal thing. You feel it in little bars and cafés all over Montreal when it is very cold outside. And going out into the night, if there are great banks of snow at the roadside, is also something special that gives a new little tang to your taste for life. If you have been drinking and talking at a party and getting a little tired, and thinking it's late and you'd be better off now in bed, you come out to the street, the cold air suddenly makes your flesh tingle, and you are ready to go somewhere else and start the night all over again.

One of my secret Montreal pleasures used to come from being near Peel and St. Catherine's about two-thirty in the morning after a heavy snowfall when the ploughs came out to attack the snow. There would be big snowploughs on the road, but the little snowploughs with the caterpillar treads, looking like small tanks, would be working on the sidewalks, swirling around, rushing furiously at each other, spinning, attacking the drifts, and I could pretend that I was watching General Rommel's tanks in the desert. And then sometimes I would have a nostalgic regret, watching these machines. All over Canada the machines have ploughed away the lovely old days of the horse and the sleigh. Deep in the countryside, on the farms, there may still be horse-drawn sleighs with jingling bells, but not in the big cities now, not that I know of, and for a city kid winter, with its horses and sleighs when the macadam roads had tracks in the snow and were not stripped clean as they are now by the ploughs, was a time of happy excitement. The delivery sleighs from the big department stores would come around and the milk trucks, and the bread wagons, all on sleighs, and the kids would hitch a ride. And there used to be sleighing parties, school parties, just as there were skating parties at the outdoor rinks. Now the automobile, changing all this, gives you indoor warmth right in the car itself. Skating goes indoors, curling too. The comfortable winter!

Yet the rinks are still in the parks for neighbourhood skating, and in Toronto right in front of the new city hall there is a rink where they skate all day long and far into the night. Not long ago, watching these skaters put me in a nostalgic mood and I said to an old friend, "Speaking right off the top of your head, what is your fondest winter memory?" And right off he said, "Teaching my son to skate when he was little." "Well, well, well," I said, thinking that all along, secretly, he had been one of those Canadian fathers who dreams of having his son grow up to play in the National Hockey League. The country now is full of such fathers. There was a time when they dreamed of having their sons become rich plumbers, or rich doctors; now in their mind's eye they see the boy becoming a whirlwind on skates, a beautiful stickhandler and, above all, a tough hardrock who terrorizes junior hockey so colourfully that one of the NHL clubs will be compelled to offer him a contract at hundreds of thousand a year. The American clubs in the industry have to have these tough players. Where are they going to get them? Why, from Canadian fathers, of course. They are like the old-fashioned stage mothers. They see that the boy gets on the right midget team, gets up often a five in the morning so he can find ice time in one of the arenas. "Yes," said my friend with a happy smile. "Teaching my boy to skate, watching him getting used to them on a pond we made with the hose in the backyard and gradually becoming sure of himself." Then my friend fooled me. I had him all wrong. He hadn't wanted his son to be a hockey player. "You see, for a kid, once he can really use the skates and is sure of himself, it's like discovering another mode of locomotion," he explained. "First he crawls, then he walks, then he finds he can run, and then he finds he can whirl on skates, or speed along and stop, throwing up a shower of ice. Yeah, that was a real pleasure, watching my boy gradually make these discoveries and then exult in them."

All this is part of the winter warmth of my own home, my winter, but in this country there are many other winters where I am as much of a stranger as would have been that young French poet if he had come to Canada. Going north or going west always seemed like a trip deep into another winter, deep into the cold. In the summertime, the land above the north shore of Lake Superior has such a wild operatic beauty a man hunting and fishing or just camping feels small and unimportant, yet even at that time of year when you are at a little settlement, a few log cabins, or in the small towns on the edge of the bush country, or the muskeg country, you are always asking a native, "What do you do in the wintertime?" Up there, even that haunting sense of abandonment that you feel in the Gaspé is missing completely. This is no deserted place, the life lived there all hidden or gone. The big mining companies – and this is the Ontario mineral belt – the hunters and the loggers too – don't seem to have made the land their own; they have only scarred it. Deep in the winter, if you are on a train or a plane, you see the little snowed-in cabins, the small settlements, and at night the gleam of lights, just a little cluster of lights, people huddling warm, actually very warm in another elaboration of the big-bellied stove. A good log cabin will have its big stove, and the stove pipes will run just below the ceiling, and no matter how cold it is outside, the hunter when he comes in actually feels hot. Canada may have been called Our Lady of the Snows, but in the summer, if you are on a plane on your way to Winnipeg, you can see that this countryside, all the way out to the plains, is really an astonishing pattern of lakes. It should have been called Our Lady of the Lakes. In wintertime this stretch of lakeland looks as if it were actually dotted with air-fields. Hunters know it. They come in on planes or snowmobiles and where there is a highway there is always a car coming down the road with the slain deer or moose slung across the hood. But it was beyond this lake country in Winnipeg – where they used to have air maps showing that for fliers Winnipeg was the centre of the world – that I felt colder than I had ever been in my life.

It was a night when I was with Sydney Smith, president of the University of Manitoba. It was about nine in the evening and twenty below zero. We were on our way to visit a professor friend. We couldn't get a taxi. We decided to walk, it was only ten blocks to the professor's house. There was a bitter wind. I was wearing my city overcoat, and it was no protection against the heavy, icy wind. We stopped at a crossing and I thought we were having an animated beautiful intellectual discussion about whether England's future lay in an acceptance that it was simply part of Europe. I began to shiver. The wind tore into my bones. My jaw began to tremble. I felt dizzy. Our voices, the discussion about Europe, sounded idiotic. Voices from a faraway, fantastic, warm other world. Then I really believed in those stories of the Winnipeg winters of '36 and '37, when it had been 50 below for days. Those winters seemed to be all around me, slowly killing me as they had killed others who had wandered away from home. They tried to hide in snowbanks. Outside the city, cows and dogs had stood stiff and dead – bizarre monuments. All across the prairies, farmers had huddled around stoves, praying only that the fuel would last. They had used cow dung for fuel. Now I felt a numbness in me as I stood there holding the arm of my friend. It was the wind. I asked myself, What am I doing here? Is all of Canada a longing for Spring? "Faster, for God's sake, let's walk faster," I said to my friend. While the wind chewed away at my face I seemed to have a profound insight into the growth of the astonishing Indian civilizations that had developed in Mexico and Peru. It had been a simple matter. Thousands of years ago Indians had come across the Bering Straits, moving south. The quick Indians, tasting this prairie winter, kept moving very fast. They kept running all the way to Mexico. The placid, slow-moving, Indians were left behind in what is now called Canada, where I was too, in the centre of all the cold in the world. Why? Then we came to the house of our friend and into the incredible warmth, and the relief I felt made me tremble.

Well, my cold night in Winnipeg was admittedly a shameful experience – for a Canadian. I wasn't myself. I was caught off-guard by the bitter heavy wind. It must have weakened the spirit. It made me, for the moment, give in when I knew that the wonder of the country was that people never gave in to the winter. And anyway, the truth is that those western cities, Winnipeg, Regina, Calgary, Edmonton, seen in the fantastic winter sunlight, have a lovely sparkle. That's what should be remembered. Why, in Regina, come to think of it, it often didn't seem to be cold at all. It's the dry air, so crisp and exhilarating. One night when it was twenty-five below zero I was walking along blithely with a friend, feeling light and lively, with the northern lights swinging overheard as if a giant ribbon counter had been caught in an electric fan. When we passed under a street light my western friend said casually, "You better watch that ear. I think it's turning white." Hands over my ears, I headed for the nearest restaurant.

I think of that frost-bitten ear now, seeing it in my mind against the prairie wheat fields just before harvest time when you are looking across flat land for miles and miles from some high office building or hotel room, and this land with its ripening wheat is one big warm golden bowl in the sunlight. The contrast! The frozen ear, the warm glowing bowl, the bowl becoming, when winter settles in, an endless howling winter desert, always – summer or winter – a terrible presence of loneliness, the prairie loneliness of those unpainted farm houses looking so bleak and cold against the wild winter extravagance of the northern lights. Then a sense of isolation literally reaches through the train window at you. The winter loneliness is worse. It's not like the summer prairie loneliness that has a touch of pleasurable melancholy to it when the moon rises and a dog barks and the land and the sky seem to come closer together in stillness, and evenness: no grandeur, nothing wild. Nothing wild? It is a prairie winter wildness that I always remember.

The blizzard snow, coming in whirling patches, made a shifting cold grey screen against the window; then would come sudden clear patches that seemed to have endless depths till they too were screened. The man had been telling me that wild horses still roamed the prairie. I had never quite believed in these horses. But there, now, out there in the blizzard about a quarter of a mile away a herd of horses came charging along. Sometimes screened off, they became part of the blizzard. Sometimes they came into one of the clear patches as they raced along, ghost horses, tossing their heads, all white in the swirling snow, and I watched them raptly as if I suspected they were trying to tell me something with their ghostly dance.

There is a myth growing in the country, pushed by some painters and poets who have gone into the Arctic, that the Canadian psyche has a subconscious awareness of the vast Arctic ice pack, the tremendous lonely frozen distances at the top of the country. This masked awareness is supposed to shape all our moods, our whole view of life.

I have only had a fugitive glimpse of that endless, frozen, silent land glistening in the sun a hundred miles north of Edmonton. I was with a friend who knew a man who ran some kind of a station for trappers. We drove in a car. The station manager and his Indian helper met us. They had a sleigh pulled by six huskies. That day there was a lot of sunlight. I stood looking north at the unbroken sweep of snow reaching to the horizon. You could say it had a kind of beauty, yes, but it was the beauty of a desert – if deserts have beauty in changing light – and it was monotonous.

The Indian now was attending to the dogs. The manager asked me how I would like to go for a ride on the sled, driving the dogs myself. "Okay," I said. He gave me the two words for go and stop and showed me how to handle the reins. It was like driving a team of horses, he said. I drove across the snow, all by myself, saying "Mush, mush," and wondering how they would catch up to me if the dogs wouldn't turn back. But the dogs did turn, and my friends, watching me, were having a good laugh. Finally the Indian touched his head, he kept touching it as he grinned. At that time I was seeing many political dignitaries and I had been told that in Ottawa I would not be taken into the confidence of such men unless I wore a black homburg hat and a dark double-breasted overcoat, and there I was now on the dog sleigh, crying "Mush, mush" to the huskies, wearing my black homburg and city coat. How, then, could I ever believe that I was secretly a creature of the Arctic ice pack? What a comic notion. When I left that vast desert of sunlit snow I knew I could never be one with it. I knew I could never believe that an awareness of this snow silence and the infinitude of pure white space lay buried in my soul as a shining bowl of pure white light: no!

In a Vancouver hotel one February night, a middle-aged man, who had left the prairies to settle in Vancouver, started talking to me. He looked old for his age. Wiry and healthy, but old! "Yes, I miss the prairies," he said. "But let's face it. I was born in this country and in February too, and now I know I've had enough of the winter. No more prairie winters for me. Last year I said to myself, 'I really don't have to put up with this anymore.' So here I am. I like it here." But next day it was raining. For three days it rained, it was this damp heavy air that made me feel inert, I knew. Some clean bright snow would have been a relief; and that night I found myself thinking of an elderly doctor friend who had retired two years ago to California. He had sold everything; house, books, the old Ontario pine furniture – everything, and for two years had basked in the California sunlight. But two months ago I had met him, he was back in Toronto – to stay. The things he had missed you simply wouldn't believe, he said with an odd smile. Driving his car in the winter, for one thing. He had a special skill with it on ice. And rocking the car out of a deep snow rut; you use the gears, never racing the engine, you rock back and forth, back and forth in a gentle easy seductive motion and just roll out.

I was at my window now in my city home with my big white pup who had never known a snowy night. The snow had been falling for hours. It was nearly midnight. No one passing on the street had broken the path. I had to take the dog out so I went looking for the galoshes I hadn't used since last winter. Bundled up, I stepped out, the big young dog moving just as gingerly as I do in the deep snow. Then the pup began thrusting his nose in the snow, turning sometimes to look at me. Suddenly he started a slow leaping gallop, then, just as suddenly, whirled around, hurling himself forward fifty paces, then whirling back and leaping in the air as if he had found some magic in the snow that had to be celebrated in this wild ritual dance. Well, dogs and children love the snow, I thought. It wasn't cold out, there was no wind, and as I looked around I could remember very poignantly other city nights after a heavy snowfall with a little leap of satisfaction. It was not satisfaction that the hunter, the skier, the snowmobiler, the skater, all those who go hurrying out to the countryside for their winter pleasures feel at the time of the first heavy snow. No, it was an awareness of the loveliness of the city in the snow, when the night is mild as it was now, and how I have liked being on the streets late at night after a heavy snowfall when the city has a white mask that hides the daytime ugly scars, and when the moon coming out suddenly touches with its winter light all the snow-covered roofs and spires and hardly anyone else is on the street. You can keep on walking for hours, feeling quiet quickening within you. It was on such a night, I remember it so brightly now, when I walked with a girl who had taken millinery lessons so she could design her own hats, and she had made this Chinese-looking hat, triangular strips of pink and black silk. We walked for hours in the city streets, not noticing that it had begun to snow again, and talked about going to Europe. When we finally went into a restaurant the new hat had turned into a bowl full of snow. It was ruined. But it didn't matter. The night had been given some kind of haunting beauty by the snow, a beauty that touched us, and I know this beauty is often felt by others in cities from Montreal to Regina. And, come to think of it, that old man I used to watch when I was a boy, the man who came out late at night and shovelled his neighbours' sidewalks, that man who bewildered us all, maybe in his own way he had been touched by this mild night city snow magic, as my dog was now, rollicking wildly on the corner under the street light.

*Winter*, McClelland & Stewart, 1974

# THOSE MEN OF ACTION

In times of war, in almost all countries, the intellectual becomes a despised and rejected man. That's understandable. These are the times of the men of action. Men of action win wars. Of course, the Canadian intellectual, that lonely and pathetic creature, has never actually been rejected. He flourished in such a solitary state that he never had much influence in the cultural life of the nation. That cultural life has been shaped by intellectuals from other lands. So our homegrown intellectuals may feel no uneasiness in this wartime subjugation. But what happens to the intellectuals throughout the world happens to the Canadian intellectuals, too. The men of action, having full possession of the field now, have no intention of abdicating the cultural field after the war. In fact, they never miss an opportunity to attack and destroy the intellectual when he raises his small piping voice these days. They blame the war on him. "Talk, talk, talk," they say. "All this talk led to Munich."

This is a slightly comical criticism of the pre-war intellectual. The suggestion is that he was listened to and that the critical faculty, the faculty that the intellectual should stand for, was dominant in France and England, and that the statesmen of these countries, and of America, too, had become so rational, or so intellectual, that they had no spirit left to withstand the Hitler attack. Actually, this point of view is a mockery of history.

All of England may have been talking and discussing political affairs before Munich. Conceivably they may have talked themselves into exhaustion, but the men of Munich could never be called the intellectual leaders of the life of England or France. The men of Munich were the haters of the intellect in critical action. They were completely impervious to what they called and still call "intellectual chatter." It wasn't the intellectuals who built up Germany; who subsidized German industry; who partitioned Czechoslovakia.

So, when someone comes along these days and starts attacking the intellectuals and repeats the old lie about "all this talk leading to Munich," then it can be pretty well taken for granted that such a person has in mind some particular cultural objective in the achievement of which the intellectual, trying to exercise the free critical faculty, is not expected to play a very large role.

It is surprising how dominant this anti-intellectual trend has become. It has eaten into the very vitals of our educational system. There was a time when the word "progressive" in educational or cultured circles meant a man who was pushing the critical faculties to the very frontiers of knowledge. In these debased educational times, a progressive educator is a man who either scorns the human intellect functioning freely, or believes that philosophy and metaphysics have been the ruination of the world and have been a very poor substitute for beautiful action. So what do we get in education? We get everything that can be a substitute for thinking. Not that the objective isn't entirely laudable. These days everybody has a lofty social conscience, and therefore we must produce useful citizens. A useful citizen is a man who does something, who functions in society, or so they say, and naturally that means that the man who is running around in circles always doing something is a far more useful citizen than a man sitting at home in his armchair looking out on the world.

Recently, I've had the pleasure of attending some educational conferences. These conferences have had to do with the preparation of particular educational programmes. And always there was a kind of pathetic eagerness for what is called "action." No one seemed to be concerned much with what the action might lead to as long as it was pure and undefiled action. If an educational program merely leads a man to sit down and think and come to some painful conclusion about what's going on around him, that is regarded as defeatist and out of date: you see, it gets nothing done! And take my word for it, there's nothing more irritating to these new men of action than to have an irreverent fellow merely trying to use his head and sitting around in an armchair asking what all this action is going to lead to. "You're corrupt," they say. "You're out of date." Well, maybe so, but it seems to me that the only thing that can save our cockeyed world is a restoration of the dignity that used to be attached to the meditative, reasonable man.

Our country has been poverty-stricken culturally because our people have never developed the critical faculty, the critical approach to policies, art, music, and literature. This has been a godsend, of course, for all the mountebanks in the land. In all civilized countries public men have had to be watchful of contemporary cultural opinion; they have had to fear the quick flash of critical minds turned actively against them. In Canada, a politician fears only a rival politician. There are few sages to brood over the wilder antics of politicians on the hoof and jab the critical scalpel deep into their thick impenetrable hides.

Our homegrown intellectuals live in a kind of pathetic isolation. They have very little effectiveness as a group; they practically never move on an objective together. A conniving citizen, contemplating some slick gesture, has only to fear political reproach or general public indignation. He rarely has to deal with the laughter that ought to greet his antics. He is rarely destroyed by a flash of wit. All our journalists run to the somewhat sober side. They go in for what is called constructive criticism. Their editors, like products from the new progressive schools, want to be useful.

After long hours of meditation, I have decided to make a choice between the useful citizen and the man who is almost anti-social in his desire to sit still and think and come to his own conclusions. And I'm not choosing the useful citizen. I'm tired of men running around being useful and never asking what it may all add up to. I'm tired of the whirring of dynamos who create nothing. A certain kind of action can be its own opiate for the people. Give them action and give them enough of it, keep them busy and they may never stop to ask why they are busy. We are in grave danger of having our world flooded with busy little men. The aim of our schools, under the new dispensation, is to produce such busy little useful men. So I suggest, for the sake of the future of the nation, that one scholarship be given in every school in the land for the little boy who refuses to be busy, but with a frown on his face while lying in the sunlight merely keeps saying: "I want to know why."

*New World Illustrated*, 1944

*Go! and make cat calls!*
*Dance and make people blush,*
*Dance the dance of the phallus*
*and tell anecdotes of Cybele!*
*Speak of the indecorous conduct of the Gods!*

*Ruffle the skirts of prudes,*
*speak of their knees and ankles.*
*But, above all, go to practical people?*
*Say that you do no work*
*and that you will live forever.*

—EZRA POUND

# IN HIS IMAGE

In Ottawa I have a friend who long ago stopped thinking of people as persons. In fact, he has no time to be concerned with the fate of individuals and their little griefs and hopes. Nowadays he thinks of the "masses." And since he is interested in education he deals in mass education. Sometimes he breaks down and concentrates on the community, but that's about as far as he will go. There was a time long ago when a personal tragedy could break his heart, but now he regards that part of his life as a shameful adolescent period, a time of decay and intellectual corruption.

These days everything seems to come my friend's way and he is positive that he is marching in step with the times: across the world he sees great armies hurled into action, the fate of one soldier is unimportant. Civilians die by the thousands, and as the days pass and it keeps on happening, I sometimes think that, as far as my friend is concerned, no one at all seems to have died.

One time I said to him, "Why is the death of one man sometimes more moving than the death of a hundred thousand men?"

"Because a man like you concentrates on the death of an individual," he said. "You're a decadent writer. You must have tragedies."

As you can see, my friend is a man of strong social purpose which means that he has little time to be bothered with the relationships of human beings. This is his hour. These are the days of national objectives, of world goals, or broad social movements. Naturally my friend has no time to read novels. Lyric poetry bores him. A movie, to please him, must have a social purpose and no emphasis whatever on character. The last time I heard from him he was developing a new plan for group, or functional education, and when I said to him that it was all excellent and even admirable but that I couldn't see why he called propaganda education, he smiled as if he pitied me. "You're still off there by yourself trying to make everything personal," he said.

But in the rest of the human race in these times there is a great hunger to discover the essential humanity of someone against the tremendous backdrop of armies in motion, of thousands of deaths, of the daily reports of cities in flames. And suddenly a personal issue between two men can push aside in the newspapers the reports of tremendous victories. The American General Patton slapped a shell-shocked soldier in a hospital and accused him of cowardice. It was a simple story, a little incident that told of human failure, yet it stirred people on this continent more than anything that had happened that day on the fighting fronts.

My friend in Ottawa would shrug and say that people magnified this incident out of all proportion, but somehow I believe that the people who were so stirred were right, and that they represent whatever hope there is for the human race. Something had happened that they could understand. Something had happened that touched their own lives, that reminded them of their relationships with one another. There had been a violation of honour on the part of the general. Dignity had been destroyed. We were all deeply humiliated.

The character of the two men was suddenly revealed to us. The swashbuckling, Wild West, blood-and-guts general, a martinet, a brave man himself, and familiar to the human race for thousands of years, stands over the helpless soldier and curses him and strikes him. Suddenly the whole world has an awareness and respect for the dignity and sanctity of the person of that poor soldier. Whether the general, when he apologized, was actually ashamed is not important. Millions of persons in America were ashamed.

The afternoon when the story appeared in the newspapers I was having a cup of coffee in a restaurant. In the next chair was a poorly dressed, tired little man in a threadbare grey overcoat who was reading the paper. Putting it down excitedly he reached over and touched my arm. "See, see that," he said, pointing to the story about the general. "Why, it's terrible. Something should be done to that general. Look, mister, I was in the last war. Maybe you don't understand." He was excited and distressed. A light seemed to have been thrown on his whole life.

While I listened to the shabby man in the grey coat I had a feeling that the story of the general who had slapped the sick soldier would be remembered long after some of the great historical events had been forgotten. Unwittingly, but at an enormous expense to himself, General Patton did a great service for the American people: he reminded them that no matter what was happening in the world, certain human relationships could not be trampled upon.

There was one other incident in recent months that must have shocked my friend in Ottawa and which touches on the same problem. A young man in the RCAF named Wayne Lonergan, who had been separated from his rich wife, took a trip to New York, where they had lived together, and he killed her in a fit of passion.

For a week this story crowded some sensational war news out of the headlines. Columns were devoted to the wretched man and his dissolute wife. Of course, my Ottawa friend would smile and say that the newspapers knew how to play on the craving of the masses for sensational scandals. But I would say, "Nonsense," to him. People were excited by the Lonergan murder because it was a story of human corruption and passion. It was a story that is a thousand years old. In these times when great armies clash and millions of men die – when the Russians are launching a great counter-offensive – the imagination can't grasp the enormous scale of it all; the mind gets blurred. When Lonergan killed his rich wife, people wanted to know why. They had a craving to get inside the minds of the people who were involved in the murder, to understand, to fathom the impulses, to bring the man and his dead wife so close that they could be seen and understood.

That curiosity about what goes on inside a man is like a great hunger. It can only be starved for so long. For a while it may be denied for the sake of other more important goals, but it is always there in men and women. Slogans cannot kill it, mass movements cannot blot it out.

In time of war and of national crisis there is, as my friend in Ottawa very well knows, a heroic willingness to sacrifice personal relationships. But the sacrifice produces an abnormal way of thinking and feeling; the craving for proper human relationships, or a mere awareness of each other as human beings, lies hidden and then breaks out startlingly in a universal fascination with the story of the general who slapped the soldier, or the airman who killed his rich wife.

The Bible is full of similar stories: the stories of Cain and Abel, of the woman taken in adultery, of Salome and St. John the Baptist, of Ruth, of David and Jonathan, of the Good Samaritan, of Samson and Delilah, of Paul on the road to Damascus, of the conscience of Pilate, of the suffering of Job, of the prodigal son, of the woman with the box of precious ointment, of the kiss of Judas. These are the stories that have haunted the heart of man for centuries, stories of the virtues and vices of men and women created in His Image, not in the image of the Mass Man.

*New World Illustrated*, 1944

# KAFKA

No writer has been so continuously celebrated as Franz Kafka. Kafka wormed his way into the blood of most of the writers I knew when I was young. Some got him out of their blood. Some didn't. The poet, W.H. Auden, went to his grave believing that Kafka had the scope and influence of Shakespeare, which is absurd. Auden believed in a myth: – that ours was the age of anxiety. Surely Kafka had a hand in creating that myth. It was also the age of Freud, an age of neurotics, men eating their hearts out. Men flat on their backs talking their way into the cave of the womb, the cave of night. But being flat on your back in Kafka was something else, something more – you were a bug.

Kafka shaped many writers by seeming to open a door (for many, it became a trap door), with *The Trial, The Castle, Metamorphosis, The Penal Colony*, works that held a troubling mystery and seemed to speak ominously to our time, and there was a two- or three-year period when his great book, *The Trial*, got into my blood. In this novel, the hero K is arrested; he has done nothing wrong, and from the time of his arrest K is on a quest to find out what he is accused of, or who his accuser is.

Of course, he can't find out, and will never know why he is condemned, or even why he was on a list. Is it any wonder that this story made such a powerful impression in the thirties and forties when the police, SS, the NKVD, were operating with such full insidious, inscrutable force. "Men are disappearing before our very eyes." I had friends who argued with me over what the book was about. They said it was a story of the police state . . . the knock on the door, the arrest, but no, it was more than that, such an accusation implied much more than that . . .

Kafka, it seemed to me, had restored a sense of destiny to the novel, but destiny with an Old Testament, Calvinist twist to it: some were saved and some were damned, and there was no knowing why. A world in which you knew you were doomed because you knew there were only questions, or worse, only questionnaires. The mystery of it, the unseen hand with a grip on your life, on your heart, must have got into my mind.

At this time, I was working on a long story. I couldn't get it right. In a way, I didn't like the story. In my bones I didn't like it. I showed it to a friend. Delighted, he said, "It's Kafkaesque, mysterious, and your hero is a demoralized man!"

Since I hadn't wanted my hero to be demoralized, I was upset for days. Maybe even demoralized. Then, I saw what the trouble was. I was going against my whole nature, writing against the grain of my temperament. In my life, if I'd felt that a mysterious hand had tapped on my door and I was never to know why, could I have gone off on a tireless quest seeking the answer which could never be given to me, and could I go on and on and on suffering a terrible anxiety till I was demoralized?

No, I was no Calvinist.

I was not like Kafka, on an endless prowl for some sign that my mother might bestow on me her fulfilling love, and unlike Kafka, too, I did not hate my father. Those anxieties had not nested in me. I had other problems. There were other mysteries, other strange wonders that moved me more deeply.

I put Kafka aside, and now I believe that the age of anxiety, so widely accepted, is the product of those two men of genius, Kafka and Freud, and their own temperaments. Kafka had such a powerful imagination and he was such a singular artist that he succeeded in making a whole generation of writers believe that he was dealing with a universal truth but it was not universal, at least, not universal for me.

# SLITKIN AND SLOTKIN'S

Of a Friday night, toward the end of the War, I used to get off the
train in Montreal and take a taxi to a bar and eatery on Dorchester
Street, JACK & LOU'S BAR AND GRILL. Lou was the little guy
with the cigar. He had come from Central Europe before the First
War. The big guy with the cigar was Jack. He was out of New Jersey.

Partners in the fisticuffs racket through the thirties, they had
worked with thugs and pugs in walk-up gyms, first as coaches and
then as promoters, staging fights in Boston, Buffalo, Philly, Brooklyn, and Montreal. They'd had one good fighter, a thumper named
Maxie Berger, and one they still loved to talk about, Jasper O'Hanley, who had a delicate glass jaw. As starving fight managers they'd
wangled and chiselled their way into some towns and been chased
out of others, travelling under their names, Lou Wyman and Jack
Rogers. After the War started, they had given up promoting and
they had settled in Montreal and had opened up their eatery. Elmer
Ferguson of the *Montreal Herald* had referred to them as the firm of
Slitkin and Slotkin, and everybody said that they were probably
called Slitkin and Slotkin in heaven, and so the name had stuck.

They didn't have a bartender. They were the bartenders. They
didn't have a greeter at the door. They were the greeters. They wore
homburg hats, black tuxedos, and four-in-hand ties "to make sure
the air of dignity is truly dignified."

Those were great times in Montreal for a storyteller, for anyone
interested in characters: Premier Duplessis, who took payoffs from
gangsters and a hundred "protected" *barbottes* (gambling houses);

Camillien Houde (Mister Five-by-Five, His Worship, the 350-pound Mayor); eager young soldiers and sailors on leave; Lili St. Cyr at the Gaiety; reporters, racketeers like Frankie Carbo; the boxing clan, hoofers, public relations men for the breweries, and stars in show business. The walls in Slitkin and Slotkin's were papered with signed photographs: Two-Ton Tony Galento, Rocket Richard, Tommy Dorsey, Frankie Filchock, The Ink Spots, Frankie Sinatra, Sugar Ray Robinson and Jack Dempsey, Judy Garland and Lucille Ball, Jack Kearns and Gratien Gelinas, Jackie Robinson and Gypsy Rose Lee. Though there were city curfew liquor laws, the police never closed the grill room doors. The police themselves often stayed until dawn, crowding into the bar with men who were bending an ear.

Presiding over them all, serving thick excellent juicy steaks, were Lou and Jack. They thought of themselves as private guys who – as Slitkin and Slotkin – had a public. They knew who they were. They took immense pride in being who they were.

The first time I met Lou Wyman it was late at night on St. Catherines Street where I was walking with "whispering" Dink Carroll, the sports editor of the *Montreal Gazette*. A quiet little guy stopped Dink on the street and they chatted, while my feet got cold and I started to sneeze. After I pulled my friend Dink away, I asked, "Why talk to the guy so long? Couldn't you get loose?" Dink smiled and said, "That's Lou Wyman. They call him Slitkin now. He's an amusing guy."

Slitkin was short, broad-faced, bald and had a wide smile. His speech was the argot of the ring, the racetrack, the street; only it came out of him in a strangely gentle tone. One night I asked him about a quiet young woman who had been sitting at a table by herself. "Ordinarily we don't like girls hanging around. It's no good for business," Lou said, "but she's all right. What I mean is, if she had ten bucks and you needed it, she'd loan it to you, because then she doesn't mind borrowing five from somebody else."

Lou wasn't married, but the story was that he got along well with women while, men, it seems, saw only a hard wise guy, grinning and playing all the angles, men who told funny stories about Lou's banking system: he was apt to produce his money roll from his shoes, his hat, his stockings or his underwear. I liked him because he was a good listener.

There weren't many listeners there in the eatery. They were all talkers. Even the gangsters couldn't button their lips. There was a little man known as "Derle" (Doyle) – who was a henchman for the gangster, Frankie Carbo, who managed Jake Lamotta. Carbo was in Slitkin and Slotkin's all the time, and so was "Derle" – who was officially the trainer for the Montreal fighter, Johnny Greco. One night, Carbo and everyone else got up from the table and I was left alone with "Derle."

Here was this guy looking at me, wanting to bend my ear, but we had nothing in common so he began telling me how he would go about getting the vote out in certain districts for Carbo in New York, telling me about the very strong-arm tactics he used. The point is, in normal restaurant life, I would never have heard anything like this, never have come up against Carbo, a very much feared man, and "Derle." But this was, shall we say, a mixed society. In Slitkin and Slotkin's you'd see newspaper and PR guys, yes, but you'd also see Jack Dempsey, Jackie Robinson, and A.J.M. Smith the poet, and all the fight managers were there, too, and Deacon Jack Allen would drop in with a fighter from Toronto and you could talk boxing all night.

One of Slitkin's ex-pugilist protégés, Maxie Berger, had hung up his gloves to go into the clothing business. He tried to sell suits any night he was in Slitkin and Slotkin's and one early hour he persuaded Peter McRitchie, who was the managing editor of the *Gazette*, to buy one of his suits. Weeks later, McRitchie got into a brawl at the bar and Slotkin threw McRitchie out, ripping the lining of his new suitcoat.

After a period of penance, McRitchie returned to the bar, but every time he saw Maxie Berger, as a joke, he would open up his suitcoat and say, "See, Maxie, you make lousy suits." Berger was humiliated. He pleaded with McRitchie to let him make a new suit. McRitchie refused. He wore the suit everywhere. No one bought Berger's suits. Eventually Berger went belly-up, a broken man. Everyone at the bar thought the situation was amusing but I couldn't help myself, I turned the situation into a story, my novel *The Many Coloured Coat*, with McRitchie as Harry Lane and Berger as Mike Kon (in much the same way, the quiet young woman who loaned ten bucks so she could borrow five had quickened my imagination: I'd seen something about her, a guilelessness that was dangerous – she, among other things, refused to see that as she socialized openly with men, and with black men, too, she aroused rage not only in white men but in black women; anyway, she became Peggy in *The Loved and The Lost* – a woman who refused to see that her sense of unsullied aloofness might just as easily be a pig-headed self-indulgence, as night after night she sat having a lamb chop under the towering eye of Slotkin).

The ineffable Mr. Rogers, Slotkin, had a lot of bounce and a much more florid air than Slitkin, as became "the heavyweight champion of Belgium by default," a title he had never explained. He wore hand-stitched suits, had an exultant and airy wave of the hand and a cold, shrewd eye. Unlike Lou, Jack was married and slept at home two nights a week, Saturday and Sunday. In a certain light and at one angle, his face was hard, and I wondered how the local police in any town in Vermont or upstate New York had dared to chase him out of the place when he was a fight manager, but then when he was oiled up a little and he was sitting down with the boys, a warm expansive grin and a vast amiability softened his face and he wanted to clown around and go in for ham-handed rowdy horseplay. He fancied himself a dialectician, a natural comic, especially when he wasn't trying: he had set up the drinks for the boys one night as a lady said sedately, "Who, or should it be whom, should I thank?"

"Ah, we have a grammarian present," someone said.

"A grammarian," Jack said, "what's a grammarian? I'm a Yiddel myself."

On another night he said, "Moderate your language, gentlemen. There's broads in the joint."

Slitkin and Slotkin liked being themselves, they had a belief in themselves, and they didn't hold themselves cheaply. One night when my friend the broadcaster, John Fisher, took a party of Hollywood celebrities to the establishment, it was afterwards pointed out to gentle Lou that possibly he hadn't made enough fuss over the stars.

"They were celebrities, see Lou?"

"Celebrities," he said with dignity. "Hell, we're celebrities ourselves."

I had dinner there one night, and it was a dignified occasion – dignified for about ten minutes, and then eight people gathered around our table and the banter and insults flowed cheerfully, and someone shouted, "Why doesn't somebody sing? Where's the tenor?" and out of the next booth leapt a young business executive, who sang tenor arias for the edification of all the diners until he was interrupted by a strange sound like the whining of bagpipes.

It was a middle-aged, red-faced fur merchant, holding his nose and pounding his throat to make the bag pipe sound. He wanted to join the party. And ten feet away at another table, a woman was talking to an elderly gentleman who dozed in his chair, as if all were peace and quiet and he was in the seclusion of his private club while she kept talking and talking, louder and louder, and when she paused, someone else started up, another monologue.

The monologue! I came to see on that night that ours is the time of the endless public monologue, of men and women who are stage-struck, and so, not long after that night in Slitkin and Slotkin's we formed a group we called the Earbenders Club. We talked and talked and talked and told wild stories, each man waiting breathlessly to get a word in edgewise, and then, as that man took the floor and held it, nobody listened. It was good fun if you'd had enough to drink, but at the end you were left feeling rather lonely. Lonely among the earbenders, who we would, now, a few years later, call communicators.

And so, Slitkin and Slotkin's is gone and Jack is in the grave. Lou is carrying his money roll in his socks, selling newspapers. It strikes me that more than ever, the earbenders are with us. Public talkers are bigger than ever, but the thing to remember is – no public talker is really interested in you, or me, and what goes on in us.

Today, nobody needs a bar, nobody needs an eatery, everybody talks out loud, and as often as possible under the eye of the camera. Some of our communicators tell me that television will give me a new freedom in my choice of involvement in what is going on in far away places. Others say that the great gadget will enslave me to the hucksters – I am to be doomed to inertia, to becoming a man with no soul of my own, just part of a tribal mind. Well, maybe, but I know something else, too. I know that many civilizations have come and gone. Those that were really bright places on this earth for a time were those where the private citizens, not just the king, or the chief of the secret police, or the rich man, had won respect for the dignity of his private life. "I'm a Yiddel myself," such a man might cry, a man who thought of himself as more than a part of an apathetic audience stuck watching someone inoffensive like Perry Como who stood singing "Do You Love Me" while idly – as if his mind were somewhere else entirely – picking the lint off a studio chair – singing to an audience that was waiting, always waiting for the message, never asking who sends it, who controls it.

I can hear someone saying in that presently tired, inane inside language of the hip – "Come on, man. Talk the talk. Get with it. It's film, man. Orson Wells. Eisenstein. The novel's not happening, man."

As a writer I know that this is sales talk. It's a pitch. It's the Seventh Avenue textile designer, it's the man working on the TV ratings abacus, and the dope peddler, too. I know that if I have any perceptions of my own I can never be totally in tune with this talk talk talk world of men in grey flannel suits. Was Joyce with it? Or Proust? Or Kafka? Why, they were so far out of it they could hardly find publishers. The trouble is, when the dedicated artist finds that the "get with it" men have caught up to him, it breaks his heart. No, he has to be like Baudelaire's old voyager. He has to be forever seeking something new, even if it is in death, and so sometimes he kills himself. And when Hemingway, losing his mind, kept complaining desperately, "I can't write any more, I can't," he was really telling the great and terrible story of the eternal artist who could no longer see why he had any right to go on living, not among the earbenders, the medicine men of the airwaves and the big public communicators because I am convinced that those communicators have succeeded in doing at least one thing. They have made and will go on making a lot of people lonelier than they ever were before. It's a new kind of loneliness. It's a great field for a writer. It is the loneliness of men and women who are always in an audience watching and being talked to from a screen and shown pictures and talked to again and told they are being involved in famines and deaths in Vietnam and Biafra because they see moving pictures that in fact don't move them very much.

Anybody who really knows anything about people is aware that a person can get truly involved only with another person he or she knows. The death of a hundred thousand Hindus in a famine, cruelly and sadly, becomes something watched one night and forgotten the next. Out of this vast superficial kind of awareness of what is going on comes apathy, and out of this apathy the terrible loneliness that men and women feel in crowds when they dare not raise their own voices in any discovery and assertion of themselves.

When Mark Antony shouted, "Friends, Romans, countrymen, lend me your ears," he was making the request of all great communicators. Lend me your ears, lend me your eyes. You must never say to such a man, "Okay. Now it's your turn, you do the same for me. How about your left ear at least." He'll say, "What is this? Who's the communicator here?" There is never to be a relationship, not with the communicators, those public faces appearing "this week only" in private places.

I believe that the human being emerged from the prehistoric swamp and slime, and then from the whole crazy tribal voodoo world, when he discovered himself as a person. This is why I write. I'm interested in persons and what they do or fail to do with each other. Since man has endured so much on this earth and since he has been able to keep alive that mysterious spark in his soul, I think it'll be a struggle but he will be able to handle this new kind of loneliness, this new kind of electronic belittlement.

# KINSEY'S REPORT

No book in recent years has created such a bother as that large tome called *The Sexual Behaviour in the Human Male*, by Messrs. Kinsey, Pomeroy, and Martin. The book is a survey made by members of the staff of Indiana University. It is impressively supported by the U.S. National Research Council with Rockefeller Foundation funds. In an age of surveys this survey was inevitable. But just why so many citizens who have read the book are going around with troubled or startled expressions I can't quite figure out.

One learned gentleman wrote that this book shows how right Freud was. The book, of course has nothing to do with Freud, and offers no theories about the significance of sexual behaviour. The book goes in for facts. The gentleman who conducted the survey, in effect, went around America counting noses. Some citizens made love one way, some another. Some liked the gleam of a shoulder, some liked a lot of clothing. Some liked the dark. Some liked the light. And when the authors had sorted out these little preferences and broken them down into tables and graphs and put them in print, a lot of learned readers gasped and exclaimed, "I had no idea so much of this went on in America!" although Cole Porter, no sociologist, but a man who can write a catchy tune, had told them some years ago that "Even oysters up in Boston do it." In fairness to the great American public, it should be pointed out that the survey does not suggest that Americans love the ladies or are more perverted in their inclinations than the citizens of any other nation.

None of this so far is news. What has attracted so much attention in the survey is that there seems to be evidence of a sexual caste system in democratic America. It's not exactly a class war in sexual behaviour: I'm not even sure that the Communists could get much comfort out of it, because, for all I know, the same authors may be conducting a survey in Russia, to show that the Russian upper classes have little preferences in sexual behaviour that are not shared by the factory worker. But in democratic America, a little class war in sexual behaviour could go on almost any night in the week. It is well-known that college men, or lawyers, or even doctors at times get tired of consorting with college girls, and take a liking to easy-going dancing ladies whose fathers may be unskilled labourers. And sometimes the college gentleman and the girl who only went to grade school agree, after some dubious sparring, to come together for a regrettable purpose. But no matter how ardent they may be, if they follow the rules of the survey, they get caught in a new kind of nocturnal class war.

The college boy, having a beautifully developed aesthetic sense, leaves the light on as he kisses his new-found friend.

"You forgot to turn out the light," she says quickly.

"No, I didn't. I deliberately left it on," he explains.

"I'm not going to stand for that," she says angrily. "What do you think you're doing?"

"I'm looking at you. You are beautiful. If I turn out the light I won't be able to lose myself in contemplation of your beauty."

"Listen, mister. What do you think I am?"

"I think you're very pretty, and I don't want to lose sight of your prettiness even for a moment. If I turn out the light . . . well, I'm not going to turn out the light," he insists with all the stubborn dignity of a college man.

"Why, I never met anybody like you," exclaims the angry girl. "There must be something funny about you . . . You're certainly not going to keep on eyeing me. I didn't think we came here for that. Why . . . why, it's positively indecent this business of keeping the light on."

"But you don't understand," he protests. "I have an aesthetic sense."

"I knew there was something queer about you."

"That only means that I'm a college man."

"Okay, college man. You don't get away with that stuff with me. Give me some taxi money and I'll go home."

If the girl had only read the survey she would understand that the great majority of college men who were interviewed made it plain that they preferred a lady in the light rather than a lady in the dark. But unskilled labourers, in the main, liked to have the lights turned out. Just what would happen if a college-bred woman married an unskilled worker who got rich quickly won't be known until the companion book to this one, dealing with the sexual behaviour of women, appears, but clearly such a marriage might result in a delicate reversal of some of the accepted modesties.

No one should get the impression that there is evidence from the survey that the highly educated are more licentious than the intellectually underprivileged. On the contrary, they seemed to be more restrained. But they have their little customs which are simply not those of the mechanics. And the mechanics, being skilled labourers, have little peculiarities that are alien to the unskilled workers. Morals are not involved. It is simply a matter of custom. If a boy grows up with a hearty direct approach, his girlfriend, assuming she is of the same class, accepts him on those terms. Anything outside these particular terms of reference tends to be regarded as indecent. It all depends on what you do yourself. But whatever you do, you have the consolation of knowing that a definite percentage of American males are doing exactly the same thing. Anyone looking for the salacious touch in the making of this record is going to be disappointed. The book is a cold analysis. It is as cold as the professional touch of a mortician. And what strange and demoralizing evidence it offers of the lack of democracy in sexual behaviour! What required reading it should be for the social service worker who arrives at a client's home and judges the sexual behaviour there according to the rules she plays in her own little caste – rules which seem just as outlandish to the client as the client's seem to the social service worker. And certainly many a judge who has passed sentence on culprits found guilty of sexual irregularity, must blush a little if he reads this book.

However, I find myself doubting a lot of the facts, figures, tables and graphs so neatly recorded in the survey, because I know what incredible liars men are about their sexual behaviour. They always put themselves in a bright light, they boast of their prowess, and they don't even believe they are lying. And no matter how carefully the interview with them is conducted they are going to go on lying. Yet, in spite of my lack of faith in the interviewing system, which is the basis of this survey, I now suffer from a weakness I find I share with other men who have read this book.

The graphs and the tables get into the mind. You find yourself referring to them again and again in the most unexpected places. If you go into a drawing room where there are 50 guests all happily engaged in drinking cocktails and chattering cheerfully, you find yourself eyeing them and breaking them down quickly into classifications according to the tables. Which are the university professors? That tall, tired man over there? Imagine! In his case it is unbelievable, but figures don't lie. He's the hope of America because he has restraint, although there's a one-to-five chance that he has consorted with another woman. And as for my friend, Fred, he told me that when he meets a strange girl he begins to fit her into the chart. "Did you go to college?" he asks. "No." "What do you do for a living?" "I was married to a truck driver but now I'm looking for a job." While this amiable little conversation goes on my friend is muttering to himself, "Don't expect her to go in for long kisses. Don't expect her to let her children run around the house naked. She won't go in for nudity at all. Don't be over-attentive and too intimate with your caresses. Grab her by the neck and be direct, be brutal."

*National Home Monthly*, 1948

# OWLS AND PUSSYCATS

Why shouldn't owls turn into pussycats if this helps a story? And if the story becomes simply a fable, what's the matter with fables? Fables usually have a larger general reality than common sense stories. And anyway, surely there must be a larger reality than the one we know and touch every day. Only the free imagination can deliver us from the conventional face of things we tire of!

All artists, touched by the divine afflatus, long for the acceptance of a condition where the untrammelled imagination can find ways of expressing new things. During World War One and after, the Dadaists had their innings. All accepted traditions in art were laughed off as garbage, conventional works were seen as obscene. In France, that writer of perfect French prose, Anatole France, was made the butt of risqué jokes. Free the imagination, free it from all accepted and sanctified forms, was the cry. Ten years later, in prose and poetry and in painting came the surrealists, offering the splendour of an enchanting dream world that was to bring death to the dreary logical mundane world, the waking conscious world, and give us the wonder of the anti-logical relationships of the dream. In those far-off days of Dada, with all the mockery and scoffing and the surrealist days, too, I was sympathetic, believing as I did, that all of this was good in that it meant a clearing of the ground in preparation for a new freshness in prose and a new simplicity and directness in tall and short tales. But now, with the new fashion for fantasy in prose, with the new breed of fabulists telling their fairy stories, and all doffing their hats respectfully to Marquez, I am growing very dubious about the impulse behind all this.

Very late one night I sat at my window, watching people passing my house in the moonlight. I knew as they passed that they threw shadows, but they were real people going to their homes. They looked so ordinary and yet each one had relationships with another, and each one had a world within himself or herself. Maybe behind the thrown shadows it was a terrible world. How did I know? But they were out there on the street at night in a real objective world, and that night, sitting there watching, I knew there could never be any end to my wonder at the mystery of real people, especially if one of them happened to believe deep in his heart that he was actually a pussycat and another believed that he was actually an owl.

# A THEOLOGY OF ART

A writer I knew, but not very well, asked me to read his novel. He was a man with a singular but difficult talent who had gained my respect through little stories I had seen printed, so I sat down and read his book. It was a work of dreams and fantasies, a work which began to trouble me for I knew how desperately anxious this man was to get a book published, and I could see that no publisher would take this book as it was. But I could see, too, that in the work there was a story; it was all there, a dream-like, almost surreal love story; it was there all worked out, all of a piece, an imaginative work.

But then I was in a quandary. Years ago, Gertrude Stein had pointed out that if you want to offer helpful criticism to a writer you should deal with the work generally and avoid going into detail! Try and see the thing as a whole. But it is not my nature to withhold in this careful professional manner. This man had been trying for years to get a book published. He had been heroic in his acceptance of rejection. And apart from the personality involved, I was sure that I, as an old hand, knew what was required aesthetically in this case. All that cluttered up the fine thread of the one poetic love dream should simply be thrown away. But could I say this to the writer? Well, it all depended on how much he respected me, how willing he was to believe that I was not only concerned about his welfare, but even more concerned about the good of the work.

A week later at a big party, I encountered my author. From the beginning, his eyes were on me; mine shifted away. I ducked aside feeling squeamish, even a bit abject, and then a little later, his hand was on my arm. He said, "Well, did you read it?' Suddenly I wanted to kick myself. It was as if I were ashamed to ask *him* to do something for *me*. This was incredible. I was trying to do something for him.

I told him I had read the book. "Now, here's something to think about. Maybe it's just a wild idea, myself, though I'm sure of it. Just think about it, please."

I told him about throwing away all that got in the way of the one fine lyric love fantasy. "Will you just think about it?" I asked.

Without any rancour at all, he agreed to spend the night thinking about it. He even said the idea was attractive. "Yes, I'll try it," he agreed, and though, naturally, he was upset, I could tell by his eyes that his imagination was already at work. "You could do it tonight," I said. "Yes. I could. I'll try it," he said.

Later in the evening at this big party, I encountered the editor of a large publishing house. "I think I've got something for you," I said happily, and I took her arm and, guiding her to my author, I introduced them, told her about the lyric story, and how he was trimming the manuscript and how he could have it for her by the end of the week.

My author beamed happily. The editor was opening her arms to him. Before leaving them I took her aside. "Call me after you've read the story," I said, "I'll help in anyway I can."

A week passed, and then she did call me. Yes, she had read the manuscript, but she was only calling me out of a sense of obligation. The manuscript went off in so many directions she had wanted to toss it aside. "Wait a minute," I said. "There is this lyric story—"

"Oh, it's so obscured by all the other stuff . . ."

"You mean he didn't change it, didn't do the cutting . . .?"

"Not at all. It must be just as it was," she said, and I cursed.

Soon, I felt ashamed of myself, and even sympathetic to the stubborn but blind author. As soon as he had got home and looked at the manuscript he had found that he loved his own work, all those pages I had told him to throw away, and he had grown fiercely resentful, saying to himself, "I'm letting that guy tell me what to do." And he had wanted the editor to see the whole thing as it had come out of him. Unfortunately, the editor had lost all interest in him.

I hadn't tried to rewrite his book, not even a line of it, and so I ended up believing the author to be a foolish man willing to remain unpublished simply for the satisfaction of his own vanity. And yet, I'm aware that he, for his part, must believe that my vanity is wounded because he wouldn't take my advice. And even if he remained unpublished he would go on nursing the joy that comes from having expressed himself fully in his own fashion. And here, thinking about these things, I get a little impatient.

What I am interested in is a kind of theology of art, the striving for perfection in the made thing. Supposing a man does not express himself fully, does let the sprawl of his imaginings loose on the page. What do I care? What has it got to do with art? Self-expression, the satisfaction with one's self-expression – this can be mere therapy, or it can be the romantic enlargement of one's ego, and the fact that the writer or the painter must believe in himself has little to do with the worth of the thing that comes out of the belief.

I can see now, thanks to this author's absolute rejection of my advice, that during all my life as a writer I never wasted time wondering if I should believe in myself. I wanted, I had always wanted to believe in the good of the work and I knew I should be willing to sacrifice my pride and even squirm with disappointment for the sake of the good of the thing being worked on. And I think I knew, too, from the beginning that if I could have this attitude I would be a professional.

# TURN OUT THE LIGHTS

It was after midnight when we came out of the hotel. Six inches of snow had fallen and it was still snowing. While we waited for a taxi she held her fur collar across her face, but I could still see her eyes, and I said, "Satisfy my curiosity, will you?"

"If I can," she said.

"Lying on the bed, I was sure you really wanted to . . ."

"Yes, I think I did," she said.

"What happened?"

"You didn't turn out the light."

I nodded, "Tell me something. Didn't you go to college?"

"No," she said. "I was privately educated in France. Why?"

"My mistake," I said. "College girls always like to leave the light on."

"No kidding?" she said, shrugging. When the taxi came along, we got in and she remained silent, and riding slowly in this silence through the snowbound Montreal streets all my confidence came back to me.

After Morley had been to Montreal time and again hanging out at Slitkin and Slotkin's, he felt guilty about Hugh MacLennan, well-known for his novel, Two Solitudes. MacLennan had written little notes to Morley wondering why they never saw each other. Morley decided that he had to be courteous, so he phoned MacLennan and they agreed to meet late one Saturday afternoon at MacLennan's flat for a drink.

Morley knocked on the door. MacLennan was disgruntled and peeved and, above all, tired. He'd had almost no sleep. The problem, he said, was a joint just around the corner, a joint full of loud lowlife who caroused till dawn! He had complained to the police but as usual the police did nothing.

"Have you ever been in it?" Morley asked.

"No, never," MacLennan said sternly.

"Never been in the joint?"

"No, and last night was terrible," MacLennan said. "I got no sleep at all."

After a while, Morley finished his rye-and-water and said he must go, that his friend Dink Carroll had tickets to the Canadiens hockey game.

"When I was out on the street," Morley told me, "I didn't know whether to laugh or cry, I hadn't had the heart to tell him that I was one of the lowlifes, that it was Slitkin and Slotkin's, and even worse, even more sad, MacLennan had just written to me, saying how much he admired The Many Coloured Coat, my novel that is set so much in that joint.

"Sounds apocryphal," I told him wryly.

"Yeah, maybe, but it's true," he said.

*It was also true that Morley had many of the same kind of friends in Toronto. In fact, the local writers he seemed to be most at ease with were reporters and sportswriters – Jim Coleman, Ralph Allen, King Whyte, Ted "the Moaner" Reeve, the dapper owner of the baseball club – Jack Kent Cooke – and the boxing promoter, Deacon Jack Allen.*

*The editors of the somewhat raffish, right-wing newspaper, the* Telegram *– knowing their man, and probably having read sports stories he'd written for* New World Illustrated *– advanced an extraordinary proposition, which they announced to their readers in the summer of 1957. For a year, at high pay, he found himself in print on the sports page "In the Gallery" as a feuilletoniste (not that anybody knew then, or would care now, what a fueilletoniste was):*

---

### INTRODUCING MORLEY CALLAGHAN

Every week in *The Sunday Telegram* Morley Callaghan, eminent Canadian author, will turn his fine literary talent to tales of the sports world. As a refreshing newcomer to this field he will approach sport, not as a specialist, but rather from the angle of one who sees it as part of the human comedy. Morley Callaghan is the author of seven novels, two books of short stories and two plays. He has won the Governor General's award, a Maclean prize and over the years has contributed to a wide range of U.S. magazines, including the *New Yorker* and *Saturday Evening Post.*

---

# IN THE GALLERY: ONE

There may be innocent souls in this world who do not know how to tell when a man has won a fight. If they see two fighters coming out of a ring and one has his arm in a sling, his eye cut and bleeding and his face knocked lopsided, and the other is unmarked, they may jump to the natural conclusion that the unmarked man won the fight.

Then the boy with the battered puss cries out, "Look, Mom, I won." His mom may burst into tears and say, "Oh, son, did you let that brute do that to you without doing anything to him?" And out of swollen lips he whispers ecstatically, "You don't understand, Mom. You see, I forced the fight. Hey, you guys, tell her," and twenty-seven assorted sportswriters of long standing speak up and say it is a fact that her boy forced the fight and got the decision.

Carmen Basilio, holding his mangled head after the fight, said he knew he had won because he knew he had forced the fight.

He was right, too.

But what I want to know is how did this lazy and artificial view of a fight get so solidly established in America? Everybody who reads the newspapers now knows how to watch a fight and judge it. You pick the boy who is plodding forward determinedly, taking six punches to get in close, spitting out his blood along the way, but always going forward. You may be admiring the skill with which the other boy is eluding and punishing the grim, angry plodder and think he is winning easily, but sitting beside you there may be a piano player, taxi driver, a lawyer, old fight manager, or anybody else who reads the newspapers, who will explain wisely, "Oh, no. Can't you see it's the other guy who is carrying the fight to him?"

It's a way of looking at a fight, of course, and there is no reason why experts and judges shouldn't agree that it is the sacred way.

Basilio is lucky.

Admirable as he is, he fits into this antique and rigid view of battle. But surely Sugar Ray Robinson was doing what any successful general is supposed to do; make the enemy bleed and avoid getting marked himself.

But to be elusive, to know when to retreat and, with masterly generalship, keep your opponent lunging after you, is called "getting on your bicycle," and any self-respecting judge properly hypnotized by those voodoo words, "forcing the fight," knows that any master of rapid manoeuvre is to be grimly discouraged.

Have you noticed that with the rise of the "forcing the fight" school the good straight left is now treated with splendid contempt? Robinson probably popped Basilio with fifteen straight lefts in a row, but twenty-seven of the writers and two of the judges were too wise to be taken in by those jabs. All Robinson was trying to do, they would insist now, was keep Basilio away from him. Anyway, they agree, with a light air, that a left jab is just an irritant, it causes no real damage, it inflicts only superficial punishment. A man like Basilio, forcing the fight, will take six jabs on the eyes and nose to get in close to inflict his murderous clubbing blows.

So they say.

But this is just an agreed-upon legend, a dream, as anyone looking at the picture of Basilio's face should be able to see. A left jab used to be considered the basic blow in boxing. Used by a man like Robinson it is like having a pole thrust again and again in your face.

It is not a knockout punch, true enough, but it can cut a face to pieces and close the eyes.

Look how Tunney used it against Dempsey.

What I can't figure out is why there is such ready expert agreement that the six jabs Basilio takes to get in close are not to be taken too seriously, but that when he is in close he is landing "murderous punches." Who told them they were murderous? When you get in close holding with one hand you are banging away at the body and the back of the head and mauling and pushing, but why the ready agreement that this kind of punching is devastating. Did Robinson look as if he was being murdered?

The general popularity of the Basilio victory may really be a secret tribute to Robinson's mastery. When you watch a smaller man getting cut up and he keeps going on and on, sometimes staggering at the bell, then returning as grimly eager as ever and refusing to back away, you forget that he may be getting the worst of it in the ring. Your heart goes out to him in admiration. He becomes the grim, tough, fierce little underdog with his fantastic faith in his own power, and you want to see him rewarded in some way. The reward doesn't come in the fight. It comes in the decision. It is all against your own judgement, yet you can't help feeling pleased.

*Toronto Telegram*, 1957

# THAT WOMAN'S A SLUT

*❧✦❧*

"That woman's a slut. Why're you trying to turn her into something else? She's just a slut," I said to the blue-eyed woman I was having a drink with, a woman I had only known for one hour. We were talking about a character in a book. This blue-eyed woman, who was quite pretty, thought the character in the book caught with fine abandon something close to complete female sexuality.

"A slut?" she said bridling. "Well, what's a slut? What's the male equivalent for slut? Isn't there one? Slut! A male word. You don't understand me at all, do you?" she said.

"Not yet," I said.

"Not yet?"

"Would you really like me to understand you?" I asked.

"Sure."

"After only an hour that'd be terrible, I wouldn't feel I had to see you again." A new interest came into her blue eyes, and while she sipped her drink I told her that no woman should want a man to understand her completely. Nor should any man take delight in a male friend who believes he has a perfect understanding of him. I know men and women rush around crying, "If only someone really understood me." They assume that if they're understood they'd be loved and appreciated. It never occurs to them that the understanding friend, able at last to see them clearly, might also see that there was nothing left to hold his interest, or he might even wonder why he had ever been interested in the first place. When we see right through a character in a book, or someone we know in our lives, we possess them, we have risen above them. We can forgive and even pity them; we can be generous, or we can be bored. But whichever it is, this superior understanding never can be the basis for an electrifying relationship. A comforting relationship, yes. Peaceful, yes. But without moments of mystery, without moments of magic.

The woman with the very blue eyes was staring at me and frowning. Finally, she shrugged and smiled. "What has all this to do with you and me?"

"You said I didn't understand you."

"So I did."

"Well . . ."

"I'll tell you one thing," she said. "I really don't understand you."

"That's great. I'll be seeing you again."

# IN THE GALLERY: TWO

You wouldn't think a fight manager with a boy of his own would go out of his way to thrust the boy of another fight manager into the limelight, would you? But they will, they really will.

Wanting to talk to a boy of Al Weill's, Dave Rent, I got in touch with Deacon Jack Allen, though I knew he had a boy of his own to worry about, but the Deacon couldn't have been more affable or more concerned with my little problem.

He got hold of Al Weill's boy, who had a job somewhere, made arrangements to have him at the Toronto Athletic Club that night and at the appointed hour when I climbed the stairs there was the gentle-voiced Deacon, his hat sedately on the top of his head, yet looking twenty years younger than he should, and he led me into the office.

No man could have been more helpful. He got a writing pad for me, he gave me his own pen, he made me comfortable in the chair. If there was anything I wanted, just call him, he said. A picture of Al Weill's boy in fighting togs? Of course he had one. Opening a drawer in his desk he drew out a sheaf of pictures and, without comment handed me the picture of Al Weill's boy.

Then he did an odd thing. Puffing his cigar, his head on one side, he seemed to forget about me in the sheer aesthetic pleasure he got in contemplating another picture he had come across in the sheaf he had been thumbing through to get the one I wanted.

"There's a boy for you," he said, idly handing me this picture.

"Oh, who's that?"

"Chuvalo."

"So it is. A fine boy, Jack. Say, they tell me this boy of Al Weill's is only twenty."

"It's a fact," he agreed. "Very anxious to learn, too. I'll get him for you." Starting for the door, he stopped, looking thoughtfully at the floor, then he smiled. "Did you know Chuvalo was only nineteen? Well, no matter, just a minute."

He brought in Al Weill's boy who sat in the corner shyly, and he left us. He closed the door so the noise coming from the gym wouldn't disturb us. For twenty minutes Weill's boy talked earnestly.

Then the Deacon's fountain pen ran out of ink. I swear the Deacon wasn't listening. I would have seen his shadow against the glass. But the door opened. There was the Deacon with a pencil of his own. Naturally, he asked how I was doing, peered thoughtfully at my notes. His concern was touching as I thanked him. He again started for the door, but he hesitated, looking at Al Weill's boy. Suddenly he smiled hopefully.

"Get all you want?" he asked me.

"Not yet."

"Going to be quite a story, eh?"

"Well . . ."

"By the way," he said at the door again. "I was just talking to George."

"George?"

"George Chuvalo."

"Oh, must meet him sometime. Well, thanks, Jack."

For the next half hour I was busy making notes. Sometimes shadows passed across the closed glass door, but I went on with my interminable questioning of this boy of Weill's. I forgot all about the Deacon.

Suddenly the door was pushed open and a big, broad-shouldered, opulent-looking, six-foot, handsome fellow in an overcoat and hat came leaping at me like an old, happy friend, his hand out expansively.

"Why, Mr. Callaghan," he cried with a charming air of surprise.

"Yes?"

"It's George Chuvalo."

"Hello, George," I said, not too friendly, since I was being disturbed.

"How's Barry, Mr. Callaghan?"

"What?"

"How's your son?"

"You know him?"

"Why sure. I was a year behind him at St. Mike's. I just wanted to say hello."

"Well, fancy this," I said, feeling happy and friendly. There we were shaking hands warmly and naturally we had to do a little reminiscing. The whole focus of attention was now on Chuvalo with Al Weill's boy for the moment forgotten in the corner.

The Deacon stood modestly in the background.

"That's a funny thing," he said, when his own boy, George, had left, "I was talking to George and he happened to mention your son."

The smiling Deacon didn't look at all restless and thoughtful.

*Toronto Telegram*, 1957

# IN THE GALLERY: THREE

With every sportswriter in America looking down his nose at him, Hurricane Jackson should have a high old time in his bout with Floyd Patterson. They say he can't box and has no real punch, and that Patterson has already beaten him with one hand. Yet he has the pleasure of knowing that a big crowd is there to see him anyway.

They want to see him against the champion because they're not sure what he will do. Since he is so unpredictable, he's a sporting event in himself. With the odds so heavily against him, all he has to do is be himself at his best, a wild, sprawling, tireless, flailing happy-go-lucky brawler, and he may have astonishing success.

Since he does everything wrong, and is a clown in the bargain, he would make a rather ridiculous champion. But the experts seem to have forgotten that in the previous fight, even before he broke his hand, Patterson wasn't doing too well against him. At no time did Patterson dominate the fight.

I know that no one else agrees with me, but on what does Patterson's new and enormous reputation depend? Not so much on his previous victory over Jackson. That was too close. But on his masterly knockout of that old dignitary Archie Moore.

There was one thing in particular worth noticing in that fight. Moore was much slower with his hands than Patterson. A cagey old fighter like Moore can have extra pounds of suet around his waistline and can even get to the stage where he is so slow on his feet that he hardly more than shuffles, and yet he may still win fights because he remains faster with his hands than his opponent.

Archie's speed of hand had gone in the Patterson fight. It had to happen sometime, and it happened at the right time for Patterson.

It marked the end for Moore as a first-class fighter. Yet, as I say, Patterson's great reputation seems to depend on that fight with Moore rather than on his split decision over Jackson.

When the bell sounds and Jackson and Patterson leap toward each other they'll be offering more than a contrast in styles.

Watching them you may wonder what it is that prompts one man to try and lift himself up by his bootstraps while the other is content to stay as he was born.

Both Patterson and Jackson came from poverty-stricken neighbourhoods and both were illiterate. Patterson hasn't exactly become a scholarly fellow, but when he makes a personal appearance, or a little speech, you can see him trying carefully to get the right words, and he sounds grave and modest and rather winning. Nobody would think of laughing at him. He sounds like a man who is determined to conduct himself with a sobriety becoming to his high station.

Jackson, on the other hand, is the happy illiterate. But in his little appearances before the cameras he is even more moving than Patterson. Bewildered by the words the reporters use talking to him, he flashes his big happy smile and clowns around shadow boxing, while the men doing the interviewing laugh at him openly. Everybody seems to be sure he has no feelings at all.

Maybe he has some feelings, and maybe he has some awareness too, that Patterson, facing him in the opposite corner, has determinedly improved himself socially and culturally, and is being discovered as a sensitive and tender-hearted fellow, very acceptable indeed.

Jackson, the man they laugh at, the illiterate, the clown, may have some strange envious thoughts as he looks at Patterson and remembers that this polished reformer now so highly respected, was once as poor and unlettered as he was himself. Like all the unaccepted and laughed at and rejected clowns of this earth, he has nothing to fall back on but his primitive fury. That'll be all right for him, too.

If he can only manage to feel deeply incensed at being told so often that he is in the presence of his betters, his style may get so unpredictable in its wildness that Patterson could have a very rough time trying to control this happy-go-lucky flailer turned brawler in his fury.

Toronto Telegram, 1957

# TIME

Time is the melancholy enemy of all writers. When a very good writer has been around a long time, other writers, in the course of time, go back and look at him, his work, and they start re-examining the work, and no matter who the writer is, sooner of later he is up for assault. Sooner or later he must be reduced to ashes just to see if he can rise from his ashes.

I've been around long enough to wonder: which one is next? Which great literary fortress, hitherto impregnable, will be under assault? In a magazine article where writers were being named as overrated, I saw to my astonishment a few lines from that interesting and excellent writer, John Updike. He said he had found himself taking another look at William Faulkner. Faulkner? No one is sacred! Faulkner, the writer who has always been so respected by those who have ruthlessly cut down Hemingway, Fitzgerald, Farrell, that whole generation. But Faulkner. There's always been Faulkner! Jean-Paul Sartre's Faulkner. But that little note from Updike. Watch out, watch how the word spreads. If at first Faulkner, can Sartre be far behind.

# IN THE GALLERY: FOUR

Watching George Chuvalo working out for his fight with Mederos on Monday I was wondering if he would ever show that knockout punch that seems to be suggested by the hard, vicious glint that comes into his eyes when he swings. What has the look in a man's eyes or the way he feels got to do with a knockout punch? Just about everything. This came out in an argument I got into with Deacon Jack Allen as we watched and brooded over Chuvalo.

A man who didn't have a punch couldn't be taught to punch, I said pontifically, and no one seemed to know why this was so. A man might have the natural strength, the shoulders, the skill, and spend months or years punching away at the heavy bag, and yet, in the ring, he surprised himself if he ever knocked a man down. Maybe a punch was like a talent. If you weren't born with it you were just out of luck.

"What about McLarnin?" the Deacon said.

"What about him?"

"When I first knew McLarnin he was just a boxer."

"Are you sure he didn't just change his style, discovering he had a wonderful punch?"

"He certainly changed his style," the Deacon said. "I'm not saying anybody gave him his punch, although you can certainly work with a boy and correct his faults. What about the great Benny Leonard?"

"He was like McLarnin, wasn't he?"

"Yeah, though he started off as a boxer," the Deacon admitted grudgingly, "I guess he must have always had the punch."

So we went back to watching Chuvalo, the big eager kid with his natural savagery, and in my mind was this question; this time, against Mederos, would he be free of the nervousness and tension he showed against Baker, and would he show that he could get set for that one punch? With his great shoulders and huge legs and fine eagerness, would he also discover that he had the gift denied to a fine fighter like Willie Pastrano?

Pastrano is the best boxer among the heavies. It is true that he is not as fast with his hands as Patterson, but he moves around better. Those two other highly rated heavies, Machen and Foley, fight in the same flat-footed style, bobbing and weaving, both fast with their hands and always set to punch. Pastrano has restored some of the lost art of footwork to the division. But if you owned a piece of Pastrano you could break your heart wondering why he couldn't develop a punch. Of course, he can knock a man down, even sometimes knock him out. But with him it is all a matter of timing. He needs the cooperation of his opponent's jaw in its movement toward him. Like a lot of other fighters, he has the timing, but as for the natural punch, the murderous gift, he must wonder what it depends on.

A little old guy, who had been standing beside us, snorting sometimes to show his discontent, said suddenly, "I don't go for this. All these things can be taught. Look at golf. Is it such a mystery?"

"Up to a point, no."

"Why can't a fighter's punch be developed just as a golfer's swing can be straightened out? Why, even a woman, getting the right swing and improving her timing, can drive over 200 yards. Why not the same thing with a punch?"

The little old guy had a point, but there's more to the murderous punch than the timing. A Dempsey could hit from all angles, and even when off balance, and with the timing all wrong he could really hurt his opponent.

"Maybe there was a kind of desperation in a knockout punch," I said. "Why couldn't a scared little man turn suddenly and lash out with all the despair in his heart and knock you out?"

"It never happens," said the Deacon lugubriously, "because the scared guy in his heart is really running away. You see, a rabbit can't really hurt you. No," he said after meditating profoundly, "I'll tell you what the knockout punch really depends on. Temperament."

"But what kind of temperament?"

"The gambler's temperament. The kid with the great punch just naturally shoots the works. That's it. He risks all."

And come to think of it, we have all known such kids in schoolyards and back alleys and sandlots, all willing to take the reckless chance. Many of them weren't fighters, but in their own line they carried a knockout punch.

But now we were looking at Chuvalo thoughtfully. He was still green. He was in a strange position in his hometown, he was having to start his career by fighting only name fighters. We were wondering if he would at last show against Mederos that he was one of those lucky fighters who had the gambler's temperament.

*Toronto Telegram*, 1957

# SPEECH

I have the habit of listening to speech. I believe that each single word has a meaning. Each word is almost a living thing, and I have come to believe that when men and women use words believing they are saying one thing, the actual words often imply something else. The other night, I heard a young man and his girl engaging in a brief brawl of words. The young man was tired and irritable. The girl hadn't done something he had asked her to do. He blew up. "What the hell . . ." and then came a flow of intimate sexual abuse. She, in her turn, God damned him, offered to take his head and . . . In a minute or two they were on affectionate terms again. The words meant nothing, they might say. Well, I don't think words ever mean nothing. The man and the girl would be shocked if I insisted the brutal words represented some brutal contemptuous view they had of each other. I'm aware that it is a fashion now for those who call themselves lovers to address each other in this coarse style. Lovers of each other they may be, but they don't love words! And if they don't love the words they use on each other, or respect the words, then they can't really respect each other. The truth always begins in the words. The words are incarnational! Speech is incarnational.

# IN THE GALLERY: FIVE

It was Christmas. I was wandering about in the hockey crowds, then in poolrooms, bookie joints and back alleys, asking if anyone could tell me anything new about Christmas. I got nothing but broad smiles till I came upon Deacon Jack Allen in his gym.

There he was, lean and straight and ageless, his shoulders held back stiffly and with that mournful expression on his face that he got from counting the house too often at the Maple Leaf Garden fights.

"Jack, you have promoted hundreds of fights in forty years," I asked. "Were you ever a Santa Claus?"

"A Santa Claus! Me?" he asked. His voice was filled with dreadful uneasiness, as if he had a frightening picture of himself standing on the corner of Yonge and Albert, a lean Santa in a red suit and a long white beard, shaking a tambourine. "Things have been bad along the way," he said doubtfully, "but never that bad."

"But you've had such a stable of fighters, don't they come to you at Christmas?"

"Well, I'm no Christmas tree."

"Why not? Everything else has happened to you in the fight business."

"Just a minute," he said slowly, and I could see why he was called 'the Deacon.' With his best sad and tolerant expression he was looking back over the flock of fighters he had ministered to for the last forty years.

"Come to think of it – well, do you remember Bobby Eber?"

Indeed I did. Bobby Eber in the late twenties was as clever and cunning a mitman as ever fought around Toronto.

Sometimes he was known as Elbows McFadden.

"The trouble with Eber was that he was a bad boy," said the Deacon with the sigh a good church worker reserves for lost souls.

Eber wouldn't train, he said; he was a spendthrift and he was hard to handle. Well, one wintry day, a week before Christmas, the Deacon encountered Eber and he knew he was talking to a desperate man.

The cunning little fighter was destitute. His wife was going to have a baby, Eber said, and he had no groceries in the house, no money for a doctor, or stuff for the baby and it was Christmas time and he had nowhere to turn.

"Now Eber had been a bad boy," the Deacon repeated, as if this raised the question whether the peace of Christmas was only for good boys.

The Deacon had known all kinds of boys, good and bad, but he got to brooding about this bad boy's wife having a baby and he decided that possibly he should go to them bearing gifts.

The Deacon could have waited until Christmas Eve and like one of the Three Kings he could have shown up at the Eber place with gifts of gold, frankincense, and myrrh.

He decided that the role of one of the Kings didn't suit him. On the other hand he had always been one of the Wise Men of the East.

In his wisdom he pondered over the proper gifts for a down-and-out fighter whose wife at Christmas time was ready to welcome a little stranger.

With the right kind of gift he knew he should be able to say: "Peace be with you," but he himself had never known any peace that didn't include groceries.

Strange as it may sound, he saw that Eber could only find peace with a fight. The trouble was the Deacon had no fight card coming up before Christmas.

He looked far and wide in many cities till he came to Washington. There alone was a fellow Wise Man, alone at the time of the Feast of the Nativity.

The Deacon got on the phone and told his colleague about the baby coming to the Ebers and he told the story in such sad and beautiful tones that the colleague, in a panic of fear that his heart would be broken unless he got off the line, agreed quickly to give Eber a spot on the card and expense money to Washington.

So just before Christmas, with the Angelic Choir singing, Eber, out of condition, was in the ring taking his painful lumps and handing them out, knowing each blow he took brought him closer to his purse and home.

When he came home he was able to have groceries and gifts and the baby was born and had the proper swaddling clothes.

As for the Deacon, it didn't occur to him to say to Eber, "May the peace of Christmas be upon you, my son."

It would have been too horrible a thought.

It was the last thing a fight promoter, living on beak-busting, could wish on any tough, cunning fighter.

Yet, to this day they do say that a certain stiffness in the Deacon's shoulders comes from bearing the weight of a whole flock of angels that had settled on them during that particular Christmas week.

*Toronto Telegram,* 1957

# BAUDELAIRE

One night, when I was eye to eye with our giant white poodle, Nikki, talking to him, my wife asked why I kept calling him Baudelaire. I said I had just remembered he was a French poodle, and that his grandsire had been owned by Françoise Sagan, and that anyway, he seemed to like the name. Baudelaire, Baudelaire! Then, I found myself thinking of days in the thirties when two young American Jews, converts to Catholicism, had come to the Pontifical Institute of Medieval Studies to work under Etienne Gilson.

These two spiritual comrades had lived in France and had grown intoxicated on Peguy, Max Jacob, Cocteau, and Maritain, and I had grown very fond of one of them, Chapman, from Chicago. He had a rough time at the Institute. Outspoken as he was, wearing his heart of his sleeve, he was easily hurt. His aesthetic superiority, his French friends, his special bond with Maritain, exasperated some of his colleagues, but he and the other Jewish convert had each other. Maybe I tended to separate them. Chapman alone was my friend.

Then, one night after Christmas vacation when the returning Chapman came straight to see me, we got into my car to go and pick up his returning friend. After embracing each other, they got into the back seat of the car where they sat in silence. As we drove along, I heard Chapman say softly, "Notre Baudelaire." His friend repeated just as softly, "Notre Baudelaire," and in the silence that followed I felt quite left out, and a stranger to them, even to Chapman who had become the closest of my friends.

# FRANÇOIS MAURIAC

The death of François Mauriac, at the age of eighty-four, touched off some nostalgic memories for me. Mauriac, the master of French provincial life, wrote beautifully. I knew he was great, but I resisted every novel of his I read. Yet, often, I would go back and reread some pages, filled with admiration for his art, for his insightful thoughts. Indeed, I could recognize that he was in such mastery of the craft that his whole method had become a demonstration of temperament reacting to the human material; there seemed to be no separation between the thing seen and the way it was seen. In his hands the thing just was. Only a master can create this effect. And yet in my heart I always turned away from Mauriac.

The Catholic novelist *par excellence*. For thousands of Catholics he was. Yet was he? For General de Gaulle indeed he was, yet I went on believing that the Mauriac view of life, Christian though it might be called in the highest circles, wasn't for me. The book that made him famous was *The Desert of Love*. The very title of that book underlines the great theme that runs through all his work: the desert. The absence of love, the failure of love, a world without Christian love, or love of God. Now no one could turn away from the nobility of this theme. But Mauriac, it seemed to me, when he depicted men and women in their intimate carnal relationships, always loaded the cards on the side of the spirit, at least as he thought of it.

Every young man or young woman knows that physical love-making can become something ugly, yet just as easily – it can be something rapturous and exalted, too. Any man, coming to the end of his life and looking back on his lovemaking and finding the memory disgusting or empty of that flash of rapture is a man who, as I see it, failed love in the deepest possible terms; the spirit and flesh when they are made one in physical love.

Back in the thirties, I remember, I used to complain to Jacques Maritain, the French philosopher, and a friend of Mauriac's, that Mauriac refused to see that a loving woman with a man in her arms would not be noticing his blackheads, the large pores of his skin – not always anyway. Maritain, smiling, said that he believed Mauriac suffered from a dualism, the spirit and flesh always at war. It may be that this dualism, this Christian dualism, which a reader feels as a kind of coldness in him, made it hard for the North American reading public to embrace him. Another Catholic novelist, Graham Greene, who is not as great an artist, manages to be extraordinarily popular. Indeed, with Greene, the whole Christian machinery seems to make it easier for the reader to understand him and perhaps, too, the reader feels a large human sympathy in Greene. Mauriac wrote mainly about narrow provincial life – the countryside around Bordeaux. I asked Edmund Wilson once if he didn't agree that Mauriac wrote beautifully. To my astonishment Wilson said that he had never read Mauriac; he simply refused to read novels about Bordeaux and French provincial life.

Though Mauriac was devout, all his work shaped by his Catholicism, he was never simply an establishment Catholic. His monumental integrity as an artist shines in every line of his work and he evidently carried this integrity into his life because there was a nobility of independence about him. He was a Christian who was his own man, and he proved this during the time of the civil war in Spain, when the dictator Franco was offered to the world as the perfect Christian knight by the Pope, and the Pope asked Maritain and Mauriac to write about the issues involved from their Catholic point of view. Mauriac and Maritain denounced those who espoused Franco as a Christian hero. Mauriac told the world that the Spanish war was simply a civil war.

Some have hailed his last novel, *Maltaverne*, written when he was over eighty, as a masterpiece. It is a tightly written, beautifully controlled story of the adolescence of a young man who is to become an artist, a novelist in Paris. The boy is in revolt against the ugly Catholic puritan world of his mother, a world centred around Bordeaux. Her lust, her passion, is to pass on to the boy her vast property holdings. Also, she wants him to coddle and marry a very young local girl who will bring him more property. Never having seen nor known this girl, he nonetheless despises her, he calls her *the louse*. She knows this. The blight of his cold contempt is on anything they might become.

But then one day he sees the girl bathing naked by a pond in the woods. Startled, she recognizes him, and runs from him because she knows his feeling for her. Later, she is raped and killed in the woods by a woodcutter. What was so moving for me, and what seemed to bring into focus all my feelings about Mauriac's work over the years, was his description, as seen through the boy's eyes, of the naked young girl. She had for him an ecstatic beauty that made him shiver, a glimpse of the warm perfect beauty of the flesh. Reading that description for the second time, I was bemused. I had to fit it into my view of Mauriac and my certainty that for him the flesh was a mean experience, and then I thought, how ironic, yet how moving, how wonderful and beautiful that Mauriac, at the end of his life, should have the compassion to offer the warmest and most exalted glimpse of life as he saw it in the body of an unspoiled, untouched young girl.

*CBC Anthology*

# WOULD YOU GIVE THIS BOOK
# TO A FIFTEEN-YEAR-OLD?

❧❧❧

The news that Attorney General Kelso Roberts of Ontario has set up a panel of four to review "objectionable" books took me back to my appearance in a Montreal court where I acted as a witness for the defence when the crown charged that D.H. Lawrence's book, *Lady Chatterley's Lover*, was obscene. In that case, the censor stood out in the open. The kind of censorship being offered by the Ontario panel will be hidden and hard to cope with, but I'm sure that some of the questions put to me at the Montreal trial are bound to come up again and again in the minds of those on the new Ontario panel.

At that trial I was asked a question I found some difficulty in answering readily. The question was: would I give this book to a fifteen-year-old boy to read – assuming I had a fifteen-year-old boy?

It struck me, at the time, as an unfair question because it could not be answered with a "Yes" or a "No." It is also an unfair appeal to watchful and innocent parents. I am not ducking the question, though. I have never regarded the book as a manual for the sex instruction of fifteen-year-old boys. It is a novel.

The more I reflect upon it, however, the more unreal the question becomes, the more unreal the role the fifteen-year-old boy is supposed to play when we try to judge whether or not Lawrence's book is obscene. So many lawyers, clergymen and parents seem to assume that these boys, and girls, too, would read *Lady Chatterley* if it was within their reach. Is this true? It is not. I say it is utterly unreal to draw them into the matter and pretend they should influence our judgement. Any lawyer or clergyman may check on this statement by visiting cigar and drug stores of those provinces where the book is on sale.

I took the trouble to ask some questions, and while I'm aware that those who hate all such books will say dealers would not tell the truth, there was one dealer I knew very well whose store was always crowded with young boys and girls, who made such good sense that I believed him utterly. Not once, he said, had he sold a copy of *Lady Chatterley's Lover* to a boy or girl of fifteen or sixteen. The book, he said, was far too literary, too intellectual for them. On two occasions he saw boys of some education thumbing through the book. He gathered that they had heard adults talking about the book. They didn't buy it. Maybe they were looking for the four-letter words, he said. On the other hand, they could hear the same words outside on the street.

In any general discussion, then, I think we should stop pretending boys and girls of fifteen and sixteen are reaching out with hot, eager little hands for books of the quality of Lawrence's book. They aren't. What the book is really doing is testing the workability of our new definition of obscenity in the Criminal Code: "A book, a dominant characteristic of which is the undue exploitation of sex."

I was talking to Frank Scott of the McGill law school, a poet himself as well as a brilliant legal mind, and I asked him how he would define obscenity. We agreed you probably couldn't get a better definition than "dirt for dirt's sake." How clear and beautifully simple this definition is! I wish it were in the Criminal Code, for not only can it be readily understood by most men and women, but it has the advantage of considering the intention, the purpose of the work. It is the intention of the work as a whole which has been considered of the utmost importance in all the recent great court decisions, whether in the United States, England or Norway.

It seems to me that only the people who thumb through books, or have single paragraphs called to their attention, or those who find any revelation of the intimate relations of men and women disgusting in themselves, could mistake Lawrence's lofty intention. His desire to give a basic dignity to the sexual relationship is so apparent, of such a tract-like determination, that it weakens the book artistically. There is fun in sex as well as this high-minded sense of harmony that Lawrence exalts. To me, Lawrence is a born puritan who came to hate that withered world of the colliery town in England. He hated it for its drabness, its lack of colour, its inhumanity, and it seemed to him that, in this world, sex had become a drab, shameful and inhuman thing, too. He is, it seems to me, still a puritan moralist, with a deep sense of what is right and wrong, and he was convinced that if the basic relationship between a man and a woman was wrong, if it had no glory, no ecstasy, then the man and the woman were truly part of that drab world.

It is true, of course, that a book with this message delivered with great frankness of language could not have been openly circulated fifty years ago. Does this make our attitude to sex more morally reprehensible than that of the Victorians? Well, some of the attitudes to sex that were publicly accepted by respectable people in our fathers' times were simply lies about life. Some of these lies, hardening into conventions, must have been accepted as the truth by respectable men and women, and heaven knows the damage they did to homes. For example, there was the conventional belief that no respectable woman was really interested in sex. It was understood, of course, that she submitted to her husband, but only as a dutiful wife. If she abandoned herself with any rapture, then the poor husband was supposed to understand he had a hussy on his hands. How many sour failures in marriage were concealed by this stern puritan respectability? On the other hand – and this is surely one of Lawrence's points in *Lady Chatterley's Lover* – maybe many good women went to their graves too ashamed to wonder what they were missing. Is it any wonder that the giant Tolstoy said the greatest of tragedies were the tragedies of the bedroom, and they didn't get written about?

In our time, though – and it is the time when some are wondering if Lawrence ought to be banned as an obscene writer – novelists, playwrights and advertising agencies have enjoyed the greatest license. In fact, the pendulum has swung so far the other way that a normal sexual relationship shown in a book or on the stage fails to attract much attention. Look at the success of *Lolita!* It is the story of a middle-aged man's lust for a twelve-year-old girl, and it was read with avidity in hundreds of thousands of homes. A story of perversion! On the stage, Tennessee Williams offers shock after shock and Norman Mailer goes on projecting those strange sexual fantasies of his in his work, and in the world of commerce as many commodities as possible on billboards and on television are sold by way of some sex symbol.

The sex symbol, the great North American sex symbol, dominating our world, Lawrence would say, is without any real sex behind it. The symbol takes the place of the sex. I think that Lawrence, in our time, emerges as a kind of innocent. In this commercial world of sex symbols, of perversions, of violence and sadism, a world in which all the sexual problems are even discussed freely in the women's magazines – the discussion made respectable, of course, because it appears in what is called a medical column – Lawrence in his novel wanted to glorify only what was natural. In *Lady Chatterley's Lover,* far from being his best novel since it is too much of an intellectual thesis, he shows a truly religious respect for sex. That's why he seems to me to be an innocent in our time.

But there is a simple explanation. Lawrence uses the four-letter words. He uses them not as men use them for cursing or just as marks of vulgar bad language; he uses them accurately for their true meaning. The lady's lover, it should be remembered, is a game-keeper. The words come naturally to him. And besides, the game-keeper must use them in his lady's presence to shock her into an awareness of the primitive reality of their lovemaking.

These four-letter words are Anglo-Saxon. Polite people in our society use words of French or Latin derivation instead of these Anglo-Saxon terms, for it has come to pass that the more privileged and better educated classes – those, in short, who have the money – make it a mark of gentility to use words of foreign extraction. Surely snobbery as much as decency is involved here. Or do we believe that the poor and uneducated who don't know the words of Latin origin are indecent? Anyway, it is surely obvious that for Law-rence to have his gamekeeper using the words of great gentility rather than his own native words, would have been false to his char-acter.

A lawyer said to me, "Oh, come on now. Would you yourself use those four-letter words in your own living room if you had company? Or would you read aloud some of those brutally frank passages?"

It is a ridiculous question, a silly comment on the book. These words, these paragraphs are of the most intimate nature. A man would not read the passages aloud to a woman unless they were sharing a most intimate relationship, nor should he. No one has yet suggested that *Lady Chatterley* ought to be read aloud at neigh-bourhood gatherings as a form of togetherness. And here is an im-portant point: there are words, scenes and descriptions that can be permitted in a book because the reading of a book is a private matter. To put the same scenes with the same words on television or on the stage might be socially offensive and in very bad taste. Reading is a private matter; a performance is a public affair, so it should be obvious that in a civilized society the reader should enjoy the widest latitude according to his taste.

While recognizing that the puritans, those who feel uneasy about anything that delights the senses and especially the delights of sex, can never accept a book like *Lady Chatterley's Lover*, I have one suggestion to make: let them in their turn at least recognize that Lawrence was fiercely honest; he was without despair; in no way was he negative; he believed in tenderness, sex, without it being hateful to him. Above all, he was always on the side of life.

*Toronto Star Weekly*, 1960

# PAESANI, COME STATE?

If you have ever been out at the end of the Bloor carline in Toronto, east or west, at 6 in the morning, you may have seen the trucks loaded with Italian labourers. They usually stop there for a few minutes waiting for workers who weren't picked up at their homes, and these come hurrrying off the streetcars, husky men in lime-marked, blue-denim pants, sweaters, old hats and heavy, mud-stained boots. Ditch diggers, bricklayers, carpenters and their assistants, they climb aboard and head for the construction job in the suburbs.

One of the men you might have seen is Rino Pellagrina, a man of 30, not big and powerful, just about five feet nine, but well-knit and sturdy. Nothing about him makes him stand out. He has no exotic immigrant touch or flair, he has no more formal education than the others. Yet just because of what he is, a builder, he is an important person now in this country.

With his own hands and his tools Rino is one of the Italian immigrants, the builders who are helping to shape the structure of the new city in these days of boom construction. Whenever the soil is broken, wherever dilapidated structures are torn down so that towering new office buildings and vast blocks of apartments may rise, wherever giant expressways are carved from the earth, wherever bungalows and shopping plazas appear, Rino and his compatriots have a hand in it. A hundred thousand of them have come to Toronto in the '50s, as many as 15,000 a year. They come, in the main, to get in on the construction work, because for 2,000 years building has been in the blood of Italians.

When Rino, along with 400 other Italian labourers on the same ship, came into Halifax harbour one day seven years ago, he did not feel very important to anybody. All these labourers were being brought to Canada to work on the CNR tracks. They were from the little places of Italy – the small towns and the villages – and they seemed to be leaving behind not a country but those separate little places. A man was proud of his town having the biggest bell or specializing in a famous dish or a style of dress. The things like that were home.

That day while they waited in the harbour, Rino, standing with the others at the ship's rail, bemused by the strange frame houses on the hills of Halifax and not knowing what was ahead for him, had one profound conviction: he had come to the shore of a nation where there would always be steady employment for a man willing to work at building something.

Rino had lived with his mother and sister in a little town in northern Italy near the Alps. His father was dead. His six years of schooling, mainly technical, had been broken up by the war. Working in a lumber mill, he had come to dread the long seasonal lay-offs. A man couldn't save a cent. His life could never be any bigger than the life he had had, the life his father and grandfather had known. One day in his town he saw a notice on the bulletin board in the station announcing that labourers were wanted to work on the CNR tracks in Canada. It stirred his imagination, for he could not think that in such a big, new, rich, growing country there could ever be real unemployment. So he spoke to a young priest in his town who arranged for his name to be put on the list. His passage was to be paid for out of the salary he would earn in Canada. And so he said good bye to his mother and sister and Italy.

Before the 400 labourers could look around Halifax, they were put on a train for Montreal. On the long ride they watched the country unrolling under their eyes; then they were in Montreal, which looked to Rino like a big new temporary structure for a city, and 120 of the gang were quickly put on a train for Manitoba; 80, Rino among them, took another train for Hornepayne in northern Ontario. So, within about two weeks, Rino seemed to have been hurled from sun-splashed Italy with its pink cottages and its golden-brown old buildings to a boxcar on a siding at Hornepayne at the edge of a vast forest wilderness where he was to live for a year with 11 of his compatriots. The boxcar became their home. It had the bunks, the stove, the food. They weren't a section gang, just assistant labourers getting 90 cents an hour for 10 hours a day in the summer, nine in the winter.

Without knowing it, Rino, cooped up in that boxcar in a wilderness of woods and tracks, was in a similar position to hundreds of other immigrant Italians who have come straight to Toronto. As many as 12 of them have been cooped up in a private home, the landlord making sure he gets the money for their room and board. Sleeping on floors and sofas, cut off from any real contact with the family of the house, they huddle together and wait for the jobs . . . Steady work! It doesn't matter how heavy or dirty it is, they'll take it when it comes. They'll do it and pay off the debt for their passage. Marvellously, they won't become public charges. Their strength is in their willingness to work, to build. But when I said to Rino the other day that the Italians had always been builders, that 2,000 years ago they had built all the great roads of Europe, he looked at me, smiling slowly, shaking his head, and said with dignity in his slow, careful English that he didn't know anything about that; the plain fact was that the Italians coming to this country were willing to start at the bottom with the dirty, heavy, unskilled pick-and-shovel work no one else would do.

From Hornepayne, Rino and his companions always moved up and down the line to points like Armstrong or Capreol, working on the tracks with nothing to do in the evenings but sit around their boxcar home and look at each other or play cards or sing or joke. They hardly ever saw a hotel or a woman. When the fierce Canadian winter came with its silent, long nights, Rino used to dream of the sunlight on the fields of Italy, of his mother and sister, and wonder sometimes what he was doing so far away from home with his life spent in a boxcar in the woods. But he thought he was needed in this country; after all, they had come after him.

It never occurred to this young Italian labourer, shovelling snow from the frozen switches, that there were some Anglo-Saxon Canadians who were uneasy about having him and his kind in such numbers in the country. What were the grumbling complaints? Well, these Italians, for one thing, were Latin; they were Mediterranean and too emotional, and they went in for those gaudy pink colours; and they were noisy, content with a low standard of living, and they weren't a people with a stiff upper lip, and besides, they were Roman Catholic, and they cluttered up the sidewalks, standing outside their churches on Sunday, and anyway someone ought to call the Minister of Immigration about it. Rino, in his boxcar with his shovel, didn't think of himself as an exotic child of the Mediterranean. He simply thought he was doing a job no Canadian wanted to do.

In this longest, loneliest year of his life, it often seemed to him he was in a country where they had strange, frightening customs. His boss had told them that when they stopped work to eat they were not to have animated conversions; they were just to say, "Pass the salt" or "Pass the catsup," then keep quiet; Rino thought this must be the way with Canadians at meal times. A pretty grim, sober country; people keeping away from each other. Later, however, he found out that the company had made this rule because it had learned from experience that men often get into arguments and fights while eating.

But there were other things that fascinated Rino. In one of the gangs was a Canadian college student, doing the same manual work as the others yet teaching them English in the evenings. How astonishing this was to the Italians. A university student working with them! An educated man telling them that Canadian students often worked as waiters or diggers without feeling they were belittling themselves! In Italy such a thing could never happen, the Italians said to each other. In Italy the university student was always "Poppa's boy," too proud to demean himself with menial heavy work. What an upsetting, wonderful country this Canada could be, Rino thought, if educated people, students, had this good opinion of humble labour.

Toward the end of his year, the gang moved as far south as Stratford in their railway car, and Rino caught his first glimpse of the settled farmland of southern Ontario. Soon, however, he was back up north again. Then, one day in Capreol, a fellow worker, who had come over on the ship with him, told Rino he was going to Toronto where he had a relative . . . That's the Italian story in this country – the story of the relative! Anyway, the fellow was going to become a carpenter's assistant, and he asked Rino to go with him.

Rino, the young immigrant, the unskilled worker, had made the break from the bush, the railroad tracks and the pick and shovel – as has happened hundreds of times. He moved into a house in Toronto's Bloor-Dufferin area and he and his friend got the job with the relative as carpenter assistants. He wrote home proudly to his mother and his young sister that he was in Toronto, a big spread-out city not like those pictures they had seen of New York, a city rising in the sky, and yet when you got downtown this Toronto did have the look of a towering city; he wrote, too, that he liked the way the houses, no matter the neighbourhood, had the little patches of green lawn in front of them.

Rino could have made himself at home very easily in Toronto, spending most of his spare time in the heart of Little Italy among his own people. Though there are 120,000 Italians in Toronto in a neighbourhood beginning at Bathurst and College Sts. and fanning out north and south to Dundas and Bloor Sts. as it goes westward to Dufferin St., the old Italian colony is in those blocks off Bathurst St. adjacent to Grace St. and Manning Ave. There you can walk in the sunlight and see only the warm Italian faces, the boys with thick, shiny, carefully combed hair, the women with opulent figures and languid movements, a laughing earthiness in the faces of the children. It is a neighbourhood of grocery stores with the smell of spices and salami and coffee. Little groups stand at doorways, each boy cutting a figure. Crowds loiter at the curb after mass at St. Agnes' Church, their voices, their expressions, their gestures bringing something of the vivaciousness of the Mediterranean world into the gray Toronto streets.

Fifty years ago in Toronto it was assumed that an Italian immigrant would turn out to be a musician, the owner of a fruit store, a restaurateur or a waiter. Then they went into the construction business. They became contractors and builders and some grew very rich. Today they have their own newspaper, the *Corriere Canadese*. They have the Italia soccer club with its rabid following. They have produced doctors, lawyers and musicians but few political figures. In New York the Italians have had their La Guardia as mayor, and they are deep in Tammany Hall. Nothing of the kind has happened here. Only the other day a woman said to me, "Why haven't the Italians risen to the top?" But what was it like here in Toronto just 30 years ago when the Italian colony was small? Toronto was overwhelmingly British and Protestant, and so were most of the public figures. They had to be. In the new polyglot metropolitan city with the great influx of Italians since the war, it ought to be different for them, and yet it isn't. I asked Rino, the newcomer, why things hadn't changed.

The Italians of his age have a bad memory of politics in Italy, he said, for they were children of Mussolini's time, when politics was a dangerous game. But an Italian parish priest shrugged at this explanation; he said the thousands of new immigrants simply hadn't been here long enough to have a good understanding of Canadian politics; they were too busy trying to get established economically. The New York Italians, he said, had been in America at least a generation longer. A little more time was needed here.

During those first months Toronto's Italian colony was there for Rino, but he was determined to live outside it, if he could, so he would lose the feeling as quickly as possible that he was a stranger in a big alien city. The loneliness he had felt on the streets was worse than the loneliness he had known in the boxcar at Hornepayne. He wished their were street cafés where he could sit and watch life flow by, but Toronto seemed to be an indoor city, everything hidden away and locked to him. There were bars and taverns, of course, but they seemed dark and cheerless. When he wasn't with his own people he felt conspicuous, as if all the strangers were waiting for him to do the wrong thing. He could laugh later on, listening to another Italian immigrant telling how he had been on a street with busy traffic and had started to cross at the intersection when suddenly there had been a grinding of brakes, shouting, a cop's whistle, angry yells. As he scampered back to the pavement, frightened, he believed he was such a monstrosity he had stopped the traffic in the city.

Then Rino did what the Italian immigrant always does. In Toronto four churches have mainly Italian congregations; he turned to one, St. Mary of the Angels.

The parish church is always a haven for Italian immigrants. It draws them gently into a community, opening a door to a wider life in the city. St. Mary of the Angels offered a night class in English, and Rino took it. He began to sing in the choir. In the *Corriere Canadese* he read about a recreational club for young men, and he joined it, too; he also joined the church dances, meeting some Canadian-born girls, but not quite joining in with them, for he had got the idea that he would be come kind of a disappointment if they had heard all Italians were wildly romantic Latin lovers.

Speaking much better English meeting Canadians everywhere, Rino became aware of that uneasy criticism of Italian immigrants that is voiced in some circles. No one called him "wop" or "dago," as might have happened in the old days; those words now are used mainly by Italians when laughing and kidding each other. Nor did he stand in Union Station, as I have stood, hearing somebody muttering, "Look! Bringing more of them dirty Eyetalians in, and who's going to support them?"

By this time, though, Rino had gathered that he was not quite welcome in the country, particularly by those who fancy they have nailed down the cultural pattern. The Germans, they say, are businesslike; so are the Dutch and the energetic Swedes – all the solid Teutonic Europeans, but not the southern ones!

This didn't worry Rino. He could have curled his lip, of course, and pointed out that the two great sources of civilization in the last 2,000 years have been centred in his country – the Roman Empire and the Renaissance. But these facts of history were too remote for him or the critics. Instead, his pride was soothed by little things; he saw going on around him every day. A man could even laugh a bit to himself about it. How can you feel your country is looked down on when you see established citizens proudly wearing Italian silk suits, or stylish women sporting Italian shoes and handbags and adopting Italian haircuts, and department stores take page advertisements of Italian styles in dresses? It made him a little proud of himself. And Italian food and wine seemed to be all around him, too, and when he passed a movie house he might see the lovely faces of Sophia Loren or Gina Lollobrigida, all these little things making him feel that he, an Italian himself, ought to have a place in the Toronto world.

A year passes, two, three, and Rino had moved westward to Bloor and Runnymede. He had left the carpentry one winter after his landlord got him a job in a large grocery story – working in the fruit department, of course, because he was Italian, although it is only the southern Italians who know abut fruit – then he had gone back to carpentry, building bungalows for an Italian contractor. He was a skilled worker now, getting $1.70 an hour. Yet gnawing away in his mind was the feeling that he wasn't completely established in this country. A part of him still seemed rooted in Italy . . . It was his mother, his sister, his family, for that is the way the Italian story goes in this country. When the immigrant begins to dream of bringing his family over, he knows he has established himself and is going to stay.

Having kept his accounts carefully always making the payments for his passage, Rino managed to save some money, and three years ago his mother and his young sister came to live with him. Italy still drags at his mother's heart, but the young sister loves it here.

The thing Rino, the carpenter, likes about this country is hard to put into words, so he expresses it by telling again abut that Canadian college student, the first Canadian he had known, who had worked with the gang of labourers on the tracks in the bush. Work is respectful here, Rino still thinks. The vast new country needs the city builders. He is a builder. If you do a good job, he says, you have importance and dignity.

*Toronto Star Weekly*, 1960

# AN OCEAN AWAY

By the time I came to think of English literature as the literature of another country, not my own, much of it had been ground into me. Happily for me, and most influentially, my parents were of the generation that took to the English poets as the general public now takes to the most popular novelists. As a boy I could rhyme off hundreds of lines from Tennyson, Byron, Keats, Moore, Wordsworth, Kipling, without thinking of them as literature. This was a fine thing for me.

When I was about twenty and at college, I began to write stories. From then on, even though I was supposed to be studying English literature, all my reading was done to serve my own selfish purpose. Which English prose writers could help me, which ones did I feel close to? By this time I had become aware that the language in which I wanted to write, a North American language which I lived by, had rhythms and nuances and twists and turns quite alien to English speech. When I showed some of my first stories to academic men highly trained in English literature, I could see them turning up their noses. "A failure of language," one said to me; and feeling contrary I said, "No, a failure on your part to understand the language." I had decided that language of feeling and perception, and even direct observation, had to be the language of the people I wrote about, who did not belong in an English social structure at all. Under these circumstances my reading of the traditional English novelists was having a strange effect on me. The reading deepened my desire to write, and that was wonderful. But I was a young man looking for a master, sometimes thinking I had found one, and then walking out on him, impatient and irritated.

I had this feeling only about the English novel – the poetry was another matter. From every period came some English poetry that seemed to belong to me, teach me something about the use of words in the expression of new ways of feeling. The very great writers are always one's contemporaries. And while trying to learn about prose I would find myself watching the clean relationship of one word to another in the poetry of Chaucer. I would wonder if that freshness and brightness could ever be achieved today in prose. Or I would brood over the Border ballads. A storywriter had so much to learn from them. In them was the mystery of what could be left out. And coming into our own time there was always a poet, a Hardy, Hopkins, or Yeats to convince me, oddly enough, that for the prose writer the dew could still be on the grass.

Of course, from the beginning I had to forget about Shakespeare or Marlowe. Such a glorious cascade of words coming out of such a spectacular time could only drive a young writer mad, or stop him writing.

But English prose and the novel! Since I had to be always reading an English novel of another century I think now I was using so many of them as splendid irritants, provoking me into finding out what I wanted to do myself. There is no generosity of appreciation in this approach. None whatever. But young writers are always most arrogant, either openly or secretly, in thinking only of the enlargement of their own work. Fielding, I liked. I liked his directness, his humour, his worldliness, his health, his point of view. I admired Defoe. The scene in *Robinson Crusoe* where Robinson discovers the footprint on the sand seemed to me to be unique in literature; the heart of all storytelling was in that scene. And *Moll Flanders* was a delight; the *Journal of the Plague Year*, too. In the early years, I thought the prose of Swift might be great for narrative; later on I wasn't so sure of him. Anyway, with these writers I felt at home. I loved the way Jane Austen wrote, but Mr. Darcy spoiled her for me. And there were two other writers who were quite outside that quarrel I had taken up with the great English novelists of the past. Sterne's *Tristram Shandy*, for one, Sterne being in that book what biologists would call, I suppose, a "sport"; the other being Emily Brontë's *Wuthering Heights*, a lonely, isolated work in English literature. In atmosphere, mood, scene, action it was all one. Isolated though it was in English it seemed to me to be perfectly in the ancient romantic European tradition of *Tristan and Isolde*, and love beyond the grave.

As for the great ones in the language – Dickens, Thackeray, Scott, Trollope, Smollett, Richardson – well, Dickens will do to make my point. I wish earnestly I had been able to give myself to him. What other writer ever had as much talent, such a wild boldness of imagination, and sheer reportorial skill? And yet he could not influence me. I found I simply didn't believe in the story he was telling – never the whole story. Friends of mine would say, "Don't be ridiculous. No one who reads Dickens bothers about the coincidences, the vast improbabilities, the endings, or what the thing adds up to as a whole. You read him for the characters and the wonderful things along the way." The characters are indeed so grand and colourful that they do exist in a separate world of the imagination. But I wanted a novel to have an impact as a whole – to offer some one vision of life, giving the whole thing its own reality. This was my prejudice, the way my mind worked. And it seemed to me that whether I was reading Smollett or Trollope or Dickens or Thackeray I was in a tangled English garden in which I might come upon rare and delightful flowers which oughtn't to have been there at all. It was the novel as an entertainment, a loosely knit variety show. With this prejudice in me I naturally turned away to the French and the Russians.

But even in these literatures the great English novelists pursued me to confound me. I discovered that Dostoevsky did read Dickens and liked him. And Richardson, whom I thought rather dull and sentimental, was Laclos' direct influence. I regarded Sir Walter Scott's novels as rather preposterous as writing (and by the way, what a mockery of writing that an author like James Hogg, of the same period, and who had a clean and beautiful style, should have been left in limbo while Scott was exalted), yet I found Goethe speaking of Scott with admiration and Balzac doing the same. What could I say but, "It's something in the air at the time. The first fresh wind will blow it away."

Back in 1929, just when I was coming out of college, the big name writers in English letters were Wells, Galsworthy, Shaw and Bennett. For Galsworthy I had a complete blind spot. He didn't mean anything to me. The younger Wells of *Tono Bungay* I enjoyed immensely. Bennett was another matter. In *The Old Wives' Tale* and the *Clayhanger* series he was a serious writer, deliberately following a method, the creation of character and scene by the slow deliberate building up of physical detail. But here was the rub. Here was the change taking place under my young eyes. Wasn't this the kind of thing that Zola did much better? And wouldn't Galsworthy have liked to think that he was under the influence of Flaubert, and didn't this mean that the erratic, irregular, sprawling, fanciful, episodic native English novel that irritated and stimulated me was yielding to the international influences? It was as if these novelists, who flowered before the First World War, were like the young men of fashion in the eighteenth century; they had taken the Grand Tour and made it even grander by including Russia too.

My real sense of personal involvement with English and Irish writers, the drawing of them into my life, came at this time, and it was a fine time, for it was just when I was starting out for myself. New impulses, new feelings, new forms, new glimpses of reality seemed to be coming from England. I had to know all about D.H. Lawrence. I used to get into excited arguments late at night about whether Virginia Woolf, with her technique, had added a new dimension, a new eye, or whether her work did not represent simply an over-refinement of sensibility, a lady who could not have written any other way. And were the stories of Katherine Mansfield to be compared at all with Chekhov's? Weren't they rather like Japanese prints? And Joseph Conrad! He was so utterly un-English in temperament and yet he was getting strange new effects and bringing in new people too; lonely superior men of honour, and a view of women that eluded me completely. It was a happy time. A writer knows he is happy in his reading when he gets carried away in his imagination, as he did when he was a boy of fourteen, say, and is reading *Treasure Island* for the first time; and the writing that was coming from England in those days I read in this way.

The two writers who came closest to me, whose work I would have liked somehow to have influenced my temperament, my equipment, as a writer, although I knew they hadn't, were James Joyce and William Butler Yeats. Yeats gave back to me something I hadn't had since boyhood – lines, stanzas to remember, verses that came singing readily in my head, though I had never tried to commit them to memory. And there was real elation in the discovery of Joyce's *Dubliners*. Young writers I met in New York would agree it was one of the important books. A book that had to be known. For me it belonged with Sherwood Anderson's *Winesburg, Ohio,* and Chekhov, and the good stories of Maupassant. And to go along with Joyce from the *Dubliners* to the *Portrait of the Artist,* and then into *Ulysses* was the joy of pure discovery. One's own little window on the world kept widening.

Looking back, those Irish writers, and their Abbey Theatre, must have brought a kind of new magic into the British writing scene. I remember that Thomas Wolfe used to complain sourly that every third-rate Irish poet who came to New York was crowned with laurel and given too much to drink. But who was more under the influence of Joyce than Wolfe himself. And I remember, too, that when I was only twenty, Hemingway refused to share my enthusiasm for Synge; he was even doubtful of Yeats, but I thought at the time he was dead wrong. Synge was perfectly what he was. Frankly, the Irish Twilight movement, or what Joyce called "the Irish toilet," didn't appeal to me at all. But there were beautiful talents involved in it, and George Moore could tell me all about it, Moore who was so determined to write like a Frenchman himself.

I had never included Shaw among these Irish writers. Shaw was all around me, and everyone else – he saw to that – but I thought of him as an English writer. I knew that Yeats, too, was Anglo-Irish, but I did not think of him as an English writer. Years later, when I read the St. John Ervine biography of Shaw, I understood why I had had this feeling; he convinced me I had been right. For that matter, my attitude to Shaw always puzzled me. From my undergraduate days on, I applauded him, was amused, and delighted he was in this world, and yet as a writer he never came close to me. The great dramatists of the time, for me, were O'Casey and O'Neill.

Having said at the beginning that I had always found myself carping at the traditional English novel, trying to draw away from it, one must wonder how I managed to get such vast stimulation out of English and Irish writers of the generation just ahead of me. The answer is: though an ocean away from me, those writers seemed to be of my world. It was as if fiction writers of the whole western world, since the turn of the century, had begun to share the same sources, the same influences and were becoming recognizable to each other. In some ways, of course, this is a pity. Nowadays, when I pick up a novel by an English writer, I find myself hoping that in structure and view and level of insight, it may be radically different from any novel by an American.

In the last few years, I have found myself involved and fascinated by a trend in the theatre and the novel in England. It may be that Europeans, North Americans and English writers are all trying to cope with the same problem, a sense of spiritual rootlessness that is general in the hearts and minds of men these days. It is no longer a matter for an island literature. The island days may have passed. Take Beckett's *Waiting for Godot*. Where does it belong? And the dramatist Pinter? Isn't the human condition he tries to make something of as true of New York or Stockholm as it is of London? And Golding's *Lord of the Flies*. Where does it come from? Graham Greene went off in another direction. And I found it provoking and stimulating. Greene, accepting man and his relationship with God as something revealed with finality within the Catholic church, had found a whole dramatic apparatus for a writer. Yet the thing that was so interesting, and which I felt to be exemplifying one particular English tradition, was the kind of dank and dismal Catholicism that came out of this apparatus. Greene, in the novels *The Heart of the Matter* and *The End of the Affair*, and the plays, *The Living Room* and *The Potting Shed*, may have been coping with what are called "spiritual problems," but after putting down a novel, or on the way from the theatre, I would find myself muttering "arsenic and old lace." What a hopeless spiritual trap men got caught in. And this awareness of evil! Wasn't it the old English Puritanism being fanned into flames again? Yet hundreds of thousands of readers found it new and attractive. What was going on?

The same thing in Golding. In his *Lord of the Flies*, critics and a million undergraduates were enchanted to discover that children, left to themselves, were naturally "evil." This ancient view of things, which is not too far away from Greene's, seems to be strangely acceptable to the young. One wonders why. Why do they take to it so readily? Is it a comforting looking back?

Pinter, on the surface, seems to be wildly at odds with Greene and Golding, but is he? He has great skill at dialogue. He deals frankly with fantasy. Anyone can see he likes playing with his fantasy. Yet don't the hypnotic trivia add up to a belittlement of all purpose, of all man's claims to have some dignity – man is really a bit of a worm – and doesn't this mean that Pinter's next and inevitable step is to be towards the discovery that man is so trivial and groping because he is flawed: he is "evil" and needs grace?

Each of these men, Greene, Golding and Pinter, have picked out different fantasies, which give their work a striking power. Yet what has been so absorbing these days is a growing conviction, born of my reading of these English writers, that the old English puritan view of life, which Lawrence tried so desperately hard to free himself from, and could not, is appearing again in these chosen fantasies as a new light, and I am completely bemused that the young find it novel and attractive.

*Times Literary Supplement,* 1964

# SCOTT FITZGERALD

❧❀❧

Scott Fitzgerald has a high place in American letters, but strange things have happened to the Fitzgerald reputation over the years. Without batting an eye, one of Scott Fitzgerald's scholarly admirers said the other day that Fitzgerald had come "to grips more fully than any novelist of his generation with modern movements in western culture and philosophy," and that in his own person, Fitzgerald had not only acted out the role of the genteel romantic hero, but in his work he had transformed the whole genteel romantic tradition. Slightly bemused, I had to ask, "Was this really Fitzgerald?"

The view that Fitzgerald was personally acting out that role is derived from all the familiar information, but certainly the word "genteel," if it has any meaning at all, is not to be applied to Fitzgerald's life. A romantic? Of course. Extravagantly so. In his way, he was a kind of Madame Bovary. He was quite an actor, too. But as for being a critic and great thinker – a student of western culture and philosophy? Really!

Fitzgerald had his insights. He had a remarkable sensibility. But even in these areas he was always personal – and a truly great dramatic character in the sense that he could say one thing, do another, and think another.

The real Fitzgerald dilemma was neither romantic nor tragic. It was utterly commonplace. He wanted to make a lot of money, yet he wanted to rise above the practice that gave him the money. It sounds elegant now to say that in turning out all those stories for the *Saturday Evening Post*, Fitzgerald was mastering the genteel romantic tradition, but other writers – his then admirers – said he was writing "formula stories," and indeed he was. The stories were a triumph of packaging. They were written in his unique lyric style. He could make a thing look better than it really was. It was like this in real life, too – his natural eloquence, his spontaneous charm, could make you feel he was so much better than the regrettable thing he had just done.

The truth is that Fitzgerald, without his special lyric touch, was a knight without armour. His Hollywood experience proves it. Fitzgerald was not a successful screenwriter. Yet he could have got from Hollywood all he wanted from the *Post*, and more; the money was there, and he had all the training to look at life out of someone else's genteel romantic eye. Isn't it likely his failure as a screenwriter lay in the circumstances of picture making, circumstances which denied him the totality of his lyric flow; and that without his lyric flow, he was simply another hack screenwriter?

As for this genteel romantic tradition and Fitzgerald's place in it, there are those who believe that Fitzgerald was like a saint in our world: in it, but not of it; and as he increased in strength as an artist, he finally saw the tradition for what it was, and reached beyond it to a new power and wisdom. If you believe this, you have to believe that *Tender Is the Night* is a better book than *The Great Gatsby*, and that *The Last Tycoon*, if he had finished it, would have topped them all. This is a very dubious point of view.

In *The Great Gatsby*, there is no revolt at all against that strange mixed-up world of commercial romanticism and Calvinistic veneration of success that has enchanted the American imagination. It is the world of the *Post* editor, the established clergyman, the Rotarian, the social climber, the banker, and it is Fitzgerald's world, too; but he was able to find a magic pattern in it, the one right story to bring out all his talents. For the only time in the Fitzgerald novels, the lyric gift was more than beguiling surface; it actually seemed to deepen the insights and the revelations.

# THE CHAIR

My brother-in-law's wife gave us a chair. It was unlike any other chair in our house, a chair upholstered in burnt-orange velvet with a rather high narrow back cut straight across at the top, the velvet back sewn in a quilted effect, and the sides of the back sloping into the seat so that the chair had no real arms. When I first looked at it, wondering where we would put it, I thought it looked like a medieval chair, or something you might have called a princess chair; in spite of its velvet elegance it seemed to be essentially a chair, a seat with a back, a comfortable back. It couldn't have had a simpler line, and I liked the richness of the burnt-orange velvet. The only thing required was the right place. After putting it in places where it clashed with other pieces of furniture, we found the place in the large hall near a white panelled wall and a black marble mantel.

That night some friends came by, younger people who get out in the world. They say I don't. They looked at the chair and said nothing. Finally, I said, "How do you like the new chair?" They glanced at each other. He hesitated, the woman smiled politely. The man said nothing. "Oh, come on," I said, "how do you like it?"

"Where did you get it?" he asked.

"Well, I didn't buy it," I said.

"I hope not," he said.

"It would have been too expensive," I said. "A relative gave it to us, a present."

"So you have to use it?"

"No, we like it," I said, and the young woman, who had hesitated, and who now seemed to be downright offended by my approval of the chair, said firmly, "Well, I'm glad to hear it was given to you because I can't believe that you people, of your own accord, would buy that chair. I think you just feel under an obligation to have it around. I think it's awful."

"And why is it awful?" I asked, knowing that this is always an unfair question. People squirm when you ask them to explain why they don't like a thing, just as they squirm when you ask why they do like a thing. Usually they say with dignity, "It's simply a matter of taste." Of course. It's always a matter of taste. But the young woman was exasperated enough or sure enough of herself, to throw up her hands and say, "For one thing I don't like the colour. Pumpkin. It might look all right with that quilted back in some woman's bedroom. I could take you to them, people who've just struck it rich and have three interior decorators."

"I know where you'd find that chair," the man said.

"Where?"

"In Miami," he said. "Or maybe Las Vegas. Are you going to keep it around?"

When I said we were going to leave it just where it was, they were not only disappointed in me; they were positively disgruntled. The next time they came around I was aware they were trying not to notice the chair in its place. Little things like this can come between friends. I grew more attached to the chair; for them, it was an eyesore that had to be tolerated; for them, it revealed my growing unawareness of the relationship of things, the relationship of objects to people. You knew about people by the objects in their possession. This is true, and because I had divined the attitude they expressed with their patient silence, I raised the subject again one night.

I shouldn't have done this. You can't win victories in the field of taste, not honest victories. Yet I said, "Look, I know how you feel about that chair and its place in the world, but here is how I feel about it. First, I like it for what it is in itself. It is a very ancient style and I like very much that burnt-orange velvet. And look. Supposing some woman up in Don Mills or Miami has such a chair in her bedroom. What the hell do I care? I won't ever meet her. I'll never be in her bedroom. What do I care what goes on in her bedroom? And since it's a free country, why should I worry if she likes something I like? If I write a story and such a woman likes it I'm delighted because it is one of my stories. And as for Las Vegas – what do I care if a hotel manager has picked something I too like? I'll never meet him or his customers. I don't care. The relationship is between me and that chair. That's all."

My friends seemed to regard these remarks with a certain hostility, as if they believed I was trying to tell them something about themselves. All this reminded me of an occasion when an older friend, an English professor, had asked me if I would come to his college and have a little informal talk with him and five or six colleagues from the English and Philosophy Departments. He had said they wanted to talk about prose and poetry. But after we had been talking some twenty minutes my friend said suddenly, "What we really want to talk about is this matter of taste. You must have some strong opinions. Years ago when you were a student I remember you saying of someone, 'He has no taste.' Well, what is taste? What is good taste? Who has good taste?"

"You ask me this?" I said, taken aback. "Well, I haven't the faintest idea." But they said, "Come on now, let's talk about it," and of course we did. I found that my trained academic friends tended to rely on guidance from the ancients. Aristotle was quoted and Plato and St. Augustine and Croce. It became a general discussion about aesthetics. I was enjoying it until I saw that my old friend, the professor, looked discontented. "This is not quite what I expected from you," he said. "I mean, when you say right out of hand, this is bad prose. Or that's a bad poem. Or that's an ugly dress, or that's a bad picture or an ugly building, what do you go by?"

"Just myself," I confessed.

"And it may not be my view at all," he said.

"Exactly," I said.

"Then which view is to prevail and be called good taste?"

I said I could only tell them how I feel about these things myself. It is true that there is always an accepted taste – and here my quarrel with my young friends about my velvet chair is involved. It seemed to me that certain social factors – their circle of friends – people they know and respect had got into the act. These social factors have a powerful influence on us all. But they can obscure the value of the particular object in itself.

If all the people you respect dislike a certain poet, you tend to give in to these people. But surely this only means that you are in the fashion business, or are bent on proving you are one of the tribe. Then, too, for a poem or a story, or even a style, there is supposed to be the test of time. But even this is suspect. Sometimes a work is kept alive by a schoolmasters' agreement through generations. Yet, time can be wonderful, the way it exposes the affectations of a period.

For example, the very affectations that make a writer's style so attractive and so contagious in one period may look ridiculous only twenty-five years later. I don't slough aside the test of time. It certainly does clear away the phony graces, but over some three thousand years, the definitions of beauty that the philosophers have come up with are scant. There is only one comment I remember that justified my remark in answer to the question, "What do you go by?" – when I said, "Just myself." The comment is in James Joyce's *Portrait of the Artist as a Young Man*, and it is, "The true test of a work of art is out of how deep an experience does it spring."

I extend this to the matter of taste and the judgement of beauty. Out of how deep an experience does it spring? When I say, "I like this. I think it is good," my life, my experience, is laid on the line. For better or worse, the judgement tells something about my life. If I surrender the judgement, I'm trying to hide my life. So I like my chair. There it is. And here I am. Incidentally, a very attractive woman who has lived in many cities but never in Miami, came into the house the other night and said, "Oh, that chair looks lovely there." I told this to my young friends. I don't think they drew any closer to me.

For another view of this chair and the story surrounding it:
*Barrelhouse Kings, A Memoir*, Barry Callaghan, pp. 421-426

# BLAISE CENDRARS
# AND RÉJEAN DUCHARME

The spiritual condition of our time, vast, desolate and stricken, was reflected in the ugly canker we recently saw bare and raw during the 1968 Democratic Convention in Chicago. It wasn't bared only by the shameful violence in the streets, the police rioting; it was within the walls itself of the Convention hall, among the delegates who frankly cried out again and again: "Who is running this convention? Why are we being treated like sheep?" – as if they felt themselves in the grip of some great cop, some higher authority they could not reach. Something monstrous was afoot. Over the whole scene lurked the shadow of a big cop's club. Under his stick, or in front of the wheels of his great revving motorcycles, men and women became sheep, or monsters.

I was reading two books at the time; a novel by Blaise Cendrars, *To the End of the World,* and *The Swallower Swallowed*, by Réjean Ducharme. Cendrars and Ducharme are a generation apart. Cendrars, long a legend in French literature as an uninhibited scallywag, is just now being translated. Ducharme is the young Québécois who, with this novel, raised the eyebrows of the Paris literary critics. With the Chicago Convention in my eyes, with all its grotesque conceptions of law, order and authority shaking my imagination, I was caught up in the lives of two Cendrars and Ducharme characters, a child and an aged woman who are utterly free from the jackboot sense of order that flowered so voluptuously in Chicago (and which is just as deeply admired in our own city). The two characters are, of course, monsters themselves.

Ducharme's monster is a young Québécois girl, her story a nine-year-old telling it in the continuing present. She is the product of a Jewish-Catholic union, each doctrinaire. They have given birth to a monster. Her idea of amusement is to kill the family cat and bury it with its tail upright out of the ground. Ducharme creates a weird affect in the book by giving the small child the mental processes of a graduate student. As psychology, or as observation, it is utterly false. Even so, Ducharme makes it true: his sureness – his deeply felt sense that the little girl could think in no other way – makes his depiction of the Québécois family – a scene that Marie-Claire Blais has also described – absolutely authentic; at its core, there is a terrible privation of the spirit.

Our child heroine, a child-witch starved for love, ends up in Israel of all places, in the army. She saves herself from death by using her girlfriend as a shield from enemy bullets, letting her friend die. Ruthless as she is, free as she is from the old morality, free as she is, too, from the recognition of any other kind of morality, she belongs in those Chicago streets alongside those cops who behaved like animals, those cops, whose right to be inhuman had been given to them by a righteous authority. Ducharme's little girl, free from this authority, with no respect for the law, is not only inhuman but loves being so. What is the answer?

Cendrars is an old hand at deriding god-justified monsters. His heroine is a great Parisian actress, an eighty-year-old nymphomaniac. Yes, at eighty! She is without a shred of conscience, without a scruple – free. The reader, following the old harridan in the making of a play she is about to star in, is no doubt supposed to be amused by her astounding energy, her will to live, and her agility as she proceeds from one set of soiled sheets to another.

Cendrars, a writer of astonishing gusto and originality, with a gift for the sentence on the page that is artlessly Proustian, has created an old witch who is an animal. I've no doubt that she would shock Mayor Daley, or President Johnson, or any other truncheon swinging cop. But the more important point is: they would amuse her; her old ribs would split with laughter; how could anyone like her take their kind of club-swinging morality seriously. She had known such a morality all her life and she knew what it did to people, which would lead her to laugh at delegates asking, "Who is running this convention? Who has the authority?" As for love – to hell with it – she is too old to love. All she needs is excitement, the excitement she could have got in the streets of Chicago, free as she is, to be a monster.

For the writer, then, in these times, as for millions of young people all over the world, and particularly those who followed the Democratic Convention in Chicago while also watching what was going on in the streets, it seems all too plain that the world of some supreme cop wheeling his commandments from church to police station to polling booth is now just the world of a naked and withered old lady clawing for power and admiration over the souls of men, a lady like Cendrars' eighty-year-old nymphomaniac witch. Those, however, who have managed to remain young in heart are now, all too often, confronted by a present dilemma: with public authority cankered, how do you in a world in which there is no inner sense of authority, or love, if you want to call it that, resist becoming a monster in a world of animals in the street.

Where is the love that makes someone more than an animal to come from? Ducharme doesn't know. Cendrars doesn't know. It is not going to come from the Mosaic Code. That's been tried, the cop's billy club tried again and again in the cities. It's not going to come from a Papal Encyclical. Not from a President Nixon, not from a television huckster or Hollywood trick-or-treater, not from any retired general nor from Messrs Mao and Ho smiling into Ché's eyes. It is a strange time for a young man or woman to be alive: the young wondering where to look for something that will leave them feeling free to trust their own hearts.

Toronto Telegram, 1969

# FEMALE VIOLENCE

Lady Macbeth, the strong-minded, ruthless, ambitious woman, exercised a terrible influence on her husband's heart, goading him to murder. For the sake of the story, the knife had to be in the man's hand. A Lizzy Borden who took an axe and killed her pa with forty whacks is regarded as a crazed human being, her deed a violation of the very nature of a woman.

One of the great turning points in the long history of civilization, men have told us, was when man, the nomadic hunter, discovered the art of agriculture and came into harmony with the earth and domesticated animals, allowing his woman to work in the fields beside him, giving him a home and a family.

From that time on, women were supposed to be against the marauder, to want peace. And I think that from that time on, so many thousands of years ago, men have nourished in their imaginations, even if grudgingly, the belief that a woman by her nature is not only the custodian of life, the sacred vessel, but that she also has a kind of ethical wisdom that is superior to his because this wisdom is always on the side of life.

She might be abused, beaten, raped, slapped on the mouth, told to shut up, degraded and defiled as little more than a beast of burden, but a man told himself that he had to do these things so that, as he followed his own nature – the wild brawler, the killer ape, the lout, the warlord or the slave master – she could be the keeper of his conscience.

This notion always used to pop into my head when I was watching movies, especially those grand old westerns, full of vicious outlaws and cheap dance-hall girls. No matter how degraded those girls might be, there had to be some little radiant moment to indicate that she had remembered to shed a tear, to remind us that she was on the side of life. A dreadfully sentimental view of women? Of course. I knew it by the time I was twenty. Even then, and even now, I believe there is some primitive truth in it.

If I'm to write about women, there is an aspect to woman that has been overlooked in fiction: the love of violence, of ruthlessness, of the cold will to kill and dominate through the sword, the gun. When I meditate a little, I can see that all through history there have been ruthless bloodthirsty, dominating women from the one-armed Amazons to the warrior women of the ancient Irish clans, from Elizabeth of England to Joan of Arc to Catherine of Russia to the Catherine in France who ordered the St. Bartholomew's Day massacre. Looking back I can see that my mind should not have been boyishly chilled when a woman on stage or in my imagination whispered, "Put the dagger in my hand." The fact is, throughout history, the destructive weaknesses of women have always been there to match the destructive weaknesses of men. Thackeray could show that Becky Sharpe was a scheming little minx, or Defoe that Moll Flanders was a successful trollop, and every man who writes a novel today has to have one woman in it who is a neurotic little bitch competing with a neurotic bastard.

But the woman I'm talking about, the woman who invites not a caricature but a portrait, is the woman with the gun in her hand.

In recent weeks, there have been two attempts made on the life of President Ford. Two women with guns in their hands. It doesn't matter that these two women are rushed to psychiatrists, or that a third one, Pattie Hearst, the poster gun girl, is also in the hands of doctors now. A man, clinging to his ancient views, has to believe that a woman with a gun in her hand needs a psychiatrist. What the man himself may need, as I am beginning to see now, is a little more knowledge of the nature of women. Ma Barker, that legendary lady of the thirties, was as tough and violent as any man and she proved it.

I was reading some reports of jailed juveniles, jailed for muggings and beatings, and found that the girls worked with the boys. They could use knives just as effectively as the boys, and had done so, and with just as much relish. And then I remember hearing Margaret Mead, the noted anthropologist, say, in a discussion about taking women into the army and whether they should handle guns, "Don't give women guns. Under no circumstances should they be taught how to handle guns. It would be terrible," and I had the conviction that she, a woman, knew they would become more bloodthirsty and reckless than men had ever been in the use of guns.

I said to an older woman, "Why are women taking to guns now?"

After pondering for a long time she smiled and said, "Because they are bored. They're looking for some excitement." I snorted, thinking this was an easy dismissal of women. Men take up guns for great causes, or conduct assassinations, shouting, "Death to all tyrants," or launch great wars. Or, go off singing to wars. But – forced to consider it – how did I in fact know that men with their great causes, launching their great conquests, weren't just bored and looking for new excitement?

We learn that the general public these days has a tremendous insatiable appetite for violence. The violent woman is being overlooked when obviously such violent women are all around us. Articulate feminists have been bent on having women emerge from all the antique shadows that men have used to guard her from herself. This is great. Coming out of the sentimental protective shadows she can be looked at freshly by the writer and some great new portraits may emerge. Soon we will have a new crop of popular heroines, violent women.

This, however, won't entirely satisfy me as a writer because I can't see a future for men and women living together while aware of and afraid of the violence in each other. One or the other would have to give in. Nietzsche said, "When thou goest to women, take thy whip?" But who could want an intimacy based on the whip? It is plain that there is as much violence in women as there is in men and this may become the basis of a new respect, a new concern that a man and a woman could have for each other. If so, I would be able to say to a woman: "All the violence I now know to be in you I know is in me, too, just as nothing that is in you is foreign to me."

*CBC Anthology*

# DAYDREAMING

The other night, lying around and enjoying daydreaming, these words popped into my head: "Man can not live by bread alone?" For heaven's sake! Why that? Tolstoy was fond of the line. Then, a little later, back daydreaming I suppose, I thought, "Man's built-in computer. Maybe the genes." By now, really interested in the meaning of these phrases, I began to put them together.

Some time ago, I had been thinking that if a man had a religious novel to write – now was the time to get to it, and yet I had rejected the notion. The intellectual world, the intellectual critics – let us say the boys represented by the *New York Review of Books* or the *Globe and Mail* and *Saturday Night* – may write respectful reviews but they are not going to show much excitement over a Christian novel, Protestant or Catholic.

In fact, a New York publisher said to me about a good Catholic novelist who had just won a book award: "Twenty-five hundred copies. That takes it all in," as though there were an agreed view among sophisticated literati that a superior reading public was apathetic to religion – unless drugs went with the religious experience, or murder, or homosexuality, or devil-possession.

One can say that our days have been days of deliverance, a time of the death of the gods, a time of the withering away of the influence of the great formal religions, a time of the loss of papal power in the Catholic church, the loss of all Protestant intellectual fervour, a time of liberation from conventional moral strictures in business, in politics, and especially sex.

Sex, even, has been liberated from love. The first-class writer now ought to be having a field day. He, too, now is utterly free. There is no part of the mind or body that he can't touch publicly, no words he can't use.

And yet? And yet what? Why is it an agreed upon thing that the writer is only daring and adventurous, and ruthless in his explorations, when he shows the depths of a man's pigishness? Can it be that what used to be called the spiritual places, the places in a man's heart that are just as secret as the slimy corners, are too hard to explore in a city whose every street and alley and lamppost and temple and graveyard is known too well?

Take a writer like Graham Greene. He is a religious writer, and one of the most widely read authors in the world. His novel, *The Heart of the Matter*. A woman in an adulterous relationship. A woman who is an orthodox Catholic faces a tragic climax because she can not go to confession, receive absolution, and then take the bread of Holy Communion. But with the intellectual climate of today being what it is, and with even the Catholic climate blowing hot and cold, I doubt that even so adroit a storyteller as Graham Greene could have the success he has had. I say I doubt it, I'm not sure. I am sure only that publishers, critics, and booksellers shy away from religious themes.

And yet, here is a paradox. Today, Dostoevsky is far more widely read than is Tolstoy. And Dostoevsky is a profoundly religious writer. Then too, André Malraux, in his book, *The Psychology of Art*, maintains that the greatest periods in art were the religious periods, and that behind great works of art is always a religious impulse.

I tried to think of highly praised and critically fashionable novelists at work today – men or women of whom one might say, "They are driven by some kind of religious impulse." Most writers like to believe they have readers, a constituency that will understand them. Few say, "I can't count on having any readers but this is my own feeling – this is the way I see it." Such writers are usually out of season. And yet, while few books are being written by first-class authors out of any moving religious impulse, think of what is actually going on in this continent.

Millions of young people, certainly all of whom, having found new mental and sexual liberation, couldn't be dragged to orthodox churches, are behaving very strangely. Millions who would smile at the notion of going to confession to a priest go every week to a psychoanalyst. Instead of saying absolve me from my sins, they say, absolve me from my obsessions. Or they consult tarot cards. And all over the continent grown men and women meeting for the first time, don't feel they can truly know each other until they learn each other's zodiacal signs. "OK, you're an Aquarius. I'm a Leo. Good. Now we know where we stand." Men and women who can't believe in the efficacy of prayer, or sainthood, or the mystery of love, can believe in astrology.

And who can count all the strange new cults! The ever-present television evangelical cults. The strange new prophets running around loose. Many of them imports. A living God from India. Another from Korea. The Moonies. And the strange part of it is that the young men and women, leaving their fathers and their mothers and their brothers to give their lives, and of course, their possessions to the cult leaders, often seem to be reasonably well-educated. What are they up to? What do they want?

If this is the age when the old faiths are fast-waning, then it ought to be a period of scepticism, of disillusioned rationality, especially since it is the time of democratic mass education; instead, it is, I believe, the most gullible period in North American history.

The novelists who would do a job on these cult figures and their followers and place them in a milieu where astrology is taken seriously, and throw in a few shivers from demonology, would have no trouble interesting a publisher. If the novel were well done, it would be regarded by the critics as an exposé of the silliness of contemporary life. The critics would be embarrassed only if the novelist himself had some profound religious convictions of his own.

And now about those lines that popped into my head when I was daydreaming: "Man can not live by bread alone," and the other; "Man's built-in computer." I think that in my mind for a long time I must have been dwelling secretly on all the moon madness of the cults with their gullibility and need of superstition in these commercial times. I must have been wondering if this kind of terrible fun-and-games wasn't inevitable and necessary when there was only spiritual emptiness. Can it be, then, that all men and women, even the greatest dullards, came to a time when they realized they could not live by bread alone? And then I wondered – and this was a strange thought – if the hunger was not built into man, programmed into him – as if his destiny – as if his genes might be his destiny? Or, going even further: in fact, in his genes there was this religious instinct and though civilizations rose and fell, and religions flourished and waned and were, in turn, tyrannical or liberating, nevertheless, the instinct, the intuition could not be escaped, it had to be expressed, even if in some ludicrous or inhuman form.

If there is any truth in this perception, then the religious novelist, the man with a view that is merely a recognition of the deepest part of his nature, should never be out of date – as Dostoevsky is never out of date, his audience growing even in our time.

# THE PLEASURES OF FAILURE

The attitude of men enjoying success to those who are failures has always fascinated me. Businessmen in particular grow uneasy in the company of someone they can see is on the way down. They seem to feel a little chill in his presence; a reminder that success is a slippery pole.

The failures men run from are not failures on a grand scale, like the general who lost a great battle, or the industrialist whose schemes put in him into temporary bankruptcy. Nor do I have in mind the stupid man who has been devoting his life, say, to trying to sell insurance when it is pathetically obvious that he was never cut out to be a salesman; or the man whose life may be a series of passionate failures worth far more to him in enlarging his life than a series of cautious little triumphs. No, the one the successful shy away from uncomfortably is the man who, obviously having gone down in the world, has let the sense of failure get into his blood so anyone can almost smell the panic in him.

When I was fourteen I caught a glimpse of how the conviction of failure could demoralize even a healthy boy. Alex, a chum of mine, a good-looking, imaginative, active fellow, had invited me to his house for dinner. At the dinner hour we came together to his place, entering by the back door, and we could hear his father saying vehemently, "No, it's another failure, and I don't mind saying I've lost all faith in Alec."

My chum tried to smile at me, but he looked desolate and bewildered. It was as if he had suddenly found himself entering the wrong house. At the dinner table he was subdued, pale and brooding. While I talked to his father and mother, my chum was trying to accept the fact that those who knew him best, those he loved, knew he was marked for failure. I remember that his eyes were scared. It may have been that his father had found him a little hard to handle, but he wasn't a dunce; he was an intelligent boy. Within a year he had dropped out of school. He became a mechanic.

Later on, whenever I met this boy's father, I used to look at him uneasily and vow that if I ever had a son of my own I would try and convince him he hadn't failed, no matter how disastrous were the reports from his teachers. Years passed and I used to listen with distaste to fathers who would say of a son, "I'm taking the boy away from school. He had his chance and he failed." One failure! And it would seem to me that these fathers themselves had been desperately afraid of failure in their own lives.

Since the classroom is indeed the first arena for public failure, I used to wonder why all high schools weren't required to have one teacher who could give a yearly lecture on how to handle failure. Of course, in our society, no high-school teacher would want to be known as an expert on failure. His fellow teachers might shy away from *him* uneasily. But if such a teacher could be found, he might say to the students, "Some of you will make a lot of money. Others won't. But whether you are ever to have any inner security in your lives will depend on your ability to cope with your failures. Never hide from them. If you are any good, you are bound to fail a hundred times. Get used to the idea. Anyway, failures are often more interesting than successes. They can toughen your spirit. But no matter how you fail, never let them see you have your tail between your legs. Console yourselves by taking a good look at some men who are called successful. They are often driven, restless and neurotic. They nurse their blood pressure and their heart attacks because they are scared stiff – of failure."

And this teacher would go on: "To fail again and again is merely to lead a normal life. Judge a man by his ability to cope with failure. Look at the lives of so many great men. Take Winston Churchill. If he had been a poor boy he might never had got to college; he didn't seem to be too bright at his public school. And Einstein had difficulty getting into universities. And the great dramatist, Eugene O'Neill, flunked out of Princeton, as did Scott Fitzgerald. The thing is that these men never accepted the fact that their academic judges had marked them for defeat. Besides, there is a hairline division between success and failure which the life of Scott Fitzgerald makes very clear. He had all the early success and wealth of a golden boy of his time; then his audience rejected him. No one wanted his work. But he couldn't believe he was a failure; he writhed, groaned, debased himself, tormented his spirit, but kept on crying out that he was as good as he had ever been. Though he died alone and half forgotten, as soon as he died, his work immediately made him a greater figure than he had ever been in the days of his early triumphs. He was right about himself."

And the teacher would also say, "The main thing to remember is this: the sense of failure begins in the feeling of panic. Get used to it. Play around with it and other men will never smell it in you."

Some men can't hide it. It gets into their blood. A few years ago I was talking with one of our Ottawa statesmen, an old friend, about men from our year in college and what had happened to them. "What about Johnny Henderson?" I asked. Henderson is not the real name, of course. The powerful politician, looking genuinely distressed, told me Henderson had no luck, one job after another, a marriage and four children. One day he had heard that

Henderson was living in Ottawa. He asked him to come and see him and was sure he could give him a lift up in the world.

Next afternoon Henderson now seedy, but neat, and with an apologetic air, came to the office in the Parliament Buildings. The politician, busy at the moment with someone else, greeted him warmly and asked him to wait in the outer office. When he returned to this outer office, Henderson had gone.

"Where's Mr. Henderson?" he asked his secretary.

"I don't know what happened to him," she said. "He was sitting there, and suddenly he looked sick. He had such a funny, scared look in his eyes. It was downright panic, absolute panic. He half stood up, then mumbled something and hurried out."

I could understand the man's panic: I had once felt it myself.

Back in 1938 I had begun a period of spiritual dryness. The rise of Hitler and the Spanish war had made me profoundly cynical about the Great War that was approaching. For years I had been writing stories for the *New Yorker*. Suddenly I couldn't write such stories. Any story I attempted was done half-heartedly. Soon no one wanted my work. I had either lost my talent or no longer had anything to say. But I had a wife and two children. I tried to borrow money, using my car as security. No one even wanted my car.

I can remember the summer night when I was out on the street at twilight, walking slowly up and down in front of my house, asking myself what was going to happen to me. I was broke. I could not write anything anyone wanted to read. Was I a morning glory? After all the quick early success, was I all washed up? I remember wondering if I could start to practice law, and what would be required of me. Going back to the fold would be like a public proclamation of failure of course. But wasn't it too late anyway? There on the street I felt an apprehensive chill, thinking of the life ahead, and then a moment of blind panic that bewildered me and left me in a sweat.

Though I wasn't aware of it at the time, it is this panic that is the classic condition for the establishment in the heart of the sense of failure, and as I was to learn, too, from watching other men, it establishes the condition for a nervous breakdown. This panic is like a little old guy, who, if he gets into your house and is offered any kind of welcome, stays around forever. But the little old guy has one weakness; he can't bear to have you get bored with him. As soon as you can say, "Here he comes again, and exactly as before," he gets the hell out.

For a few weeks I was morose, depressed, incapable of doing any work, and then, hating my own apathy, I did the right thing. Accepting the fact that I couldn't write stories in this period, I turned to something else. I took out an old play that had once aroused some interest in New York, borrowed money on an insurance policy, and went to work. Within the year the Theater Guild in New York had taken an option on the play. For a year and a half they paid me advance royalties. Buoyant again, I wrote another play, sold it to two charming young producers named Curtis and Blackwell, drew option money on it, and was billed to have two plays produced in New York in the one season.

In the theatre, even after the contracts have been signed, you live in a state of uneasy hope, but it did seem ridiculous to me that I had been able to tell myself and believe, if only for a few weeks, that I was from now on marked for failure. They were exciting days. I remember meeting Lawrence Langner, who, with Theresa Helburn, *was* the Theater Guild, under the clock at Grand Central Station so we could go to his home at Westport, Connecticut, and that night look at an actress who might be right for my play. It was a little after the time of Dunkirk, and on the train, still being coldly objective about the war, I told Langner that the British, having been driven off the Continent, had lost the war, but they could still be on the winning side, if the U.S. entered the war. He was angry. We had a violent argument. Yet we looked at our actress that night and rejected her, and I could still believe that all was going well.

All those days were lively and exciting. Days crowded with theatre people, new faces, men-about-town. I would meet my agent sometimes for breakfast so we could exchange the gossip of the night before, and try and figure out just when my plays would open on Broadway. I remember I often met William Saroyan at three in the afternoon and did not leave him till five in the morning. I sat around with the boys in Lindy's. The word was that the Guild people were trying to get two well-known movie stars so the production cost would be mainly covered in cities on the road before the play came to Broadway. I returned to Toronto.

But the movie star, who had quarrelled with his studio and who said he was interested in my play, suddenly returned to the movie field. The Guild dropped my play. Shaken though I was, I told myself I still had another play. I had read in the New York papers that my two young producers were now casting this second play, a director had also been signed, and I waited to hear when rehearsals would begin.

But a letter from the producers seemed to me to be so evasive I grew uneasy. Now I was looking about superstitiously for little signs that my luck was running out. I had strange hunches that I was in trouble. I wondered if that sense of failure I had experienced on my street, which I had ducked away from neatly, hadn't really belonged in my life and was now to have its inning.

One night I got on a train for New York, and in the morning I appeared in the office of my two producers. It was early. Neither of the boys was there. But at the sight of me, a startled expression had come into the secretary's eyes. Then she smiled, fiercely bright, fiercely quick, fiercely cheerful, and she might just as well have screamed at me, "Trouble. Trouble."

While I waited for the producers I tried to tell myself that all the odds were against the collapse of two plays at the same time. Then the two boys arrived. When they saw me there was such embarrassed pain in their eyes they made me feel I had played a dirty trick on them, being there, waiting in their office. But they were men of sensibility and gentleness, and they took me into the big, inner, broadloomed office and confessed that one of the principal backers, just before putting up the money, had got drunk and boarded a plane for the west coast, and his wife, having tracked him down, had had him committed to a sanatorium as an alcoholic, and, of course, had cancelled his investment in my play.

Ridiculous things are always happening in the theatre, especially at the time of the financing of a play. I didn't say, "Isn't it incredible that one of our backers should get drunk, get on a plane and vanish." No, we sat in the broadloomed office, considered the matter as if it were a normal occurrence. It was very comfortable in that handsome office, and my young producers were men of delicate insight and consoling voices. They knew how I felt, I knew how they felt, and though we talked about finding another backer, I could tell they had shopped all around and the jig was up. They had taste, discernment and style, but it was known they hadn't made money in the theatre.

That night I had a funereal drink in the Algonquin with the man who was to have been the director. It was up to me to tell him the bad news and crush him completely. My own mood bewildered me. I was so heavy-hearted I could hardly smile. When I had parted from the director, and was walking over to Times Square, I was filled with superstitious uneasiness, a kind of recognition of the fact that failure was following me; I had seen it coming two years ago on the street outside my house. Now it had caught up with me. For two years I had been kidding myself that my luck had changed. Now I had to go home to my wife and children and tell that all the hopeful plans had collapsed, and I was right back where I had been two years ago. Soon that feeling of panic would possess me again, and this time the little old guy would really feel at home in my breast. I remember I waited almost impatiently for this touch of panicky fear. I could have been saying, "Come on, come on. Here I am. What are you waiting for?"

I had friends, a professor and his pretty young wife, living on 26th Street, and I called on them, and when they had given me a drink I told them of the collapse of both my productions.

The professor, who had soft blue eyes and a bald head, kept looking at me incredulously, and I thought his nice, sympathetic young wife was going to cry. She understood that all the hopes held out to me after two years of work had vanished; the two years of work had added up to this incredible failure. I began to make ironic jokes about the two young producers, and then about the alcoholic angel. I laughed a lot. But finally the professor stood up, staring at me. I remember that he was white-faced, his mouth twisted. "Cut it out," he pleaded.

"What's the matter?"

"I don't know," and he groped for words and then blurted out. "This offends me. Something is wrong. You shock me."

"What can I do? What should I be doing?"

"I would be more sympathetic if you were out somewhere dead drunk and lying in the gutter. Both plays! It's incredible. And you sit there turning it all into a farce."

Because he was so disgusted, I knew he couldn't smell failure or panic in me. And I became almost apologetic. I had to explain that

I understood indeed what had happened to me. Having tried to change the direction of my work, I had failed. My number hadn't come up. If I was going to go on writing, I didn't know which way I would turn, and I didn't know what I would say to my wife and children when I went home. I understood, too, that out of pure sympathy my friends were trying to stir up some rage and despair in me. The truth was I felt no real panic at all.

Looking back on that rather memorable night, a turning point in my life, I think I avoided the dreadful chill a man feels wondering if from now on he has been marked for failure, by saying to myself, "Well, here I am. If I'm going to feel demoralized, let's hurry and get it over with. It has happened before. It may happen again. I'm still here." The little old guy, Mr. Panic, didn't come. I think it was because I had spotted him and was waiting.

I was accepting the failure as a normal part of my life. I was becoming aware that there might be other times that would be like little deaths, dreadful depressions, but if I didn't get to like these deaths – that's the great trick; not to have a secret liking for them so you court them as some men do – then the spark in the spirit would flame again just because I very much wanted to remain alive.

The odd part of it was that I didn't start in desperately to try to write stories. No, I had a hunch I wasn't ready. I would wait. I would know when I was ready. And I felt strangely in full possession of myself, more than ever my own man.

I went down to Halifax to do some work with the navy. Afterward, I went back and forth across Canada, doing wartime radio programs for the national network. Often my pride would be stung by a remark made by a chance acquaintance: "You're not writing anything these days." And once I met a writer who told me a famous New York editor had asked, "What in the world happened to Morley Callaghan?" But never again did I feel that sense of failure. There wasn't a time when I wasn't thinking about writing. I seemed to be quietly waiting to get some new view of things. I started to write a monthly magazine column, and then in 1946-47, I began to write stories again. Editors wanted them. I was spending a lot of social time in Montreal. Toward the end of the decade I began my novel, *The Loved and the Lost*, writing with great confidence.

Along the way I had grown more interested than ever in the successful men who avoid the company of those they call failures. Aside from the fact that they are betraying their own sense of insecurity and are wearing their crowns uneasily, they seem to have a fantastically limited view of personal success. If a man is a financial success they seek him out, cultivate him, hope some of his success will rub off on them. That such a man may be a dreadful failure in all his personal relationships, unable to love, avoided by his children, neurotic and in and out of sanitariums, and after the day's work is done, calling for the bottle just as he did when he was an infant, doesn't upset the nervous success boys at all.

*Maclean's*, 1965

# A NAME IS A NAME
# IS A NAME

In this matter of being a writer – and at once I sound a hopeful note – no poet or novelist should worry about having only a few readers, or being practically unknown. Take Gertrude Stein.

There's a name. A name! Simply a name! A household name in literature. Who do you know who has read a book by Gertrude Stein? Indeed, one book was widely read in the United States, but that was called *The Autobiography of Alice B. Toklas*, and by the time it was written, Gertrude had become such a famous name that when she stepped out on Fifth Avenue, passersby immediately recognized her. Everyone wanted to hear her lectures because Miss Stein had written two lines that everyone, simply everyone, could quote knowingly: "Pigeons on the grass, alas," and, "A rose is a rose is a rose."

If you were out of an evening and could say with a smile, A rose is a rose is a rose, you implied that you had a way of looking at things, and a love of those figures who were said to be on the frontiers of literature. When Miss Stein was touring the United States at the time of the publication of Alice B. Toklas, she was asked what was the basis of her great fame, her enormous prestige. How did the thing get going? And she replied with candor and marvellous shrewdness that it was important to have very few readers. You can see how accurate was this observation. If your work is practically unknown it has a sense of mystery about it – the unknown is always mysterious, isn't it?

But Miss Stein didn't tell the whole story; why should she have done so? This unknown thing, the body of work, and the great unknown writer, must have runners, dedicated little priests who at some time have got into the inner sanctum, who indeed, under the spell of some incense, can feel they are in on something very rare, very special, very knowing, above all very exclusive. These selected devotees must never explain anything. This is important. They create an aura. If you want to get in on it, you have to come to them; and night and day they repeat and repeat and repeat. They don't get paid for this, of course, but they have that deep inner satisfaction of those who are truly exclusive, and gradually but inevitably – the journalists who keep track of these things will begin to write about the devotee, treating him as a source. Who can say he isn't a source?

Only one thing can destroy the source. The crowd! If the crowd moves in, if too many eyes are looking, if the work is there and finally read by the masses, the jig is up, the illusion vanishes. Sadly then, I have to warn our young poets and prose writers, all running neck and neck, that if any one of them is to bob up, wearing the crown of the great reputation, he and his two or three backers must recognize, as any good politician does, that everything depends on creating the illusion.

I remember the time of the national Liberal Convention that selected Pierre Trudeau as the national party leader. A man of good repute came to my door, some weeks before the names of the candidates had been thrown into the hat, and he wanted me to sign a telegram, which surely was to be two or three feet long, urging Pierre Trudeau to enter the leadership race.

I said I was sure Pierre Trudeau was an excellent man, but I did not know anything whatever about him. Just the few stories I had read in the papers. My caller understood my position, and my effort to be honest. Then, it turned out that he had never met Trudeau, either, and didn't know much more about him than I did, except that word had come to him from people he respected.

A little later, I too began to believe in the word, and by the time the race was on in the convention, I was rooting for Trudeau and exulting in his victory, happy to forget I had said I knew nothing whatever about him.

The writer who is to cultivate the great reputation must have this kind of charisma hanging over the reputation. It seems to me, now, that the essence of charisma is simply a great expectation of the unknowable or the inscrutable. The hint dropped here and there that can lead to expectation! Gratification for expectation? Only the expectation!

So, if you have a few friends who want to make you into a reputation of some grandeur, make sure these friends don't insist that people read your work. Feed them the delightful sense of expectation that they will have looking forward to the day of the reading of the work. It might even be useful to suggest that the work should be left there like an untapped treasure. Untapped! A sunken treasure ship. A whole legend could be developed about the treasure that will someday be found and appreciated.

Above all, repetition of the assertion of the writer's greatness is important. Sooner or later, if the statement is repeated, scholarly expeditions will set out to find this writer. Trapped in the created illusion, the scholars are bound to believe that the scraps of work they find arouse the greatest scholarly expectation. The writer, however, should never make a statement about himself. A Mona Lisa smile from him is enough. Norman Mailer is not nearly as smart as Hemingway was. Hemingway remained enigmatic about himself and his work. Mailer gets into trouble because he keeps yelling, "I'm the champ, I'm the champ," out in the open, no mystery left, no inner temple, nothing left to say to him but, "You're not the champ, you're a bit of a chump."

I have to pass on one last observation. I have never met a writer of reputation who wouldn't give his eyeteeth to feel that he was considered truly important because of his work alone.

*CBC Anthology*

# THE TIMELESS HUNGER
# FOR A STORY

Yet another announcement that the novel is dead has come in – this time from the ubiquitous Gore Vidal. Such a funereal notice usually means that the man making it is about to palm off a few tricks he has learned as a masterly piece of fresh storytelling. Anyway, what is a novel? A long story, that's all it is. The boys who believe there are only so many ways of fixing a pipe are just as sure there can be only the old ways of telling a story. Since the methods have all been worn thin, they say, few people now are interested in storytellers.

But I thought of a quote from Karen Blixen's *Out of Africa*. If, she says, you start to tell a native audience "there is a man who walked out on a plain and there he met another man," you have them all with you, their minds running on the unknown track of the men on the plain. The hunger for a story! A hunger that I think is universal and timeless, too.

Yet, if you followed the last few years in film and in literature, followed the critical fashions which change as rapidly as women's fashions change, you really would believe that the story as a form is exhausted. The underground filmmaker tried to prove how deep in the ground he really is by shunning narrative as if it were the plague. Even a good filmmaker like Jean Renoir, the French director, said that he is no longer interested in suspense. And, again and again over the last 10 years, pronouncements have come from New York or Paris that narrative is a 19th century device. Well, I'm both bemused and amused. I don't think these writers and critics know what is involved within themselves. They say that a writer should no longer play around with narrative. But in saying this aren't they simply confessing their fear, caution and inadequacy?

Closer to home, I also read that Farley Mowat said he would not advise any young writer to try a novel. Now – aside from the fact that any young writer of real talent couldn't possibly take this business-like advice – this is simply an invitation to quit on your own imagination and sensibility, and do journalism. We must try and understand the despair of those who try to make a virtue out of their disappointment in themselves. Of course, it is hard to make a story sound fresh and new. It always was. But it has been the eternal quest of the imaginative writer. I'd say to those abdicating writers and tired critics, do you really doubt that there is a hunger in all men to hear a story? There's a catch in it, of course. The story really must sound like a new story.

To come back to the African quotation, "there was a man who walked out on a plain and there he met another man . . ." Well, if the native audience has heard the rest of the story they'll shrug, or walk out. Just as a Canadian audience would. But the everlasting quickening in the audience comes in the question, "What happened when these two men met on the plain?" Well, the trick is in the telling. There are a thousand ways of telling it. No matter how old the essential facts are, the differences will come, or should come, from the different sensibilities, the difference of imagination and insight in the storytellers. So, remember this. The hunger for the story is always in people.

Now, when storytellers, professionals, realize that their sensibilities and imaginations are so shopworn and beaten up they can only tell the story as other men have told it again and again, they get frightened. Their jobs are at stake. They turn to journalism.

Nursing their hidden wound, the disappointment in themselves, they say to eager young writers who may still have fresh imaginations and some audacity, "Narrative belongs to another century. Don't waste your time on it." There's a slight misrepresentation here. In reality it is these writers and critics who belong to the previous century.

However, just imagine! A group of young writers is presently looking at the life around them and making stories out of what they see, just as if they hadn't heard the lugubrious word that you can't make stories out of life around you any more. The good thing about it, the very rare thing in Canada, and a most hopeful sign, is that these young writers are looking around and putting down what they see and trying to give it a form shaped by their own temperaments. And they are all bent on writing honestly. They haven't the knowing commercial eye. The eye that is now the worn-out eye.

What astonishes me is that these young writers, being in Canada, haven't been content to write poetry. What came over them, I wonder. An astounding amount of fairly respectable poetry is turned out in this country. Why? I have often wondered why. Are young writers afraid of prose? The story, you see, especially the short story which in its impact or totality scores the same effect as a poem, has to reveal more than an isolated sensibility, more than one's own feeling for a situation; 9 times out of 10 it deals with the relationships of people. The story always lies in the understanding of these relationships. So an isolated sensibility is not enough; nor is the very subjective awareness of the writer. As soon as you begin to deal with the relationship of others, you reveal your maturity or silliness as an observer of the ways of men. You risk appearing as a dummy. Lyricism can only help to make you seem a little wiser than you are.

I recently read a review of some of these new storywriters. It was fair enough, admiring, too, but the reviewer wished that the writers showed more avant garde influences. The world of pop art and so on. The contemporary ferment in form, I suppose! Now, what in the world is avant garde in writing? Experimentation, you say. If pop art is to be dragged into it then we are dealing with the world of trends. No real writer with his own authentic vision goes in for this kind of nonsense. An authentic writer with his own vision may never have heard of pop art or Andy Warhohl. So much the better! Avant garde, as it is understood these days in painting, writing and filmmaking, is a junk dealer's phrase. A phrase for hopeless amateurs.

By the way, who are or were the experimental writers? The days of so-called experimental magazines was back in the twenties; the days of *Transition* in Paris, Ezra Pound's *Exile, This Quarter,* Ford Madox Ford's *Transatlantic Review*, and Robert McAlmon's Contact Press. I doubt very much if any writer appearing in these publications thought of himself as experimenting. What happened was that publications appeared with editors who were anxious to print authentic stories or poems, stories as the writers saw them, not as editors or critics thought they ought to be seen. At that time, my own beginning, I was in Toronto. I wrote in all those Paris magazines. It never occurred to me that I was experimenting. No, I wrote a story in my own way because I didn't know any other way to write it. And that was the only thing that counted. Many years later, reading a book about the writing in those Paris magazines I discovered that I was listed as a writer of experimental "vertical prose." Vertical prose! It was news to me. To this day I don't know what it means.

What the great storyteller does whether he be a Maupassant, Proust, Joyce or Chekhov, is give you a new effect, a new sensation in literature. Even if he is telling only about a man and a woman in a room, he is making you feel he sees something going on between them that was never quite seen in this way before. A Robbe-Grillet tries to do this with a technique. Simple technique! Fine! An experiment! But what is really new in seeing and feeling comes out of the storyteller's own temperament, his own eyes, his own heart, his own sensibility. If he has great talent he'll make ordinary things seem remarkable. For him, there'll always be thousands of new stories because there are thousands of people around him, all begging to be seen as they were never seen before. The ancient hunger. Well, if young writers in this country now are turning to prose and storytelling it means that at last we are beginning to look at each other and wonder about each other, in our relationships. And what a sign of growth that is.

*Toronto Telegram,* 1970

# JOHN DOS PASSOS

When I was young, John Dos Passos was one of the great new shining stars in American letters. He had written *Three Soldiers* and *Manhattan Transfer*, the big novel about New York. Experimenting with the form of the novel, he had become enormously respected. And even more, Dos Passos in his work and in his personal view of society had seemed to mirror perfectly the whole intellectual climate of the thirties. He was the writer that students read; now they don't read him at all. I want to protest against the tyranny of the taste of all students, but then, maybe he had mirrored the students' taste of the thirties too perfectly. Anyway, student taste aside, in the thirties he was the one who was splendidly committed to being a good writer. He was a withering critic of the capitalistic structure. All other writers in his scene – in New York or Paris – respected his scholarly knowledge of his craft.

I remember in 1929, when I was driving from Paris to Chartres with Hemingway, we were talking about style in prose; the decorative or elaborately literary beautifully decadent poetic style, as opposed to the straightforward clean and lucid concrete statement. Hemingway said that he trusted Dos Passos' judgment in the writing of English. No one he knew had a better knowledge or judgement of what had been involved in the putting down of words in English from Chaucer to the present time, he said. And Dos Passos believed that for our time the clean direct statement was the only method that could have relevance. It was enough for Hemingway. He trusted Dos Passos. In those days they were great friends.

Just a year later, when I was in New York, I remember talking to another young writer, Nathan Asch, a friend of both Dos Passos and Hemingway, and Nathan said, "Dos is great, I have enormous respect for him. Among all the writers we both know he is the real intellectual. Yet his work lacks heart, doesn't it?" This observation stuck with me over the years.

Dos Passos wrote his great trilogy, *U.S.A.*, which was an examination of the whole face of America, with particular emphasis on the trade unions and the radical movement. There were a hundred characters. An ambitious book, it was offered as the whole fabric of American industrial society. Dos Passos was at the height of his power and influence. In the thirties and the forties he was the darling of the students. Yet, reading him then I felt a little out of it. I even felt disloyal to my own time, for while I could read sections of these books and agree that they were admirably written and that Dos Passos was wonderfully observant, I was never really moved, never in my heart. And the devices he used, like the Camera Eye, a separate section on a page or at the end of a chapter, a fiercely intense picture almost from an Olympian height above the narrative, used to strike me as artificial. Then I would remember walking in that New York street with Nathan Asch and Nathan saying "He's the great intellectual, but there's something wrong about the characters. His work lacks heart."

Not only in his work but in his own character, Dos Passos seemed to embody the best traits of style, the best modes of thought of his time. He had something more than an awareness of the social direction. He had great personal integrity. Political though he was, he couldn't be a party hack. He had to trust his own eyes and his own judgment. The Spanish Civil War was a torment for him. Ultimately, his whole mode of thought was to turn on what he saw was going on in Madrid. Of course, he had to be there. All the big writers of the left were in Madrid. Among the loyalists there was a bitter struggle for power. The Stalinists were as much, if not more determined on the destruction of their political enemies, the Trotskyites, than they were of Franco's men. What Dos Passos saw going on sickened him. He spoke out. He quarrelled with his old friend Hemingway. The American writer, Josephine Herbst, who was also in Madrid, and a friend of both Hemingway and Dos Passos, told me about it. Hemingway thought Dos Passos should keep his mouth shut. Hemingway was alarmed. He said you had to go along with the Stalinists. And so the Dos Passos-Hemingway friendship ended in this sad lack of personal respect.

After the Spanish Civil War, Dos Passos' life took another turn, almost too severe a turn, I thought at the time. He put himself against the whole fashionable apparatus of the intellectual left. Looking back on it, this could explain why he gradually lost his influence among students and radicals. A popular writer is supposed to be loyal to the readers and critics who have got used to what he stands for. Critics quit on a writer who changes direction; most of them are too lazy to try and look at him freshly; and the public quit, too. It may be that Dos Passos, the disillusioned radical, still doing imaginative work, found that this work was even colder in the heart than in his earlier work. The dew was off the grass. Another strange twist in his life also has to be mentioned. Let it be asserted firmly, though, that the change in direction after the Spanish Civil War took place before this new more personal twist.

Dos Passos was the son of a rich Wall Street man. Through a complication that had to do with his birth, he had been cut off from his father's estate. He had always lived frugally. And then magically, the legal complications ended and Dos Passos was affluent at last, living in a great house in the South, working as a farmer and travelling a lot. You can see a picture of this house on the back of his autobiography. So there he was – a conservative, a man of property.

Though I had many friends who knew Dos Passos intimately, I had never met him until a few years ago. I felt instant affection for him. He was so soft spoken, gentle, still unyielding in his loyalty to his own view. For years he had been a friend of Edmund Wilson's – in view of their vast political differences I wondered if they ever saw each other.

"I see him once a year. I make a rule of it," Dos Passos said.

"But don't you find yourself in political opposition? Don't you grow angry with each other?" I asked.

"Not at all," he said. "We just avoid certain subjects."

This satisfied me and I said to him, apologetically, "But even now I want to know why you are so far over on the other side – in the conservative position."

"I didn't see that there was such a change in me. No, not at all," he said. "When I was young I was against the established thing, the status quo that always becomes stultifying. Now the new ones in power, the intellectual left, it's a new status quo. It's just as stultifying. I have to be against it." Is this the explanation of Dos Passos? Or just the way he explained it to himself. But there he was, still his own rebellious man and in his very person – and this was strange to me – since I had always felt his work lacked heart, he seemed so full of warmth.

*Toronto Telegram*, 1970

# MAKING IT NEW

A friend I was lunching with told me that a young writer, who had just discovered the Russian Solzhenitsyn, said to him with genuine surprise, "I didn't know a writer like this was around. He seems so big, so fresh, so contemporary. I thought he would be old stuff." This young writer was excited by the nearness of the work of the older Russian writer, my friend said. So I fell to musing about writers who are supposed to be the new thing, new mainly because they are depicting a very contemporary scene, and older writers who are automatically rejected by the young as they feel compelled to reject their fathers. But the father and son relationship in terms of the aging and the fresh, doesn't work at all in literature. The father may be a wildly imaginative innovator, the son, if he is caught up in a tired, sterile conservative scene of his own, may actually – in the spirit – be closer to his great grandfather than to his own father.

Teaching methods, critical schemes, the newspapers and the love of fashion are so often responsible for the false placing of writers, for the burial of writers who could still be wonderfully alive for the young. In writing, the dead sometimes have more to say now than they had when they were alive. But the critical historians usually deal with writers by grouping them chronologically. There are supposed to be the men of the nineties, or the men of the twenties, the men of the thirties, the forties, the "after the war writers" and so on. Writers are supposed to have something in common because they have been locked in the one time slot. Well, this is absurd. The calendar is no guide if you are a writer seeking a relationship with another writer. All writers feed and flower on secret, joyful, sacred chosen relationships. There is always an ancestor who seems to belong to your own blood, light up all your own perceptions, and to be walking with you, even pushing you when your work isn't going well, and even calling to you in a familiar voice. Yes, he may be separated from you by a hundred years. But you have the distinction of knowing that this voice is alive today, for your own time. Your distinction is that you know the voice is true in the most contemporary sense. No good writer belongs only to a decade. Indeed, the best of them are sometimes wildly out of step with the men of their own decade. The great Stendhal, with his style and insights, has been speaking to us now for the last fifty years, yet he had little or nothing to say to the young writers of Paris in his own time. He was way ahead of them. So, for a long spell he was just a dead old writer. A hundred years pass, and he's a great new writer.

Not long ago, I was talking to a young professor who was telling me about a young contemporary writer.

"Have you read Tolstoy?" I asked.

"Why no," he said. "But Dostoevsky, yes! I love him. His ideas, his themes still belong to our time. But Tolstoy. No."

"Why not?" I asked. "Isn't the way he writes still wonderfully of our time? Isn't it a prose and a view of things for all seasons?"

"Nobody I know reads Tolstoy now," he said. "I don't know why. Nobody talks about Tolstoy and the way he writes."

Yet he looked a little worried. My own eyes had been filled with astonishment because I knew he loved literature. Well, a few weeks passed and he came to me and said, "I have just read *Anna Karenina*. I think it is about the greatest novel I have ever read." He went on talking about this book. He talked about Anna in the same way I talk about Tina Turner. He was filled with excitement. Tolstoy, who had been on the shelf for him, had become his new writer. Tina Turner, that forgotten rhythm and blues singer!

"*What's love got to do with it?*"

Anna was showing my young friend what love had to do with it!

An old story somehow made new. That's what Ezra Pound, my first editor, had said when I was a young writer: MAKE IT NEW.

But when is a writer doing something new in the language with old stories? Well, he may be doing it as James Joyce and Virginia Woolf did, their language like a new eye on reality. Or, whether or not you like Hemingway, the way he wrote at a particular time – his mastery of a style – shaped the use of language in American literature. Then there is the writer who has his own vision of life, his temperament that is always new because he can't be imitated, and you may ignore him, you may abhor him, but you cannot imitate a writer like William Burroughs.

It suddenly strikes me that great writing – Solzhenitsyn in the *Gulag*, Stendhal, Tolstoy's *Ivan Ilytch*, Joyce's *Ulysses*, Woolf, Hemingway's *In Our Time*, Burroughs' *Naked Lunch* . . . like the singer Tina Turner, they give great new legs to old stories.

*Toronto Star*, 1976

# ARTHUR MILLER

The other night, after reading Clive Barnes' wildly enthusiastic review of the revival of *Death of a Salesman* with George C. Scott in the lead, I sat back and fell into a reverie. I was remembering an afternoon years ago in New York a week after the play had opened when I was sitting in the office of my New York agent. He was slightly baffled by the praise being heaped on Miller for this particular work.

The play, for my agent, had a terrible dramatic flaw. As soon as that salesman, Willie Loman, had come on stage carrying those heavy bags as if they were breaking his back, his spirit already broken, my agent said that he had got the whole story. A broken beaten old salesman at the end of his trail, who up and died for my agent as soon as the curtain rose. So, why go on with the story? How could there be any dramatic progression? No matter how the thing was to be dressed up from then on, my agent insisted, nothing much was going to be added to the story that hadn't already been told in the beginning.

A few nights later, when I was in the theatre, watching the play myself, I could see what my agent meant. The heavy bags, the weight of death right there in the beginning. Any worldly fellow might want to turn away, saying, "I've known hundreds of guys like that." By formal dramatic rules, the thing was all wrong. Imagine Macbeth being a beaten man with the smell of death on him as soon as he appears on the stage! And though I was enchanted, feeling I was seeing Arthur Miller at his very best, I nevertheless could agree with my agent; Willie Loman, the salesman, became a figure of infinite pathos rather than tragedy.

Pathetic, pathetic, pathetic! The fact that George C. Scott now seems to be playing Willie Loman for the fierceness and rage in him, rather than the pathos, and scoring an immense success in doing so, is beside the point. I am fascinated when the artist, doing the thing that seems to be structurally all wrong to the trained observer, nevertheless brings it off.

Again and again a trained observer, looking at a story, can say truthfully, "It is all wrong. That is no way to tell a story." The more highly trained you are professionally, the more difficult it becomes for you to free yourself from your traditions and certainties, to look at a thing with fresh eyes and a fresh heart, and ask yourself the one important question, "Does it work? Has the thing got its own authenticity?"

The history of painting is, of course, a history of men who broke all the established rules, set up their own aesthetic structures, were damned as heretics in paint, often to the tune of rioting in the galleries, and then later, they were hailed as masters of a new school. I think, however, that even nature itself delights in making a mockery of a man's rigid aesthetic structural sense of beauty.

Take a woman's face. Men have celebrated a perfect harmony in a woman's face, from the Egyptian Nefertite to Elizabeth Taylor today. In the public arena now, there are two female faces that satisfy my taste. There is the classic beauty of the actress Catherine Deneuve, who has an enchanting face, satisfying all that one remembers of the beauty of other ages and here she is, a beauty in our own age, too, a beauty that gives no trouble to a noon's repose, to a remembered delight.

And then there is another face, another great beauty, Sophia Loren. But the Loren face, if you examine it with the trained eye of a scholar or critic, or an academic painter, or an editor who knows from his training that he has a structurally irritating story on his desk, is all wrong. The Loren face is a mystery; break it down and you find the mouth far too large, the eyes too widely set, the nose at times even seems to jut out too sharply. Yet the parts come together to make a moving impact, the whole is worthier than the parts.

So, about a play, or a poem or a novel, there should be only one question concerning style or the structure. Does it work? Yet it can never work for the editor, the critic, the viewer, or even the copy reader if he can't first of all divest himself of all the rules that have been ground into him, the rules by which he lives.

There doesn't seem to be an editor on the continent now who isn't convinced that Henry James was merely stating God's law when he proclaimed that a story must be told through the eyes of someone vitally concerned in the action. It is a device that James himself found very useful. But I like to think there are a hundred ways of telling a story. In *Death of a Salesman*, Arthur Miller was simply breaking an accepted dramatic progression to achieve his own effect. Any artist who breaks an accepted convention, whether he be a painter, a musician or a novelist, is a law breaker, a kind of criminal or outlaw, a man following his own instinct even if it shatters all the accepted codes that men have agreed to live by. I think the bosses in most totalitarian states have an understanding of the nature of an original artist and so they view him with distrust, watch him suspiciously, and ultimately may have to suppress him unless he agrees to learn to play by their rules.

The Chekhov play, in the beginning, had a bewildering impact on English-speaking audiences. To this day, there are those who shy away from a Chekhov play: they explain that he breaks every rule of the theatre; they say there is no dramatic line at all in his plays.

An intelligent editor, a friend of mine, confessed to me one night that he had never been able to understand the enthusiasm for Chekhov because he could see that time and again, according to his best editorial judgement, everything went wrong, and according to this judgement whole stretches of Chekhov dialogue could be shown to be irrelevant, in the sense that they did not carry forward the dramatic line at all.

He listened very sympathetically while I talked to him about the little things that create a mood, and how little things going on on the stage, even a thing as irrelevant as the chiming of a clock, were all building to a total effect, an ambience that left you, at the end, going far beyond the play into a sense of the deep poignancy of life itself. But I knew by the patient baffled expression in his eyes that he himself would never print a play by Chekhov. If he should do so he would grow so uncertain about his editorial judgement that he might have to give up his job, which would have been a great pity, because he was very good at his particular job.

I have said: the thing is good if it works. My editor friend would say: who says it works? He was right. For him, Chekhov doesn't work. Who is ultimately to say? I don't know. Yet if the editor were to start reading the rule book to me, from Aristotle to Shakespeare, and Ibsen, then I would know that to my satisfaction, at least, he was wrong. All he would be proving to me was that he had never looked at Chekhov with his own eyes, something we all do, because in a sense we have all gone to the same school. The original artist, of course, longs for an audience of intelligent perceptive people who never went to school.

*CBC Anthology*

# COLLEGE OF ONE:
# FITZGERALD

Back in 1937, Sheilah Graham tells us, she grew tired of being a decorative wallflower in the Robert Benchley set of Hollywood, a gossip queen who could be easily exposed as a fake; and she turned to her tormented lover, Scott Fitzgerald, for an education. In *College of One*, she opens the window again on her familiar Hollywood-Fitzgerald landscape. But it is not as it was in her *Beloved Infidel*, where the accent was on the splendour and misery of life with the doomed and alcoholic Fitzgerald. Here, the accent is on another side of his character, a bright, good and true side, and he is presented as a gifted teacher who could give an ambitious woman in a hurry a liberal arts course in about two years of directed reading.

The good thing about this record is that it is so compellingly authentic. If Miss Graham has had to retell her own life story and throw in odds and ends, hoping to enlarge her original portrait of Fitzgerald, no one should complain. Sheilah Graham has a fresh and valid point to make about him; he had a great natural talent for teaching.

Indeed he had! I can recall that you couldn't be at a café in Paris getting a view of a church, or riding in a taxi with him and passing a monument, or going down an old street, without getting a lively and interesting discourse from him. Even when he was quite wrong in his information, there was no pleasure to be found contradicting him. His desire to impart the information seemed to be his way of celebrating his enthusiasm for being alive.

To educate Miss Graham he had prepared a curriculum and there were sheafs of notes. Much of this appeared to be lost. As the years passed and Fitzgerald rose so splendidly from his own ashes, Miss Graham realized she had lost a treasure in those notes. Then, just two years ago, she found the treasure among Fitzgerald documents in the library at Princeton University. The curriculum is given here in *College of One*, along with many of his bright and sardonic comments. In its way, this outline of an education is a kind of period piece, but interesting, for it not only reveals what Fitzgerald thought a bright woman of his time should know; it reveals the slant of his own mind.

The period's fashionable historian was Spengler. Miss Graham was certainly to know all about him. And Proust! Of all things she began her reading of the novel with Proust.

The real delight, however, is to be found in the offhand Fitzgerald comments about the master works. They are bright and pungent and so often wise. "Poetry is not something you get started on by yourself," he noted. "You need at the beginning some enthusiast who knows his way around." And about Palgrave and his *Golden Treasury*! Palgrave was "that Protestant pansy." His view of Dreiser is surprising: "As a storyteller, the best of his generation." And surprising, too, was the fact that he could ignore those beautiful early stories of Hemingway's in his short story list, yet recommend Gertrude Stein's "Three Lives."

Miss Graham's desire to get an education from the man she loved was obviously part of an ancient yearning; a woman's desire to share her lover's inner life. If Fitzgerald, the tutor, hadn't loved his pupil, there couldn't have been this happy involvement with her in which the whole world of learning is made part of the ritual of love.

They could read poems aloud, they could clown and kid, they could in this way draw all the learning into their daily lives.

But some questions come up about those days Sheilah Graham shared with Fitzgerald. At the time she was making very good money herself, and if she was so close to him, how is it that she has to say now she didn't know how broke he was? And a question about Fitzgerald, an old nagging one. In those last years, he was working on *The Last Tycoon*. The legend is that with all the drinking and the hack work he couldn't find time to get on with the novel. Yet he planned and worked on these studies for Sheilah Graham, studies aside, as she says, he catalogued everything, simply everything, only so he could then compose all those fine letters.

This means he was spending long serious reflective hours at his desk. Why couldn't he get to the novel? Were those reflective hours, busy creating a curriculum for his lover, just a way of avoiding that novel? I wish Miss Graham could have revealed that story.

*Washington Post*, 1969

# HUGH GARNER

Though I had known the storyteller Hugh Garner for at least twenty-five years, our meetings were always casual or accidental. On only a few particular occasions did we plan to see each other, so I really knew no more about him than he did about me.

When we did meet, he would talk about himself, and if he was in a desperate situation he would tell me about it with astonishing candour, he didn't mind bleeding openly, and yet, afterwards I would feel that I didn't know what really went on in him any more than he knew what went on in me.

Writers often remain strangers to each other. I had wanted to tell him that I had extraordinary admiration for the way he had lived his life, but I was afraid that if I did, he would have been insulted. I admired him for having made up his mind in his twenties that he was a storyteller, that he had his own talent, that he would show he belonged with the best storytellers, and above all, he would live as a writer – which he did until the day he died.

There are not many writers who have done this. The country is full of semi-professional writers, weekend writers, teachers with another string to their bow, men with other jobs who dream of writing what is known in the trade as the big popcorn novel.

Hugh Garner was a natural storyteller. Some of his stories, stories like "The Conversion of Willie Heaps," are excellent. Who could have done that story any better? Some were careless . . . too often he was a man in a hurry. Anyone is apt to write one good story because a short story is the revelation of one immediate experience making one impact. But in Canada there haven't been more than three or four writers I'd call storytellers with the work there to show it, and Hugh Garner, whether up or down, or careless or very sensitive and perceptive, is surely, with his good stories, among the better four or five. Yet, he had no success in New York, and this was, I think, because he fell somewhere in between John O'Hara and James T. Farrell. He lacked O'Hara's sharp-eyed worldliness and was without Farrell's great scope and powerful sense of inevitability, but his real weakness was that he lacked angularity of temperament; some particular view of life that was his own.

My encounters with him were rather strange and baffling. In the thirties and forties, when he was trying to get launched and was absorbed in reading, I was writing stories which were appearing in the very magazines he was aiming at himself, and though he lived in my home town, I never heard from him. It wasn't until I wrote *The Loved and the Lost* in 1951 that he phoned me and asked me to have a drink with him.

He was a good-looking man. I liked him. But he never mentioned my short stories. I decided he didn't read me at all. After that, I would run into him occasionally. The encounters were amiable, but I thought I had got the hang of him. He seemed to be saying he didn't go in for intellectual conversations, he preferred the company of earthy and gritty buddies who sat around drinking in the old Savarin.

This attitude of his bored me. It was a throwback to those days when a young man was afraid of being taken for a limp-wrist if he didn't talk tough in a fraternity of beer-drinking knuckleheads.

The fact was, Hugh Garner was actually a sensitive and compassionate man, and I think he trapped himself as a writer, pretending to believe that the men in the lower deck of a ship were more real than the officers on the bridge. This was and is an affectation which, in a writer, tends to make his world small. Yet, Hugh Garner made a point of hating all affectations. He had a drinking problem, and I used to wonder if this alcoholic loneliness or despair came from a realization that he had to act out a role which really didn't satisfy his heart.

As I say, my own encounters with him were always something to mull over. One night after we had done a radio broadcast together I took him to my house where he encountered one of my sons. "How old are you?" he asked the son. "Twenty-three," the son answered. "What do you do for a living?" Hugh asked. "I'm going to school," the son said. "Law school," I put in quickly. But Hugh, not hearing, said, "You're twenty- three years old and you're still going to school? What the fuck for?" and he looked disgusted. The difficulty for me was that he not only sounded virtuous, he really believed that any good man would agree with him, so it was hard for either me or my son to laugh without offending him.

Then, in the sixties, I got three short letters of apology from him. The first came after he had written a column in the *Telegram* – in effect, he had said that I was done as a writer, that I was on the shelf. I said nothing to him. He wrote again, a note. I didn't have time to answer. A final note came full of profuse apologies, insisting he hadn't realized what he had written!

Okay, I thought. Okay. Anyway, over these years I still wasn't sure whether he had ever read any of my short stories. But then, as the months went by, on at least two occasions when he was being interviewed, he took little cracks at me, perhaps being in a boozy state of mind, and then came the note of apology. Always the apologist. The odd part of it was, as prickly as I can sometimes be, that I didn't get angry, just thoughtful.

Another year or two passed, a newspaperman interviewing him asked him about other writers and mentioned my name and Hugh said, "I wish he'd take his money and go off around the world." The note of apology came promptly saying that as an old friend I should know that his liquor had run away with his tongue. That night he came to the house bearing gifts. Two volumes of my early stories he had had for years and wanted to give to me. At last I knew that Hugh had read all my stories.

My most moving encounter came after a phone call from him. He had just come out of the hospital. They had thought he was dying of cancer of the stomach. It turned out he didn't have cancer. He wanted to have a drink. So we met and drank and he told me all about the hospital, and just before it was time to part, looking me right in the eye he said solemnly, "You're ten years older than I am."

"That's right," I said. "What about it?"

"Nothing" he said with a mysterious satisfaction.

Yet I understood what he meant, and was I moved. He had ten years to write books, ten years still to do more than I had done, just give him the ten years. Writers. Strangers to each other. Yet why was it that I could never hold to a harsh sentiment about Hugh Garner?

*CBC Anthology*

# ON BEING GENIUSES
TOGETHER

❧❧❧

The two writers, Robert McAlmon and Kay Boyle, whose memoirs of Paris in the twenties are offered here in the form of a dialogue in *Being Geniuses Together*, belong to the scene they write about as authentically as do those cafés, the Dôme and the Select on Montparnasse. Kay Boyle and Robert McAlmon, in the lives they led in the Quarter, earned the right to the expression of their intensely personal views of their old friends and their enemies, too, and since at the time Paris was the one lighted place drawing to it talented people from all over America and Europe, most of them to become friends or enemies of McAlmon, this book becomes the place you go to find out what the people with the great names of the time, Joyce, Pound, Eliot, Hemingway, Stein, Wyndham Lewis, Sinclair Lewis, William Carlos Williams, and a half a hundred others really thought of each other.

Kay Boyle, still alive and writing well, is widely known. Robert McAlmon has been dead for some years. He seems to be remembered only in the books of those who knew him personally. Yet he was one of the most admirable, infuriating, contemptuous, generous, malicious, interesting, insulting, unbudgeable men of his time. The reason for all these adjectives may be found in this memoir of his, first published in 1934.

McAlmon, a young American from the middle west, in New York at the beginning of the twenties, and determined to be a writer, had married Bryher, the daughter of Sir John Ellerman, one of the rich men of England. It was strictly a marriage of convenience. McAlmon now had money. Soon he was off to Paris, off to Spain, off to Berlin and meeting everyone and respecting no one.

But he had a touch of greatness about him. He established his Contact Press. He was the first to publish Hemingway's work; he also published Gertrude Stein's *The Making of Americans* when that well-off old girl wouldn't risk a nickel of her own on it. He was that unique thing, a writer willing to spend his money on the advancement of other writers. And of course, by the time he died he must have been nursing the bitter thought that all those he helped had soon forgotten him.

But the key to McAlmon's fate, and surely Kay Boyle sees it, or remembers it, is in this book. He had to cut you down. Even if he liked you and was drinking with you, he turned the knife. You winced, and if you liked and respected him, you laughed it off. I can still see him sitting there at the café with his little grin growing more disdainful as he got really drunk. The fact is, though, that his cutting down, his cattiness, was always based on some shrewd perception: high and splendid irreverence and happy malice. In the memoir he treats Wyndham Lewis as a grovelling tradesman, T.S. Eliot as a kind of English undertaker's assistant, Gertrude Stein as a rather dim-witted lady who had conned a little public into believing her childish repetitions profound because she was so heavy herself.

And Hemingway, his old friend? Something happened between them the first time they went to Spain together. McAlmon doesn't really tell about the incident. From then on his bitterness about Hemingway won't let him rest. Hemingway owed him a lot. He paid off by punching McAlmon in the mouth. In the end, he sees Hemingway simply as a cheap publicity seeker.

Of the great names, only two held his affection to the end. His old dear drinking companions, Joyce and William Carlos Williams; they are spared his amused disdain. All this seems to put McAlmon in a horrible light; indeed, he often was in that light. But if he was bent on belittling everyone, dozens of his friends were bent on belittling him. All I can say, as one whom he often made wince, then grin, is that I would love to see him coming along the boulevard with his disdainful smile, ready to sit down at the café with us for the evening; and it would be very refreshing to hear some of his cutting perceptions into the work of Joyce, of Eliot, of Hemingway – perceptions rooted in his first hand contact with their texts.

Kay Boyle's memoir in this same book, it seems to me, should be dealt with separately and not taken as a dialogue with McAlmon. But that's the way it is presented and this arrangement irritated me. The Boyle memoir, about the same years and often about the same people, is a charming and beautiful story of a romantic girl in love with the idea of being a great writer among the most interesting people of the time. Yet, there is reason for having her memoir in the same book as McAlmon's; her touch is so different; in happy contrast, she is free from malice.

The central incident of her story has to do with her love affair with Ernest Walsh, who was the editor of *This Quarter*, one of the important magazines then publishing Joyce and Hemingway. She had a child by Ernest Walsh. Her picture of their relationship and how her love for him haunted her after his quick death is quite moving. But this picture also has another value that makes it belong in the literature of our time with a note underneath explaining it should be always read in contrast with the picture Hemingway gives of the same Ernest Walsh in his *A Moveable Feast*. The Hemingway portrait is all malice and viciousness. Is this the way Paris was in those days? Backbiting and needling! Or did it all depend on who the teller of the tale was? Because it wasn't all hate and malice. It was a wonderful time to be alive. These two memoirs in the one book bring the period and those people very close, all vivid and angry and alive again.

*Toronto Telegram*, 1968

# SAROYAN
# AND ANDERSON

Reading William Saroyan's autobiography, *Obituaries*, I came upon a comment that stirred up many old and moving memories. He remarked rather casually, as if there could be no doubt about it, that Sherwood Anderson had had a greater influence on American writing than any other writer in the first fifty years of this century. I was delighted. Anderson had meant so much to me when I was twenty. He gave me a whole world. He must have done the same for Saroyan, and for a hundred other writers, too.

When I was twenty, reading Anderson, who had a very small audience at the time, had suddenly forced me to wonder what made good writing good. Was it the balanced sentence, the rhythmic grace of a Walter Pater, the English master. It couldn't be this. In those days if I read such men closely it was because I was observing the techniques of English prose and trying to learn something. I got no leap in the heart out of it. But soon I discovered there was another kind of writing, writing that had such freshness I could almost smell the dew on the grass. I could get a world, a new world, or rather have the old world made new by the freshness and wonder in the author's eyes. Only a few times in the life of a writer does any other writer come along, who disturbs him and makes him restless and finally touches some chord in him that makes him want to start writing feverishly and with the greatest confidence.

I'll never forget Anderson because after one year at college when I was wallowing in English prose, trying to get going, I read a few stories of Anderson's in magazines. Suddenly my writing became easy for me and exciting. All around me seemed to be people who were stories or as Anderson himself called them, unlighted lamps. They had their own language which was my language, a spoken language that had its own rhythms and its own ripeness, and it seemed that all I needed to do was listen and use my own eyes.

A few years later when I met Anderson in New York I startled him, saying solemnly that he was my father. Rather uneasily he asked my name. When I told him he started to laugh, he knew my work, and we embraced, then he said seriously, "Don't kid yourself. You would write as you do even if you had never heard of me."

Maybe so. But I still have a vast wonder about those magic moments when a writer reads a piece by another writer and wants to get going immediately on his own work – as if a door had just been opened – as if he had just been shown something he had never seen before.

I remember, too, my reading of the first few pages of James' Joyce's *Ulysses*. I quickened almost nervously. Something was happening on the pages; things under a camera. But where was the camera, and then with me came the hunger, the hankering to start trying to write this way, then the realization that a thousand other writers would be having the same hankering. Yet it was one of those rare times when another writer added to my awareness by way of a method. Though I have never tried to use the method myself, one writer tends to read another writer with a watchful professional eye. As a Canadian, I can read a story by Mavis Gallant and admire it, I can admire a story by Alice Munro, and I can appreciate a comic chapter in a Richler novel, and going on afield, I can admire the cleverness of a Phillip Roth, and be astonished that Mailer can change his style and can become simple and direct in the *Executioner's Song*, as easily as a man gets a haircut. I read to quarrel, or admire, or appreciate, always as a professional, and yet I know that in the back of my mind is that hope that I will hit on a writer who will so shake me up that the whole world of writing will become new again. I'm like a man on a train. I'm watching the landscape flowing by the window, sooner or later I must see something going on out there which will make me jump up and shout, "Stop the train, I want to get off." It can't happen very often.

Years ago there was Kafka. When I read *The Trial*, then *The Castle* and some of the short stories, I was troubled and restless. Kafka had come along at a time that should have been just right for me. I was writing little or nothing. He set me off again because he seemed to have a new sense of destiny which was intoxicating, but I did nothing of any consequence. A little later I realized Kafka was not opening a window for me. His people weren't my people, my temperament wasn't his. What he was doing was troubling me intellectually, which is of course, very good for a writer. But it couldn't make me write. Indeed, that kind of influence can become a block to a man's writing.

The last time I had the delight in recognition of my open widening eyes, was when I read Marquez's *A Hundred Years of Solitude*. Here was something new and exciting that made me want to start writing. Joyce in *Finnegans Wake* had combined in a dreaming mind all of a man's racial memories and myths, the world's river of dreams flowing through the man's mind. Marquez, in his Colombian town, had layers of faces, myths, tall tales, memories, and an action taking place under our eyes, a living present. I marvelled at what he had done. I rejoiced because I saw that there was no end to what could be done in writing. Yet I had the sense to know this wouldn't be for me. That town was Marquez. A million miles from my train. I knew there would be a hundred writers who would try foolishly to follow him.

A great British editor said to me, "A writer, once he passes a certain age, gets set in his ways, set in his style. It took him a long time to develop it. Why should he change?" It's true. But a man who is set in his ways avoids too much excitement, he avoids passion, he avoids all wonder about the world. I can't help believing that there is a new writer just around the next corner, who will shake me and fill me with new wonder just as Sherwood Anderson did when the dew was on the grass for him many hears ago, and I'm glad that Saroyan now reminds me of this.

*There come now no kings nor Caesars*
*Nor gold-giving lords like those gone.*

—EZRA POUND

# HEROES

At midnight when I was walking my dog, I passed some tall bushes alongside a house, got a spray of water on my head as if it had started to rain, and a voice coming out of the shadows called, "Just a minute," and a neighbour, who was watering his lawn turned the hose in another direction, joined me on the sidewalk and said, "Tell me something, will you? I've just been wondering why it is that only hockey players are heroes in this country. Why is it that this country has no other heroes?"

And so there at midnight with the dog waiting patiently I listened and wondered if it was true that we in this country were embarrassed by the appearance of greatness in men and women. My neighbour then asked if it wasn't true that as soon as a local writer or an actor or a musician or scientist was called great by someone in another country we felt compelled to belittle him.

"Well, since you've been here behind your bushes swishing your hose around and thinking about this, tell me why it's so," I said. He said he wasn't sure, but was wondering if it all was due to the Scottish cultural influence. He was of Scottish origin himself. In English-speaking Canada, he went on, the dominant cultural influence was overwhelmingly Scottish. It had shaped the Canadian temperament, and so we were all cautious in our appraisal of all human achievement, and suspicious of flamboyant men, and certainly we wanted to do good business without being noticed.

Well, a frugality of the spirit was never a good climate for heroes, he said. "What do you think?" But my dog, bored and impatient, was pulling me away, so I said, "I'll see you tomorrow night at midnight," and went on my way. Heroes, I thought. Who were our greatest heroes if not hockey players? Well, maybe happy, healthy, democratic people don't need heroes. Happy the land that has no history. Heroes usually emerge from times of bloody conflict. I suppose that's why Louis Riel gets bigger for us every year: he was one of our few periods of bloodshed. Anyway, one man's hero is often another man's thug, and I remembered that when I read Carlyle's *Heroes and Hero Worship*, he made Oliver Cromwell sound just like Hitler and yet he was one of Carlyle's heroes. In the United States they were lucky, I thought. They had all those outlaws. Jessie James, Billie the Kid, the Daltons, and it was as if the Americans realized they needed these outlaws to remind them that the human imagination can't be forever satisfied with the banality of eternal frugality, caution and commercial respectability.

The imagination reminds us that the human spirit has to be lifted out of the stultifying pattern of an ironclad law. The saint is really an outlaw, and so is the great artist with his own shattering vision. Oh, where will we find a wild west of the imagination? The hockey player, my neighbour said. Well, yes, maybe he is our figure of violence. Violence put on ice. Hasn't it been bred into us in our schoolrooms that the great heroes, the ones who have enchanted the world, are masters in the world of violence, causing the slaughter of millions? They came at us through all our formative years at school. The Greek heroes of Homer, then Caesar, Hannibal, Tamburlaine, Alexander the Great, Napoleon, Wellington, Marlborough – on and on. Masters of violence were they all, and we haven't had anyone like them in Canada, so maybe my neighbour is right. The poor dear hockey player, teeth long gone to a cross-check, is the best we can do.

# FOSTER HEWITT

Early in the 1920s, when I was at college and working in the summer months as a reporter on the *Toronto Daily Star*, I used to see occasionally a thin-faced, slightly built man about my own age who, whenever I saw him, seemed to be hurrying from one office to another. I never saw him at a desk in the newsroom. When I asked who he was I was told that he was Foster Hewitt, the son of the sports editor, W.A. Hewitt, and that he was fooling around with the idea of a hockey broadcast on radio. At that time the *Star*, across the road from Child's restaurant on King Street, had a remarkable crew of reporters. Gordon Sinclair was there, and for four months Ernest Hemingway was suffering and bleeding under the whip of the legendary city editor, Harry Hindmarsh. Hindmarsh later described us as a raffish crew, too big for our britches. But there was nothing raffish about Foster Hewitt.

If Hewitt had any boon companions, they were not on the editorial staff. I used to like going across to Child's for a coffee and long conversations, but I never saw Foster Hewitt – trim, dapper, pale – sitting around with the boys. If anyone had told me he was a boxer, I would have thought the idea absurd. Nor could I have dreamed that one day he would become a great actor, powerful enough to draw the people of his country together.

I had played hockey in the old Toronto Hockey League until I was seventeen. I liked watching hockey games. Only when I could not see them did I listen to a radio broadcast. When the 1930s came around, Hewitt's Saturday broadcasts had a huge and loyal audience, a tribal family around a national hearth. I thought people listened to Hewitt on Saturday night because they couldn't get to the Gardens.

One night I called in on my father and mother at their home and found them sitting in the dark, near the radio, listening to Foster Hewitt. I turned on the light. My father had a happy smile and my mother's blue eyes were shining with excitement.

I was bemused – I had no idea either one of them had any interest in hockey. My father had had no interest in sport. Though I had played baseball in all the city leagues, I could never get him to come and watch me pitch. Yet there he was listening to Foster Hewitt with my mother, both of them breathless with pleasure. About a week later I phoned, expecting to have a long conversation with my mother. She told me rather hurriedly that the Leafs were losing three to two and she would call me back.

They had never seen a hockey game, so I got them two tickets for a Saturday night game at the Gardens. The next day I went to see them. How had they liked the game? It was confusing, they said apologetically, almost upsetting and very strange. I said I'd get them tickets again. No, they said, looking at each other uneasily, they were more comfortable listening at home.

I thought the trip to the Gardens, the crowd, the traffic, must have been unfamiliar and tiring for them. But a year or so later a friend – Bertram Brooker, a painter and writer and later vice-president of MacLaren Advertising – asked me if my wife and I would come to his home on Saturday night to hear the Hewitt broadcast of the hockey game. He had friends, cronies, painters, musicians, and writers, who came to his place every Saturday for the game and a party.

"I didn't know you liked hockey," I said. "But since you obviously do, then why don't we go to a game together?"

"I don't want to go to a game."

Baffled, I said bluntly, "Then you don't like hockey."

"So you say," he said curtly, and a silence fell between us, a kind of hostility. We dropped the subject, and I imagined that he and his intellectual friends were like my father and mother. A real game of hockey might have bewildered them.

Why so many people preferred to listen to Foster Hewitt rather than seeing a game continued to baffle me until the evening a neighbour asked me if I'd go with him to the Gardens to see a Canadiens-Leafs game.

His wife came to my house to visit with my wife and listen to the broadcast while we went off to the Gardens. Hockey is a peculiar game, a little like ballet. At its best it has a flash, a suspense, a grace, an elegance in the pattern of the playmaking. At its grinding worst, it's dull, heavy, and monotonous. That night we found ourselves watching a dull game.

When we got home my wife said, "My, we were wishing we could have been with you. It must have been quite a game."

"It was a tedious game," I said sourly.

"What's the matter with you two?" my neighbour's wife asked. "Foster was so excited, and we got so excited too."

Now I thought I got the hang of Foster Hewitt's powerful magic. With amused and satisfied cynicism, I thought that he was one of the world's greatest salesmen. He could take the most ordinary game – the product – and package it by selecting what he saw on the ice, so exciting himself that he could draw around him a million listeners – much of English-speaking Canada coming together under his spell. And I decided there and then that the National Hockey League owed him about $10 million for what he had done for the game.

In the 1940s, the National Film Board hired a director of documentaries to make a film about hockey. This director, a fellow from New York named Irving Jacoby, asked me if I would write some narration. Jacoby and I became friends, and he wanted to use my voice for the whole narration. But the Film Board guy said he wanted a voice that sounded more like that of a BBC announcer, an impersonal voice.

On the day we were doing the voice testing, Foster Hewitt joined us. He was to do a two-minute broadcast of a hockey game, for use in the film. He came in looking exactly as he had when I'd first seen him in the old Star building – just as slim and trim, just as inconspicuous. Wasting no time, knowing exactly what was expected of him, he went into the sound booth.

I could have believed I was at home and he was at Maple Leaf Gardens – that slightly high-pitched voice, deliberate pauses, mounting tension, the sense of some fierce impending action on the ice when he said, "He dumps it in," then the exultant cry, "He shoots, he scores!" I wanted to stand up and yell. I could have sworn he was at least watching a movie of a game. But there was no movie. There was no game. He didn't need a game. He was just as good without one. He was alone with himself in the booth. Astonished, I realized what an extraordinary creative artist he was. In his own way Foster Hewitt was as good as Marlon Brando. He could give life to things!

When Hewitt had finished his job he came out of the sound booth. I walked to the door with him but he had no time for idle conversation. As I watched him get into his big grey Cadillac and drive away, I remember thinking, "There goes the greatest dramatic artist in the whole country."

Remarkable as he was, though, he had his limitations. He was like a dramatist who had done only one play. What made him unique was that, for two generations of Canadians, he became bigger than his play. He became the play.

*Saturday Night*, 1985

# THE HENDERSON GOAL

On the morning after the Canadian National hockey team defeated the Russian team in Moscow, the game in which Henderson scored his incredible goal, I came to a stunning realization.

Getting up in the morning, I grabbed the *Globe and Mail* and started to read the big front-page story. In the first third of the column, right after the lede,[1] and even in the headline, the goal was referred to as "the twenty-five thousand dollar goal." And down into the column, the discussion went on as to whether Henderson could get his contract with the Toronto Maple Leafs changed now, and I was given a report of the emotional dialogue between those two all-time great Canadians, the agent, Al Eagleson, and the owner, Harold Ballard. Their outpouring of emotion led straight to business. With a kind of puritanical surprise, I blinked my eyes and asked myself if the conversation of a couple of businessmen about a property, a player, was the really big news out of Moscow. And did the news editor of this great national journal really believe this was the right lede for a national triumph.

I tried to imagine a smash hit on Broadway, and a newspaper story about the play, in which the first third of the column was given

---

[1] As a word, "lede" is not in the Oxford Dictionary. It is, however, in various newspaper style books. Reporters and editors use the word, but often are never quite sure how to spell it; "lede" or "lead," as in "leading entry." The word "lede," in fact, comes from that period when newspapers were printed using hot lead. Newspapermen, to distinghish between the metal – "lead" – and the lead to a story, that is, the opening paragraph, coined "lede" as an in-house spelling for "lead."

over to a dialogue between the author's agent, and his Hollywood boss who had him under contract. I couldn't imagine it. It was too incredible, too commercial, too much like a satire on a little shop-keeper's world.

And then I thought, wait a minute! The job of that news editor at the *Globe and Mail,* and the reporter who wrote that kind of story, was to sound the note, at the start, that would warm the hearts of my countrymen. What, then, is more fascinating in our society than money? What seems to unite us all in an emotional binge? Money! And this was a special case. Usually, there is envy and bitterness in many hearts when a man has a claim to a huge jump in salary. But Henderson was a heroic figure, he had done what we wanted him to do, he had satisfied us all, and so it was all right, it was lovely, to think of dollar bills and not angels floating around his head.

It is apparent that the news editor with his headline, and the reporter with his story, were right: they were much closer to a good hard understanding of native exultation than I have been in my work. It is as if they understood instinctively that when Henderson scored his fabulous goal every man in the country turned to his wife, and with tears in his eyes, said, "I'd like to be there when his agent talks to his owner."

Looking back on it, it's clear to me that in a perverse way I have ignored the fascination with money in all my work. There was no excuse for this attitude. In the early thirties, most writers, especially those under the Marxian influence, agreed that money and sex made the world go around. It must have been, however, that I had some strange conviction that money did not alter intimate relationships, that the rich in their intimacies were just as twisted and unhappy as the poor, and I wanted to deal with the intimate relationships. It's my only excuse, this belief that the real world with all its triumphs and failures in what we do to each other is a world where all men, in their hearts, are equal.

But no. That Henderson goal, with the agent rushing to the owner, for the gratification of the nation, made a few things clear to me. Why not a television show dealing strictly with people telling how much money they have and how they got it, the mistakes they made, how they corrected their mistakes, and above all, what the money got them in houses and cars?

A really interesting show could be done by a loose lady out for hire who would spend very little time telling about the physical details of her encounters, but giving a careful account of the cash involved, those who had to be cut in, and the amount saved and banked. She would make it perfectly clear that only the money fascinated her, as it so often does anyway, but the convention has been to play this side of hooker sex down. Now, she would be playing it up and she would be telling of the struggle she went through as she increased her stipend and how she heroically resisted other temptations of the flesh, and as her bank balance really grew we would become fascinated, we would be at one with her, and rooting for her to make a million, and then on the morning after her biggest score with her biggest-ever john, we would wait expectantly for word from her pleased-as-punch pimp, word of a new contract.

*CBC Anthology*

# NORMAN MAILER

Since Norman Mailer has always had an uncanny instinct for a style that mirrors the taste of his time, I have been fascinated by the change in his new book, *The Executioner's Song*. Everyone has noticed this change. In fact, Mailer has talked about it himself at great length, and unless I misread the signs and portents – this means we are soon to say goodbye to a kind of journalism that he made so popular.

He wasn't just interesting as a journalist, he was compelling. It was as if his longing to write a distinguished novel had got twisted in him, a longing that had emerged as a method of reporting, and this method, this approach to journalism, consisted simply of making himself more important, and in fairness, often much more fascinating, than the event he was recording. Objective analysis, the objective story, no matter how brilliant, seemed to be dead.

There was, indeed, a kind of reversal of Chekhov's advice to Gorki; if you haven't got the facts then be lyrical; now it was, easy on the facts if you can be lyrical and personal. These were big days for men like Mailer and Tom Wolfe, who could explode personally in every paragraph. This method, this right stuff, became so beguiling that it was picked up by ambitious young journalists in every town, and I remember reading a story about a hockey player, and somehow the hockey player, great as he might be, had reminded the writer of his grandmother, and so the journalist recounted his experience with the grandmother, a chain of Proustian memories opening up, the writer, in himself, becoming much bigger than the great hockey player, and stunned, I wondered what had happened to the editors.

But there it was! The writer, bigger than the object, the material. Essentially, this is the romantic enlargement of the self, the self so enlarged, in fact, that it can never be truly contained. The romantic! The self reaching out in a discontent or profound melancholy for measureless distances. Grand or pretentious as this may sound, it did get into journalism. But, why? Why was this attitude to material so acceptable at this time, and why the change in the attitude of the general public?

It seems that we have been passing through a romantic period. Signs of this should have been read: in lavender, not in old lace, not in the gallantries and sentimentalities of the hour, but in signs of a more honest, truer, more brazen and more brutal romanticism – represented by a longing for some wild feverish raw enlargement of the self through everything from drugs to clothes to language.

That time of signs, that decade, the sixties, the unpredictable dizzying sixties, were days in which there were supposed to be no dirty little secrets; everything was to have been hung out at high noon in the market place. Even in economics and sociology! Marcuse! Remember? Romantic Marxism?

Then, suddenly the attitude changed. It's baffling, it's heartbreaking, it dates us. Yes, it changed as suddenly as Norman Mailer has changed his attitude to his material in *The Executioner's Song*. It is now to be reporting. Reporting! The objective observer. After all, Tolstoy was a pretty good reporter. So, out goes the style of the seven veils of the Mailer ego. Maybe just in time. Just in time! Margaret Thatcher now reigns in London. Ronald Reagan is among us, smiling.

A sudden change in the temper of the times can bring about a change in attitude toward a writer's style. About ten years ago, an

American writer I know wrote a lean hard clean intensely objective book, brutally clear in its impact. The book was not only a great critical success – he also made a lot of money. Shrewdly, he waited ten years and then he wrote another book in the same hard style. It was a flop. Worse still, no one seemed to know he wrote it, that it was his style. Why? He wondered. Why?

The publisher said, "Times change."

That's all.

Times change. People take a different attitude. So this writer, as perhaps we all have to do, went around wondering if his success, his critical acclaim were not simply a record of changing attitudes, meaning that the smart editor, or publisher, is the one who has a long wet finger always held up to the wind. Yet, where do you go to feel a change of attitude coming on? What high mountain did Norman Mailer climb? Where is the mountain?

Any artist, writer or painter, who has self-respect must loathe the roadrunners who rush in with news of the change of attitude, a leak in the pipe, the leak soon to be a flood. It is as if no one can ever know what is really good or bad. I don't buy this. If I did, I'd have to believe that no civilization could ever flower, no writer could have a style and a temperament that bridged the ages. This is a lie about life. Catullus and Sappho and Chaucer and Villon are there in themselves, and in the long run, it doesn't matter a hoot what attitude we, in a particular decade, take to them. They sit in judgement of all changing attitudes.

And so, I find myself thinking about these matters because of Norman Mailer's new book, *The Executioner's Song*, about a strange man, Gary Gilmore of Utah, who committed two murders, a man who – once he was convicted – refused to go through the long delaying process of appeal after appeal, insisting instead, to the consternation of a vast instantly created public, that the state execute him.

This Gilmore, the murderer, turns out to be a remarkably interesting man. The central character of the book, he creates suddenly a whole world around himself. Because this man chose death, his public feasted on every intimate little detail of his private life. He became a commercial event. He became, too, a mirror of our society. A mirror mounted in the prison, with all of us dancing around outside the prison: dancing images in his mirror, and certainly looking worse than he ever imagined us to be when he chose death, rather than be confined for life – on the other side of a wall to this circus we call our society.

Though he is the central character of this scene, a man who, at the end, commands our sympathy, can he be thought of as "the hero"? Give me liberty or death is a heroic statement that comes easily to a man's lips. Few men mean it. This man did. He was prepared to pay the price – his life – to escape confinement – death itself. Going his own way, by going to die, he affirmed the legal system, but not for us, not to purge us of our fears and our pity, but for himself, entirely for himself. Gary Gilmore as a hero is at first glance preposterous but he suddenly embodied an idea that lifted him into a realm where, as a man among men, few had ever walked. What is it that troubles me, then, about his being heroic? After all, even a murderer can enter the heroic realm. What about Dostoevsky's Rashkalnikof of *Crime and Punishment*, the student, with dreams of becoming a superman above the law who kills a poor old woman. He is a hero because he is alive as the representative human being in the eternal story of *Crime and Punishment*, he is the man in torment who gradually realizes that he is a wretched human being, who in the end discovers his humanity. He is all of us, only more so. More! But what is the "more" in this wretched Gilmore?

Wherever we go we rarely find our heroes leading exemplary lives. This is true, I imagine, even for our saints, who are of course, heroes in quest of a spiritual perfection, and yet even in the field of saintliness, it is those who are obsessed, those who burn with a passion, those who can only go one way, their own, who catch the imagination and make us want to follow them in one leap of the heart.

In fiction, it seems, there is a vast difference between the hero, or heroine, and the merely sympathetic character. If a book is to do well, they tell me, the leading character, commonly called the hero, must be sympathetic. Gary Gilmore is not sympathetic. I remember talking to that great American editor Max Perkins, who had just published Ernest Hemingway's *A Farewell to Arms*, and he asked if I had noticed that Hemingway had taken pains to see that his lover soldier never put himself in a bad light, so the reader had to be sympathetic to everything he did. This was very true, and maybe in so lyrical a story, this was needed. But surely now no one could think of the lieutenant in *A Farewell to Arms* as a hero. He's a nice guy who never violates our sympathies. The world is full of these guys. No, that book succeeded for other reasons.

In *Gone with the Wind*, Scarlet O'Hara is a fiery little bitch. Yet among movie heroines she remains with us. Why? Because she is more of what she is, and in the end, we sympathize with her, and many a girl has tried to emulate her. Or Flaubert's *Madame Bovary*. For me, she is a genuine and almost perfect heroine. If Hemingway was careful that his hero should do nothing unsympathetic, Flaubert is just as careful that Emma Bovary be shown not only as self-centred, envious, and ungrateful to her husband while all the while nursing a fantasy about herself as a lady caught up in the throes of great romantic passion. Her dream, her false view of her little life, ruins her, but she is truly heroic for me, she lives on in literature, possessing more than anyone else the embodiment of that pathetic romantic view we can have of ourselves – now called Bovarism. She has it more than anyone else in literature. More of the thing! All around we see people following her.

I don't know where to go looking for heroes today, where do I go looking for someone who makes me want to be like him, someone who gets into my dreams? Who is he? What is he like? What has he more of? More of something stirring in him, like Ulysses. And now, just now, after saying there was an aspect of Gary Gilmore, the wretched murderer who had never been able to live with any dignity outside a prison, that struck me as being heroic, I know why Ulysses comes suddenly to mind. Ulysses, the voyager. Ah, Ulysses! More cunning than other men, more courageous, more unyielding in purpose, more resourceful, more wily, more of everything, while he voyaged out widening the margins of his world till he was old and it was time to come home.

Gilmore believed intensely in an afterlife. So did his girl. Rather than be confined, he preferred to plunge into that unknown after life, and he did. A hoodlum Ulysses. Finding his liberty in death.

*CBC Anthology*

# WOMAN'S WORLD

Back in the pre-feminist days, when I was at college, I used to read Katherine Mansfield, Virginia Woolf and Dorothy Richardson, and ten years later Katherine Anne Porter – and I never thought of them as being women writers. They were writers as I was a writer, and it was what they did with their material, their sensibility and their insight, that was fascinating, never the fact that they were women.

And later, when I was writing stories for the *New Yorker*, the managing editor, who handled my work, was Katherine White. That she was a woman seemed utterly irrelevant, and I never wondered if she had any views about the role of women in our society. It was the work, only the work, that counted.

When the militant feminists took over, their movement seemed to me to be a thing apart from imaginative writing. Politics can, of course, get into writing, and what was supposed to be so interesting about those fiction writers who were so committed to the feminist cause was that in writing from the view of a liberated woman they would come up with astonishing new insights into human relationships; men would be seen as they had never been seen before, seen at last through the eyes of an uninhibited woman.

Well, I ask mildly, diffidently, did any of this really come off? Surely we can now ask the question, now that it is supposed to be the post-feminist period. Did any one of these militant feminist fiction writers, with no holds barred, tell us as much about the feminine sensibility as, say, Katherine Mansfield did?

The other night I heard Erica Jong – she wrote *Fear of Flying* – being interviewed on television, and she was asked about women writers who seem to dwell exclusively on women and their problems. She said, why shouldn't women write mainly about women? After all, men wrote mainly about men, didn't they?

For a woman writer who has, I believe, some academic pretensions, this balderdash was incredible.

There are men, the macho men, who love locker room stuff, the brutal horsing around about women, all boys towel-snapping together, the bold tough gestures that have little to do with human relationships. And there are now women writers, just as brash and limited, who give you only their own locker room rowdiness, and – forgive me the corny expression – but they sit around talking about sex and men as if men were only sex objects, dildos wearing shoes.

Well, these women are just as boring as the macho men.

Other men, however – the writers – have always loved to write about women. The great portraits of women in fiction have all been done by men. Is there a lovelier or truer picture of the heart of a woman in all literature than Tolstoy's *Anna Karenina*? And there is Henry James' *Portrait of a Lady*. And what woman writer has created the dreaming reverie of a woman as Joyce did in his Molly Bloom soliloquy in *Ulysses*? No woman has touched it. And Flaubert's *Madame Bovary*? She is immortal, for she is the very soul, in herself, of all those women, rich or poor, the factory girl or the college girl, who have had a false view of themselves which led to their destruction.

To put the matter in balance, it is well to remember that a woman, a great writer and a mistress of human relationships, was not at her best with women but with a man. Think of Emily Brontë's great portrait of Heathcliffe in *Wuthering Heights*, a book in tone and style and treatment that doesn't date. The style is so crisp and clean and yet so sensitively poetic without affectation that it strikes me as being the kind of style many modern writers aspire to, and in Heathcliffe, she gave the reader a wry, twisted yet masculine and thoroughly understandable human being, Heathcliffe, the product of the piercing imagination of a spinster, and this English spinster, of all things, understood romantic and desperate love as it can grip the heart of a man as well as a woman, Cathy and Heathcliffe like nothing else in English fiction, their love having its own odd, jagged impact.

No, no, a great writer is a great writer whether male or female. Wouldn't it be rather ironic if it turns out that, in the end, our time of determined feminism not only limited, but actually blighted, the talent of many a greatly gifted woman writer?

*CBC Anthology*

# JAMES T. FARRELL

Among American academics, big or small, perceptive or dumb, James T. Farrell's masterly creation, is *Studs Lonigan*. Lonigan stands as a monument of the time, but ever since that time critics have had their vision blocked by the monument's shadow. The critics think they know all about Farrell.

A few years ago, he wrote a short novel, *New Year's Eve, 1929*. It was something of a master work; a poignant, intense story with a beautiful unity of tone and an utter fidelity to life. Certainly Chekhov could not have done that story any better. I remember I watched for the reviews, and of course soon grew dismayed: not that some of the critical pieces were not pretty good, but behind the pieces was so often the half-articulated determination of a young academic to assert that he had known about Farrell a long time ago, and knew exactly where Farrell stood in the literature courses. I wanted to shout, "I don't care about your credentials in Farrell awareness . . . For God's sake look at the piece there under your eyes."

I think if someone would closely examine the novels between *Ellen Rogers* and *Invisible Swords* he would find passages of poetic intensity in the delineation of a character that would make him feel he was in touch with a Farrell he had hardly known. In search of this new Farrell I have sometimes wished I could cut down the even, naturalist flow of the prose that his method seems to demand, although I know it is the proven strength of the work.

But this is the world of Farrell, and, I suppose, readers hesitate to enter it when the circus barkers of literature are shouting that the contemporary masterpieces are about meditative seagulls or vaginal wailing. Farrell is out of step but sooner or later people will want to know what life was really like in Farrell's time, which is now as well as forty years ago, and then they will read him.

*20th Century Literature*, Volume 22, No. 1, 1976

# JOHN O'HARA

There is a new biography of John O'Hara. Alfred Kazin has written about the book in the *New York Times*. Kazin, accurate and just in all his perceptions, offered such a dismissal of O'Hara, the man and his work, that I grew depressed. O'Hara had been a big man all my writing life. He had made a million dollars, he had a Rolls Royce, a big house near Princeton, and not long before he died, *Newsweek* in a cover story had pronounced him about the best writer in America. Yet here is his biographer, Mr. McShane, just five years later, declaring he is trying to restore some interest in O'Hara's fiction and here is Alfred Kazin declaring O'Hara a parvenu who toadied to the rich and successful.

I was always of two minds about O'Hara's work. From the beginning, he had shown he had a great ear for dialogue, and then as time passed, his ear seemed to be a mimic's ear. Everything said was immediately recognizable. In the *Pal Joey* stories, the characters, whether from the bars or showbiz, were immediately familiar, as were all their needs and passions. Each turn of the page offered a kind of perfect surface, the surface always under the one eye, and that shrewd cynical and hardboiled eye saw little that was not known to me, too, so I stopped reading O'Hara.

In the sixties, Edmund Wilson asked me why O'Hara did not seem to excite me at all, even though I claimed he was a fine writer, and I remember I said, "Well, it's all of life seen through the eyes of your favourite taxi driver." This delighted Wilson and he made a note of it, saying he agreed.

But what depresses me is that Mr. McShane, the biographer, within just five years of O'Hara's death, should be explaining that he is trying to arouse some interest, or any interest in him. Students in English courses now don't know his work at all. Many have never even heard of him. According to McShane, this can happen to a writer in just five years.

O'Hara was a good honest writer, and that was the trouble; his work was a portrait of his own spirit, which, as I say, I didn't think much of. But I'm convinced that every honest writer who has great skill and great ambition secretly believes his work can not die. He secretly believes he may be overlooked, forgotten for a while, but in the end, he believes his work has to be rediscovered; it can not die simply because it is good and true.

Why does a man write?

Dr. Johnson, the old pundit, said, "Unless he's a fool, he writes for money." To understand what drivel this is, apply it to painting: Van Gogh sold one painting in his lifetime. Could Dr. Johnson imagine that Cézanne, Utrillo, Rouault were driven to paint as they did by the desire for money. It's the same with the poet and the real fiction writer; they do what they have to do, and this I swear, though it may seem to be wildly romantic, and beautiful, it can not die because there will be someone in some strange corner of the world who will discover it and turn a small light on it. Yes, it is whistling in the dark. But it is the kind of whistling that has kept civilization alive.

I go on believing this though my common sense tells me to look around and survey the desert sands that have blown over so many beautiful writers, even in my own time.

Erskine Caldwell! Dead only a number of years. Does any student turn today to *Tobacco Road*? Or *God's Little Acre*?

I can't find students who'll talk about Saroyan's stories.

Or Bernard Malamud's novels.

Or is it possible that each new batch of college students listens only to its own writers. Can it be that writers and their reputations are now in the complete control of the academic world, and is it possible that any writer who does not make it in this academic world is doomed to be quickly forgotten?

Or is it a matter of luck? I don't know. But perhaps it's true, mournfully so, that the sun can shine again on a forgotten or neglected writer, but only if it shines first in the mind of some wandering academic reaching for attention, for tenure.

O'Hara, then, appears to be lucky. Here is his biographer trying to launch a revival. Unfortunately, according to Alfred Kazin, the biography only buries O'Hara a little deeper.

The fact is, though, that O'Hara had sublime faith in his own work, and the fact is that he pictured, with the utmost fidelity, the people who interested him in the America of his time. Though I could never understand why a man of his obvious talents should have had such awe of the rich and worldly, maybe he was on to one of the great themes of his time: making it! Maybe O'Hara and Norman Podhoretz are secret-sharers to a degree that would shock Podhoretz.

Anyway, O'Hara got what he wanted. There are some who say that that's what hell really is. No matter: in his time, in his place, I don't think there was a more honest or more skilful writer than John O'Hara. His work was the man. If he could only have got out of that taxi he could have been a great writer, but for him there was no other world, no other way to get around town, no other kind of wisdom.

*CBC Anthology*

# CANADA: A WOMAN
# WAITING AT A WINDOW

A Turkish journalist, here to write about this country, came to see me, and of course he immediately asked how I felt about the impending breakup of Canada.

Looking at him in surprise, I told him calmly there wasn't going to be any breakup, he could forget about it.

When he looked let down, I explained quietly and firmly that what was really involved was a constitutional dilemma. All the provinces, and not just Quebec, sought more autonomy.

So, in effect, in an apparent titanic struggle to keep Quebec within federation, the provincial premiers were really holding Levesque's coat for him, knowing their own provinces could only gain in autonomy when the final constitutional agreement with Quebec was worked out.

Baffled, not quite believing me, the Turkish journalist shrugged.

I shrugged, too.

Others had given him a vastly different impression, he said. Others had been deeply moved. Surely it wasn't all just pretending. In this country, did we go in for this kind of pretending?

This was in some ways a unique country, I said, and then I gave him a rundown on all the right things one should say in our public places, especially: the country is going to be bilingual all across the land . . . Unlike that dreadful American melting pot, this country is now a mosaic of many races and in the separate segments of the mosaic, each race will be encouraged to develop the ancestral culture . . .

I was hot. I was going good. Then suddenly I gagged in embarrassment. I didn't believe what I was saying to the journalist. Changing the subject we began to talk about literature. But after the Turkish journalist left I fell to brooding over my country.

This mosaic. These projected cultural ghettos. Some fifty years ago the idea of the mosaic was just a nice neat academic dream. The thought behind the dream, it seems to me, was that there should be some recognition that Quebec was a uniquely separate segment in a federation. At the same time, other races would be encouraged to remain culturally where they'd always been. Two founding races would heroically watch over this mosaic.

In short, for all the years to come, a status quo would be preserved: Italians, Ukrainians, Germans, Caribbeans, or whatever, would remain locked in their cultural past, even in this new country. It was a conservative cultural locksmith's dream. Instead of Hugh MacLennan's two solitudes, we were to have twenty or thirty solitudes held together in a unity in which the people would remain separated.

So what has happened? Already, the segmented new people are being called "ethnics." Newspaper editors, politicians, public speakers, and many other establishment figures are using this meaningless and insulting name. The ethnics. Well, fortunately, if a man has any imagination he does not have to serve his ethnic sentence very long.

The life around him, now a great swelling river, washes over the ethnic walls. Men and women, working together, get to know and like each other. They meet and part, they fall in love, they separate, they come together again. Above all, they come together in the use of the language.

These things are far more real than the moonings of any cultural mandarin.

The Québécois have understood one simple basic truth: the wonder and mystery of man and his culture is his language. The Québécois have already won because they understood that all the wisdom of the people, all the racial memories and the imagination that plays on those memories is in their language, and it is now established that French is to be forever the language of their province.

As for bilingualism in the rest of Canada? Well, as Premier René Levesque knows – indeed, as he has said – Who cares?

It is true, they say in Ottawa that there will be education in the French language any place in English-speaking Canada where numbers warrant it. And there'll be French in post offices, courts, maybe in banks, maybe in restrooms, when French is asked for. But surely this is only institutional French. The language in which the current flow of life will be articulated will always be English because it is language that claims and conquers as no army can.

Men love illusions. They live by illusions so long as they serve them, and all this stuff about the mosaic and bilingualism is a form of national pretending. I don't think anyone is really being served. Yet the vision may only represent something that has always gone on in this country . . . a kind of neurotic need to pretend, a kind of wild flight from the reality of the country as it is. For some, this flight has always been necessary.

This country has been like a woman waiting at a window of an old house at a crossroads.

She is an ageless wild hard beauty. Men riding by come to her in the night. They use her, but never really possess her. They leave her and ride on afraid of her fierce domination over them, knowing they can't handle her; she leaves them feeling small, so she is like the old woman who lived in a shoe; she has had so many children she doesn't know what to do because none of them want to claim her and call her Mother.

For most of us in Canada, the motherland is always somewhere a thousand miles away.

Our people came here as losers. Most were in angry flight, most were bent on cherishing the traditions of a land they'd fled from in a wilderness without security. Others came willingly, hoping to have a better life than they'd had at home. And yet, there were some who, unlikely as it sounds, immediately settled here as lovers.

Years ago, the American poet William Carlos Williams, in a book called *The American Grain,* celebrated beautifully those few remarkable explorers who came to this continent not just to claim land, but to loot and ravage it and steal gold from the Indians.

The great American poet was fascinated by those explorers who were in such awe of this land that they had to open their hearts to it. And one of those great lovers, his journals reveal, was our own Champlain. He looked hard at the lakes, he knew which way the rivers ran, he endured the bitter winters, was awed by the grandeur of our mountains, and what he saw didn't make him feel small and unimportant, and full of apathy.

Because he loved what he touched he was enlarged within himself. He was here as a lover.

Sometimes this wild hard rugged country can be so hostile a man shudders and believes it was never intended to be a habitation, a place with a name. Cartier called it the land of Cain. It easily defeats a man.

But those who are dominated, subjugated, depressed by the land and soon in flight, trying to pretend they are somewhere else, are the real losers. The lover, as is always the case with the lover, has the all-consuming fire of a Champlain; he has to possess the object of his love. He takes the land into himself; he dominates it and lovingly molds it.

For such people, since they have been here for some time and are at home with themselves, the new fascination is in watching the land work on the strange mixture of peoples west of Quebec.

They are like seeds caught in swirling winds, seeds all mixed up, falling in new soil and in the end, making a tangled garden of a hundred new blooms.

In the meantime, there has been endless talk about a Canadian identity. What is it? Where is it? Who's got it? Open your hand. Look under your boot sole. But it is like trying to get a fix on one image in a revolving mirror.

In our literature, I gather, there is only one authentic Canadian story. It must be about the flat lands. If possible, the story should deal with a lonely prairie spinster in an unpainted frame house twenty miles west of a grain elevator, who dreams of getting to Vancouver.

Mind you, other academic writers have tried valiantly to find the real Canadian myth in the northern badlands where lonely figures, one of them preferably an Inuit, reach out gropingly for each other, as their ice floes pass in the endless night. But what have the badlands got to do with me. I'm a city person.

Still, others write that the peculiar Canadian psyche can only be understood if one's soul is haunted by an awareness of the Arctic icepack. Whether we know it or not, it is always supposed to be there in the back of our minds, reminding us we're in for an eternal hangover. But why do they keep looking in the wrong places? Why must there always be this flight away from people and places?

Indeed, the Northrop Frye vision of Canada leaves me wondering and bemused. Frye is, of course, a justly celebrated literary geographer. But surely there was some faulty map reading in his vision. He looked at the map and saw all the great waterways mysteriously reaching toward the west. I had always thought a lot of water went flowing into the Atlantic.

No matter. It is flight again, flight from the people around you, and we are all supposed to be pilgrims with this secret yearning for the western sea, ultimately Vancouver I suppose, where we end up wondering what to do on a rainy night, and do we dare wear our trousers rolled and go to Victoria.

No, if you want to look at what is really shaping the Canadian imagination right now, you must look at the great centres of population, at the big new oil-rich cities of the plains, at Montreal, and Toronto, for these cities now are a giant smithy wherein is being forged a new consciousness and a new spirit.

In Toronto, the place where I was born and still live, one old city seems to have been piled on another, and now there's another, and it is a strange new crazy quilt.

Where I live, there is a ravine enclosing the neighbourhood and a footbridge across the ravine that leads to a subway entrance on the other side. Crossing this bridge, leaving a clutch of founding Presbyterians behind me, I come to the subway entrance where, after 5 p.m., the people of the great new crazy quilt stream out on their way home from work.

They head for over-jammed, over-packed St. James Town with its blocks of massive high-rise apartments. There they are. People with pale faces who look as if they might have been born in small towns near here, people with faces so black they are tinted blue, sallow brown faces, saffron-brown faces, sepia faces, and slant-eyed faces, too.

Germans, "Wessindians." Greeks, Pakistanis, Punjabis, Portuguese, Labradorians, and Laplanders, and the rash of neon fire along Dundas Street at night, Chinatown.

They aren't aware that, to me, they all look different. They don't notice each other. Why should they? They work side-by-side, they live side-by-side, and they share the wonder of the one language in which they now think and remember and love and build dreams, and maybe even make poems, knowing that their fresh use of the founding language is needed, now that our Anglo-Saxon poetry has grown so pallid.

As one Italian told me, his people tend to keep apart till they get the language, and then, life itself and the language won't let them remain apart. So the town, with its new exotic bloom, is full of energy, the wonderful confusion of life, with a row of Bay Street banks, the glass laced with gold dust, proclaiming it the new counting house of the nation.

All these things, I'm sure, could be said of other big cities, Edmonton, Vancouver, Calgary. The voice from these cities is the new Canadian voice. It's a city voice, shattering forever the mosaic. In spite of the efforts of the arts councils and the CBC, there is no regionalism left in Canada. A voice in Moose Jaw, if it is authentic enough, can be heard anywhere else in the world.

But a neighbour of mine, living right where she was born, said to me with a troubled air, "I went downtown today. Do you ever go downtown?" Imagine. Do I ever go downtown? "It's so strange," she went on. "It's really rather awful now. Right there on Yonge St. near Eaton's I saw a lot of young men with shaven heads and in saffron robes trailing in single file and chanting. Can't something be done about this?"

The trouble is, if you describe the people of Toronto to such a woman, you are trying to name the people of Canada, and you can't do it because they are changing, becoming another people. You can only watch and wonder as the new, tangled garden grows. All of Canada outside Quebec is a new, tangled garden.

The extreme nationalists, on the run, turn out to be very much like the old United Empire Loyalists in their prejudices; they can't bear to think that the heart and the imagination and the voice of Canada is now in the big changing cities. They would rather look to the bush or the snow cap.

The original natives of this continent, whose children are still here, even if we keep putting them in our jails, understand these things; they, like their forefathers, know that their land is without borderlines. The same was true of their culture. Now there is another great continental civilization, and whether we find it beautiful or repulsive, we are in it and of it. We're all in the same arm-chair as the citizens of the United States, watching the same games.

Our hockey is in American control. Our baseball cities are in the American big leagues. We have their television. We have the same entertainment darlings. We too, pack them in to hear Billy Graham. It used to be comforting to know that if there were a continental depression we would come out of it as soon as business improved in the United States. After all, we had the natural resources; we were the wheat basket of the world, the nickel lode of the world, the lumber king. We had everything and, the economic nationalists said, all we had to do was own it, free of the Americans. But even in these matters, in this country, everything changes and becomes something else.

We see now that we can't count on the Americans to carry us along out of a recession. The underdeveloped nations are as rich in natural resources as we are, and they have cheaper labour. We don't know, and can't quite admit, that we are at a crossroads.

We may be left to cultivate our own garden, a garden among many gardens all freely linked, a little earlier than we had planned.

Yet, the Americans must be always near us and around us, for after all, we are North Americans, too, in spite of our elaborate pretending. When one of them came here in the sixties to look around and see what he made of us – the critic Edmund Wilson – he looked at our literature, said what he thought, and he has never been forgiven. But one of the things he said to me was, "I like it here, I like Canadians very much. There is something in the air here, or in Canadians that makes the place more attractive than the United States now. It must be like the Republic was some fifty years ago, before things took a turn for the worse."

Then he made a remark which still baffles me. "I keep meeting men here," he said, "who are pleasant, educated, intelligent, and who seem to have done well, yet I feel in them some disappointment."

Each man should have his own reason for liking his country. Mine is this: while it is true there is less nervous intellectual excitement in my town than there is in New York, and many of the things I think important are not fought for as fiercely as in New York, yet there is one area of life working some grudging magic on Canadians, maybe it's the loneliness of the land touching them, and this area in life is the gold citadel of any superior civilization.

It is the area of a man's private life. A man's private domain where he has his dreams, where he has his own law, where he is his own government. In this, his domain, lies the source of all creative things.

In all of Canada, and so in my town, too, there is a wonderful respect for a man's privacy, no matter what is going on in a parochial, provincial or comic public arena. For me, a writer, it made life in this country very worthwhile, and I think this is what Edmund Wilson felt when he said there was something in the air here he liked very much, that reminded him of the Republic. Here, a man could keep to himself and be himself. A man at home with his own people.

Then, in 1970, we got the news that there was an "apprehended insurrection" in Quebec, and the War Measures Act was imposed.

With this act, all our civil liberties were taken away from us. The Act was accepted, it was approved, it was applauded by our Parliament, and after the farce was over and the engendered hysteria had faded, no accounting was asked for in what I am sure historians will see as the most shameful moment in our Parliamentary history.

I say that the War Measures Act and its popular acceptance may have altered not only the tone but the very structure of our society. It was a police gesture on a grand scale.

The current Mounted Police scandals, the police crimes, the desire to tamper with the law, these acts would have been unthinkable a few years ago . . . especially the proposed legislation permitting the police to open first-class mail, and the use of the word "security" to cover any police crime. And, above all, the police's authoritarian contempt for the private domain – for me, the one last sacred grove – all these stem from the lemming-like acceptance of the War Measures Act. And so has begun in this country the erosion of all privacy.

In the beginning, the sponsors of these strange ruthless shenanigans may have expected only applause, for how could anyone see that they had no real evidence of an insurrection; but were they surprised by the general apathy outside Quebec, or did they count on this apathy? It is this terrible apathy that is being exploited now. And I see this as the terrible spiritual sickness of Canadians.

Out of apathy men will accept any crime, anything done in the name of security, if it will promise to make them comfortable. An apathetic people hate anything that is first-rate, everything that is singular; it only upsets them.

In this time of the acceptance of a secret police erosion of the private domain, we should recognize that the country's real enemy is not some Mafia thug in a back room, or some drug peddler or even a security cop with his burglar tools; the enemy is this sickness of ours, this dreadful spiritual apathy which makes us willing to accept not only any crime done in the name of the law, but accept too a false mosaic vision of this country, its people and even our language, too.

*Toronto Star*, 1978

# A CONTEMPORARY
# NOSTALGIA BINGE

One night I sat in my hotel room reading a laudatory review of the Eugene O'Neill play, *A Long Day's Journey into Night*. I was moved. I had loved O'Neill. Then, I wondered if the critics' enthusiasm might be due to the revival binge New York is on right now. No, Clive Barnes of the *Times*, was certainly not writing about this O'Neill play with the affectionate tenderness that the public is now bestowing on those happy and innocent show pieces like *No, No, Nanette* and the *Ziegfeld Follies*.

Nostalgia, in itself, is something I have fled from all my life. I never reread any of my old books. A writer is in trouble when he starts looking back. Sooner or later he starts imitating himself. Yet, that night in a hotel room far from home, I found myself wondering if the craving for revival now being shown in the theatre, and in the fashion world, and in the novel, too, might not be a cultural necessity. It might even be a built-in balance wheel in all cultures if those cultures aren't to die.

I know, of course, that a theatre given over to the productions of another day, or novelists who want to capture fondly only the temper of another time, represent a kind of death. Nothing new is happening for them. And the great legends warn us against looking back. Lot's wife or Orpheus losing his Eurydice when he looked back! Is the theatre now, or is the novel now, to turn into a pillar of salt?

I remember as a boy how impressed I was by Carl Sandburg's line, "The past is a bucket of ashes, a sun gone down." And in those days, too, Henry Ford, the carmaker, had said that history was bunk. Everybody in those days was under the spell of the myth of progress. We were to have no past. Only a future. Everybody loved the future. But surely this love of the future is escapism as much as any nostalgic backward glance. So, what about the present.

On the publishing vine, strange fruit is growing.

Why are some young writers frankly dealing with witches and ghosts and poltergeists, possession, and evil spirits? Is this a frantic leap back into Gothic times? Do these writers, being young and with the advantages of a scientific education, really believe in witches and ghosts and the devil? I can't imagine that they do. Why, then, the success of a picture like *Rosemary's Baby*? A good story. A fantasy. A nostalgia for the superstitious tall tales of our great grandmother's time. Yes, but there is something else, a needed thing, something needed by the contemporary imagination, what with our dreams of the moon and the stars resting in the hands of practical men, the big master mechanics.

The mechanics, in tune with the technological times, tell it like it is. The journalist, telling it like it is, displaces the novelist; human conduct is measured not by the moralist, but by the behavioural scientist. The artist is fierce in his pride, but not in the seeking of new forms, the eternal quest. No, his pride lies in freeing himself from all form. And the mystery that is in lovemaking, the mystery that has its very private and secret form, is stripped away, until lovemaking is like eating a hamburger on the open stage.

With everything out in the open, the private world would be deemed unworthy of respect and subject to invasion by electronic snoopers seeking information. "Like it is, tell it like it is," they have been saying. Yet a man knows that this isn't the way it is at all. A whole caboodle of who he is that can't be measured by the slide rule or by the behavioural scientist. The fantasies, the dreams of men have shaped history as powerfully and as a bewilderingly as other rational forces.

So, this contemporary binge we're on is, of course, an escapist binge. But an escape from what? Not just the social ugliness of a period. Maybe it is a kind of witless, built-in protective apparatus in us, that says to us about a prevailing view of man and society, "We've had it. We're not gonna take it anymore." We turn then to something old, familiar and secure. We console ourselves. We manage to get rid of something that was boring us. The thing we are looking back to will soon bore us, too, but in this painless way we manage to clear the ground to be ready for something new, and hopefully, new forms.

If I'm to know where I am now, where writing is now, I must occasionally look back, not to be drawn back, not to be snatched away from the present and lost in sentimentality, but to get my bearings. Maybe to change direction and then move on. And so a binge of nostalgia, a love of the thing left behind, may also be a great thing for a public that has no other way of measuring what's been set before it.

Socrates suggested that Orpheus was a coward and betrayed Eurydice when he looked back. Maybe so. But Lot's wife is another story. It's an authoritarian story. The higher authorities didn't want the lady to look back, ever to look back, because they didn't want her to ever understand what they had done and where she was.

*CBC Anthology*

# EVERYTHING HE WROTE
# SEEMED REAL: HEMINGWAY

Hemingway was something more than a natural writer. When nerve-wracked, sleepless or desperate, he took to writing letters for relief as another man might take Valium. He wrote strange and sometimes wonderful letters although they have nothing to do with the art of the charming letter. Since he knew he would order that they never be published, most of them come pouring out exuberantly, or furiously, or maliciously, or humorously, the stuff of his own wide gaudy wonderful world. We get, too, the part of his inner world he wants to reveal; he was always very canny about this.

Since he had a searing power to make everything he wrote seem real, the letters are captivating because we can never be sure whether he is telling the truth, or whether he is being seduced by his imagination into believing the legends he created for himself. And so, after reading Carlos Baker's *Selected Letters* for some hours I suddenly remembered an afternoon in the middle '30s when I dropped into Scribners in New York to have a drink with Max Perkins.

As soon as I entered the office Perkins said, "Sherwood Anderson was in here earlier and he was telling me that at that dinner you had with him last night you gave a splendid defence of Hemingway's Catholicism." Seeing the astonished alarm on my face, since Hemingway's Catholicism had never been mentioned at the dinner, Perkins stood up and said hastily, "I know. Now don't get Sherwood wrong," and he explained that Anderson had a trick of the imagination that was often misunderstood. After such an evening, Anderson would find the event still flowing on after we parted, a daydream, and in this daydream he would hear himself saying things he had wanted to say, and get answers to questions; he would even hear the answers, and later on, the daydream would be remembered as part of the evening, having become just as real for him as anything that had actually happened.

Hemingway had a touch of Anderson in him, and, as with the author of *Winesburg, Ohio*, a compulsion to create a new reality that was not necessarily malicious or self-serving. In the end, of course, he called Anderson a slob and a liar. But, as with many artists, the truth was there only when it satisfied his imagination. I mention Anderson not only to make this observation, but because he actually was a turning point in Hemingway's life. Before reading these letters, I wondered, how did the young unknown writer from Chicago manage to leap from Chi-town right into the open arms of Gertrude Stein, Sylvia Beach and Ezra Pound? Well, he had letters of introduction from Sherwood Anderson. But if all the Paris doors were opened for him by Anderson, he himself had something rich and strange to offer – his personality. As Archibald MacLeish has noted, he had presence. You felt it when he was with you listening intently, or explaining something himself, then giving you the delightful excitement of sharing some acute secret awareness of all things. Of course, not all people got this impression. Edmund Wilson told me of his first encounter with Hemingway, an evening in New York with Scott Fitzgerald, and he had thought Hemingway was "just a little too slick."

The letters from these Paris days prefigure the pattern of relationships to follow in Key West and Cuba; a lot of love at first, then resentments turning sometimes to hate. He is all love for his wife Hadley as he writes adoring letters to Gertrude Stein and warm appreciative letters to Fitzgerald. He comes to love Ezra Pound, and he tells how much he likes Bob McAlmon, his first publisher – and then the dark brooding side of his nature begins to appear. Soon he is talking about his contempt for Ford Madox Ford, he comes to loath Ernest Walsh, the editor of *This Quarter*, and he soon hates Bob McAlmon for making up stories about him. Yet, at the same time he remained wonderfully generous and helpful to other writers, as I know; but having written Anderson, thanking him for being the one who gave the necessary push to open the publishing gate for him at Liveright, as soon as *In Our Time* appeared and some New York reviewers likened him to Anderson, he took off after his benefactor. He wrote *The Torrents of Spring*, heavily satirizing him. Then, as if he didn't know what he had done, he wrote Anderson, telling him that a thing that is really good cannot be hurt by satire. There it was again, that trait: the truth was there only when it satisfied his imagination. What a weird triumph for Anderson.

Those days in Paris were a mixed-up time for him. He had written *The Sun Also Rises*, and was on the edge of great fame, but he was divorcing Hadley and writing with great emotion to Pauline Pfeiffer, soon to be his second wife. He wrote good love letters. The ones he wrote years later to Mary Welsh Hemingway are natural and good, too. But his father and mother, who had not liked *The Sun Also Rises*, nor anything else he had written, were on his mind. His sister Marcelline, writing to me after reading my memoir, *That Summer in Paris*, said it was true Ernest was a mixture of the light and the dark, but she didn't think he had ever been fair to his family. Yes, he may have hated his mother, but the letter he writes to both his parents trying to explain *The Sun Also Rises*, has a genuine boyish concern and dignity.

When he moves to Key West and later to Cuba, becoming bigger and bigger as an international celebrity, the letters keep flowing to the old friends: Mike Strater and Waldo Peirce, Gertrude Stein, Archibald MacLeish, Ezra Pound, the beloved John Dos Passos, and a host of new friends who seem to come swarming around him, helping him struggle against the dark forces and those who might challenge his place in the sun. And there are all those letters to Max Perkins and Charles Scribner about the making of his books. They are fascinating. They are full of gossip, business details, the making of big deals, and full of mean backbiting, too. He writes in high glee to Sara Murphy, explaining how he thrashed that big lovely poet, Wallace Stevens. He is always threatening to punch out someone.

But the style of these letters is probably unique in literature. He may start off vilifying some enemy, but then, suddenly, he is out in his boat fishing and he soars off into vivid prose like a man driven to prove he was a lovely writer no matter what his state of mind. The vitality, the passion for writing, is amazing. But as time passed, this man who could be so gentle and generous, became murderous about other writers. He litters the literary beach with casualties. Sinclair Lewis he loathed because he got the Nobel Prize. The vilification he heaped on James Jones, in a letter to Charles Scribner, is simply shocking. At this time, he seems to be right off his rocker. What was going on in him? What was his secret despair? It's not in the letters. Everything else is, including of course Fitzgerald, who runs repetitiously through these pages as if Hemingway knew all his life he would never be able to make up his mind how he felt about him.

As for the letters telling about his dashing military feats when he was a war correspondent in France, I can't be sure if it isn't all leg-pulling, or a love of storytelling – yet he had such great wisdom about what was good and true in writing. One of these letters is very funny, unwittingly so. He wrote to Bernard Berenson, describing how the beribboned André Malraux had come to the Ritz after Hemingway and his friends had "liberated" it. These two men of high talent, both flamboyant adventurers, both always determined, as Ezra Pound has it in his poem – "we do high deeds in Hungary to pass all men's believing" – faced each other, bearing all their legends. Instantly, Hemingway hated Malraux. A fake, he tells Berenson. Malraux's legend was his own creation. It's these versions that fascinate me: changing, shifting, full of contradictions. No one should care now, but the many versions he gives of his boxing bout with me in Paris, with Fitzgerald acting as timekeeper, are strangely revealing and perplexing (in the same way that one wonders why he made up the story that the great middleweight Harry Greb stuck his thumb in his eye when it never happened).

In an early letter to Perkins, Hemingway explains how he slipped and fell when Fitzgerald let the round go on too long. Some years later, writing to Fitzgerald's biographer, Arthur Mizener, he gives another version; now he is full of wine and Fitzgerald lets the round go 13 minutes. A 13-minute round? Incredible! And he was not on the floor at all! Is this plain lying? Or is the daydream now the real thing? Was he always shaping and reshaping reality to suit himself, to soothe himself, carrying on conversations or fights or jungle treks in the night he wishes he'd had. I don't know, but if this was the case, how terrible it must have been for him at the end, having a nervous breakdown, with his wild imagination working away, seeking the right end to his story, his life.

The fact is, all the gossip and daily routine aside, all these letters help explain why he is a great storyteller, a great artist, a great actor, and the great Romantic of the period. As Edmund Wilson, whom he had so often reviled, wrote to me on the news of Hemingway's death, "After all, he was one of the pillars of our time."

*Washington Post*, 1981

# INTELLIGENCE GATHERING

Facts are sometimes called intelligence. Intelligence implies the gathering of information, and with electronic equipment, these facts keep pouring in. A new set of certified facts always superseding the old set of certified facts, until the men in charge, facing a moment of decision, grow bewildered. They have no choice but to make a tragic mistake. They drown in their sea of information.

Being a writer, a novelist, I long ago discovered that I could have too many facts, too much information about a scene or character. I would be so close to the details that I couldn't bring them to life. Not until I drew back and forgot half of the facts, with my memory or my intuition rejecting all that clutter, was my imagination able to take hold. Only then was I able to see the thing as a whole.

So, now I feel free to make a traitorous, treasonable statement that mocks our time. It is this. Only the imagination can give us any wisdom about all this information being dumped on us. I go further. The man full of information, who does not use his imagination, the program director in radio or television who says he's only interested in information, or the publisher who prints only factual books – they should all be committed, they should all do time in rest homes as men spreading a plague that's stunting our civilization.

The theory is, I suppose, that any man who has an amazing amount of information stuffed in his head is an educated man. I don't want to call him a scholar, scholars can usually recognize when a colleague has insights of his own. But what this man has, and what usually drives me to drink, is called "useful information." Some very distinguished men have believed that all information is useful, and therefore, good. I remember I once had an argument with Edmund Wilson, who had an astonishing amount of information on, of all things, the first chapter of a Hugh MacLennan novel. Some readers had said the chapter was dull and boring. Wilson asked me if I liked the chapter. I said I didn't. He said he liked it. I said I had read it determinedly out of respect for the writer, and then I said, "Why in the world do you yourself like that chapter?" and Wilson said, "I found it was full of information, useful information," and all I could say was, "Well, there you are," because we had then touched on a difference in our temperaments.

All the information programs, and the outpourings of books of factual information by the publishers and the gradual domination of the literary reviews by the critics and the schoolmasters, seem to me to be based on the assumption that the audience is made up of yokels and peasants. You are supposed to be doing God's great democratic work if you are telling these people about something, and the light of our times shines upon you if what you are telling them is free of all personal slant, and you make it clear, too, that the listener or the reader should never be encouraged to have his own private view.

We go in for this.

We do.

We have been seduced at last by the nineteenth-century notion that education consists of the collection of useful facts. The blind belief that information by its very nature and in itself must be useful. The good, the true, the useful. What is most pleasing to God, is the useful thing! You see the fine flowering of this perversion in educational circles where students, trained in this harsh discipline, haven't the slightest interest in wisdom, or what makes for human happiness, but only in the questions, "Will this discipline get me a job? Will it help me to make a buck?" In the universities, some professors have told me, there is a declining interest in the English language. Isn't this inevitable? The wisdom of the human race is in the language. You can do a business deal with a sign language and a few grunts and groans. When language ceases to be the instrument of the imagination, and only a tool for the noting down of information, it dies.

When our heads are jammed with information we are suffering another plague of the locust, and this time the locusts are feeding on the person. Writers, broadcasters, publishers, and listeners and readers who are bent on eliminating the personal slant, the personalized view of wars and rumours of wars, and even accounts of what goes on from day to day in this country, bring everything under the grand umbrella of information. But they dehumanize life. No doubt they believe they are being objective, impersonal, educational, too. But they make men smaller than facts about men. They are caught up in the current drift away from the value, the mystery of personality. Instead of saying, "Nothing that is human is foreign to me," they say, "Only that which is impersonal, factual, is valuable to me." Behind this, of course, is the strange embarrassing hatred of the story. Why this hatred of the imagination? Why this pathetic eagerness to forget the ancient dictum? – "If you want it to be interesting, put it into a story." Well, it's a skin game! A sudden new opium for the semi-literate, life as a game of *Jeopardy*: possessing the answer, what is the question? Bogus, ever-changing information that won't give you any wisdom, just a skull jammed with facts.

*CBC Anthology*

# EDMUND WILSON

Edmund Wilson has died. One of the most embarrassing moments I had with Wilson was very early in the game of my relationship with him. Most people found Wilson a rather intimidating man. Because he had the air, I suppose, of an aloof bishop, but of course I knew from the beginning that that wasn't the man at all. He never struck me that way, as aloof. But he conveyed, let us say, the vast competence of his scholarship, and – aside from his scholarship – the vast confidence of the strength of his opinion. He had an enormous sense of himself.

One time, we were having dinner, in a place called the Hungarian Village on Bay Street in Toronto, just the two of us, and he'd been drinking a lot of champagne, and I suppose I was helping him along the way. We had one of those big bottles, a magnum, and suddenly he said to me: "What do you make of me?" I drew back a little and said: "What do I make of you? What do you mean make?" He said: "How do you place me? What do you think I stand for? What is the direction, the whole direction of my work?" If, in all America, if anybody had asked me that question, I would have been a little surprised, but when Wilson asked me this question, I was stunned, because I don't think Wilson went around asking people what they made of him. I was somewhat aghast, so I thought, that's an honest question, I must try to give an honest answer.

I fumbled around and told him what, first of all, I thought of his prose style and his general feeling about the objective world. I thought that he could be traced back to the 18th-century tradition. And then I said that even in his concern with the objective world and his utter faith in the rational as the basis of sound knowledge for everything he wrote – and his Calvinist background, which I thought he had very determinedly, early in the game, tried to shuffle off – I said that though these qualities be admirable, and might even be the basis of his strength as a critic, it wasn't that aspect of his work that interested me, those weren't the qualities that had recommended him so highly to artists, to writers.

When I was about 21, I remember Hemingway wrote me a letter from New York – he hadn't published *The Sun Also Rises* yet – he wrote me with some pleasure that he had spent an evening with Edmund Wilson, because Wilson meant something to all the young writers at that period. What he had – and it's a very rare thing when writers believe in a critic – they believed that Wilson had perception, a gift for the recognition of what was new and fresh and good.

So, I said to him as we sat at the table, that the interesting thing about his work, and the whole structure of his work, was his ability to look at a thing, look at it with cold objectivity, and his hope, I could feel this hope – that the thing would not be contained within the structure of his criticism, that it would require from him a recognition of something that was outside the critical structure that he seemed to adhere to.

He just nodded, he didn't say anything. He was obviously quite pleased with what I had said. I was a little embarrassed because Wilson had always made the point that he thought we tended to think rather alike, that our view of things was somewhat the same. I've never been sure of this, though I know what he meant: I think he meant that we tended to look at the work for what it is while the whole critical baggage of academic criticism especially had to do with trying to fit the object, trying to fit the thing under consideration, into a particular system, which was usually within the man's mind.

Wilson's distinction was that he had always tried to see what the thing was in terms of the thing itself. This is why all writers from the time when I was very young had had such admiration for him. I doubt if the academics are now or ever will be as crazy about Wilson as they once were when he wrote *Axel's Castle*, when every academic and every student in the American colleges was reading *Axel's Castle*. Now, they tend to regard him, if they regard him at all, as a bishop-like figure sitting upstate in New York in an abandoned old stone house, an anachronism; they think they are the younger theologians who have long ago upset the bishop.

But that is exactly the point I'm making: the younger theologians, the critics, are boys with a system, and Wilson's everlasting distinction in American letters will be that he was not a man with a system. The academic mind, by its very nature, had to view Wilson suspiciously, because he was apt to write something or recognize in some writer a quality that he thought made that writer great, when this quality was obviously quite outside the stream of some ready tradition. He'd always been ahead of the game.

What has been amusing, in this context, is that everybody has assumed a kind of overwhelming scholarship in the man, that is, the man seemed to have read everything. This would mean a kind of catholicity which suggested that he was free of all prejudice. But I found over the years that Wilson had some rather laughable prejudices, that he had not only prejudices about writers, but he had what I think was a kind of vast stubbornness. For example, one day, and I don't know how this subject came up, I was talking to him about Prescott, *The Conquest of Mexico* and *The Conquest of Peru*, and I was saying that these were really very great books. He listened and he said, "Really, do you think so?" And I said: "Oh yes," and, "Well, you agree with me, don't you?" And he said: "I've never read Prescott." I said: "You've never read Prescott's story *of The Conquest of Mexico* and *The Conquest of Peru*, never read them at all?" And I said: "Why?" He said: "I don't know." And I started very ardently to say that Prescott had a narrative power that was most extraordinary, how Prescott in *The Conquest of Peru* gradually built the narrative till it had all the qualities of a novel of suspense. He listened very respectfully, and then he said to me: "Well, I suppose I must read it." And then I suddenly got the point. I said, "If you've gone this far and have not read Prescott, you're not going to read Pres-cott." He said: "That's probably true." And then I thought about it for a while, and suddenly I said: "Don't you like Spanish writers?" He said: "I am not particularly interested in Spanish literature." And I said: "Oh, then you don't like Spanish literature, is that it? Do you read much of it?" And he said: "No." I asked what it was that he had against Spanish literature? He said: "I don't know. There is something about the whole thing that turns me against it, and I just don't read it." So, I had to assume that all of Spanish literature as far as Wilson was concerned was way out in left field. And he had never turned that way, to that field. Not even to *Don Quixote*. No, without apology, he just was not interested. It was thumbs down on the whole Spanish temperament.

Another thing, and this was rather strange. Not so long before he died, he wrote me that he was reading Balzac, and he said he had never really read Balzac. I didn't like to say to him, Why have you never read Balzac? Which led me to remember that he would not read Mauriac. He had not read Mauriac. And I'd said to him, "But Mauriac writes beautifully, aside from the fact that you may not like the Jansenist element in his work. You should read him because he writes so beautifully." He said he didn't deny it for a moment, but he said Mauriac writes about Bordeaux. Yes, he writes about

Bordeaux, and he said if there was one thing he could not stand it was novels about French provincial life, and since Mauriac was the great novelist of French provincial life, he would not read him. A very curious remark from a man who was then devoting the last years of his life to his notebooks, his everyday investigation of upstate New York provincial life. But then, because he lived in Talcottville, his ancestral home, I guess he felt that he was writing about his own flesh and bone in context of the whole wide world of his life as he'd lived it.

Still, to carry this further, this business of provincial life, I remember I was talking to Margaret Laurence one night, and she said: Oh Wilson wouldn't like her work because she wrote of the west, and she was quite right. He would not read novels about Canadian prairie life, western novels, as he would not now read novels about the American Middle West. So, if you look at the Wilson body of work, you find that he made no effort, no pretense to put himself in the position of the man who had read everything, who had looked at all the ends of the earth, and who had judged them. And this brings me back to my original impression. He was interested in the thing that quickened his own imagination; he was not the eternal professor who would give you a footnote on everything written in international literature. He refused to turn to stuff which, after having glanced at it, did not quicken and stimulate his imagination. In his early days of course, he had read Anderson and Lewis, he'd engaged the great discovery of the American Middle West in literature. He'd read them all, but for some reason he came to a point where he was simply no longer interested in that scene, so he skipped it.

And finally, he was a great believer in temperament, in the temperaments of other men. He could make astonishing quick judgements about people. In fact, he said an awful thing one of the times when he was here in Toronto. He'd met a number of people. He'd met the boys, and he'd got along very well. By and large, he liked Canadian people, but he made an odd remark.

He had been thinking and he said: "Would you agree that Toronto is a city full of disappointed men?" I laughed and said: "Just exactly what do you mean?" "Well, I mean I've met men who I know have done rather well, but who are at a certain stage of life, and," he said, "they are all extremely amiable and they are all rather nice and often very gracious and good humoured." And he said: "I get the feeling that underneath there has been some kind of an abdication or rather a resignation, an air of resignation, to make the best of it. You sense the air of agreeable men making the best of it, a man who is secretly in his own heart a disappointed man."

This, of course, being my native heath, I hadn't really thought it was a city full of disappointed men, but I could see what he meant and I thought it was a very shrewd judgement. I began to watch men around town from then on, men who, having started off with a kind of wild ambition, like a Canadian writer, when he is very young in the game he aims at Paris or he aims at New York or he aims at London; he thinks his work belongs in the big metropolitan centres. Then, time passes and he decides that he's really a fervent Canadian nationalist, because he knows people here at home, or some of the local reviewers, and so he then accepts their care for him, he accepts this beautifully. He thinks he has some special distinction in the world as a Canadian which can only be recognized by fellow Canadians, but in his heart, he's a disappointed man. I think this is a kind of Canadian quality, this refusal to keep on reaching.

Wilson spent all his time here in Toronto and Montreal examining Canadian work, with many many volumes to read and study, so of course when his book *O Canada* came out, there was rage and disappointment and many sneers because much about Canadian culture had been left out. But after all, he had described his book as a footnote. Aside from that, however, what he had been looking for was stuff that would really interest his mind. Hugh MacLennan said a very accurate thing about him. He said: the reason why so many Canadian writers were disappointed in what Wilson had to say was that Wilson simply was trying to apply international standards of taste to Canadian writing. That was the real shock and the good thing that Wilson did in that book. No matter how inadequate in scope it may have been, he had looked at Canadian work through international eyes.

Now, looking at his place in America – as he'd asked me to do – through my own international eyes, I can say that Wilson will occupy an astonishing role in American letters. In the first place, his style is everlasting in English literature, because his style was based on observation, and it's that lean fine prose which will belong to every period; as long as English is written, Wilson's style will be a good style. And I think that when the time comes and readers look back on Wilson, they'll find that he will be there as a Proustian figure, because if you read all Wilson's work, you'll find that you're getting a whole view of America. His greatest single book, however, is *Patriotic Gore*, the history of America through America's writers, and this is a very strange history, a history of the country as a kind of gathering of angels, all the voices of all the writers of the period are there giving their views of the country. It's an astonishing work, and my only regret is that those people who go in for gossip – they like the short pieces Wilson wrote – would not read this grand soaring choir of authentic American voices, all sounding their own notes, and all under the direction of Wilson.

What was rewarding about the man, now that we can look back over fifty years of work, is that up until the end, you'd find that Wilson could always tell you what was going on, he was – despite his disclaimers – always looking out at the world, and his appraisals were always the most just appraisals of the time. If the academic world at present is tending to be patronising to Wilson, this is a dreadful reflection on the academic world.

*CBC Anthology*

# MY LOVE FOR MIRACLES

One night back in the '50s, when television was making its first big impact, my friend Ralph Allen, at that time the editor of Maclean's, said to me: "We'd better all start learning to handle pictures and images. From now on there'll be less and less reading of stories or anything else. In fact, we should be worrying about whether reading is on the way out."

I couldn't believe this. We argued.

I saw, then, that watching television and reading are two entirely different experiences. You can love one and hate the other. You can get so drugged by television that you can't take the time to read anything. Reading becomes an effort. Television is a spectator sport.

What you are watching is all outside you and it goes on, even as you are falling asleep, even as you sleep. I watch a lot of television; I get comfortable in the big chair and half the time I'm daydreaming, I'm thinking of something else, half-hypnotized, mentally inert, but comfortable, very comfortable.

But reading – this vastly different experience – requires work from me. My inner eye must come to life. If it's a story I'm reading, the characters come to life on the screen of my inner eye. They come to life in the language.

Language, just words, are making the miracle. The greatest wonder of humankind is the development of language, and the second wonder, growing out of the first, is learning to read. A man sits alone with a book, the whole world around him grows silent, a voice so secret it can't be heard, just felt, is whispering to him and leading him deep into the world of the greatest wonder and power – his own imagination.

To this day I remember the first long story I ever read. It was called *The Fall of the House of Garth*. I was nine years old. The book was a cheap pulp horror story. I forget who gave it to me. But I had discovered reading and how it could enlarge the whole world, and as time passed and I grew much older, and though I read and read a thousand works, I think I was always looking for some writer, some book that would give back to me the rapt attention of a child.

Ripeness is all, freshness is all – how do you get it? Where do you get it? And looking back, and looking around at others, I can see that the person who keeps stimulating his or her imagination, stretching it like a rubber band through the visions of others coming through lovely reading, never grows old in the heart.

I had a friend, a Russian Jew, who had a serious optical problem. He wore glasses with very thick lenses. I asked him what had ruined his eyesight. He said that when he was a boy in Russia his parents had been very poor. He had had to work hard. His mother always got him to bed very early and turned out the light. But he would have a flashlight in the bed, and pulling the covers over his head, he would read by the flashlight.

He read the stories of Chekhov, then book after book of Tolstoy before his eyes weakened and he was almost blind. Thinking back, he said he couldn't regret the damage to his eyes. Tented under the covers, his beam of light had opened up new towns, new city streets he would walk for the rest of his life; crossroads that took him far beyond his poverty-stricken home, making him aware of lives far different than his own.

As this man knows, now that he is middle aged, you don't have to have money, or go to college, to find the magic that lies in reading, the new planets and their several moons that swing into your kenning. It happened in a big way for me in my first year at college. Up to that time, I had been a boy reading all the boys' books, and then I read Dumas and the *Three Musketeers*, and so on.

But one day, sitting in the Hart House library, I picked up a short novel by a Russian I had heard of, Dostoevsky. The book jarred me; I knew I was being forced to look at things in a new way, at how thinking could be like a rage of energy, how a question could become a whirlpool of accusation. I had got my first taste of real writing. A crime, and of course, a punishment, but . . .

Flaubert, in one of his letters to the Russian, Turgenev, had said that there was nothing new for a writer to say, there were no new stories, but there were certainly new ways of saying the old stories, and all my life I've kept this in mind as I've read and read, waiting and waiting, and when I find a writer who has his own way of saying and seeing things, I get excited; yet again, yet another angle on life; again the new planet, again the new moon.

Naturally enough, there are times when I am not in the mood for new things, I don't need angularity, and so, as I read I'll watch television out of one eye – just relaxing. This is how I read all of Agatha Christie and all of Raymond Chandler, and that's how I read newspapers, too. Newspapers are in my blood. I have to know what's going on.

But in the back of my mind, despite vast bouts of one-eyed laziness and lethargy, there is always the longing to read something that will not only stir me, but give me the unspoiled freshness of imagination that I had as a child when I read *The Fall of the House of Garth*. Though I'm in trouble there, too. I'm a professional writer, and even when I'm reading a good book now, my critical intelligence is too often getting in the way of my imagination. I can see what the writer is doing (or not doing) and even worse, what he is going to do.

Another troubling thing I have to guard against as I grow older is finding it easier to read non-fiction than fiction. A thousand papers on Ezra Pound. Those incredible memoirs by Mandelstam's wife, Natasha, memoirs of hope abandoned and regained. A book like Barbara Tuchman's *Distant Mirror*, about the European 14th century, can completely absorb me. I don't have to use my imagination at all. That worries me!

My imagination might someday wither.

I know what it's like for a man who finally comes to realize that he has let his imagination wither and die and has grown old in the heart. He knows he is half-dead. I saw it one night in a man I knew who was with me at a party.

He was a very successful executive, only fifty-five. He was having trouble with his wife. Crouched on the stairs he called, "Morley, sit with me. I want to tell you something." Holding my arm, he said desperately, "When I come home at night I'm tired. I eat, I have a drink, I pick up *Time* magazine. I read three pages and fall asleep . . ."

He started to cry. Tears were running down his cheeks. "I know I'm a little drunk," he said, "but I used to read all the time. When I was at college I was crazy about Katherine Mansfield and Virginia Woolf. I read Melville and Poe. I read . . . what happened to me?"

I often think of this man, particularly when I'm about to fall into a sweet little sleep, watching television.

*Toronto Star*, 1986

# "MAKE ME INTO A STORY"

I met a man who had come to realize that we are all doomed to be forgotten unless we get into a story, and then have this story told about us. Of course, for a few short years, there is often a memory of us in our friends. An anecdote here, an anecdote there. But beyond that, it is as if we had never lived.

This friend of mine, made rather desolate by this view, said to me, "I found myself going around asking, 'Am I a story? I'm nothing till I am a story. And who would want to tell my story? No one, of course,'" and then laughing cynically, he said that maybe many politicians and business men know instinctively that they can be forgotten overnight unless they get into a story, so, what do they do? – they pay someone to write their stories, their memoirs, and if the writer, by an incredible stroke of luck, has talent and imagination, then these men, maybe years later, are there to be looked at when some historian examines the period in which they flourished.

Think of Pepys' *Diaries*. Who is a more famous figure of his time than Pepys, who simply kept track, with some wit, and great humanity, of his daily goings and comings, and imagine the delight of some big political figure of those days, if he could have foreseen that since only the story survives, if he could have bribed Pepys to devote a dozen vivid pages to him – getting him to tell a few tales intimating his importance – imagine his delight at knowing that he would be alive forever in English literature.

And so, the very rich, as many of them do anyway, should go climbing narrow stairs to those cold attics where men of genius suffer and rage, and in the attic they should say to the poet or to the novelist, "Make me into a story. Draw on your imagination. I insist that I am a story. Go ahead. I'll pay thousands, a hundred, two hundred thousand. I want to live on beyond my time."

Many a man, particularly if he be a composer, a dramatist, a painter or a novelist, has realized — no, it does not have to be such a conscious awareness — I should say, instead, if a man or woman has the actor's instinct, then he can so shape his life and so mix it up with his work, that he and his work become the one story.

In a man's own time, as his story gets told over and over again, he becomes a legend. Everyone has to know about this man's work if they want to be in on the story, and sometimes the story becomes bigger than the work, and sometimes, just as with most of us in our lives, the work fades away, and there is only the story . . . the personal story, the legend.

From the beginning of his career, Hemingway had that peculiar faculty, an innate talent for making men want to tell stories about him. He was a beautiful writer, but as he knew himself, and as he said, a writer often gets praised for the worst aspects of his work. As the stories about him gathered, as the worst aspects of his works were praised, his legend grew until he became one of the most celebrated men in the whole world.

A broadcasting company in New York, editing a program about him, tried to get me to tell stories about Hemingway. I said, There are dozens of people who knew him . . . well-known people. The producer said desperately that he couldn't find anyone who knew him as a writer. There were people who had had a drink with him or fished with him. But they had nothing to say about Hemingway the writer. With them, he never was the writer, he was Papa.

And now, with the times changing, times when there is a silly denigration of Hemingway's work going on in the flaky critical world, especially the feminist world, what the scribblers are really doing is beating down or rejecting the legend their fathers helped to create. The Hemingway story! Since they're sure that they don't like the story, the legend, they turn away from the work. The work, however, freed of the legend, can be seen clearly for what it is: some of the most striking, original, and beautifully written stories in the language.

Fitzgerald, his friend, had been the fair-haired boy of a decade, he'd had all that success, all that money in the twenties, and a beautiful wife who was a bit of a dingbat to boot, but then came the Depression, and it was no longer fashionable to adore the rich and the beautiful, and Fitzgerald, out of favour, sank into the oblivion of Hollywood and alcohol.

Yet, he kept on writing. Then, in the fifties, it was as though some god had said, "This guy Fitzgerald, remember him, he's a hell of a story. His wife, sometimes out of her mind, goes up in flames in a burning nursing home. And he named the jazz age the Jazz Age," and so, with the rediscovery of the story, came the rediscovery of his work.

In the fifties, Fitzgerald had become a kind of river god. At the time, I ran into the well-known American writer, Louis Bromfield, whose early success had been comparable to Fitzgerald's, and for a moment Bromfield mused over the new lustre that had been given to the Fitzgerald name. I said, lustre or no lustre, I thought *The Great Gatsby* would go on being read because it deserved to be read. Finally the musing Bromfield said, "That Fitzgerald-Zelda story, well, to tell you the truth, I think the Fitzgerald story is better than his work."

The work!

Am I suggesting that the poet's work, the painter's work is liable to die off if there are no stories about him? No, not at all. In the long run, the work is what lives, but the stories help. Think of Byron. Think of Oscar Wilde. And some writers are lucky enough to have had it both ways. Take a writer like François Villon; there are wonderful intriguing stories about his life, but his work is also so singular that it will sustain itself forever in French literature. He is alive in the stories, he's alive in his poetry.

And then there is the singular presence of Shakespeare, perpetually with us, about whom there are no stories, just surmises, guesses, a few names in a registration book and many cunning professorial fantasies. Yet he lives gigantically. His work is the work that has also become the legend, because giants of the imagination like Shakespeare are forever in their work as themselves: the work tells their story. Not just the facts about the man, but all the corners of his soul, moulded, passed on, all his sensibilities.

As it is with the forceful Shakespeare, so it is with the quiet Chekhov. His story is his imagining of himself in his people, all those characters we have come to call Chekhovian, as we sometimes call ourselves Chekhovian. His legend, those stories, will be with us forever.

So, a man, any woman, wanting to be known, should not only ask, "Am I a story?" but also, "In what way am I a story?"

*CBC Anthology*

# LILLIAN HELLMAN
# AND MARY MCCARTHY

I read that Lillian Hellman, author of *The Children's Hour*, *The Little Foxes*, and whose story, *Julia*, was such a successful movie, is suing the equally celebrated Mary McCarthy for over a million dollars because of some scathing remarks made on the Dick Cavett show.

I find it a fascinating story. Authors rarely if ever sue. The puniest reviewer is free to insult the most gifted author. In many of these reviews there is, of course, some hidden venom, some personal dislike of the author whom the reviewer imagines he knows. If a slanderously malicious piece is printed and the author complains, the editor will usually say, "Well, we thought it was fair comment, an honest opinion."

The laws of libel and slander, by general agreement, do not seem to apply to a writer and his work. Usually, when a man feels he has been libelled he goes to a lawyer, taking along the statement alleged to be libellous in the scurrilous review, and the lawyer asks, "Is this statement true? Is it made with malice aforethought? Does it defame you, bring you into contempt, cause you to lose your hard-won reputation and cause you financial losses?"

The author answers that the statement does all these things. The sensible lawyer, though, will advise against a suit, asking: aren't all these things merely a matter of taste? And if the reviewer who made this statement has no taste, isn't he honestly revealing this?

And as for honesty – supposing a bad writer is praised as a genius by this same reviewer. Aren't all good writers consequently slandered by this lover of bad writing? No, in the long run, unless a plain unvarnished lie is involved, the author can't do anything about malicious attacks on him and his work, unless he is standing very close to the attacker. Then, a punch on the nose helps to heals.

The novelty in the Lillian Hellman suit against Mary McCarthy is that two writers are involved. It has been my experience that the most outrageous attacks by reviewers on authors tend to give wounds that fortunately close quickly. These days, you can just as freely insult an author who is well known as you can insult a politician, and the author, as time passes, tends to take the personal insult as an occupational hazard.

But the one wound he can not forget, the wound that seems to deepen as time passes, is the wound that comes from another established writer. Ah, these are the cuts that rankle in the night when you can not sleep. Your mind goes back to those words you are sure will always be remembered by your contemporaries, who are really the only ones whose opinion you respect.

I would like to have been near Jack Kerouac when he heard that Truman Capote had said of his work, "This isn't writing. This is typing." And I've heard Capote, chuckling with satisfaction, say that his quip destroyed Kerouac. Could Kerouac sue? No. Capote would claim that his comment was fair, that it served the cause of all good writers. The terrible wound is made all the more terrible because it comes from an established writer.

I remember one afternoon, sitting in my hotel room in New York with Thomas Wolfe – this was in the middle thirties – and he was incensed that the left-wing critics had turned on him. Incensed – but not really troubled in his own mind, not deeply hurt, more contemptuous than hurt – he then told me about a remark Scott Fitzgerald had made about all the Wolfe work.

Fitzgerald had said that as a writer Wolfe was like an Italian heavyweight fighter, Primo Carnera, who for a brief and unexpected few months had been the heavyweight champion. Carnera, like Wolfe, was about six feet-five and proportionately huge, but he was so awkward and clumsy he seemed to be falling over his own feet and you knew it was a fluke that he had become champion. Telling this story, Wolfe's whole tone changed. He was really troubled and hurt; he wanted to know why Fitzgerald would make such a remark. I knew he would go on thinking about it and hurting, wondering what was in him as a man and as a writer that had annoyed Fitzgerald, an artist he respected. When the scathing attack comes from another writer, the one attacked always takes it as a personal matter.

If the things said about Lillian Hellman had been said by a run-of-the mill critic, instead of by Mary McCarthy, we probably would have heard no more about it. Miss McCarthy said, "She is a bad writer." Well, you can't sue on that; it's simply an opinion, a matter of taste. She also said, "I think every word she writes is false, including *and* and *but* . . . the truth isn't in her," and here I think is where the fur began to fly, and where, I suspect, a fascinating can of worms could be opened up if the 2.5 million-dollar case ever comes to trial.

The phrase, "Truth isn't in her," is often applied to a writer. I remember walking up the street once with John Grey when he was president of Macmillan and he was talking about a friend of his, a man he liked who had written a war book, a very successful book which Grey thought, however, was a falsification of war, and Grey, laughing, had said, "I'm afraid the truth isn't in him," but there was no rancour in Grey; it was obvious he was talking about a certain kind of writing. But Lillian Hellman is a strange story. She's told the stories of others, but she's also told her own. It's dangerous to get caught up in your own story. Just like Madame Bovary, she, too, came to believe in the myth of herself. So, strange indeed is Hellman's ascension into grace. For years she had been very political. Well to the left. With Dashiell Hammett, she suffered during the McCarthy years in the States, forced to appear before the Senate House Committee of Un-American Activities (1952), where she testified about her own political actions but took the Fifth Amendment when asked to testify about the activities of others. She has since flowered as a noble and heroic relic of the resistance to those days. She has become almost mythic. But Mary McCarthy remembers that Miss Hellman supported the Stalin great purge trial in Russia. There are those who say they still think of her as a steadfast Stalinist. And then there is "Julia." Is "Julia" her story? My guess is that this case, which could be a dandy, a real beauty, will never come to trial.[1]

---

[1] Editor's note: The legal action died when Lillian Hellman died in 1984. As part of her argument, McCarthy had alleged that Hellman had made up heroic details about herself in her autobiography, *Pentimento*, suggesting that she had played a real role in funneling funds to anti-Nazi groups in and around Austria. A Hollywood film based on the story in *Pentimento* was made, starring Vanessa Redgrave and Jane Fonda, a film called *Julia* (1977). A woman named Muriel Gardiner persuasively challenged this story in her memoir, *Code Name 'Mary': Memoirs of an American Woman in the Austrian Underground*, (1983) claiming she was the real Julia, and in a documentary released after Gardiner's death, *The Real Julia* (1985). Till her death, Hellman stood by her Pentimento version of the story.

# SACRED PROPERTY

There it was in the newspapers, the ultimate confirmation of a view of life that has disturbed me for years. I used to ask myself the question: what is really sacred in our society, what has really been sacred all through human history? And I've always come up with the same answer. Property! No matter the race, the nation, or the period in history – life itself, which ought to have sanctity if anything is to be regarded as sacred, has been held very cheaply. Life has always been sacrificed for the preservation of property rights, whether the society was pagan or Christian. This is a rather sour view of man and his gods, of man and all his spiritual reflections and his humanitarian concerns. It is a hard view for an artist, a writer, to live by. So, I would often try to put it aside.

And then the other day there it was in the newspapers – the triumphant announcement of the testing and workability of the neutron bomb. The perfect bomb! If a large enough neutron bomb was dropped on a city the entire population of the city would be destroyed through radiation, but, and here was the great news – the beautiful and consoling and comforting and reassuring magic of this new bomb – though all life in the city would be destroyed – the property, the buildings, and I assume the expensive productive machinery would be unharmed. All the enemy people dead, but their property left in good working order.

At first I thought I had got it wrong or someone else had got confused. What had really been meant in these news reports was that the bomb would destroy all property and leave life untouched. But no. I saw this would be a violation of our whole tradition, of all the laws we live by. No, there it was, this satisfactory bomb endorsed by that born-again Christian, President Jimmy Carter . . . the final ghostly, but almost comically ghastly mockery of all of man's spiritual pretensions.

Of course, there have been apprehensive murmurings about this bomb, but it seems to me that these murmurings come from men who are made uneasy by the public declaration of the bomb's devastating peculiarities: the public pronouncement that human life will be sacrificed for the preservation of property.

The distinction of a good writer is that he has a view of life. He may be a dreamer, he may write fairy tales, but the greatest writers and dramatists, whether this be Shakespeare or Chekhov or Ibsen or Marquez or Sterne or Mark Twain make us say to ourselves, "Yes, this is the way life is. I hadn't thought of it that way, but my heart tells me it is true." I find myself wondering now about those writers who have managed to be great without recognizing what is really sacred in life, the one thing for which man has always had the greatest respect – property.

When Dostoevsky writes about crime and punishment, he tells us that the fool in his heart has said there is no god, but that a man coming to wisdom after a crime can go willingly to Siberia if he wins for himself a good conscience! Or, as in *The Brothers Karamazov*, his character tells us that the greatest thing in life is to live so that in the end you have a good memory of things. No mention of property. No mention of money. Is this real life? Is it the truth? Or is this just idealist dreaming made to seem painfully real by a great artist? Or, put it this way; is Balzac truer to life when he has so many of his characters crazy about money, as he was himself? Yet rarely in literature – at least in great literature, is the man of property regarded as a sacred figure. Powerful figures, yes, or fascinating figures, but not sacred because of their property, and yet if property is sacred above all things why shouldn't the rich man be venerated? Indeed, as they used to say, "God has prospered him." In this ancient and fine old view of the rich man and his prosperity, his property was tied to God. I am sure that those who are exultant at news that we now have the perfect bomb that will preserve property, no matter how great the slaughter of human beings, will feel it is the kind of bomb that has the approval of their property-disposing god.

The writer, it would seem to me, if he is a novelist or storyteller, has no choice; in his work, he is always dealing with human relationships and in these relationships private worlds are discovered where property has no place, where money has no place, and in a sense, the writer's characters coming alive in his imagination are all sacred figures because they are alive, even when they are ruined by property, by the law being brought against him, and the church, too, in defence of property rights.

As a writer, I know that a man has a private world, sometimes so it seems to have its own laws (try exploring it sometime in your night thoughts) and in this world there are hungers and passions and intimacies and longings where your sacred property will neither comfort you nor protect you, a world where you can think what you want, do what you want, and reach out for something in your loneliness and hear strange whisperings.

This domain is just as real a part of man as is his public domain. And it may be that the source of his true happiness is always found in this domain, and it is when I wander in this private land that I get at some of the truth – about myself at least – and I know, out of this truth, that what they are saying about the beautiful capacity of the neutron bomb to destroy all the life of a city while sparing all the property is one of the most barbaric statements ever made in all history.

*CBC Anthology*

# A BAFFLING,
# MYSTIFYING EXPERIENCE

As I have said, by his very nature, a writer keeps a part of his life in a secret world. It is the land of his own conscience, directed by his free imagination; it is the land that is the source of his intuitions, the place where, if he is any good, he is completely self-directed.

It is a very private domain where we hear whispers that no one else can hear. It is where we can dream and damn things, have dazzling ideas, reject the world around us, even if we walk around in the daytime sheets like docile, faceless little men trying to stay out of the way of men born to be cops and men born to be slaves. The Solzhenitsyn story in Russia is the story of a writer whose novels showed that he has hidden within himself this other secret government. He was a threat, and they got rid of the threat by putting him out of the country. But what a pity he couldn't have remained in Russia to remind all young Russian writers that a man could still have a domain under his own direction: an unconquered man with his own view of life.

I know there is an urge in men to surrender their own imaginations – to turn themselves in – willingly. I had a friend from Chicago, a young professor, who had come here to study at the Medieval Institute. St. Augustine was his man. One night he said to me fervently, "I want to get so I can think and feel and breathe and see things like St. Augustine, so I can be all St. Augustine." I said to him, "I was interested in you. Where did you go? What happened to *you*?" He looked troubled for a moment. "It's only for three years," he said. My friend was not the first man to yield the freedom and wildness of his imagination to the surveillance of the graduate school or a party leader.

Surveillance! A man's public actions may be controlled by cops and laws. His public face may be watched and photographed. But his private face, if only his private face could be scrutinized! If only his imagination could be controlled so that he could be turned into another more reliable, respectable and predictable man who has no sacred private places in his life. What you get is the growth of the idiotic behavioural scientists, men who believe they can control the minds of men; and so the CIA experimented with drugs; anything to invade the person, to take away from him his sense of himself as a person – in short, to make him a politically acceptable zombie. Of course, they were just seeing if they could do it! But you know the way it is with scientists. If it can be demonstrated that a thing can be done, then it will be done, no matter how barbarous the thing is. You see this in Carter's approval of the neutron bomb – at last a bomb that will not destroy property, it will only kill people. What chance do I or you, if you agree with me, have in contending for the sacredness of the private domain and a free imagination?

A well-known doctor who was having a public discussion with me said, "You talk about the person and his imagination as if it is a fixed, unique, sacred thing. But I can change that person and even all his fancies. I have seen it done in hospitals. Quite another personality emerges." But I said, "No, this unique person is still there. You have drugged him and he is behaving as a drugged man behaves, but he'll be himself again with his own fancies if you take him off the drugs." The doctor was inclined to agree with me.

Aside from the drugs and the behavioural scientists with their bags of tricks, there is a regrettable, no, a very sad, growing approval of electronic surveillance in this country, an acceptance of a kind of lawful invasion of a man's privacy. You may say, "What do you care if three or four cops are listening on a wiretap to the domestic doings of a minor Mafia figure?" Since I believe that the best part of me is in my private domain, where my imagination is free to create as it will, then, any furtive eavesdropping on *any* man's privacy can be the beginning of an invasion of *me,* too. The next thing I know they'll be trying to get into my mind. So if the conversation of some little bookie in the back room of a cigar store is being monitored, I'm there too. If a Supreme Court judge rules that evidence, even if obtained illegally, is admissible if it gives proof of guilt, I'm there too. The same thing came up at the time of the imposition of the War Measures Act. A woman said to me, "Why are you so angry? It's no skin off your nose." I said, "The fact is that for those few days my civil liberties were taken away from me; I was diminished; I was much less the person than I am."

The person! The dignity of the person! A man's own self-respect! That's the thing with me. I know that it is a man's secret, private world that gives him his true identity. Identity! I hate using that word now in Canada. The Canadian identity! A bad, tired old word. It is tossed out at every gathering by politicians, academics and editorial writers. If they mean anything, using this word, I think they really mean "image." That, God knows, is something else.

I'll tell you a little story. Some years ago, when Ralph Allen was the distinguished editor of *Maclean's* magazine, he and I were invited to lunch by a vice-president of one of the largest advertising agencies. Neither Allen nor I knew what the man wanted. At lunch, in friendly conversation, this advertising man said, "What is it that we all have in common? What is it every man wants?" Both Allen and I were baffled. I certainly had no ready answer. Our friend, waiting and growing baffled himself by our lack of awareness of these things, finally blurted out, "Recognition. That's what we all want. Recognition! Isn't that so?"

Allen and I mulled it over. The world indeed was full of people screaming in despair, "Won't someone pay attention to me?" Now, years later, I suppose you could say this has become the national cry. I don't know. However, what the man from the agency really wanted to know was whether Allen and I would have dinner with a big man from *Time* magazine in New York, a man with the grand-sounding title, Editor of the Western Hemisphere. So the *Time* man came to town. The dinner took place at Winston's. The Editor of the Western Hemisphere turned out to be a big, voluble, hard-drinking fellow, and with him, to look after all the mundane matters, was the local *Time* man, who was in awe of his powerful expansive and opulent superior.

Soon Allen and I were warmly at ease with the big man. Before dinner we had started drinking whisky sours, and during dinner he kept on drinking them, and then after dinner, too – by which time we were chums and good old boys, and finally we decided we had better move; we would all go up to my place. Then a terrible thing happened. The local *Time* man, our host, picked up the check, took out his wallet, started counting his money, looked perplexed, then terrified. He realized he hadn't brought along enough money. He whispered to the Editor of the Western Hemisphere, "Could you help me out?" You could feel the New York man's fierce outrage. *Time* magazine! Clare Booth Luce, *Sports Illustrated*, the Western Hemisphere, the whole vast *Time* empire had been humiliated by this little local representative.

We went up to my place. The local *Time* man, who obviously longed to be in other, faraway places, remained wan and silent while we drank and argued, and finally he said that if we would excuse him he would go home, he was very tired. After he left, the Editor of the Western Hemisphere said coldly, "You see, he can't drink either," and then, after reflecting, he shrugged. "A hick," he said, and went on with his lively conversation. Toward dawn, when I led the great man to his taxi, I knew that the local *Time* man was doomed. Indeed, within a few months he was out of the *Time* organization.

Now, what was involved here? Image. Not identity. The local *Time* man had in one stroke lost his image. Images. Symbols. Manufactured things and often terrible falsifications. Here today, and soon, thank God, gone tomorrow. The local man was what he was. Allen and I were what we were – as was the great editor. The images that had been blown that night had nothing to do with the reality of any one of us, except that the incident tells us something about both *Time* men and what they were before the dinner took place.

I know, from listening to politicians, editorial writers and gentlemen who love attending cultural conferences, that I, at this time in our history, am supposed to be wandering around asking people who I am. Won't someone please identify me? I'm supposed to be lost. I'm waiting for some cultural cop to pick me up and take me to a station where I, as a Canadian, like a streetwalker in Paris, can be given a card of identity. Well, people who don't know who and what they are, or who have to get together in therapy so they can tell one another who they are, are always lost souls. All their lives they wait to help the cop who is about to pick them up, they wait for someone to give them direction, someone impersonal, someone from the corporations, men from the state – the swarming bureaucrats with their computers, the lawless police with their burglar's tools and bugging devices. These impersonal men, with their strange loyalties to a monster security machine, are in hot pursuit of free men to slowly erode the area of their private domains. They are bent on seeing to it that all respect for this domain is diminished. And what is it that is being offered in exchange for our own inner light?

Security! What security? Whose security? What is the black magic of the word security that makes judges grow silent and opens any door marked Private, makes our Prime Minister want to give sanctuary to those who break the law?

Open any door marked Private! Do I sound like an editorial writer safe in his armchair who knows these things can never happen to him? Well, one winter night not long ago I got a phone call. A man with a Russian accent asked if he could come to see me. He was from Moscow and he wanted to present to me a Russian translation of my novel, *The Loved and the Lost*. That night it was snowing hard. He came into my house covered with snow. He gave me his business card. He was a prominent Moscow official. Why was he here? Why him? He had written the introduction to my book – which had sold out its printing – and then as it came out in our excited conversation, he had wanted to be a writer before going into official life. Literature was his secret passion, but his eyes had failed him. He had come at 8 o'clock and at midnight we were still talking. What did we talk about? The whole world of the imagination, as he looked at paintings on the wall and we exchanged insights on Tolstoy's work, on Chekhov, on Hemingway, on Moravia, and Günter Grass, and a story by Faulkner, too, and arguments he had had with editors in Moscow about my own work. Just literature – the world of the imagination, sharing for a few hours our private domains. When he finally left, going out into the snow again, I sat around feeling exhilarated and happy about my own work.

Some weeks later I got a telephone call from the RCMP. Could they come to see me? Their man came, and a nice young fellow he was, too, and he wanted to know what this well-known Moscow figure had been doing in my house. He expected me to tell him and I told him. How long had the man stayed? Five hours. Extraordinary. What had we talked about? Literature. Just writers. But such a busy man? This was almost incredible. The cop made me feel that any man who would waste five hours indulging in a passion for literature was, by his very nature, suspect. Then I told him that they, in their surveillance of this strange man, had slipped up. How so? Two nights later the man had come again to the house and stayed till after midnight. Really! His stunned expression gave me satisfaction. Something private had taken place and they didn't know about it. Why had he come? What did he talk about? Well, he had brought me a translation of his introduction to *The Loved and the Lost*, and we had gone over it. Imagine that! Four more hours of conversation, just about literature? A baffling, mystifying experience.

So you see, my house, my private domain, that world I shared with my Moscow man who had the passion for literature, had indeed been invaded. Would the Prime Minister and his Solicitor General condone this kind of invasion? Would it give them a sense of security to know my private life was being monitored, and would it upset them to know that one night had escaped their surveillance?

Such is the state of the nation now that the latest polls show that people have little or no concern about illegal police activities. Such may be the state of the nation that a surveillance of each and every man's private life may be welcomed and even applauded, it being understood that the real oath of allegiance in this country is to the RCMP. This seems to me to be a surrender of all self-respect. Or, to put it another way, it is a cry from the craven heart: "To hell with self-respect and the freedom of privacy. I choose security."

*Toronto Life, 1978*

# THE POPE COMES
# TO TOWN: ONE

Looking forward, I found that the Pope, John Paul II, was coming to my town. Brooding on this, I devoutly hoped that the Pope, on his visit, would put aside his views on the proper direction of sexual pleasure in marriage, views he had expressed so vigorously in Switzerland.

In that country, before a mainly celibate audience, he had stated that the sensual delights of love in marriage should come only when the act of love is performed for the purpose of procreation; that the delights of lovemaking are never to be an end in themselves.

This is a view of lovemaking in marriage that I thought had been laid to rest by Cardinal Léger at Vatican II. The Cardinal had very bravely and wisely said what all happily married men and women know and have always known – that the intoxication of sensual delight is part of true sacramental love; this delight is something that comes of itself, it can be by itself a gift, a perfection of the union quite aside from the intention of procreation. There would seem to be a wide and boundless sea of differences between the Pope and the Cardinal – their views of what goes on in the marriage bed, and maybe even about the nature of lovemaking between a man and a woman. Certainly, I began to wonder with a certain wry sadness about why the Cardinal had retired to a leper colony in the depths of Cameroon in Africa.

So what is the Pope up to? The Pope, a charismatic, bold authoritarian, is, reasserting a control and a dominion over what he knows is the last sweet little acre – the marriage bed. His view, it would seem to me, is utterly unrealistic, and worse still, it throws a wet blanket over the wild and sacred raptures that can come to those who are married when in each other's arms. It is true that men and women marry to have families – in short to procreate. But they also marry to love as they would be loved, love for love's sake, as do those who marry who cannot have children, but who delight in lying in each other's arms. Should these unfortunates abstain from the sensual delights? Or accept them as God-given splendours of a loving union, even though there can be no breeding?

The idea of respectable, controlled and directed lovemaking has always struck me as a tremendous falsification of life – of a sacred human relationship that is so dependent on a spontaneous freedom in the heart; and the wonder of it is that when anyone else, a stranger, tries to take charge and control it, or makes one self-conscious about it, the magic goes. For me, man can be aware of the possibilities of sexual union as no other animal can because sex can, in its raptures, give him a glimpse of something beyond himself. Oh, those rapturous climaxes in which, some say, there may be an intimation of the wonders of eternity. So, as for sex – just for procreation – I hope the Pope doesn't get going again on the subject when he visits our shores.

*Toronto Life*, 1984

# THE POPE COMES
# TO TOWN: TWO

❧❦❧

While the Pope was riding around in Toronto, suddenly a new window was open for me on my city. I was down at St. Michael's
Cathedral, and just a few blocks away, up Parliament Street, there is
a cemetery, and I remember thinking that those graves were probably opening and ghosts were walking around pondering this dreadful thing happening to their old British province of Toronto. They
were looking around in all their anguish and asking themselves:
"Where has this city gone? Where is old Protestant Toronto gone?"

I knew the old British, Protestant Toronto. My father, at the
time of the Boer War (1899-1902), had had the wit to oppose the
British campaign in South Africa. He was very unpopular for that
and he was a Catholic. The pro-British Protestants wanted to tar
and feather him. They chased him into his rooming house on
Shuter Street. That was stout, British, Protestant Toronto. When
I was a boy I was not particularly aware that I was a Catholic. But
when I was about 12, a new kid on the street insulted me. I started
to run across the street at him. He turned and shouted at me,
"Dogan." I was stunned. "What is a Dogan?" I said to my father. In
later years, by the 1940s, the situation softened. There was little
overt prejudice. But the old ways of Presbyterian establishment
thinking persisted: Sundays shut down to joy, to play; men and
women forced to drink spirits and beer in separate "beverage
rooms" unless eating a meal; the British-Israelite Imperial Society

headquarters (Anglo-Saxons who believed they were the "lost tribe"); the lone Catholic city Councilor, Mr. Balfour; the management of City Management by Protestants; and perhaps most symbolically significant, the 12th of July Orangeman's Day Parade featuring King Billy on his white horse, the pipes and drums behind the clop-clop of that swayback's swagger through the centre of town, known then by many as "little Belfast."

I remember in the 1940s, just after the war, I was invited to a private gathering of prominent citizens – businessmen, editors, representative Jews – to talk in private about an outbreak of violent anti-Semitism. Gangs had started to form. They were attacking Jews with baseball bats and crowbars. The late B.K. Sandwell, the influential editor of *Saturday Night*, was chairman. The Chief of Police spoke. The Chiefs of Police all my life had been Ulster Scots. He said the city had become a boil. At one point during the discussion Sandwell bowed to me and said, "We have here a man who broke through." I almost fell off my chair. I thought of Sandwell as an Englishman who had just got off the boat. All along, he had thought of me as an outsider Irish Catholic. At last, he thought of me as an Irish Catholic who finally belonged to his own city.

Now, the whole nature of the city has changed. King Billy takes his ride somewhere between cul-de-sacs in the suburbs. Orange influence has fallen away. There was discussion during the Pope's visit of a falling away, too, from church attendance. This may not be a bad thing, however, because as people tend to refuse to fight about doctrine, to kill each other over such matters, they have a tendency to approach each other in human terms. People move. Young people meet. Love laughs at cultural locksmiths. There are so many Catholics now, the educational and national political systems are so dominated by Catholics, that there is no distinction in being a Catholic. There is no distinction in being a bigot.

In fact, in Toronto, you can feel the waves of many religions, many cultures we never dreamed of living beside washing over us, washing into our language, too, and it is thrilling to realize that we can't imagine who or what a Toronto Canadian will be like in fifty years. Except, he or she will almost certainly be a shade of brown and middle class.

The other night I listened to an American woman, who had lived here for twenty-five years, arguing with two young men who had been born in Toronto. The woman was from New York. Now she preferred Toronto. It was an exciting city, she insisted, full of energy, full of money. "Any fashions that appear in Paris or New York are here within a week. Plays come here, too. Books do well here, and above all," she said, "I feel very secure here and when you feel secure in a place, that place becomes your town. From now on, you'll see that a steady wave of immigration," she said, "will come not just from the Mediterranean and the Far East but unseen from the United States, for no matter what you are, you can feel more comfortable here than in any big city in the United States."

"I agree that it is more comfortable, here," said one young man. "Yes, I thoroughly agree, it is more definitely comfortable here," the other fellow said. "Well, isn't that something, isn't it terribly important to be able to feel comfortable?" the woman asked. "Of course it's important to feel comfortable in an environment," said the first young man. "To feel secure and be able to live out your life is worth something," he added with an indulgent shrug. "But if you are alive, it is not the only thing."

"I feel uneasy in New York," said the second young man, "but I think I feel more alive there."

"Alive to what?" she asked, exasperated.

"Alive to something really new."

"Oh, that New York craziness for novelty," she said. "Fiddle-sticks."

"No," the second young man insisted. "The new in the sense of the first-rate. You see, the first-rate in Toronto usually disturbs our comfort. We're not used to it, it's upsetting. It has to be pushed aside."

The other man said, "I like it here, I'll go on living here. But I know that it is a wonderfully middle-class city. In all its happiest aspirations, rich or poor, this city is middle class."

"And what's the matter with being middle class?" the lady asked tartly.

"Nothing at all," he said. "As you say, to live comfortably is the great thing. The middle-class man, the bourgeoisie, not wanting his feathers to be ruffled, always loves mediocrity. He seeks it, praises it, exalts it and in such a society a man with a first-rate talent, whether a painter or a writer, is always left isolated in his own wilderness, till he makes a lot of money somewhere else."

The middle class, the poor blighted, comfort-loving materialistic, porky, vulgarly opulent middle class lying about in each other's arms – the enemy class of all first-class artists! Well, so they say, and I've heard it all my life. But I remember reading George Bernard Shaw when I was a student, and he had pointed out that creative energy was really in the middle class, and at the time, I had looked around and found that nearly all the great writers all through English literature had come from the middle class. There were a few exceptions; H.G. Wells, born in poverty, or Lord Byron on the princely side and O'Casey from the tenements, but Keats and Joyce and T.S. Eliot, and Flaubert, Balzac and Stendhal, and Dostoevsky and Chekhov, all middle-class men. And why not? It is almost inevitable that in this great class, the restless ambitious children, born anywhere and from everywhere, full of the energy of their class, will grow tired of the merely mundane comforts of their newly rich fathers. So if the worst you can say about a big bustling multi-racial town like Toronto, now, is that it is a comfortable place, and that all its cultural aspirations represent a love of middle-class mediocrity, you may be merely saying that you are a generation away from the emergence of a taste for something first-rate.

*Toronto Star*, 1984

# A TALE OF OUR TIME

This story seems to me to be a tale of our time.

I was at a big happy party at a young man's house. The other guests were between twenty-five and forty years old. They were all friends. There was dancing and singing and feasting and drinking. Everybody was happy. Everybody was a little drunk, yet no one seemed to be sloppy or noisy. There was much good conversation. In the house there were three big rooms, a kitchen and a little room off the kitchen being used as a bar. In the custom of the country the heavy drinkers rarely moved more than ten feet away from the bar. I was standing idly by the door of this little room talking to a pretty girl when in the corner of my eye I caught a figure in the little room swinging his arm. I heard a crunch and the shattering of glass. I stepped into the room. Someone there quickly closed the door behind me so no one else could get in. I saw a man, a handsome man of forty, with a broken bottle in his hand.

Bits of the broken bottle and spilled liquor were on the floor. Another man, bent low, his hands pressed on his scalp as he tried to stand up, mumbled, "I'll kill him. I'll kill him." But he couldn't get to his feet. A girl, her mouth gaping open in blank frightened astonishment, grabbed the one who still held the broken bottle, her husband, and dragged him away and into the kitchen. Then I saw that the man with the cracked head was bleeding badly. He was a big heavy blond young man. He could only stare stupidly at the blood on his hands. Our host, a young man of thirty-five, came into the room to get a drink; stood stunned and incredulous, then he put me out of the room, and closed the door. Nothing was to be seen by those in the other rooms who were dancing and singing. Our host opened the door again. He was pale. He cornered a young man who was a doctor, whispered to him, quietly took him into the bar and closed the door. Finally, he and two of his friends, who had remained in the bar all along and had seen what had happened, came out. The two friends were remonstrating with our host. They kept grabbing his arm. A hard glint was in his eye. "I know what I'm doing," he insisted. He sounded cold and determined.

"What about the one with the cut head?" I asked, feeling like a stranger. "Is his head smashed? Where is he? Where's the doctor?" I whispered.

"They went out the back door. The doctor has to take him to the hospital. It'll take from twelve to eighteen stitches, providing that's all that's the matter with him," my young host said grimly. Turning away abruptly, he headed for the kitchen. He wanted to tell the man who had wielded the bottle so murderously, to leave the house. He had known this man for years. "Just the same," he said, "he must not stay at this party. I know how to handle him."

His friends tried to dissuade him from creating a scene that would break up the party. It was all a misunderstanding, they pleaded. In the kitchen, the assailant sat with his weeping wife. He was trembling. She claimed she had merely said to the man who was now on his way to the hospital, "Hello there, kid, how are you?" and he had scowled and tossed a glass of whiskey in her face. Then, her husband had picked up the bottle and cracked it over their friend's head. Our host listened to the story, growing angrier as he listened. He kept on repeating over and over again that he didn't care who was insulted, it was his party; the reckless vicious violence was intolerable. His friends kept him away from the bottle wielder. All he would say to this man was, "Leave, go home." He repeated this to a friend begging at his arm. "Talk to me tomorrow, you must not be here with us."

But his friends, whispering and coaxing, held him back, soothing away his sense of outrage. Weren't they all friends? There would be apologies the next day and some remorse no doubt; few in the party knew that one of the guests had been carried off to the hospital so why make another scene that would make everyone unhappy and have the party end on a sad sour note.

Our host yielded to this advice reluctantly. "You're quite wrong you know," he said quietly and he walked away. A half-hour later the weeping wife, having dried her tears and taken another drink came out of the kitchen and drifted around with a bright stunned smile. A few minutes later her husband appeared looking very stern and watchful. I heard him mutter, "No one's going to insult my wife." But few of the guests knew what had happened. Those who knew paid no attention to him. Soon he was sitting down at the piano. He played a very good piano. The party got going again. They were all good friends.

Beside me were a young academic and his attractive wife, two of those who were aware of what had happened.

"You know I think our host was right," I said quietly.

Her eyes were full of disappointment in me. "I thought I knew something about you," she said. "You're the last man I expected to take that attitude."

"Cracking a man's head open with a bottle," I protested. "Here at a friendly party! It's barbarous, it's murderous. Recognize it for what it is. That's what our host was trying to do."

"I just can't believe it's you going on like this," the pretty wife said. "We thought you'd have more understanding."

"Well, that's our host's view of it," I said. "It's my view too."

"Oh, come on, it can't be, you're too worldly a man. Look," the young academic went on, "it's just something that happened. Everybody was having a good time, eh? Everybody was happy, then it was just something that happened."

"But the man's head is cracked open," I protested.

"Oh, a few stitches and he'll be all right. And we've all been having such a good time. You too. Come now, haven't you?"

"I was having a good time," I admitted. "I don't want to spoil it, no."

We smiled at each other, but the agreement in our smiles made me feel ashamed for I felt I, too, was just something happening, part of the general good time, part of the cheerful acceptance of an act of savagery, a little tale of our time.

# ALEXANDRE SOLZHENITSYN

In the whole world, no writer is as widely read as Alexandre Solzhenitsyn. Anything he writes – anything – is taken as a news event
in all countries with the exception of his homeland, Russia. No one
since Tolstoy has had such world acclaim. When Tolstoy lay dying,
newspapermen from the far corners of the earth hurried to get to
his deathbed. What emperor or pope in his dying so touched the
hearts of men? Yet, Solzhenitsyn, who has now an even greater
kingdom in the minds of men and women, can not be exalted as
Tolstoy was. Tolstoy had a magic spell of insights into the Russian
heart, which turned out to be the human heart. Millions of
Russians loved him as a teacher and a moving novelist . . . as if –
because he understood men and women in their relationships with
each other – he had to be a great moralist, too.

   In trying to judge the greatness of Solzhenitsyn, it is not unfair
to point out that he has a huge ready-made constituency; all readers who hate the Soviets, the Kremlin, the Communist Party, and
the whole present structure of Russian life, turn avidly to Solzhenitsyn. They don't care whether or not he is a great writer; they are
not interested in what he stands for in himself. It is hard, then, to
look at this man and see him for what he is – as a writer; to see him
aside from this great and applauding crowd who embrace him as
one of their own.

   Solzhenitsyn's *One Day in the Life of Ivan Denisovich* appeared
when I, for one, was not prepared to be excited by a book about
the horrors of life in a concentration camp under Stalin, the

monstrous and terrible ruler of all the Russias. I had lived through the thirties and forties. On this continent, hundreds of writers who had been sympathetic to the Communist Party in the early thirties had been disillusioned by the trials of the old Bolsheviks. Arthur Koestler had written *Darkness at Noon*. Imaginative writers had ended up appalled by the fanatical sense of obedience to the Party so ingrained in all Party men, and were sickened, too, by the willingness of old Communists to grovel before Stalin. But then, before a real sickening could set in, the war turned Stalin into Uncle Joe, and for a few years, he was seen in this avuncular role. After his death, in Khrushchev's time, he was denounced as one of the most ruthless and bloodthirsty tyrants in all human history.

Men of goodwill, after this denunciation, were ready to blame all the cruelties, all the prison camps, and all the persecutions that had taken place in Russia, on the monster, Stalin. By the time Solzhenitsyn came along I was a bit bored hearing about Stalin. I had long since formed my own disgusted view of him. A good deal about the war had disgusted me. Like many others, I was willing to forget. Forget? Forget? It is a word that maddens Solzhenitsyn. It is a word that is crucial to a consideration of Solzhenitsyn's words. For him, it is another word for the damned!

Aside from wanting to forget about Stalin, I felt detached from the literature produced in Russia in the fifties. A Russian official had sent me six or seven novels. I told him I couldn't feel involved in any of them: These new writers were trying to make a new literature, based – it seemed to me – on a socialist work ethic, and as I said frankly to my Russian diplomat – in a very old fashioned way, the characters in the novels seemed to have no souls. I think he knew what I meant, for he said, "Wait a while. Wait."

Those were the days of socialist realism. What did this label mean? Only old-fashioned French or American materialism, plus some laudable social objective. Who cared? Then, I encountered a young Russian journalist and twitted him about socialist realism, telling him it was an old dead horse. He shrugged, he smiled. It was I who was out of date, he said. To the writer in Russia, socialist realism could mean anything he wanted it to mean. It was a cynical remark. Life must be changing for the artist and the intellectual in Russia, I thought, and soon Solzhenitsyn began to appear in translation. *One Day in the Life of Ivan Denisovich*, instead of the tried and trite about the Stalin labour camps, had a startling freshness. In this record of one day, put down so cleanly and with such skill, the characters had souls. They were persons. Each one was there in his own little world, but they all had some kind of relationship with each other, and so, suddenly, in a sense I was thrown back into the world of Russian literature, levered out of forgetfulness, out of boredom.

The way the book was written, with a clear ordering of observations, as if incident after incident in the prison camp was happening immediately under your eyes, as if the only important thing was to get it down without artifice, without letting literature itself get in the way, made me wonder if Solzhenitsyn had read Hemingway. When he actually referred to Hemingway's direct clean use of language I was delighted. The Russian writer, in his methods, is of course vastly unlike the American. But, though the two are poles apart in their temperaments, there remains Solzhenitsyn's recognition that Hemingway could use words as if he were always making new accurate connections, bent only on having the reader see and feel for himself. That's what Solzhenitsyn was forcing readers to do, to see and feel for themselves! It is important to remember this when we come to his monumental picture of camp life in the Gulag Archipelago. The method of *One Day in the Life of Ivan Denisovich*, the method that is the art of the fiction writer – life speaking for itself, with no personal denunciation from the author necessary – was probably why he was able to get the Ivan book published in Russia, in the anti-Stalinist climate fostered by Khrushchev.

But then, *The First Circle* appeared, and *The Cancer Ward*, and Solzhenitsyn, wanting a world audience, had to have his work smuggled out of Russia. When he was given the Nobel Prize, he became a world embarrassment to the whole Soviet regime. The official attitude to the honours heaped on this man was predictable. They said he was given the Nobel award because he had proven to the satisfaction of all western reactionaries that he was a foe of the socialist order, and there was this much validity to their argument: Pasternak, the poet, and the author of *Doctor Zhivago*, had also been given the Nobel prize, and he too had been a writer of deep Christian sentiments.

*The First Circle* and *The Cancer Ward* display an amazing energy in creative power. *The First Circle* also displays an incredible grasp for detail, and from the opening pages, one becomes frighteningly aware of the demonic, all-pervasive power of the secret police. A phone call can be traced; it can be analyzed, it can be identified, it can land the hero in jail. In jail, intellectuals are engaged in some mysterious breaking down of code messages. It is a minute and complicated work, it is endless, and such work takes on a frightening and depressing Kafkaesque quality. Solzhenitsyn, still the fiction writer in this book, gives these prison characters their human relationships. But something about *The First Circle* did not shatter me. A brilliantly conceived work, it is done with an incredibly patient ingenuity. In its final effect, it was frightening, or depressing. Yet surely, in such books there should be something you cannot bear to forget. I know I do not want to read that book again. I know I can't live for long in my imagination on a secret police and prison literature. Soon or later, imagination revolts; there is a cry within for normal life, normal relationships. Solzhenitsyn could of course cry out, "This is not the time in Russia for normal relationships. If the spirit isn't free to express itself, how can any relationship be normal?"

Solzhenitsyn, himself, has been in a cancer hospital. The suffering the man has endured, and triumphed over, and used for the forging of the great weapons of his soul are incredible. The characters in *The Cancer Ward* are in the great tradition of Russian realism. As you read and admire, you wonder where Solzhenitsyn should be placed in this great tradition. He is not Dostoevskian, although he shares some feverish excitement about his characters that makes them finally overwhelm you.

He is not Chekhovian. In Chekhov, everything is tone; every little thing happening is part of the music that creates a nostalgia for all living things, and behind it all, a gentle spirit, a spirit full of compassion. No, in *The Cancer Ward*, the imaginative world seems to be more Tolstoyan, and Solzhenitsyn again and again has expressed his admiration for Tolstoy. And yet, ruminating over this, I wonder why Solzhenitsyn with all his talent, with his great eye and his incredible patience, can't move me as Tolstoy could. Is the heart of things missed? Everything else is just right; everything arouses admiration, yet that blinding flash of insight that makes something live forever in the reader's imagination, even if the insight is only a short paragraph – is this what he has missed? I don't know.

Solzhenitsyn was still in Russia. In a sense, confined to Russia, for he was not permitted to go to Sweden to accept the Nobel Prize, a writer with no place to write or publish, unless the work is smuggled out of the country. At this time, when Solzhenitsyn was in the spotlit centre of the world stage, it seemed of an enchanting importance to me that Solzhenitsyn remain in Russia, his mind full of his own characters, people around him that he whispered to day by day; and if he just watched himself a little, this world could never be invaded by a spy or a secret policeman. As Diderot, the French encyclopedist, had said cynically, "It is often easier to appear to conform." It was easy to imagine that all the young writers, noticing that Solzhenitsyn had remained among them, even if the publishing houses weren't allowed to print his work, would be reminded that every man, even in bondage, need never surrender his conscience — unless, and this sometimes happens — a man wants desperately to forget what he is and have no memory of things at all.

What, then, were they to do with Solzhenitsyn? He had become a vast problem in public relations. Put him in prison? The consequence of such a repressive measure was enormous. Exile him? Even let him take his wife out of the country? In a bold gesture, they let him go. It was as if they were saying, "We can withstand a hundred Solzhenitsyn's. Everything he says will soon be forgotten, as those labour camps he wants to tell about have already been forgotten and put down as a product of the tyrannical Stalin times."

Forget! Forget! As I said before, it is of fervently, fanatical spiritual importance that a man should not forget: for what a man is, as Solzhenitsyn sees it, is all in the memory of things. And he had been incredibly busy: busy with an energy and physical strength that almost shocks the imagination. How incredibly fluent the man must be! Does he not rewrite at all? Hundreds and hundreds of thousands of words have gone into the great work he has been preparing — *The Gulag Archipelago*. These volumes are not, as I had believed — putting off reading them for months — just another powerful indictment of the Stalin labour camps. They are an indictment of the whole Russian system of jurisprudence, of the whole growth of their socialist law. As a work, it is almost impossible to describe.

First, there is the enormous research and tabulation involved, then the blaze of creative observation that brings alive hundreds of characters; then, there is the scorn, the sarcasm, the mockery. All the tools of the fiction writer are used to bring us closer to the people. What is this work then? It is Solzhenitsyn finding at last a fitting form for his theme that can bring out all his rage, all his anguish, and ultimately – and this is a strange thing – give us Solzhenitsyn himself. A Soviet sympathizer might have objections – I would like to hear them – but this book is surely the greatest indictment of a class of people and a period in all literature.

To get a clear, simple picture of what the *Archipelago* is, you have to wait for the second volume and the chapter that deals with the "Islands Rising from the Sea." First, there was the prison on Slovesky Island in the White Sea. In 1923, the prison had three thousand inmates. By 1930, the number had grown to fifty thousand, and then these prisons began to spread until they became a network across the whole vast country. The big camps were being built before they were needed in the certainty that they could be filled. Why were they being built? According to Solzhenitsyn, because of the determination to use forced labour for the building of roads and canals across the wintry wastes. Solzhenitsyn gets a savage satisfaction in quoting both Lenin and Stalin on the need of forced labour. And how do you get such labour? The so-called political prisoners! Work! Work! The value of work. Work, of course, is the keynote in any socialist dream. The dignity of a man through his work! Tolstoy playing the peasant role; or that character in a Chekhov play, growing exalted as he watches his end-of-the-century bourgeois world falling about him, who cries, "We must work, we must work. Only by unremitting toil can the past be redeemed." The bright future to be built on work!

Solzhenitsyn, knowing about this, shows in bitter mockery how, from Lenin to Stalin, the dignity of work was turned grimly into what they called "the corrective value of work." There it was. The great degradation. Work, endless work as an endless punishment, in sentences that ran from five to twenty years or life, till a man could be shown to be corrected in his thinking by his slavery. Then, just possibly, he returned to society.

What scorn Solzhenitsyn has for Gorki, the great Russian writer of his time, who took a tourist trip along the White Sea canal built by political prisoners, and then wrote about the prisoners and their eager happy approach to their redeeming labour. Gorki, the proletarian writer, has a great street named after him in Moscow, and Solzhenitsyn, who was one of those labourers, is in exile. Gorki, the man of the people – I remember how moved I was years ago by his *Creatures that Once Were Men* and his play, *At the Bottom*. Yet, he never tried to get close to those forced labourers, those creatures who'd once been men. The man who had been at the bottom had made it to the top. But Solzhenitsyn was there. He'd had an eight-year sentence. He had been a young army officer; he had written incriminating letters to another young officer.

How dismayed all those old fellow travellers of the thirties, forties and fifties must be and how surprising it was for me, too, to read in Solzhenitsyn's record that the waves of arrests, the elimination of all who might be in opposition, not just in deed, but in word and in thought, began immediately after the success of the 1917 revolution. The plague years were, of course, Stalin's time. A plague of repression! As bad as the bubonic plague. During those years, and here Solzhenitsyn becomes the scornful prosecutor, the legalists, the theoreticians, were refining and polishing that section of the law which would permit a legal arrest of anyone. The conception of guilt or innocence became unimportant. Under Stalin this section, justifying an arrest, amounted to this; could the suspect, having his background, be capable of committing the alleged political offence? If he could have done it, then whether or not he is guilty, became irrelevant. If he could have done it, the assumption was that he did it. Guilt or innocence, in such a world, are words that have no meaning, not in the Gulag of forced labourers.

In his chapters on the law, Solzhenitsyn is touching on a great and universal theme that should trouble men in all countries. Even a man here in Canada, feeling secure in his home, has this to brood over; what is the relationship between law and justice? What about men who have a slavish respect for the law, who grovel before it, and never ask about justice? The good citizen is the man who obeys the laws. The troublemaker is the one who asks about justice. This great and universal conflict between the law and justice is at the very heart of all Solzhenitsyn's work. Obey the law? Whose law is it? Who is it we are obeying? We come back to a man's view of himself.

Arrests, or most arrests in all countries, begin with a knock on the door. There is terror in a country when no man knows which door will be next. This, too, is an old theme. But Solzhenitsyn has a dramatic point to make which is true for all countries. When the knock comes and the police step in and say, "Come with me," a good citizen goes and goes quickly. Unless we are drunk, or on the run and know the police are after us, we go quietly. We are respectable. Our respectable neighbours assume that in some way we must have deserved this police visit.

Solzhenitsyn tells of a middle-aged woman on a Moscow street, who found herself approached by two secret policemen who began to lead her to their car. She cried out, she shrieked, she called for help. She began to struggle. The astonished policemen, who had never had this happen on the street – their arrests being secret matters – grew alarmed being out in the open, and they released the struggling woman and hurried away. Nor did they come after her again in her own home.

Solzhenitsyn celebrates the wild public outcry of this woman who refused to go off quietly into limbo. He sees in it the strength and the weakness of men about to surrender forever their freedom. Being good nice people they are taken quietly. This happened, too, in Germany at the time of the filling of the concentration camps: it is so plain that if every man or woman cried out, if every free man raised a commotion and forgot his sense of respect for law and respectability, even the highest authorities would be alarmed. Everything would be out in the open.

After arrest came the interrogation. Solzhenitsyn has a hundred stories of these interrogations. There are descriptions of terrible tortures. Not just simple beatings, but obscene and sophisticated cruelties were practiced against old and young, and even against men who thought they were still Party members. Out of all these debasing and hellish scenes, Solzhenitsyn makes another one of his great points; the point that gets to the essence of all his work; man is being degraded; a man is being made to forget what he was, a human being; he is to be so humiliated that for the rest of his life it will be impossible for him to remember who he had been. As he goes on into the labour camps to suffer his "corrective labour" he is never to be permitted a moment of dignity. He must suffer years of abject humiliation. This humiliation theme is, of course, in the great Russian tradition. It was very dear to Dostoevsky. It should be clear to all mankind.

The worldly and slightly weary critic may say that this kind of fiendish and debasing torture of political prisoners cannot be blamed on the Stalinist regime alone. There were such tortures by the Gestapo in Germany. Quite true. The revelations by Henri Aleg of the tortures by the French army men in Algeria finally shocked the conscience of France. Yes, men are capable of absolutely anything. With one atom bomb we put a hundred thousand Japanese civilians in a fiery furnace. We firebombed German cities when we couldn't open a second front. Solzhenitsyn understands these things, but this is what he says: yes, other countries have barbarously destroyed their enemies, they have enslaved and tortured native populations, they have hunted aboriginals for sport, but in the Stalinist times we have the first example of a regime turning on its own people and enslaving and torturing its own people by the millions.

There were one or two little things that puzzled me in the accounts of the interrogations. Berdayev, the Christian philosopher, who had not, at the beginning of the thirties, become world famous, was arrested and interrogated. He would not answer all the questions. He said, in effect, "Here is what I stand for," and stated in principle his Christian position. They let him go. He ought to have been regarded as a mortal enemy. Why did they let him go? No answer. No matter. One horrible interrogation is piled on another till the very repetition becomes a weakness in Solzhenitsyn the writer. Supposing a great prosecutor, appearing before the jury, begins a recital of the crimes of a monstrous criminal. The list is long. The brutal incidents multiply till the listener grows numb; but as he grows accustomed to this bestiality it loses its effects on him as terror. Terror becomes almost normal, the expected thing. So it is that in the final fat volumes of this great work there seem to be repetitions. One knows what to expect. It is as if Solzhenitsyn, in his determination to leave no stone unturned in his indictment, has finally numbed the heart of his reader. We could not have wished this to happen.

Yet he is always touching some aspect of imaginative truth that is very satisfying to the reader's sense of irony. Those blue caps, this crowd of arresters and interrogators, being so deeply enmeshed in the system as they are, know that someday, and soon, they too will be denounced, they too will be confessing, they too, the very stewards of security, will feel no sense of security themselves, so that the whole thing has become a nightmare. For the truth is, as Solzhenitsyn shows by naming names, the camps were full of men who thought they were loyal Party members, or even great and powerful figures; they were there in the camps, having confessed, but believing it was all a mistake, and soon they would be restored to their former positions. All this seems to be the matter of so much that is great in Russian literature.

Neither Dostoevsky nor Tolstoy nor Gorki nor Solzhenitsyn himself could have invented this strange world of forced labour camps. If there were twelve million prisoners in the Gulag, he has estimated that six million of them at one time were political prisoners. They kept pouring in, as labour was needed, and gradually the camp world developed its own culture, even its own language and its own hierarchy. Often the wives and children of the political prisoners were there, too. While they were learning the corrective value of work, logging in the forests, or building roads or digging in clay quarries, they had to live with common thieves and other criminals.

In this twisted upside-down world the thieves were the elect, the chosen ones. They were entitled to bully and beat and steal from the political prisoners who were always in rags and always hungry. What a challenging world for the great artist! A world in which traditional moral values are reversed; in which survival depends first on unremitting toil and then, as a sideline, on successful wrangling, or sex and thieving. In these camps there were hundreds of thousands of Russians who had been prisoners of war in Germany, and now they were doing long terms, just for having been taken prisoner by the enemy. For them, surely, coming home to the motherland must have been a diabolical mockery, the ultimate in meaningless despair. What a world for a Solzhenitsyn.

What saves a man in such a world? And ultimately, what saves us all in our private nightmare worlds when we watch the flow of events around us? Here is the revelation of Solzhenitsyn himself which runs through all his work. He is able to declare through his own labour camp experience that a man who could keep his own view of himself, his own private world, and this is what I dwelt on in the beginning, the man who could do this was the only one who could finally walk into freedom as a human being in possession of his own soul.

A man in possession of his own soul! This Solzhenitsyn theme is surely one of the great themes of our time. What is the implacable force that comes against a man to pulverize his spirit and take him completely away from himself? An ideology. Always an ideology. One of the most fascinating aspects of the Gulag books is the revelation that men who were citizens of great virtue in the state were suddenly arrested and tried and actually persuaded they could have committed certain crimes against the state, even if they hadn't. These men, through the long years while they served out their sentences, truly believed that this punishment had to be endured for the good of the state ideology.

There is one beautiful little scene where an interrogator says to his victim, speaking as one believer to another, "You know I have to do this," and the victim agrees. The interrogator knows that he himself may be next: He, himself, might soon be signing a confession. There is a kind of fatalistic inevitability about it. A kind of twisted Calvinistic horror. Yet all these men are true believers in the ideology. Their lives are as nothing compared with the preservation of the ideology. True believers! The men of deep faith. The acceptors.

Such men have always been admired. O ye of little faith, is often uttered as a cry of condemnation against the pallid and indifferent souls who are unmoved by men marching in the service of the faith. It happens, of course, that Solzhenitsyn hates the particular ideology he has been dealing with. For him, the enemy is not so much a single man, not even a Stalin, or a Lenin, but an ideology that has to be served whether a man is an intellectual or street cleaner, a monster, or a man of goodwill. But Solzhenitsyn, himself, is a man of deep passionate conviction, of abiding faith. An ideologue? How far would he go against an enemy? How far could his own ideology carry him?

In Moscow, what are those in power, who are at the same time lovers of their own literature, saying about Solzhenitsyn? I was very curious about this. Last winter I had a conversation with a man from Moscow who was later described to me as a man of power in the Kremlin. He had come to talk to me about my own work. Finally, I said to him, "What about Solzhenitsyn? How do you see him?" I had expected some kind of curt or scoffing dismissal of the man, or at least a suggestion that Solzhenitsyn was a tool of Western circles. Instead, I got a mild and rather rational explanation. In the first place, he pointed out, Solzhenitsyn had had a very bad time, he had suffered in a situation born out of that Stalinist period, and this experience – for Solzhenitsyn – was all of Russia, and consequently he saw everything that was happening – even now – in the burning prison light of that period. Yet, he said, it is only a small part of Russia, there is all of Russia outside that period, and outside Solzhenitsyn's own experience.

A very good answer, yet I knew Solzhenitsyn would say, "What happened must not be forgotten." He does in fact say this: if horrors are forgotten or just absorbed into the life of a nation, then they become part of the life of that nation. They are still shaping the life of the nation, unless they are brought into the life. Everything a man is, is in memory. When he ceases to remember he forgets what he was and will never know what he has become.

So Solzhenitsyn has gone on remembering, and writing and remembering again. Sometimes woodenly, as if memory were no more than a method, and his recent novels have not been compelling, and now I wonder what he, after all this remembering, has become himself, living at home in exile in the Vermont woods.

In the past, other writers have had their great causes, and by the power of their pens they have brought down governments and upset great judicial systems. It is a tempting role for the writer who flowers in his own soul, creating a world of his own imagination; there, he, himself is king and judge and moral authority, and director of all human relationships: his own world. I wonder whether the world of the writer's own creation seems a rather small world to the writer in Solzhenitsyn's present exalted position. He is now a great personality; a great moral force. Zola, another moral force, accused a government, an army, and a whole judicial system in France, thundering against the unjust imprisonment of Dreyfus. Zola won. But only one man, one case, Dreyfus and his case, were involved.

To free Dreyfus, a whole state did not have to be brought down. But Solzhenitsyn has set himself against the Russian state as it is, and he obviously burns with a desire to end forever the ideology out of which it was born, and perhaps even end any of the connections of the heart that Russia has with the West. He dislikes the West, scorns the West. We lack moral metal. I suspect that a Russia full of Gatsbys and Updike's couples coupling as if the whole world were the town of Tarbox, just down the road from his compound in Vermont, would fill Solzhenitsyn not with fear but loathing.

The speeches he has now made in the United States are interesting and unsettling. I got a little chill out of the fervently militant spirit of some of his statements. How far would he go in bringing down the present regime in Russia? Though he believes in the sanctity of the inner private world, and he believes that men, stripped of everything else, can and do preserve that inner world, it is quite clear that he does not believe the state will ever collapse from within, from lack of faith. No, it must be destroyed from without. So, how far would he go in pushing to the limit a new American hostility that inevitability would lead to a resumption of the cold war, and even further. In short, and I know this is an unfair question, how many lives would Solzhenitsyn be prepared to see sacrificed to destroy the ideology he considers so evil?

In these matters, Solzhenitsyn, himself, has become a true believer. He is, of course, a Christian, and he has a novel vision of man as a responsible human being. But as he has noted in *The Gulag Archipelago*, Christian true believers, bent on preserving their own ideology against the heretic, used the rack and all the other tortures. How much terror should the true believer use to bring down the enemy? Solzhenitsyn has shown us how far Stalin went. What use of weapons would he have condoned in the name of moral courage in Vietnam? All true believers, whether they be Stalinists or Christians, should be judged in terms of their respect for human life. As an artist, as a novelist, as a man dealing with characters in the labour camps, Solzhenitsyn has shown a wonderful respect for human life, so I hope that he will go on being the writer, the artist, the man who makes you see and makes you feel, rather than a big man on the great white horse.

Any man can get carried away once he mounts the big white horse. Moral grandeur has a beguiling charm, and there is a chapter near the end of the *Gulag* volumes that overflows, even gushes, with this kind of grandeur. When Solzhenitsyn can write that the Nuremberg trials "killed off the very ideal of evil," I begin to wonder about him. Is he this naïve? After all, in the long run, the human race may be as much redeemed by a little wise cynicism about ourselves as by our sense of grandeur.

So, Solzhenitsyn went to Harvard, and he appeared on television, making a speech to the American people. There he was at last, and he was a presence. He seemed to be aware that he should have a great man's presence.

A long time has passed since I've seen and listened to a writer who has the kind of presence which invites almost immediate recognition of established greatness. In Europe, of course, the important writer has always been and still is viewed as a great man who should not let you down when you meet him for the first time. Yet, I have always felt a little uneasy when first encountering a man who, in his every gesture, makes me aware that he has accepted his grandeur and lives with it happily.

William Butler Yeats, a very great poet, had this quiet sense of himself which encompassed you as soon as you met him. I didn't know what to say to him because I like talking to a man casually, as if to a neighbour, and of course, this was all wrong with a man as imposing as Yeats. I remember that my wife, who was just as easily casual, asked Yeats if he had met James Joyce recently. Looking down from a great height, his eyes roving around the room, he said simply, "No, not recently," making it plain he didn't believe she was serious. When she said cheerfully that she had asked because she had known Joyce in Paris, and when he merely smiled, we knew he didn't believe a word she said and wasn't interested in such an obvious ploy, the mention of a great name, to break into the solitude of his greatness. My wife and I smiled at each other. Yet, there was no doubt about Yeats' role in that crowded room. Tall and handsome, he played the role of the bard as only the Irish understand that role.

Thomas Mann, too, had this presence. He was a much smaller man than Yeats, yet as you came into his hotel room to meet him, and especially if others were around, you knew you were in a presence, you wanted to bow as he bowed, to click you heels in his fine German style, and he appeared to be graciously available to questions. In my turn, I felt like a country priest meeting a cardinal, because my whole training had been in taking it easy, even if you are meeting the pope.

Usually, an American writer, when you meet him, wants you to feel you are with someone very much like yourself, with no interest in having you recognize his greatness as a person. Instead of the aura around themselves as persons, they have tended to go in for the great public image, an image sometimes so far removed from the real man that he doesn't recognize himself. With someone like Norman Mailer, this can be a comic and an amusing story in itself, a relief from the imposing presence. The imposing presence, what have I got against it? Nothing. But when I read in the *New York Times* that Solzhenitsyn had first wanted to be an actor as a young man, and the *New York Times* man told about being naively astonished in Moscow when Solzhenitsyn gave him an interview, for not only were the questions and answers to be pre-arranged, he was made aware that he was being brought into the majestic presence of a man he could never hope to get close to, I got suspicious. I grew wary.

Watching Solzhenitsyn and listening to him, I noted that his posture was commandingly perfect. His smallest gesture was decisive and full of authority. I began to fear he had that ancient weakness: did he have to be the man on the white horse?

As he talked about America, who did he sound like? In what he said, he sounded exactly like Malcolm Muggeridge, who is also a very good actor. Solzhenitsyn spoke of the stultifying effect of

American television, which I suppose should have been expected. Muggeridge had said the same thing. Who hasn't said this? Then he said there was a great failure of courage in Americans in their daily lives and they showed this lack of courage in their withdrawal from Vietnam, leaving thirty million Asians to wallow in slavery to the forces of evil.

Here was the rub. How many hundreds of thousands would have been killed off so he could have had his way in Vietnam? These ruthless men of principle, who find others lacking in courage. He said, too, that the American way of life would be unworthy of Russians. Even now, he would not offer it to them as a freedom, for the Russians as persons had been ennobled by their suffering and were above permissive American life. Nor did he believe there should be a freedom of information. People might hear more than was good for them. There he was. The one above all others who had stood for the sanctity of the private domain. Brave as he was, much as he had suffered, great as was his talent, marvellous as was his industry, and though he might be remembered all through modern times, I saw that he was a Christian right out of nineteenth-century Czarist authoritarian Russia, the old holy Russia, and not a man of my own temperament at all. I was in the sad position of having to admit that while I could admire his enormous talent I had very little sympathy for his view of life, this authoritarian figure on a white horse, riding off into the woods of his own imagination.

# ALDO MORO AND TRAGEDY

Long, long ago, the ancients of our western culture made up their minds about what constituted true dramatic tragedy. The Greeks gave us the rules. In those thousands of years that have passed, many a playwright has tried thumbing his nose at these rules, calling them arbitrary or artificial, calling them an ancient aesthetic perception that had been a bondage for countless generations of writers.

It seems to me that the Greeks, and particularly Aristotle, far from laying down a set of rules were simply recognizing certain cathartic emotions in the general public when a certain kind of event occurred. They must have noted, too, that this particular kind of event, varying as it did from season to season, always had the same structure. Life provides the structure. Not the rule maker. All the dramatist had to do was imitate this structure, and do it with poetic insight, then you had tragic dramatic literature. But it was life itself that was forever supplying this one structure which might simply be called The Choice. The tragic choice.

In our own dull lives, we rarely make these choices, or worse still, we aren't even aware that we are making them, but there are times when we have to be able to draw back, to begin to take sides, to be moved; we grow unbearably troubled, then shudder – or grow outraged. This is what happened for me with the story of Aldo Moro, the Italian statesman, murdered the other day by revolutionaries called the Red Brigade.

This story, as I said, was life, with a structure always there in life, always to be repeated on this earth; the same structure Sophocles recognized and followed again and again in his plays so that life, indeed, now seems to follow the plays.

What is so fascinating for me about the Aldo Moro story is the Greek inevitability of the outcome – the death of Moro. It was as if all the participants were aware that they had become figures in the ancient script; they had no choice but to behave as such great and powerful state figures must always behave. Look at the ancient pattern. A great man of state, Aldo Moro is kidnapped by murderous revolutionaries, bent on overthrowing the state. They offer to surrender Moro in exchange for the release of some thirteen imprisoned revolutionaries.

Moro is the perfect figure of the Establishment, of the law, of the state itself. Can the government men, if they are dealing with the revolutionaries, afford to give them this kind of recognition? Can they afford to acknowledge power? Would such an acknowledgement mean that the state was surrendering the power of the law to another kind of power if they agreed to set free the imprisoned revolutionaries?

Rather than do this, wouldn't it be better to have Moro, the figure who represented the best in the state, die for the sake of all he represented? If he was to die, they reasoned, he would be dying to uphold the law and the state he had served all his life. What an ancient story it is! In Sophocles' *Antigone*, Antigone herself must die because she has broken the law of Creon. She went outside the walls of the city to bury the body of her outcast brother – a merciful act, but forbidden by the law of Creon, the state. And as we watch Antigone, all our sympathy goes to her, the lawbreaker, because in spite of the law and our recognition of the law, we are human beings and know that when Antigone made her choice and did what she did, she satisfied our humanity. Yes, even if the more docile among us shudder as we recognize that for the apparent good of us all, the law must be served. No! More than that! Is the law the tyrant over the human heart? Has it always been the tyrant? The law is more than the man, they say. It is the law that is sacred, not man. Here I know I sound like a novelist, not a classic dramatist. (I'll come back to this in a moment). In the Moro story the pattern followed could have had an abstract perfection if Moro had only recognized what he stood for in himself, if he had only proclaimed, "I die willingly for the law and the state."

He couldn't do this.

Moro threw himself on the mercy of his old friends, the heads of state. He asked that the prisoners be exchanged in return for his life. Those who were closest to him, his own family, those who had love for him as a human being aside from his political responsibilities, begged for his life. But by this time the greatest and wisest figures in the land of Italy had decided they knew what was involved here, and what was sacred and what had to be faced with a terrible shudder, and with the hope, dare I say it, yes, as a storyteller, a novelist, I can say it, of possibly finding exaltation in the shudder. An exalted recognition of themselves in how far they were prepared to go in the service of the state. And so they didn't give in, and Moro was executed.

In these great and ancient dramatic structures – at least when they are set on the stage – a great truth is supposed to shine through, a truth coming out of the revulsion, and the sorrowing shudder which enables us all.

I have noted that the commentators in Italy have been looking for this catharsis. Already, they say, the Christian Democrats, Moro's Party, and the Communist Party, have drawn closer together. There is hope that the revolting Red Brigade may have wounded themselves mortally. This is surely how the writer of great classical tragedy would want to see it. But the novelist, at least one of my persuasion, with his own view of things, who wants to look into the hearts of men, knows that the tragic structure works as a structure in real life, it imitates the relentless turn of the wheel of the seasons, yet, I for one reject the values that have always been at the heart of this kind of tragedy. For me, the law is never sacred, the state is never sacred. The law is made for man, not man for the law. Nothing is colder than the state. Frankly, – as a novelist, as one who attempts to invent the possibility of individual salvation as the wheel of nature grinds on – I would have dealt for Moro's life, and would have felt I was doing it out of strength, not weakness. The principle involved? Well, it is life that is sacred, not principles. Men of principle can be utterly ruthless. For my money, you will find that the murderous thugs of the Red Brigade are men of unyielding principle. I may be an outlaw in these matters, but I remember how I felt when I first read Herman Melville's famous story, *Billy Budd*.

The root of the matter is in this story. Billy Budd, a naïve, beautiful, childlike sailor happens to kill unwittingly, but justifiably, a superior on the ship who is abusing him. Billy Budd is a sweet innocent, yet the law must be carried out. For what? For the good of the navy, the good of the law, the good of all discipline. The Captain spends hours with Billy, even winning the poor boy's love as well as his abject understanding, so that in the end, Billy is happy to die for the sake of the Law. The principle of the thing! Well, I may be way out in left field, but I find myself wanting to look very closely at men who are willing to sacrifice any human life for the sake of a principle. We'll have to wait to discover how wise they were in Italy when in the Moro story they made their tragic choice.

*CBC Anthology*

# VANITY OF VANITIES

For some thirty years now, North America has been a land where the old have to pretend they are young, for there hasn't been much dignity in being an old fellow or a dear motherly soul in a rocking chair by the fire. In China, they tell me, it is a great thing to be old. It wins respect. The assumption is that you have gathered wisdom along the weary way and when you speak, your words are venerated. In North America we seem to have reverted to the condition of men whose knuckles were too close to the ground . . . the tribe hunched around the fire, and the old fellow was the boss while he was at the height of his physical power, which was when he was about thirty, but as soon as he began to slip a little, and showed it, some younger tribesman quickly hit him on the head and took over the authority. Well, we seem to be slipping back into tribal times.

To make it worse, if you are past the first flush of youth, you are always encountering some woman, safe solid and sensible, who says scornfully, "Why not act your age? Why not let the joys of youth belong to youth?" This is a fine idea. The only difficulty is, as I have explained, it is not only the joys of the senses that belong to youth. The jobs go to them, too. Another man will say, "It is all vanity. There is nothing sadder in the world than watching an elderly woman prancing around like a filly instead of letting nature take its course."

"Vanity of vanities," sayeth the preacher. The trouble with the preacher is that he isn't saying all that is to be said about vanity even while attributing everything under the sun to it. To wash your face is a gesture of vanity. To want to look beautiful is also a vain ambition, but this kind of vanity, in spite of the lugubrious preacher may have the approval of nature, and for all I know, may be pleasing to God. For example, in our grandfather's time, a woman of thirty was considered old. In European fiction the woman of thirty, married or unmarried, was supposed to be at a desperate age. Nowadays, a woman of thirty knows she is just entering the field of fun. Ten and twenty years have been added to a woman's youth. Is this contemporary extension of youth a vain gesture? To think so may be a slander of nature. If vanity and a love of frivolity and the things of this world have led to this beautiful extension of youth in our women I can imagine the angels whispering to each other, "How these poor fools get mixed up about things spiritual. Whatever made these creatures in the past think that God was pleased when a woman grew fat and sloppy and old at thirty? The body is the temple of the Holy Spirit . . . It's about time these women started shining up the temple."

But as I look around on this scene where the appearance of youth is worshipped and then check back on old photographic albums from my grandfather's time, I'm struck by one troubling thought. The women of today all look, as I say, ten years younger than they used to, but alas, it is not quite true of the men. In fact, this has already been recognized in the advertising and motion picture worlds. Have you noticed, for example, that the glamour advertisements in the magazines now show pictures of grizzled and grey haired worldly men, standing possessively beside very young women? And it is now the fashion in Hollywood to have grey-haired and weather-beaten heroes.

This picture of ageless women and grizzled men who still have a real kick in them, real sexual vigor, not to mention just a gleam in the eye, is immensely flattering and acceptable to contemporary society. Any man of fifty who sees one of these pictures immediately asks himself whatever made him think he was out of the ball game; he begins to dream that he can bring a fine rich experience to women who look forever young. This is also immensely satisfying to the advertisers. The grizzled veteran is usually the man with the money to spend, whether it is in nightclubs or department stores.

If this North American love of the youthful appearance and eternal sexual vigor represents a kind of advertiser's dream world, I suggest you be somewhat suspicious of the crepe hangers. The crepe hangers love to talk about maturity and serenity and the peace of old age; the spiritual graces of age. Age may have its grace, its dignity, and its beauty, too, but I have done some research on these champions of serenity, and looked into my own bones, too. Too often I have found that a man growing old and lazy, with his arteries hardening, and his intellectual interests withering away, delights to kid himself that he is entering a spiritual state. All that is really happening to him, of course, is that he is becoming a vegetable; he is losing everything but his vanity. His vanity prompts him to think that his indifference, his sluggishness of mind and heart and his inability to be interested in the things of this world, is a fine spirituality.

Our American cult of youth with all its silliness may help us to keep alive in mind and heart. After all, some men of seventy are much younger in the heart than some men of thirty. The great poet Thomas Hardy, well over eighty when he died, was able to whisper, "It burns brighter toward the end."

*CBC Anthology*

*Forever and forever and forever...*
*The monkeys make sorrowful noises overhead...*
*The leaves fall early this autumn, in wind.*
*The paired butterflies are already yellow with August...*
*They hurt me. I grow older.*

—EZRA POUND

# PARIS REVISITED

I used to wonder why I did not want to revisit Paris and Montparnasse. If the suggestion came up, and it did again and again, I found myself growing thoughtful, then making excuses and shying away. Paris, 1929, the days when Montparnasse had reached its opulent and exotic flowering just before the fall, which was of course the Great Depression. That was my Paris. Moreover, I had written a book about it, *That Summer in Paris,* and I suppose I felt I had embalmed that part of my life.

I have a temperament that recoils from visiting scenes in a pathetic effort to recapture singular moments. Some years ago one of the Paris veterans wrote me a letter in which he counted the number of relics who were left alive, and he made the grand proposal that we all meet again in Paris. I fled from the notion like a bat out of hell. The editor of *Esquire* then proposed a meeting of what he called, "The Lost Generation" in New York. They would take a photograph, he said. Well, the photograph duly appeared in *Esquire,* but I was not in it. I couldn't bear the idea. My excuse was that I had never felt I was a member of a lost generation.

The Paris of 1929 and the life my wife Loretto and I lived there had remained alive only in our hearts, only there because we believed the scene was gone forever, as the people were gone. I hate reunions. I hate visiting graveyards, which means I suppose, that I hate going back. Going back, dozing in the sun, taking pleasure in a world of ghosts, always seemed to be a way of going too willingly into the dark night. When I passed through Paris with my

wife on our way to Rome and had several hours to spend at the air-
port, I knew we could easily have taken a quick trip along the
Boulevard Montparnasse. But I remembered those lines of Scott
Fitzgerald's about feeling "that he was standing on a rifle range at
twilight with all targets down," so I didn't take the run at Montparnasse. I went on to Rome and something else. Something else.
There always has to be something else.

Then one night in Rome a doubt about my attitude to Paris
began to gnaw away at me. When I was twenty-six, my wife and I
had shown up on the Paris boulevards like people coming home.
Most of my writing friends were there. Robert McAlmon, who had
first published Hemingway and had been enormously helpful to
me. And Hemingway, and Scott Fitzgerald who had urged my
short stories on Max Perkins, and the editors of *Transition*, that
great review, and Ford Madox Ford, the first editor who had ever
written to me asking for a story, and Joyce, whom we all adored,
and Ezra Pound who had printed me in his magazine, *The Exile*.

Paris had been my city of light when the world seemed to be
my oyster. My young wife and I had been completely happy in
Paris. So there was this question: did I hesitate, even, did I dare to
walk again in those streets and sit in those cafés where we had been
so alive, so elated, so arrogant, so sure we belonged at the centre of
the world? Was I afraid that I would have a thousand poignant regrets that we hadn't remained forever young? This could have been
the very core of the reluctance I had held on to for years. Yet how
stupid! Yet how like a certain kind of man to avoid the places where
he had once been happy as if that kind of happiness could never
come again if he dared, even, to revisit those places.

So again in April, as it had been in the beginning, we came
back into Paris, returning from Rome. It was late at night. The
cooling freshness of a spring night. The taxi tires humming on the

cobblestones. We were booked into the Hilton Continental, a hotel of sweep and grandeur on the Right Bank at the corner of rue de Rivoli and rue de Castiglioni – a part of town at ease with expense. Why were we not over in some little hotel on Raspail on the Left Bank where we once had stayed? Because it would have been pretending; it would have been fake. I was not the man I used to be. I knew where my next dollar was coming from. But on that first night when we came out of the hotel and looked along the rue de Rivoli and saw the Tuileries, and the Louvre, and then the Seine and the lighted bridges leading to the Left Bank, I was gripped by a kind of magic; a sense of permanence of place.

Nothing seemed to have been torn down. Not even removed. Years ago we could have been standing on this corner, wondering if it was time to cross the bridge and go home to our little flat close by the prison. Suddenly Paris wasn't just a memory, locked in the heart of youth. It was here, now, as it had been then. On this corner, men of many generations had come and gone, yet they hadn't gone, they were all around. They could suddenly reappear as I was doing. My wife and I shared this strange and unexpected sense of happy familiarity with the living and the dead; those who had come our way either in our lives, or just in our imaginations.

Around noon the next day, we set out for that celebrated café, Les Deux Magots on the left bank near the old St. Germain de près Church. It used to be such a beautiful corner, with its three cafés, Lips, the Flore – made famous by Sartre and his friends – and the old Deux Magots. In the twenties, André Gide and Jean Cocteau had often sat on the terrace, and from one of the cane chairs you could look along the splendid avenue, the Boulevarde St. Germain with its great old houses solidly packed together in a long vista, a vista right into the salons of duchesses in the world of Proust. And it used to be quietly soothing sitting on the café terrace just before nightfall watching the sun hit the grey-white stone of the twelfth-century square-towered church. This was the café where I used to meet Fitzgerald. He had lived not far away. The last time I saw him had been on the terrace. He was leaving Paris and we had met to talk about a novel I was writing, *It's Never Over*. He had been open and generous, but at this café I had also had a painful experience with him. I had called on him late one night, when he had just come back from a Montmartre nightclub where he had been very drunk and had got into a spot. In spite of Zelda's desperate admonitions he had insisted on coming back out with me into the night to the Deux Magots. At midnight the terrace was crowded. Fitzgerald, his shirt open, his hat askew, his face a ghastly ashen shade, had the earnestly sober manner of a drunk, and I could see that Americans at the café had recognized him. There he was, the golden boy, the drunk. They were laughing at him because, when it came time to settle up for our drinks, he insisted on paying and his franc notes kept falling to the ground and I kept solemnly picking them up. I hated the gloating curiosity in the faces of the tourists.

So I was afraid, approaching that café, that I would see the ashen-faced ghost of Fitzgerald coming across the square to join me as we sat down. But it wasn't like that at all. Nothing looked right. A building near the café was being renovated, workmen were chiselling and pounding. The terrace was crowded with rubber-necking tourists as the Dôme used to be crowded after Hemingway wrote about it in *The Sun Also Rises*. I felt uncomfortable. Within a few minutes I was asking myself, "What am I doing here?" It seemed incredible that I could have imagined the ghost of André Gide, or Fitzgerald could have come barging through the tables. I couldn't believe there were writers, painters, poets in this crowd, and with that incredible snobbery of the man lost in his own world, and feeling he belonged to better days, I wanted to move on. Then I was held there by the sudden realization that it was not true that this was my first return to the Quarter. In writing my book, *That Summer in Paris*, I had relived those relationships with my friends so intensely, with the place coming so alive in my mind, that this visit had become like a trip to a theater after the play had finished.

We went walking along the rue de l'Odeon to see if the store, Shakespeare and Co. that was Sylvia Beach's bookshop, was still around. Along the way I tried to pick out the lamppost Fitzgerald had used as a desk when he had given me his wallet as something to remember him by. He had scratched his name on it with a penknife, but I could not find the post. And I didn't want to fool myself into thinking that I had found the post. Though it would have made a comforting story. Then, at the bookstore, the owner told me that Sylvia Beach's desk was still there.

"Well, let's see," I said. Her store had been a meeting place, where you left your address, and people from out of town, wanting to look you up, would get in touch with Sylvia Beach who presided busily behind her desk. There had also been a backroom where a friend like James Joyce could be looked after, or hidden away. Now, I couldn't imagine I was in the same store. Maybe I wasn't. And the back room! The sacred grove! It seemed to be a storage room. Approaching the desk where a young fellow sat, I stood silent for a moment, then I said solemnly, "This isn't Sylvia Beach's desk. I remember that desk very well." Looking at me blankly for a moment, the owner said finally, "No, it isn't. That desk was disposed of quite a while ago."

Back on the Right Bank and in the hotel room I suffered from a grim sense of air-conditioned isolation and disappointment. I kept thinking, "Who do I know now in Paris?" It was plain I was not going to have the old ghosts gathering around me bringing happy tears to my eyes. Everything had flattened out, we were going to be alone! Well, I knew my son's close friend, John Montague, the Irish poet, lived in Paris and he was Beckett's friend, and I knew Mavis Gallant, and my old friend William Saroyan was reported to be living here. Already my mind was seeking a new Paris. But where did these friends live? How could they be found? Soon, through the hotel, we were in touch with a young lady who said, yes, she thought she could make the connections. That buoyed me up. And at least I had Montague's phone number. I called. But no one answered.

Later that night, for a reason I did not try to explain to myself, I did not want to go over to Montparnasse. Loretto and I wandered around the Madeleine and the Place Vendôme, poking into corners, as if we felt that in the old days we had cheated ourselves by dwelling so much just in Montparnasse. Kidding ourselves in this way, we avoided going back to our old haunts. "Things really look just the same!" I said to Loretto. "Don't they?"

"It's the same. Only no one is here," she said.

"No one who means anything to us, anyway," I said.

"It's like coming into town and finding everyone is out of town," she said.

We loafed around St. Honoré, liking the little fashion shops, then past a movie house where a Jerry Lewis picture was doing line-up business. The French like Jerry Lewis. There are aspects of French taste that I have never understood. We ambled back to the hotel where I asked if there were any phone messages. None. But who had my name to call? It had started to rain. Then, as we sat disconsolately in the spacious empty lobby, Loretto suddenly asked: "How about going to the Coupole?" It was nearly midnight and pouring rain, and in the mood I was in, deserted even by my Paris ghosts who had been so alive in my mind, I thought it would be a rather forlorn occasion, finding myself back on the Boulevarde Montparnasse at midnight in the rain, but . . . "Okay," I said, "let's go," and we got into a taxi. In ten minutes we had crossed the river and were back at Raspail and Montparnasse.

Every day, just before noon when we were young, we used to come walking along Montparnasse from the rue de la Santé where we lived and have our breakfast on the terrace of the Coupole. Breakfast would often last some two hours, for friends, passing on the street, would see us and join us. It used to be an international café. Only occasionally did a French writer come there. But American movie stars visiting Paris would manage to spend an evening sitting at the Coupole, and then dozens of citizens, patrons just for that evening, would file slowly by the great star's table. And there had been that one evening, that beautiful evening when James Joyce had invited us to his house, and afterwards feeling exhilarated, we had come to the Coupole, and in the bar where there had been music and Loretto had done a solo dance on a table and a tall young Serbian count had asked who she was. Told that her husband was sitting at the bar, he had bowed to me and formally presented Loretto with one red rose. And now all these years later, entering the Coupole once again, and feeling morose, all I could think of was, "Where did that Serbian get that red rose?"

I said to Loretto, "The first meal we ever had was right here at the Coupole. Come on. I'll show you the spot," and I led the way through the stern waiters in their tuxedos to the table. "I remember this for good reason. It was at this table on our first day on the Left Bank that I learned a little Paris restaurant trick. Our first mistake had been that we had adhered to our Toronto dining habits. At six-thirty, ready for dinner, we entered the Coupole, and were surprised at the absence of patrons. We decided the place wasn't doing very well. I remember we ordered a mixed grill, and we went on talking. We had a lot to talk about. Things were happening. We were beginning to meet people who knew me. In about twenty minutes the waiter brought in a big covered silver dish, and standing beside me, he removed the cover. I looked up at him. *"Merci,"* I said. He stood there, I thought, somewhat stupidly, then turned away with his tray to the service table and got some hot plates. But out of the corner of my eye I had caught the expression on his face. Disdain! He was full of disdain. He had even shrugged to another waiter. Well, I got the point. When he had held out that tray I should have scrutinized it with a gimlet eye, not a mere "thank you" glance. I should have examined every scrap of meat in that mixed grill, frowning doubtfully at some cuts, hesitating over others, perhaps complaining that a chop looked a bit overdone, one couldn't be sure, and invited the waiter to engage in weighing the merits of the cooking of the chop; or perhaps even sending the whole dish back for some extra touch from the chef. I had simply accepted the dish. Therefore I had had to also accept the man's waiterly contempt for a country boy. Well, never again did I make that mistake – my Coupole mistake.

But standing there by our table, the waiter was wondering what we were going to do, whether we were going to sit down. I didn't feel at home. I felt ill at ease. Familiar faces wouldn't come to mind: they weren't even in my heart; so I began to look around at those who were on the terrace just as I would have done years ago. A regrettably young crowd! No, not at all. Most of them were of the age we had been when we sat there. But not an American or Englishman. No glamour girls from *Vogue* or *Harper's Bazaar*; they looked like girls who lived in the Quarter. I noticed that everyone was speaking French, and then I realized with delight that the French had recaptured the Coupole. Why did this give me the pleasure of an important revelation?

Well, in the Nineties, and before World War One, the big cafés on the Boul Mich had been taken over by the English. In our day in Paris, the Boul Mich cafés had reverted to the students. Now the Coupole had become a spoke on the wheel: another life than the one I had known had come around. Everything looked the same yet everything was different. I began to laugh to myself. I felt a crazy exuberant exhilaration. There were no ghosts around in the Quarter, no one was missing anyone. No one was regretting that some figure had died. No one cared. This was the new life. It was something to look at freshly, and wonder what could happen if you were here among these people. The snake of the past was scotched: only new things could be here for me now. So at that hour, at the Coupole while it rained, I found I wanted to laugh about the old crowd, talk about them, keep remembering, trying to see the crowd without a moment confusing us with what was going on now. I was eager to be back in the Quarter tomorrow, especially if there was sunlight.

In my eager new laughing mood, I found I couldn't go to bed. I had to wander around a little near the hotel, in the streets washed by the rain that had stopped. I noticed one remarkable change. The hookers in this expensive hotel neighbourhood operated with a new distinction. In the old days, a man with a car would cruise along and pick up a girl. Now, on rue de Castiglione, all the hookers had their own cars. A neat little car had passed me several times. Finally, it stopped, the girl smiled. That was how I got the hang of the system. In the next half hour, while I was standing at the hotel entrance, little car after little car drove up, a nice plump well-dressed executive American would get out, lean in and kiss the girl, and come into the hotel, and the girl, turning the car around, would patrol up and down the street again.

Next day, in the strong sun of early afternoon we were back in the Quarter, and soon Loretto was sitting at our old all-night café, the Select. I stood out on the pavement looking at her till she started to laugh. She could have been sitting on that very spot years ago. Often, by herself like this, too. It was there she would meet Hemingway and me on the days when we went boxing, and Hemingway would put down his boxing bag and say, "Loretto, you're drinking Pernod. You shouldn't be drinking that stuff," and then he would sit with us until he had to go home. Now, looking across the road at the Coupole I seemed to see young Buffy Glasco, a young faun, coming across the road with his loping stride. This had been our café between the hours of nine-thirty and midnight.

Over to the left was the terrace where we used to sit with Edward Titus, who was the publisher of The Black Manikin Press. He was married to Helena Rubenstein. Every week Helena Rubenstein would come over from the Right Bank and join us. The coat! "You remember the beautiful coat, Loretto?" Titus had asked if we would like to go with Madame Rubenstein to the Paul Poiret fashion opening. Poiret was the fashionable dressmaker of the day. I couldn't go. Loretto went with Madame Rubenstein. She came home at about dinnertime with a beautiful black velvet coat trimmed with squirrel, as beautiful a coat as I had ever seen. I said, "Where did you get that coat?"

"It's mine now," she said laughing, and told me that when a model had worn it in the show she had cried: "Oh, I just love that coat," and Madame Rubenstein, a practical woman, had said, "How much could you pay on a coat?"

"Well, a hundred dollars," Loretto said.

With a shrug Madame Rubenstein, calling the director, had said, "Give her the coat for a hundred. She likes it." And he gave her the coat, and we never knew how many hundreds it did cost. We just thanked God that Madame Rubenstein was a lover of the arts, and that night Loretto had worn her velvet coat to our café.

The woman we called Madame Select, who had very black hair and a solid body, shrewdly watched over the café cash register, and all her clients, too. Across the road in the Coupole I had learned my lesson about an appreciative scrutiny of the food being served to you. At the Select, I learned that too devastating an inspection of a dish can cause disruption.

My friend Robert McAlmon, of the City of Paris, publisher – at least that was how he had described himself on the fly leaf of all the books he published – had joined us one night at about ten. Bob drank too much. He despised all people who did not drink too much. When he had money, and he had a lot (he was married to the daughter of one of the richest men in England), he had helped Hemingway. He had published writers who couldn't get published, and was the close friend of James Joyce. He had fallen out with Hemingway who, when speaking to me about Bob, had always referred to him as "Your friend, McAlmon." On this night, though deep in the drink, he was navigating beautifully: in fact, he was in good enough shape to be hungry. He ordered a Welsh rarebit. After the dish had been brought to him he tasted it and commanded the waiter to summon Madame Select. When she came smiling, ready to greet old friends, McAlmon, his lip twisting in his familiar expression of disdain, raised the dish, the Welsh rarebit. "This is not good," he said.

"But what is the matter with it? I cooked that myself," she said.

"Incredible," he said. "You should take it back to the toilet where it obviously came from."

Quivering with rage Madame Select ordered him to leave the café and never come back. But if McAlmon was banished, then we were banished, too, we said. She didn't care. We left.

The Select became an embarrassment to us. We used to pass every evening at nine. Titus would be there, looking unhappy, the head waiter would bow to us, we would bow, but pass on. Each night, Titus grew more exasperated and finally he summoned Madame Select. I don't know what he said, but that night the head waiter came out to the sidewalk, bowed, insisted on shaking hands with us and said he had a message from Madame Select. If our friend McAlmon would join us there at the Select, she would like to buy us a drink.

Those ridiculous little incidents! Everything that happened seems amusing now. And looking around the corner, Montparnasse and Raspail, which had been reclaimed by the French, it seemed incredible that it had once been a crowded lighted place at the crossroads of international letters in the western world. Writers from all nations had dropped in, and what seemed extraordinary as I stood there, was that we all had believed that it was a great period, believed that we, better than any editor in New York or London, knew when a young writer was great. We took it for granted that Joyce was the greatest writer in the language, that the young Hemingway was great, and Ezra Pound the greatest of poets. Many years have passed and the astonishing thing is those names, those Montparnasse names, have grown bigger. I could see, walking the streets again, that the cocksureness, the arrogance, the pontifications we shared, and certainly no one was more unyieldingly assertive in his opinion than I, was a mark of the extraordinary youthful vitality of the time.

Of course, there had been hundreds of poets and painters and prose writers haunting the little bars and dance halls who are not even ghosts now, yet I swear, and such now is my faith in that milieu, that if they had been taken seriously in the Quarter – then, they had to have had some real talent. And women's liberation, sexual liberation, gay power – that was just part of the scene: how could I get excited about these things years later.

But what about the strange fate of Scott Fitzgerald? I found myself thinking of Fitzgerald and the night when we had had dinner in the Café des Lilas, which is some distance from the Coupole on Montparnasse, going over toward the Observatoire. It had been the most romantic of old cafés, with tables under the trees and street musicians always playing and I used to think that the line from Hemingway's *The Sun Also Rises* about this café, "And there was Marshal Ney waving his sword among the green horse chestnut leaves," had summed up gaily and beautifully the temperament of the time. But now, though the statue of Marshal Ney was still there, where were the horse chestnut trees? It took me a while to figure it out. The Lilas had become an expensive and quietly elegant restaurant, and part of the old terrace, where there had been chestnut trees, was included now in the enclosed restaurant. Tonight the dinner crowd was wildly different from the old crowd. The men, solid, subdued, grey-haired French businessmen with young women. Appolinaire! Cocteau! They would not have been at home here. Not with these faces. The table, the green, where we had sat with Fitzgerald on many a night was gone.

We had spent one afternoon with Fitzgerald at the Ritz Bar drinking champagne cocktails and when we had parted he had said he was taking Mary Blair, an actress who had been Edmund Wilson's second wife, to dinner, but what café would we be sitting at around nine-thirty. We had said the Café des Lilas, and around nine, with the musicians playing under the trees, Fitzgerald and Mary Blair had joined us. Fitzgerald, only charmingly drunk, and he could be the most loveable and charming of men, had on an expensive ivory-coloured felt hat. Growing sentimental as the evening wore on he insisted on giving me that hat. He kept putting it on my head, refusing to keep it when I took it off. Finally I left it on my head, but when we were leaving Loretto said firmly, "That's a beautiful hat, Scott. You must not give it away like this," and she firmly took the hat from my head and put it on Scott and we left.

Since those days, no matter his personal despair and humiliation, the Fitzgerald stock has zoomed. But what did I think of his work then? And now? In the beginning I had thought *The Great Gatsby* a beautiful book. I still think it is a beautifully written book. When I first read *Tender Is the Night*, I had thought the last third of the book was slightly out of focus. I still think so. He had worked too hard on it. Edmund Wilson said to me in the sixties, "Surely those two books, the ones I have mentioned – will stand up." I told him I had reread *Tender Is the Night* and felt about it as I had done in the beginning. Later, he wrote me and said he was inclined to agree. Now, it seems to me that the tireless professors, feeding the Fitzgerald legend, treating him like a river god, have no taste at all. They commit the cardinal sin against Fitzgerald. They don't know when he was good and when he was third-rate, and so he is probably laughing in his grave.

I thought of him again next afternoon going along Montparnasse on the long walk to the rue de la Santé, the place where we used to live. As we went, I couldn't get accustomed to this old walk, nor to the Boulevarde. Cars. The parked cars. Always the cars. And to the west, high above Montparnasse, a ghastly great tombstone hotel, that one slab, violating the skyline. I didn't know, as we got to the rue de la Santé, what I expected to feel looking up at the windows of the place that had been ours, where we had loved and I, sitting in my underwear on hot days, had written stories and my novel, *It's Never Over*. The flat was almost directly opposite the prison gate. Why were there so many guards around the gate now? Up there, Hemingway had sat reading the New York Times waiting for me to get ready to go boxing. And those windows. Again I started to laugh.

On a Sunday afternoon, when Fitzgerald had dropped in, Loretto had her wet washed handkerchiefs pasted on the sun-hot window panes, and Fitzgerald had been fascinated. She had peeled them off for him, showing him how stiff they were and how they could be folded, and he, full of childlike wonder, had said he would use this in a story. So again we were laughing. Everything had become endearingly comical. There wasn't even a touch of sadness in any of our memories. The whole place had become an exhilarating backdrop for good memories. Especially later, when we went back along Montparnasse, on past the Coupole, and turned the corner to the Falstaff.

The Falstaff had been a panelled English bar, a quiet place with a famous barkeep, Jimmie, and now, as soon as we entered, I wanted to burst out laughing again and say, "Well, where's everybody?" The place looked fantastically the same. It was as if we had walked out only two nights ago. There was the shiny oak bar, the tables. This was the bar Hemingway and I often came to after boxing, and if his mouth was cut – it always seemed to be cut – he would say to Jimmie, "As long as Morley can keep my mouth bleeding I'll always have him for a friend." And now sitting on the stool where I used to sit, I asked the barkeep if he knew my friend, the Irish poet, John Montague, and he said he knew him but he hadn't seen him recently. Troubled, superstitious for a moment, I wondered, Why can't I reach Montague? Why don't I hear from Saroyan? And Mavis Gallant? What is the matter with the hotel, their bureau called Celebrity Service? Why does no one want to see me?

In this time of half-mad exhilaration with my memories, I became aware that in these places I could also have puzzling poignant regrets. Opposite the Gar Montparnasse there used to be a restaurant called the Trianon. We had dined there with Zelda and Scott Fitzgerald. We had had a beautiful night there with McAlmon and

James Joyce and his wife Nora. Around eleven, when we were leaving to drink at Joyce's house, McAlmon and Loretto and Nora Joyce had gone ahead, crossing the wide cobblestoned boulevard and I, walking with Joyce and talking, had forgotten he was blind, then suddenly I became aware he wasn't with me. I looked around. Taxis were whizzing by. He was standing alone, in the middle of the road, wildly swinging his cane. Crying out, I leaped back to take his arm. And now the Trianon was gone, and as I stood there trying to pick out that place on the cobblestones where Joyce had stood abandoned, I felt regret. I don't know why. Regret for what? It wasn't like me. Time, time! Time as the enemy. The only enemy. The mocking enemy! And then, I became aware that I regretted, too, how young painters had gone out of my life and how I missed – here in Paris – seeing some kind of painting, bad or good, in the little shop windows. I used to think that everyone in Paris was a Sunday painter. Where were those shop windows now? And why had painting been so important to me then? Why did Matisse seem so right for me, and why, standing in the Luxembourg Art Gallery, did Cézanne seem able to tell me things about writers I wanted to hear? I regretted, too, that I had never really realized the wonder of the great avenues of chestnut trees as I saw them now on the boulevarde Arrago, and in the Luxembourg Garden. I regretted that a perverse snobbery in those days had inhibited me from exploring Montmarte: I had dismissed it as a place belonging to tourists. But these weren't lost things; they were just missed things, things I would like to go on with now.

Then suddenly it was Saturday afternoon with only a day left in Paris and I hadn't been in touch with anybody. Again, I called the number Montague had given me. I couldn't believe it when his French wife answered. But Montague was in Ireland. Yes, he had mentioned me to her. She knew my name. And then, sitting on the hotel room bed, I said to myself, "What the hell is the matter with me?" and grabbed the phone book. Saroyan was listed. I called the number. A young man told me that Saroyan had left for California but he filled me in on all my old friend had been doing. Then Mavis Gallant? Of course she was in the book. Mavis herself answered the phone. "Are you so silly?" she said. "You must have been eager to see me if you couldn't even look in the phone book," and she said she would come down to the hotel within an hour. She did, and we sat in the bar till eight o'clock, when she had to leave for a dinner engagement. Lovely hours, with Mavis as vivid and laughing as ever. Mavis at twenty-four in Montreal. Mavis as she was now. Still Mavis.

And later that night I got myself into a story. Since my mind was full of stories, all the stories I had written during those early Paris days, it seemed only right that I should become a character in one of my own kind of stories. In the hotel, coming down in the elevator I was with three or four other guests. An American of about fifty in an elegant expensive suit with wide lapels was with a woman who was obviously his wife. He had iron-grey hair, and a pink and white, freshly shaved, executive's face. Under his arm was a parcel, some long object wrapped in newspaper which I thought was rather unworthy of his executive air. Then I realized his eye was on me. "Excuse me," he said just before the elevator reached the ground floor and the lobby. "Do you know anything about this stuff?" and he drew from the newspaper wrapping a two-and-a-half foot African wooden sculpture.

I thought he must have spoken to me because I was casually dressed. I had on a fawn coloured jacket, a pair of brown slacks, and a red cashmere sweater. It had to be my clothes, or my hair, much longer than his. We had stepped out of the elevator. "Well, let's have a look at it," I said. It was a trite African carving. "Hmm," I said. "Where did you get it?"

"Right outside the hotel. The fellow is out there now," he said.

"How much did you pay for it?"

"He wants fifty dollars."

"Hmmm," I said, and pondered gravely while this rich buyer waited, glancing occasionally at his wife. But I was in a dilemma. What did I owe to this rich businessman? Nothing. What did I owe to the fellow who lurked outside? Nothing. But didn't I owe something special to myself? So I said, "Where are you from?"

"Indianapolis."

"What did you want this piece for?"

"I was going to put it in my home . . . if it's any good."

"I'll tell you what to do," I said. "Tell the seller you will give him thirty-five dollars. Not a cent more. Tell him you are aware that there are dozens and dozens of these things you can buy more cheaply. They are in fact all around. Don't put it in your home. Put it in your office. I'm sure he'll give it to you for thirty-five bucks."

"Thank you very much," he said brusquely.

"It's nothing," I said.

Fifteen minutes later, I saw my executive friend arguing with an Algerian who was squatting on the walk twenty feet from the hotel entrance.

"Thirty-five dollars! Not a cent more," the executive kept repeating, and when I looked back money was changing hands.

Upstairs in our room, telling this to Loretto, I had the aesthetic delight of having achieved a balance of form. The African sculpture, I imagine, was worth about five dollars, but I, having been given the power to order things around, satisfied myself that I had behaved justly. The executive could well afford the thirty-five dollars. The Algerian deserved something for sitting out on the sidewalk those long hours. And I, too, was owed something for being drawn in on this transaction. Sitting in the hotel bedroom I felt that I had been fair to myself in having the power to achieve a neat moral balance, a moralist to the end!

In the morning we stood on the rue de Rivoli looking at Notre Dame and the Ile de la Cité and reflected that the French were very smart about their Paris. They might build it anew, again and again, yet the Paris one generation and then another loved would still be there, still the lovely woman among all cities. I felt very lucky in saying good-bye and remembered those lines in *The Brothers Karamatzov* . . . Alyosha's speech to the boys . . . "Live your life so that looking back you may have a good memory of things."

# RODIN'S GARDEN

I hadn't thought about Rodin for years, not until my last day in Paris when I found myself walking along the rue de Varenne to the Hôtel Biron, which is at the corner of the boulevard des Invalides. Entering the great courtyard, I stood facing the 18th-century mansion where the great sculptor had lived when the mansion had actually been a hotel. Some hotel, I thought. And Rodin had it all – the ground floor as his own apartment!

On the way to the main entrance I passed many rose bushes and flowering hedges. Then, reaching the entrance, I turned away, fearing that if I entered the museum I might get absorbed in the sculpture; it was the garden I wanted to see. I moved along the right side of the house, passing a row of small sculptures set in little alcoves along the wall, and I came to a pool, or pond, at the back of the house. In the pond was a figure, a naked man, and under him, their arms reaching for him, children. Or was it just one child? As I moved around the pool, the garden opened up to me. There were evergreen trees about three-metres high shaped like cones, and these cones made a little twisting alley among banks of flowering bushes leading to taller trees, older trees, and far beyond and against the sky was the tower of Les Invalides and Napoleon's tomb.

Rodin had believed that his work could be seen properly only when it was outside among bushes or trees, as if it were part of nature. While I stood wondering which little alley among the green cones I could follow, I caught a glimpse of marble or plaster heads half hidden in bushes as if they were watching me. Suddenly, I became aware that I was listening intently. I couldn't hear a sound. I could literally feel the silence. It was strange, it was unnatural, in the heart of humming, noisy Paris, and from then on I was under a spell.

Enchanted, I moved slowly through the green cones and the bushes. I reached some taller trees, the trunks wrapped in vines, and I came upon two naked figures on a rough stone base, locked in a passionate embrace. They startled me; I half expected them to look up. The limbs of the lovers seems to be moving, their rapture so plain that I could believe they felt safe and unseen among the trees. Their caressing, naked intimacy was so real I felt like an intruder, an embarrassed intruder who knew he should make no sound, just sneak away. Was it the magic in the silence of this garden, I wondered, that made the magic of nature in Rodin's work a living part of all nature?

Turning away, I remembered that when I was twenty-two and at college, I used to sit in the Hart House library reading all the art magazines that I could find. Some sixty years ago, the controversy about Rodin's romantic emotional sculpture was still going on. I dreamed of being in Paris. Rodin's critics were those who believe that sculpture should be frozen music. I was on their side. I had never seen a Rodin. Mine was just an intellectual position. I thought that sculpture should not be illustration, full of action and emotion. That was storytelling. That was literature. Well, how wrong I was, I thought now. The kissing lovers there in the bushes were not frozen music. Oh no, in the silence and in their secret place, their natural beauty had come so close to me it hurt almost physically.

The last of the sunlight was now on the west wall of the house. The green cones threw their own kind of shadow, and the taller trees and bushes shot through with sunlight made another. Then, as I went up an alley, I saw *The Thinker*. I had seen his photograph hundreds of times. There he was on his pedestal. What a grim, beaten-up, tired, primitive thinker he was. He looked as if he had come to this garden to decide if he could go one more round. I smiled to myself and began to feel a sense of elation. It was as if I had just discovered that part of this garden belonged to my own imagination.

When Rodin was living here, in 1908, the great German poet Rainer Maria Rilke had an apartment on the second floor, and I at one time had loved Rilke. Rilke, my Rilke of the stories of God. And Henri Matisse, my favourite painter from the days of my youth in Paris had lived here, and Jean Cocteau, the poet, the friend of my friend, Jacques Maritain. I was walking where they had walked. They had shared this great silence. And the great Eleonora Duse had walked here, and Isadora Duncan.

Silence – too much of it! I wanted to hear a voice, a burst of laughter. With that crowd there must have been a lot of laughter. Rodin, walking here with his beloved Duchesse de Choiseul, must have laughed with her in this garden. Laughter breaking the weight of this silence.

I was now near the pond. I could see the great statue of Balzac, and as I sat down on the base I was suddenly thrust happily back to my youth. I had read all his novels. He was so full of wit, wisdom and wickedness. There he was now, on the great stone base, a figure draped in a cloak, a hooded cloak, with that strange expression on his face! The very source of his great passion was in that expression. He, the rash impulsive man – it was in his face – had taken all of Paris to his heart. Did he not know who he was, I wondered, chasing all over Europe after a third-rate Polish countess who was trying to be superior to this first man of letters in Europe? Well, I remembered that he had seemed to be with me that day in New York sixty years ago, when, walking up Fifth Avenue, I had just heard that Scribners was about to publish a book of stories of mine and a novel. In my elation, I had repeated that cry of Balzac's young protagonist, Rastignac, "Oh, to be famous and be loved." And here I was now sitting at Balzac's feet!

*City & Country Home Gardens,* 1988

# A REAL READER

I had a friend who was quite a man about town. He led a hard life, drank a lot, got to many cities in his travels, and he liked my work. One night he told me about his experience with a couple of ladies. It was a story that I ought to hear, and it ought to impress me, he said. He had been out of town with this hooker whom he had met in a bar. She was tough and competent, he said, but very good looking, so he wanted to keep her around. He was going to take her to a nightspot.

Before going out with the hooker he told her he had to go to his hotel room to put in a call to Paris, so she came to the hotel room with him. He had been carrying around with him a book of my short stories. It was on the dresser. While he was having his long phone conversation the hooker picked up the book, thumbed through it, a title caught her eye, she started to read. When he had completed his call he turned to her, "All right, let's go," he said. Curled up in the chair, frowning, she said, "Just a minute," and went on reading the little story.

Flabbergasted, he stood there waiting for her to finish the story, which fortunately was only eight pages long. Finally she closed the book, stood up and put it back on the dresser.

"Okay?" he asked.

"Okay," she said.

Telling me this, my friend said earnestly, "You should feel damn good. You had a real reader there."

# Scrap Book

*Drawing of Morley by Arthur Lismer, 1931*

Just #remembering this morning/(*the ribbons run out*) *how
little I have cared for the past, this world of photographs,
but seeing many now, I find that I am touched and wish
there were more.*

*Morley*

Just remembering this morning (the ribbons run out) how
little I have cared for the past, the world of photographs,
but seeing many now, I find that I am touched and wish
there were more.

Morley

Morley (front row, second from right) with classmates, in Grade 2.  c. 1910

Morley (centre) with his older brother, Burke (left). Both were big
baseball fans. Morley became a sandlot pitcher, his brother his catcher.
He loved the game throughout his life.  c. 1915

Morley at age 15,
c. 1918

Morley, at age 17 or 18, with friends near his home at 35 Wolfrey Avenue, Toronto,
c. 1920

Morley married Loretto Dee in 1928. She would be his
companion and confidante for almost fifty years, and
together they travelled to London, Paris, Rome, New York
and Montreal, living a literary life full of friendships with
writers, artists, and publishers.

Morley's first novel, *Strange Fugitive*, was published in New York in 1928.

*It's Never Over,* his second novel, released in 1930.

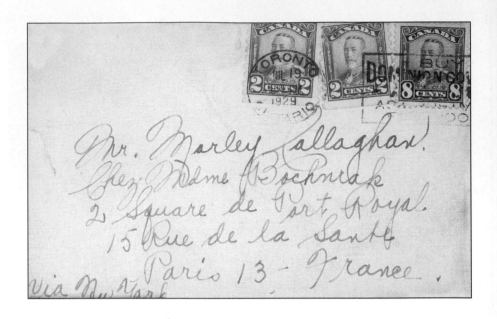

While travelling between Europe, the US, and Montreal and Toronto. Morley made the time to not only write his novels and stories, but completed many essays, reviews and reminiscences.

Above and below are lettres received from those trying to track him down while on his travels.

Morley at his 1931 portable Underwood, at the front window of his family apartment, 123 Walmer Road, Toronto, 1950.

Morley in the living room of the apartment with the family dog, Maizie, 1950.

Morley and Loretto at fashionable Café Martin, Montreal, 1951.

Morley signing Mayor C. Houde's guest book, at two in the morning, City Hall, 1951.

Morley and Loretto in their suite at the Ritz-Carlton Hotel, Montreal, celebrating the publication of his novel, *The Loved and the Lost,* 1951.

*The Night Life* – The Callaghans relive their evenings with Jack Rogers (left), who was Slotkin of SLITKIN AND SLOTKIN's in Montreal (1958). *Photo by Sam Tata*

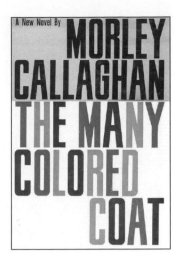

*The Loved and the Lost* was set in Montreal, and won the Governor General's Award in 1951.

Morley loved his visits to Rome. After the release of *The Many Colored Coat* in 1960, he enjoys meeting fans, here on the fashionable Via Veneto. Painter Novella Parigini, a popular Roman artist at the time, is on his right.    *Photo by Lee Thady.*

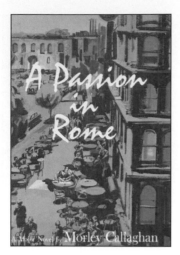

*A Passion in Rome* (1961) is a deeply moving love story, and Morley's only novel set outside Canada.

Morley whispering secrets to Michael, his first grandson, in 1965. Michael would paint the cover for *A Wild Old Man on the Road* (1988).

Edmund Wilson and Morley sharing lunch by the Sugar River, Talcottville, NY, 1963.

*Photo by M.B. Callaghan*

Left to right: Morley Callaghan, conductor and composer Sir Ernest MacMillan, actress Kate Reid, painter A.Y. Jackson, pianist and composer Glenn Gould, and philosopher Marshall McLuhan, 1967.    *Photo by Dick Loek, The Toronto Telegram*

Winner of the $50,000 Royal
Bank Award, Toronto, 1970.
*Photo by Fred Ross, Toronto Daily Star*

Standing beside his portrait,
painted by Bertram Brooker in
1932; Ottawa, 1973.

Morley visiting John Vernon on the set of *More Joy in Heaven*, being filmed by CBC-TV for airing on the *Anthology* series in the 73/74 season.

A 'Literary Masters' author caricature by Isaac Bickerstaff, in *Tamarack Review* (1975), plays up *More Joy in Heaven*'s main character, an ex-con gunman who is "redeemed."

At the Rodin Museum in Paris, 1986.
*Photo by C.W. Wilks*

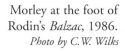

Morley at the foot of
Rodin's *Balzac*, 1986.
*Photo by C.W. Wilks*

Morley with his son, Barry, sitting on
the front porch of the Dale Avenue
house (1983).   *Photo by The Toronto Star*

In Morley's later years, the father-son
relationship blossomed, and found a
shared footing when Barry took his
father back to Paris in 1986.

Mavis Gallant and Morley at a restaurant
on the Place du Marché Saint-Honoré,
les Halles, Paris, 1986.   *Photo by C.W. Wilks*

Irish poet John Montague and
Morley share stories over a light
lunch at a café in Paris, 1986.
*Photo by C.W. Wilks*

Morley at work in his 20 Dale Avenue study, where he wrote most of his books, including his final novel, *A Wild Old Man on the Road* (1988).   *Photo by Dick Loek, The Toronto Star*

Morley with Robert Weaver and Alice Munro at the restaurant, Le Bistingo,
Toronto, celebrating the publication of *A Wild Old Man on the Road*, 1988.

*Photo by C.W. Wilks*

Morley, presumably explaining salesmanship and death to Arthur Miller,
Toronto, 1989.   *Photo by C.W. Wilks*

The Rainbow Gardens Orchestra playing amidst the tombstones at Morley's burial in Holy Cross cemetery, Toronto, 1990.   *Photo by C.W. Wilks*

Morley at 77, in Toronto.   *Photo by Nigel Dickson*

1

The     anti · American garrison in this
country, hemmed in and short of supplies ~~the last fifty years,~~
*goes on making*
has ~~recently been making~~ some interesting sorties.. ~~Into~~ what *I wish they*
*would leave literature alone. Why make literature so small a thing?*
~~territories? Well, of all things~~ literature. ~~It has been reveale~~
*I remember reading that one of*
~~that one of the judges on~~ the committee ~~that~~ *judges who* selects the
winner of he Governor Gneral's medal, a   professor, still *an* ~~A~~
Amerivan after some years in this countr, had indicated his
utter ~~unsuitability~~ for the job ; *How so?* ~~It~~ has been ~~found out~~ *discovered* that
in his critical writing he has compared certain Canadian
*similiate*
~~novelists~~ with certain United States novelists. ~~What's the~~
~~matter with that? you ask in wonder,~~ *But* aren't such comparison's
made all over the world? Sometime ago th Times Literary
Supplement trying to place my own style, suggested that it
fell somewhere between Graham Green and Hemingway. I saw
nothing sinister in this. No sign of a plot to take away
my birthright. ~~But if I have paid more attention to some of~~
~~that time I had~~ ~~read some~~ our distingu
*if I had re read*
ished conservative historians, ~~since reading~~ Donald Grighton
*I would have*
~~I'm supposed o~~ understand bhat a great liberal party
*slowly an surely*
octopus called " Continentalism " ~~has been~~ destroying th
British Amerivan nation, the part of the continent that I
*If I had paid attention I would have got the point*
had always thought of simply as my Canada. ~~Now do you~~
*dont the perfidy of a a*
see how the / professor who compares Gnadian writers
*since they all use*
with Unites States writers, ~~all writers using~~ the same
*This poor man simple unwilling  seems there been*
language , ~~gets into trouble!~~ ~~Probably to this~~ vast surprise
he ~~finds he has been~~ carrying on the evil continental
work of the liberal party. ~~He is~~ A continentalist.
~~Is there~~ *I, a writer, a story teller, am continually* ~~a writer in the country who isn't~~ astounded
by this bald political approach to our literature? ~~Can yo~~
imagine that this approach comes out of ~~any real love of~~

~~literature.~~ Yet if the sortie from the garison turns out to be effectúve and the men making it come into power, think of in the meantime the plight of the poor critic. Little party hacky ~~political literary hacks~~ would be combing his work ready out to censor ~~any~~ discovered link between a Canadian ~~and~~ an American writer, Links that threatened the as of those new national literary security. ~~Right now it's a joke, of course. Preposterou~~ in the frame of our cultural scene. Com Yet ~~at least~~ it ~~can~~ remind us that ~~Hitler, in his quest for the purely German spirit, had a similar view of German music and literature.~~

These politicians whether they be professor, histor or politician economists, write continually about the loss of our cultural idenŝity. What gives us idenŝity? When does a man or a nation have any idenŝity. [7] Does it depend, as the men seem to suggest ,only on the ownership of corporations and ŝe direction of foreign policy? Not quite. Sometimes these writers tell us how different our institutions are from those of the United States. Institutiond! It's a big wor I will, yes Our parliamentary system, ~~yes~~. But th striking differences! sent yet Our judges are appointed rather than elected. Our bar associations don't, think thiŝ is anything to be proud of. And political Both our our senators are appointed for ~~life~~ as a preferment. ~~And the proposed new Constitution amendments it senators are to go our the tendture too, do you notice that that~~ those who lament most bitterl have in the past our loss of cultural idenŝity, devote little space to any of the cultural fields oustide of politics and economics. ~~Politi and the struggle for power and our place in the empire was that all there was to our culture in the good old days. If there was something else why don't they tell us about it? If there was a flowering here innthe good old days befor the dreadful erosion it ought to have been expressed by the cuntry's own writers of the time.~~ well Read them Literature is a matter of language

3

_On both sides of the length [...] hear the same [...]_

~~and then on another and~~ heard the same songs ~~on both sides~~.

Tarriffs there may be on both sides and clashes in fiscal policies

and pressures of power, yet beyond all such controls there

is _This_ ~~a~~ recipocity of language, ~~and it is language that which a~~

~~literature~~. That grand old- National Policy, so dear to the

nation lamenters, may have been devised to protect Canadian

Industry. But it can't protect the Canadian writer. _- in his work_ It can't

protect him from _this_ ~~the~~ reciprocity of langáge. And think of this -

If that American professor is to be convicted of the cardinal

~~al~~ sin of "continentalism" because he compares Canadians always

with Americans in his critical pieces, _then_ what is to be done with

with those shameless and traitorous continentalist Canadian ~~i~~poets

who show so ~~strongly he~~ influence of the Americans, William

Carlos ~~Williams~~, Olsen and Pound

_Of course I know very well that the people who want direct_

As I said, It is my ~~beliaf~~ that the people making this

_and control and defend and select our literature aren't really_

kind of an attack aren't interested in literature at all. They

are interessted _only_ in politics, and not even in the aristotelian sense,

_and I watch the present trend to_

but in a good old party fashion. ~~And yet there is a~~

_at other times_

trend ~~here, a trend I have noticed~~. ~~It represents a kind~~ of

bogus ~~patriotic~~ encouragment at work in certain branches of

_encouraging_

the literati ~~to have~~ the Canadian writer feed on himself. _and his fellow_

_and thus this make_

~~encouragement to make~~ Canadian letters a very small

_on being_

parochial thing. Poets and prose writers ᴧ invited to gather

around their parish pump, put on blindfold, pretend that

they have a kind of excellence that can ~~only~~ be understood _only_

_when, and it is actually a mark of desiredlor_

in this countrty. ~~They can go further, they can tell each~~

other, ~~that is~~ their work is dismissed in the Unites States or

_It is a mark of this special Canadian Singularity which can't_

~~England, it is because its special Canadian quality is not~~

~~be~~ _understood by one outside the country_

understood. Now no ~~real~~ writer wants this kind of _cons_ ~~consolation~~

4 *and there is an agreement to forget that*

from ~~his friends.~~ A first class poet is a first class poet
whether he~~is~~ is published in Canada, the United States or England
~~There is no~~ *special category for Canadians*
~~And is , for one, object to the notion that in my own~~
~~country~~ there should be a ~~special underprivileged~~ category for
~~Canadians.~~ I want Canadian talent to go out to the
whole world *and as for his identity, well to hell with*
*it, identity is something that looks after itself*
As for this matter of ~~our identity,~~ ~~so dear~~
to the historians and the politicians, I don't think the writer
should concern himself at all with their tearful laments.
The writer must first of all have his own *identity.* There is *indeed*
something in the temper of our people *this is* quite different than
anything you find in the United States. Something easier, quieter
*more self contained.*
~~and right now freer~~; something that makes life more *livable* here,
Maybe it is because we are further North, maybe because we
can't get drunk on our own sense of power, maybe because we
don't have to tell ourselves the old imperial lies anymore.
*And in a climate where you don't have to listen*
~~Whatever it is in this country that makes life good,~~
*forever to no lies public lies a writer could grow*
~~whether the real writer likes it or not,~~ ~~growing here~~
like a cabbage in the sun, *it'll find at helping* shape his ~~that~~
~~identity.~~ He'll end up *as* something in himself- without the pro
tection of any *good* old national policy. ~~And~~ we should be glad
to have him compared with United States writers- the
knowledgeable critic who does so *should* be that much more
interesting. *I us* Only by such a comparison can we discover
whether anything ~~has~~ grown here is at last *a mature growth* ~~something in~~
~~itself.~~

So I say a plague on these old garrison nationalists. I suspect that the nation they have been lamenting
was never my Canada anyway.. I don't like ~~this~~ *than* latest sortie
against a teacher of literature.

## BOOKS BY MORLEY CALLAGHAN

Strange Fugitive (1928)

An Autumn Penitent (1929)

A Native Argosy (1929)

It's Never Over (1930)

Broken Journey (1932)

Such Is My Beloved (1934)

They Shall Inherit the Earth (1935)

Now That April's Here (1936)

More Joy in Heaven (1937)

The Varsity Story (1945)

Luke Baldwin's Vow (1949)

The Loved and the Lost (1951)

Morley Callaghan's Stories (1959)

The Many Colored Coat (1960)

A Passion in Rome (1961)

That Summer in Paris (1963)

A Fine and Private Place (1975)

Season of the Witch (1976)

Close to the Sun Again (1977)

No Man's Meat (1978)

The Enchanted Pimp (1978)

A Time for Judas (1983)

Our Lady of the Snows (1985)

The Lost and Found Stories (1985)

A Wild Old Man on the Road (1988)

*Published with Exile Editions*

The New Yorker Stories (2001)

That Summer in Paris (2002)

The Complete Stories: Four Volumes (2003)

Strange Fugitive (2004)

It's Never Over (2004)

A Time for Judas (2005)

The Vow (2005)

That Summer in Paris / Exile Classics Series • One (2006)

The New Yorker Stories / Exile Classics Series • Eleven (2008)

# MORLEY CALLAGHAN

*Ten Books available from Exile Editions*

order online at www.ExileEditions.com
or a mail-in order form follows this section

Born in Toronto in 1903, Morley Callaghan graduated from
the University of Toronto and Osgoode Hall. He was called
to the bar in 1928 but he never practised law. Although he
travelled widely, and lived in Paris for some time during the
golden years of Hemingway and Fitzgerald, Callaghan spent
most of his life in Toronto producing fifteen novels, a memoir
and streams of short stories. He was nominated for the Nobel Prize
in Literature and in Canada received a host of honours,
including the Governor General's Award for Fiction.

He died in 1990.

## THE COMPLETE STORIES
### VOLUMES ONE TO FOUR

Introduction by Alistair MacLeod          Introduction by André Alexis

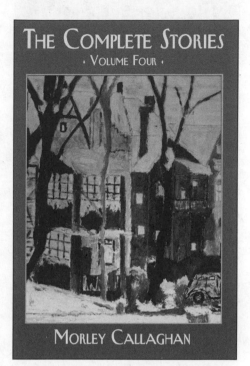

Introduction by Anne Michaels          Introduction by Margaret Atwood

The complete short fiction of Morley Callaghan is now available
to celebrate his coming into full recognition as one of the singular
storytellers of our time. In four volumes, several stories are collected
for the first time, and two of the longer stories—"An Autumn
Penitent" and "In His Own Country"—have been out of print for
decades. Hemingway said his early stories were the equal of Joyce and
Tolstoy; of his middle years, *The New York Times* said: "If there is a
better storywriter in the world we don't know where he is"; and
Edmund Wilson compared his later work to Turgenev and Chekhov.

---

**THE COMPLETE STORIES ~ 4 VOLUMES**  6x9 (pb/french flaps)

- One: 324 pages   $29.95          • Three: 191 pages   $29.95
- Two: 327 pages   $29.95          • Four: 310 pages   $29.95

Introduction by James Dubro

*Strange Fugitive*, Callaghan's first novel—originally published in New York in 1928—announced the coming of the urban novel in Canada, and we can now see it as a prototype for the "gangster" novel in America. The story is set in Toronto in the era of the speakeasy and underworld vendettas. Harry Trotter, the "hero," is a man who cannot check his predilection for brutality. Incapable of reflection, it would never occur to him that he has become a thug. He is all feeling. He wants to feel good, successful, important. If he feels good, things must be right. Given this, as Robert Weaver has argued, "there is a prophetic strain in *Strange Fugitive*." Harry reminds us "of the anti-hero of *The Stranger*, the novel by Albert Camus . . . and he has a link with something as contemporary and as subject to argument as the movie *Bonnie and Clyde*."

Introduction by Norman Snider

1930 was an electrifying time for writing. Callaghan's second novel, completed while he was living in Paris—imbibing and boxing with Joyce and Hemingway—has violence at its core—the story opens with the hanging of an ex-World War One soldier for involuntary murder. But first and foremost it is a story of love, a love haunted by that hanging. "It's never over," the dead man's sister says, as she seeks to possess the life of her brother's closest friend, John Hughes, who—"because a hanging draws everybody into it"—contemplates murder himself. The murder of the sister. As Norman Snider says, the novel is Dostoyevskian in its "depiction of the morbid progress of possession moving like a virus. This is sustained insight of a very high order."

Foreword by Nino Ricci

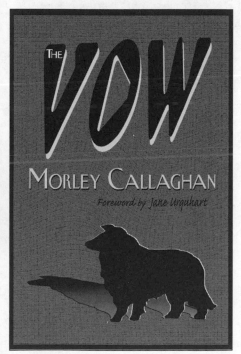

Foreword by Jane Urquhart

*A Time For Judas* is a dramatic new version of the story of Christ's trial, crucifixion, and resurrection. It is audacious and intriguing as a tale.

"*A Time For Judas* provides an engrossing set of answers to questions that have puzzled more people than Callaghan. Why did Jesus have to be betrayed? . . . Why did Judas do it? . . . Not only that, we get a new version of Mary Magdalene, and, for a hair-raising climax (and it really is), we get the truth about what happened to the body of Jesus after the crucifixion. It's all pretty daring, ingenious, and even convincing."
—*MARGARET ATWOOD*

6x9 (pb/french flaps)
- Fugitive: 255 pages   $29.95
- Never Over: 189 pages   $24.95
- Judas: 254 pages   $24.95
- The Vow: 181 pages   $19.95

In *The Vow*, Luke is eleven when his father dies of a heart attack, leaving him an orphan. Small and something of a loner, Luke goes to live with his Uncle Henry and Aunt Helen in Collingwood on Georgian Bay, where Uncle Henry has a saw mill. The aunt and uncle have no children of their own and there are difficult days as they try to get used to each other. Luke sees much to admire in his uncle, an extremely practical and authoritative man, and he wants his uncle to like him and approve of him. But Luke is sometimes a dreamy and stubborn boy, and the two often do not see eye to eye. Uncle Henry has an old collie, blind in one eye and a bit lame, who quickly becomes Luke's friend and companion. The practical uncle sees the dog is old, lame, and no longer useful, so concludes the dog should be destroyed. Luke fights to save his dog and in his struggle he comes to a better understanding, not only of Uncle Henry, but of the expedient world of adults.

# THE EXILE CLASSICS SERIES
## A Unique Series featuring Distinct Literature that stands alone as The Best!

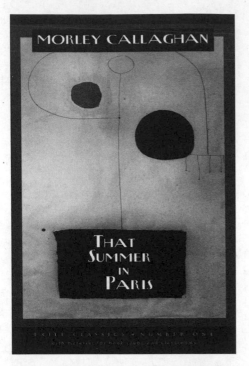

It was the fabulous summer of 1929 when the literary capital of North America had moved to the Left Bank of Paris. Hemingway was reading proofs to *A Farewell to Arms*, and a few blocks away Fitzgerald was struggling over *Tender Is the Night*. And Morley Callaghan, his first book published to acclaim in New York, arrived in Paris to share the felicities of the literary life, not just with his two friends, but with James Joyce, Ford Madox Ford, and Robert McAlmon. Amidst these tangled relations, friendships were lost, too. A tragic and sad and unforgettable story told in Callaghan's lucid compassionate prose.    *(Exile Classics No. 1)*

- Summer: 247 pages   $19.95
- NY Stories: 158 pages   $19.95

Few writers have broken into the big time so fast as Morley Callaghan. He was hailed by Ezra Pound, Hemingway, Sinclair Lewis and F. Scott Fitzgerald. In 1928, after he published his first novel *Strange Fugitive*, Callaghan wrote his editor, Maxwell Perkins:

*Do you think The New Yorker would be a good magazine for my stories? They have never printed fiction before, but are going to start with that story of mine called "An Escapade."*

Perkins replied: *As for The New Yorker I think it has a very excellent type of circulation from your standpoint and ours...*

Through the thirties, the Depression, Callaghan did an astonishing thing: he kept himself alive by writing short stories. Twenty-three appeared in *The New Yorker*. Hemingway compared this work to Joyce, it was this fiction that brought praise from Wyndham Lewis and Edmund Wilson. *(Exile Classics No. 11)*

*Each Title includes an Introduction, and an end-section with Discussion and Essay Questions, Related Reading and Further Resources: ideal for Book Clubs, Classrooms and General Readers.*

## THAT SUMMER IN PARIS (No. 1) • MORLEY CALLAGHAN
Memoir  6x9  247 pages (pb)  $19.95

A tragic and sad and unforgettable story told in Callaghan's lucid, compassionate prose.

## NIGHTS IN THE UNDERGROUND (No. 2) • MARIE-CLAIRE BLAIS
Fiction/Novel  6x9  190 pages (pb)  $19.95

Marie-Claire Blais came to the forefront of feminism with this classic of lesbian literature.

## DEAF TO THE CITY (No. 3) • MARIE-CLAIRE BLAIS
Fiction/Novel  6x9  218 pages (pb)  $19.95

City life, where innocence, death, sexuality, and despair fight for survival.

## THE GERMAN PRISONER (No. 4) • JAMES HANLEY
Fiction/Novella  6x9  55 pages (pb)  $13.95

In the weariness and exhaustion of WWI trench warfare, men are driven to extremes.

## THERE ARE NO ELDERS (No. 5) • AUSTIN CLARKE
Fiction/Stories  6x9  159 pages (pb)  $17.95

Compelling stories of immigrant life as it is lived among the displaced in big cities.

## 100 LOVE SONNETS (No. 6) • PABLO NERUDA (trans. by Gustavo Escobedo)
Poetry/bilingual edition  6x9  225 pages (pb)  $24.95

The greatest poet of the twentieth century – in any language.

## THE SELECTED GWENDOLYN MACEWEN (No. 7)
Poetry/Fiction/Drama/Art/Archival  6x9  352 pages (pb)  $32.95

"This book represents a signal event in Canadian culture."–*Globe and Mail*

## THE WOLF (No. 8) • MARIE-CLAIRE BLAIS
Fiction/Novel  6x9  158 pages (pb)  $19.95

A spellbinding masterpiece and classic of gay literature.

## A SEASON IN THE LIFE OF EMMANUEL (No. 9) • MARIE-CLAIRE BLAIS
Fiction/Novel  6x9  158 pages (pb)  $19.95

A work of genius comparable to Faulker, Kafka, or Dostoyevsky.

## IN THIS CITY (No. 10) • AUSTIN CLARKE
Fiction/Stories  6x9  221 pages (pb)  $21.95

Eight masterful stories showcase the elegance of Clarke's prose and innate sympathy of his eye.

## THE NEW YORKER STORIES (No. 11) • MORLEY CALLAGHAN
Fiction/Stories  6x9  158 pages (pb)  $19.95

"If there is a better storyteller in the world we don't know where he is."–*New York Times*

# Mail-in Order Form

*Photocopy this page, fill in the information, and send in with payment by cheque to:*
EXILE EDITIONS/BOOK ORDERS, 134 EASTBOURNE AVE., TORONTO ON M5P 2G6
*Free S&H on ALL orders! No additional taxes or charges! 5-8 days delivery (US 2-3 wks).*

❑ The Complete Stories: Volume One: 324 pages   $29.95

❑ The Complete Stories: Volume Two: 327 pages   $29.95

❑ The Complete Stories: Volume Three: 191 pages   $29.95

❑ The Complete Stories: Volume Four: 310 pages   $29.95

 • Special Price: ❑ *ALL four above Volumes, only* $95.00

❑ Strange Fugitive: 255 pages   $29.95

❑ It's Never Over: 189 pages   $24.95

❑ A Time for Judas: 254 pages   $24.95

❑ The Vow: 181 pages   $19.95

❑ That Summer in Paris (Exile Classics No. 1): 247 pages   $19.95

❑ The New Yorker Stories (Exile Classics No. 11): 158 pages   $19.95

   *Exile Classics Series:*

❑ Nights in the Underground • Marie-Claire Blais: 190 pages  $19.95

❑ Deaf to the City • Marie-Claire Blais: 218 pages  $19.95

❑ The German Prisoner • James Hanley: 55 pages  $13.95

❑ There Are No Elders • Austin Clarke: 159 pages  $17.95

❑ 100 Love Sonnets • Pablo Neruda: 225 pages  $24.95

❑ The Selected Gwendolyn MacEwen: 352 pages  $32.95

❑ The Wolf • Marie-Claire Blais: 158 pages (pb)  $19.95

❑ A Season in the Life of Emmanuel • Marie-Claire Blais: 158 pages  $19.95

❑ In This City • Austin Clarke: 221 pages  $21.95

Name: _____

Address: _____

_____

City: _____ Prov/St: _____ Postal/Zip: _____

Payment enclosed – Amount: $_____   Number of Books: _____

This book is entirely printed on FSC certified paper.